A list of the books in the series appears at the end of this volume.

COUNTER CULTURES

COUNTER CULTURES

Saleswomen, Managers, and Customers in American Department Stores, 1890–1940

SUSAN PORTER BENSON

UNIVERSITY OF ILLINOIS PRESS

Urbana and Chicago

Publication of this work was supported in part by a grant
from the Andrew W. Mellon Foundation.

This book is printed on acid-free paper.

Library of Congress Cataloging-in-Publication Data

Benson, Susan Porter, 1943–
    Counter cultures.

    (The Working class in American history)
    Bibliography: p.
    Includes index.
    1. Department stores—United States—History.
    2. Department stores—Employees—United States—History.
    3. Women clerks (Retail trade)—United States—History.
    I. Title.   II. Series.
    HF5465.U5B45   1986   381'.1'0973   85-21012
    ISBN 0-252-01252-6 (alk. paper)

For Ed:
This cannot go on.

CONTENTS

ILLUSTRATIONS

ACKNOWLEDGMENTS

Every scholar must frame a response to the frequent question, sometimes asked with ill-concealed wonderment: "How *did* you choose your topic?" Part of my answer is that I was to the counter born. The first thank-you belongs to my parents, Loraine Siegel Porter and Alvin I. Porter, for an early initiation into the joys and trials of retailing—a field that has captured my attention as much as it has theirs, albeit in a very different way.

My work on this project proceeded while I was affiliated with three institutions. At Boston University, Sam Bass Warner, Jr., provided the right mix of encouragement, hard questioning, and freedom as my advisor. Marlou Belyea and Susan Reverby helped immeasurably to lighten the burdens of graduate-student life. The University of New Mexico history department—especially Anne Boylan, Peter Kolchin, and Janet Roebuck—welcomed me as a visiting scholar while I produced the final manuscript. My colleagues at Bristol Community College graciously tolerated my repeated absences, sympathized with my problems, and unfailingly bolstered my spirits. Special thanks go to Eileen Farley, David Feeney, Lee Marvin, Tania Nicolet, Al Roy, and Virginia Winstanley.

Many people have generously given their time and attention to what I've had to say about department stores. Ed Benson, Robert Bruce, Patricia Cooper, Kate Dunnigan, Roslyn Feldberg, Alice Kessler-Harris, Barbara Melosh, Sonya Michel, Ruth Milkman, David Montgomery, Arnold Offner, Sharon Strom, and Sam Bass Warner, Jr., read this entire work in earlier drafts and gave me invaluable advice. Steve Benson, Michael Frisch, Sarah Smith Malino, John Miller, Denise Riley, Christina Simmons, Judith Smith, Bruce Tucker, and Daniel Walkowitz did the same for individual sections.

I have been fortunate in being part of a collective house whose members cheerfully tolerated this project during the ten years when it was an uninvited housemate. Edward Benson, Katherine Frankel Benson, Ophelia Benson, Christina Crosby, Kate Dunnigan, Peter Evans, Louise Lamphere, Peter Bret Lamphere, Cathy Lewis, Susan Matloff, Barbara Melosh, Ruth Milkman, John Miller, Morty Miller, Kristen Neuschel, Nancy Grey Osterud, Jane Plapinger, Wally Sillanpoa, Christina Simmons, Michael Staub, and Bruce Tucker unselfishly sustained me with good cooking, wry humor, and political and intellectual comradeship.

Friends working on similar projects have helped me to cope with problems of method and analysis, as well as offering helpful insights on and valuable tidbits from the world of the department store: Ann Bookman, Mari Jo Buhle, Anne Fausto-Sterling, Maurine Greenwald, Nancy Grey Osterud, Valerie Quinney, Susan Reverby, Nina Shapiro-Perl, Judith Smith, Sharon Strom, and Janice Weiss. Sarah Smith Malino has a very special place in this project. We shared our research on department stores and the joys and pains of reconstructing their world; I hope that we have also shown that overlapping research can be cooperative and not competitive. Kate Dunnigan and Sonya Michel, members of my work-support group, kept me on course when I showed signs of veering off. They have supplied insightful comments on these chapters and great empathy for the travails of research and writing. Even more important, they kept me laughing. All of these women know well that scholarly work is anything but a contained academic exercise and they have been of inestimable help to me in reconciling professional, personal, and political needs.

Roy Rosenzweig helped to check some last-minute details. More important, he and Stephen Brier helped me refine my appreciation of the ironies of academic life and relieved my solitary toil on this book with comradely collaboration on another.

Four people bore the demands of this project in a particularly immediate way. No one understood better than John Miller that the trials and the satisfactions of research and writing are not to be borne alone. We have long shared problems of analysis and worries about our progress, finding unexpected points of intersection between our projects. His advice on presenting quantitative data did wonders for Chapter 5, and he gave the book a title which sums it up neatly. Barbara Melosh was absolutely unstinting in her support and advice. We thrashed out together the guiding ideas and major concepts in this book, trading anecdotes from hospitals and department stores in our attempts to make sense of two very complex institutions as well as of the larger world of women's paid work. Her excellent work, and her matchless combination of involvement in and critical distance from it, have been a model for me; no small part of the pleasure of completing this project is the prospect of moving on to further collaboration with her. Edward Benson has read every page of this book and engaged with it on all levels from its analytical framework to its punctuation. He did far more than his share of child care and housework; he was always ready to listen to my thoughts on department stores; and he has generously adjusted his life to the demands of this project. But more than that, he has sustained me through two exciting and difficult decades with a steadfast faith in me and my work; his personal and intellectual comradeship have been integral to this project from start to finish. Finally, Katherine Frankel Benson helped by having a child's indifference to scholarly concerns and by being cheerful, loving, and a constant reminder that there is much more to life than research and writing.

Many librarians and archivists provided vital assistance during my research; my thanks to the staffs of Baker Library of the Harvard Graduate School of Business Administration, Beatley Library of Simmons College, Hillman Library of the University of Pittsburgh, Rockefeller Library and John Hay Library of Brown University, Tamiment Library, Zimmerman Library of the University of New Mexico (especially the Interlibrary Loan Department), and the National Archives. Mary Ruggles of the Wm. Filene's Sons Company generously gave me access to her files of the *Echo* and a comfortable office in which to read them. Ann Lyles of the Library of Congress, Jennifer Lee of the John Hay Library, William Rice (Figs. 3, 6, 7, 8), and Brooke Hammerle (Figs. 1, 2, 10, 12, 14, 17, 18, 19, 21) cheerfully and expertly produced photographs. Lynne Freed Bell, Joshua Bell, Susan Fendrick, and the other people at Verbatim typed the manuscript with great skill and good humor. James O'Brien produced a model index in record time. And, finally, Richard Wentworth and Patricia Hollahan of the University of Illinois Press consistently helped and encouraged me, graciously tolerating my offenses against their work culture.

Portions of this book draw on my earlier published work: Chapters 2 and 3 on "Palace of Consumption and Machine for Selling: The American Department Store, 1890–1940," *Radical History Review,* 21 (Fall 1979), 199–221; Chapter 4 on "'The Cinderella of Occupations': Managing the Work of Department Store Saleswomen, 1900–1940," *Business History Review,* 55 (Spring 1981), 1–25; Chapter 6 on "'The Clerking Sisterhood': Rationalization and the Work Culture of Saleswomen," *Radical America,* 12 (Mar.–Apr. 1978), 41–55 and "'The Customers Ain't God': The Work Culture of Department-Store Saleswomen," in Michael Frisch and Daniel Walkowitz, eds., *Working Class America: Es-*

says on Labor, Community, and American Society (Urbana, 1983); and the Conclusion on "Women in Retail Sales Work: The Continuing Dilemma of Service," in Karen Brodkin Sacks and Dorothy Remy, eds., *My Troubles Are Going to Have Trouble with Me: Everyday Trials and Triumphs of Women Workers* (New Brunswick, 1984). My thanks to these publishers for granting me permission to reuse this material.

ABBREVIATIONS

The following abbreviations are used throughout:

BNRDGA	*Bulletin of the National Retail Dry Goods Association*
BLS	Bureau of Labor Statistics
B & DGC	*The Buyer and Dry Goods Chronicle*
DSE	*Department Store Economist*
DGC & FGR	*The Dry Goods Chronicle and Fancy Goods Review*
DGE	*Dry Goods Economist*
JR	*Journal of Retailing*
RCIA	*Retail Clerks International Advocate*
WB	Women's Bureau

Introduction

I spent my childhood in a small town thirty miles from Pittsburgh, a city then entering the renaissance that transformed it from a grimy and dilapidated center of the steel industry into a sleek cosmopolitan hub of corporate America. But I barely noticed the new aluminum skyscrapers and the Golden Triangle development and paid only grudging visits to older urban attractions such as the Carnegie Museum. For me, Pittsburgh was department stores, in the same all-encompassing way that it was Forbes Field (then the home of the Pirates and the Steelers) to my male contemporaries. My mother introduced me to the wonders of the department store, shepherding me from store to store, teaching me more by example than by precept how to shop and rewarding good behavior with a ladylike lunch in one of the store restaurants. For many years, I thought that chicken à la king as served in Kaufmann's dining room was the summit of gourmet indulgence and genteel elegance. Adolescence opened the door to shopping forays with my peers, both as parentally approved Saturday diversion and as the clandestine object of a day of playing hooky. We bought little but noticed everything, criticizing the decor of the model rooms in the furniture departments, trying on everything from formal gowns to bedroom slippers, sampling the cosmetics on the street floors, shunning only the most exclusive departments where the haughty saleswomen withered our brassy assurance. We imagined ourselves very grown-up, worldly-wise, and glamorous. The future stretched before us as a series of department-store shopping trips: for camping outfits, prom dresses, college clothes, wedding accoutrements, home furnishings, baby layettes—the cycle of life underlined by a stately progression from department to department. In the years that I have been studying department stores, women from all over the country have shared similar memories with me. Whether they recall the heady metropolitan excitement of Macy's Herald Square store or the small-town gentility of Colorado

Springs's Hibbard and Company, they all testify to the material and imaginative hold these giant stores once had on American womanhood.

Another personal perspective shaped this book: my family life was intertwined with a small store owned by my parents and my grandparents before them. At the dinner table I listened to my parents discuss the problems of retailing. How could they build a steady clientele of customers? Why didn't their saleswomen sell more enthusiastically and effectively? Where was the balance between seeking immediate profits and investing in the store's long-term reputation? What was the appropriate mix of fashionable and staple merchandise? I was a clerk behind the counters of their store as a teenager and was curiously attracted and repelled by selling. Intrigued by the possibilities for initiative and small-scale drama, sorely tried by the need to defer to rude or condescending customers and to sell more, ever more, I vacillated between eager effort and sullen resistance.

The experiences of small-town storekeepers and department-store managers, of clerk-daughters and salaried saleswomen, of customers in embattled department stores of the 1950s and those in flourishing giant emporiums between 1890 and 1940 were by no means identical. Still, the structural similarities between them were striking enough for my own memories to resonate powerfully with my research on an earlier period of retailing and to help shape the focus of this book. I had begun this project intending to study the implementation of more rigorous management practices in department stores, assuming that I could trace the process of rationalization in the manner of Harry Braverman in *Labor and Monopoly Capital*. But the more I read in management literature, the more I heard other voices speaking in it; bosses' complaints and prescriptions revealed a great deal about saleswomen's and customers' motivations and actions. Hoping to examine life on the shop floor as more of a give-and-take between managers and workers than Braverman suggested, I soon found that the selling floor of department stores was immensely more complicated than I had foreseen. Class and gender intersected there in complex ways and the demands of service work and mass consumption exerted a powerful influence.[1]

In the end, this book became an exploration of the cultures of the three major presences on the selling floor—saleswomen, managers, and customers—and the ways in which their patterns of interaction shaped large-scale retailing for a half-century. My use of the term *culture* derives from the anthropological notion that culture, in the words of Sidney

Mintz, is "a kind of resource," as opposed to society, "a kind of arena." Culture is the set of frameworks, attitudes, and accepted standards of behavior that one draws upon in dealing with society, the real-world circumstances in which people live their lives. The cultures of department-store managers, saleswomen, and customers grew partly out of the conditions and struggles within department stores and partly out of other contexts in which each group moved. The developing culture of consumption shaped them all, urging them to see buying goods and services not simply as a way of fulfilling basic needs but as a means of enhancing psychic well-being and social standing. Managers partook of the new managerial culture, with its emphasis on productivity and efficiency. Customers and managers assumed the superiority of an urban bourgeois culture based on good taste and genteel behavior. Saleswomen brought into the store a variety of working-class cultures whose standards of esthetics and action diverged from those of the dominant culture. Saleswomen and customers, finally, shared in women's culture.[2]

This last is probably the least well recognized; a notion common among women's historians only for the last decade or so, the content and implications of women's culture are still the subject of much debate. Most would, however, agree that in the nineteenth-century United States there was a native-born middle-class women's culture, based in the domestic sphere but by no means confined to it, which conditioned women's relations with one another, their conduct as family members, and their involvement in voluntary activities, politics, and the labor market. When the arena is broadened to include the twentieth century along with immigrant and working-class women, the area of agreement narrows sharply. The decline of the domestic sphere and the rise of heterosocial and peer cultures in its place certainly vitiated women's culture, but I would argue that it was transformed rather than destroyed. The sex segregation on which it was based persisted in the labor market, parts of the education system, and much of social and family life, delineating for women a constricted but protected sphere in which they interacted more freely and exclusively with one another than with men. Refracted through the prism of class and ethnicity, women's culture emerged in countless varieties which nonetheless shared a core of outlook and actions. In this book, I assume that this core consisted of three elements: first, a consciousness that there were still physical and psychic women's spaces where men were aliens; second, a socialization which fostered cooperative and empathic traits and the ability to function through influence rather than authority;

and, third, parallel if not identical experiences of domestic and family life, of the making and management of a home, and of the rhythms and rituals of the life cycle.[3]

In most ways diametrically opposed to women's culture, the business culture which emerged in the late nineteenth and early twentieth centuries stressed tighter control over operations through drives for productivity and efficiency, elaborate accounting systems, new technology, and an intensification of the division of labor. Department-store managers shared the goals of control and efficiency but had other, contradictory aims which grew out of the peculiarities of retailing. Far more than factory managers, they were preoccupied with maintaining the goodwill of both their customers and their salespeople. They courted the former through a vast array of services, coddling them with conveniences and attractions designed to convince them that the department store was a place of recreation and sociability as well as consumption. Elaborate training and welfare programs sought to teach the selling force the skills and attitudes which would foster individual sales as well as the long-term profits and good reputation of the store. The department-store equivalent of scientific management in the factory would have been self-service, or simply letting customers examine the goods unaided in the manner of many late-twentieth-century stores; managers shunned this solution in the half-century before World War II because they feared it would undermine both their profits and their cultural message. Instead, they chose the tactic of skilled selling in which the highly trained salesperson convinced customers to buy more items and spend more money than they would have if left to their own devices. These service and personnel strategies saddled department stores with high fixed costs for lavish buildings, free services, and the personnel required for maintenance and selling. Managers were convinced that they could best absorb these costs by boosting the size of the average sales transaction through skilled selling and by building a clientele of steady customers who would return faithfully to their stores. But the cultural message of the store was equally important, for personal sales service—perhaps even more than free delivery or luxurious lounges—suggested to the customer that she was of the class which deserved to be served, that her consumption was a token of her standing in the urban bourgeoisie.[4]

Department stores were thus the agencies of a class-based culture, carrying the gospel of good taste, gentility, and propriety to those who could afford its wares. Much more immediately and intensely than advertisements, department stores confronted the customer with a dazzling array of merchandise in a setting designed to break down her resistance to spending money and to exploit her sense of her class position and personal attractiveness. The customer whose pocketbook enabled her to use shopping to affirm her class position was the ideal target of the department store; physically and socially, these firms were bulwarks of urban gentility and the culture of consumption. Yet a disruptive clash of class-based manners fermented within them: the women whom they hired to sell to bourgeois matrons were, in the vast majority, members of the working class who expressed their envy or disdain of their customers through an elaborately coded work culture. Because there was a limited supply of middle-class women who were willing to stand behind their counters and because department stores would not have been willing to pay such women what they could earn elsewhere, they tried instead to transform their working-class saleswomen into genteel but deferential workers, advisors as well as servants of the customers. These efforts were only partially successful. Saleswomen maintained a wary distance from bosses and customers who constantly pressured them to conform to the uncomfortable mold of the skilled salesperson, to adopt the veneer of a higher class without receiving any of its rights and privileges.[5]

Gender, as well as class, produced particularly intense contradictions in the department store. Managers solicited both customers and saleswomen on the basis of gender characteristics. They spoke of appealing to women's "vanity" and "whims," but shopping involved more than these. Women as customers were socialized to handle the consumption needs of their families; while men and young people of course made purchases on their own, the family's shopping was still primarily the responsibility of the wife or mother. Women shared both the knowledge and the experience of consumption in their kin and friendship networks, balancing questions of value and style against their personal preferences and the tastes of their social circle, processing the messages of advertisers and merchants in ways that made sense to them. Managers selected saleswomen both for their cheapness in the labor force and for their "female" personality characteristics which coincided with the skills of selling: empathy, habits of persuasion instead of command, and a homely familiarity with the merchandise. The saleswomen's equivalent of customers' gossip channels was the departmental work group, which built on workplace experience and women's culture to frame a work culture that provided an alternative vision of what it meant to sell. In day-to-day interaction on the selling floor, the class gulf between saleswoman and customer could be bridged by the shared aspects of women's culture, undermining managers' success in manipulating women in the search for higher profits.

These struggles were played out in two overlapping contexts: that of a service economy and that of a society based on mass consumption. Department stores did not produce goods but only conveyed them to the customers while performing various ancillary functions. Selling was generally if not always accurately regarded as clean rather than dirty work, white-collar rather than blue-collar. Even had department-store managers not stressed class demeanor so unremittingly, the white-collar nature of the work would have given it an ambiguous status. Tinged with a respectability denied factory work yet tainted with the immorality that attached to women who were too much in the public eye, weighed down by the burdens of low pay and regimented work conditions yet buoyed up by unusual possibilities for advancement and the exercise of initiative on the job, sales work was suspended more than most white-collar work in a web of contradictions. The customer, usually a phantom to the production worker and frequently absent from the scene of service work, was a continuing presence in the life of the saleswoman. In the department store, the two-way interaction between workers and managers became a complex triangle of saleswomen, managers, and customers. When managers and customers exerted unified pressure on the saleswoman, her life could be difficult indeed; but when she could play one off against the other she could create new space for herself on the job. Managers and customers similarly entered into shifting alliances with each other or with saleswomen.[6]

The ways in which saleswomen, customers, and managers jousted for power on the selling floor offer a window on the daily life of a society increasingly pervaded by mass consumption. Department-store managers shared the desire of manufacturers and advertising agencies to convince the public that buying was a panacea for psychic and social problems, but their interests diverged because they tried to ground their stores' reputations in service rather than branded merchandise. They urged customers to act out their gender and class roles in the store but then learned that such dramas were expensive and disruptive to their stores' operations. Customers found department stores seductive and exciting places and were flattered by appeals to their vanity, but they became suspicious of managers' tendency to indulge them rather than treat them as responsible adults. Those most concerned with intelligent shopping faulted department stores for failing to provide them with adequate information, while those who viewed shopping as an opportunity to exercise the prerogatives of their class found department stores insufficiently accommodating. Saleswomen viewed the department store with the cynicism of the insider and the canniness of the expert, becoming paragons as well as critics of the world of consumer capitalism. They played both sides of the counter, selling in their roles as workers, consuming in their roles as women, and merging the two roles in ways which showed in high relief the tensions in a society of mass consumption.

This book's focus on the contradictions and conflicts among saleswomen, customers, and managers should not obscure the fact that department stores were undeniably successful institutions, both financially and socially. They generated enormous profits and shaped millions of lives on both sides of the counter, blurring the line between consumption and recreation, life on and off the job. Saleswomen and customers had an important impact on life in the great downtown stores, but the structures of capitalism and gender relations ensured that neither the wealthiest customer nor the most competent saleswoman wielded the power of a manager. Nonetheless, managers seemed persistently uneasy in their position at the crossroads of business and culture and unsatisfied with their efforts to fit their firms into the mold of the twentieth-century business enterprise. Time and again, their best-laid plans backfired. Fashions in management methods changed almost as fast as those in clothing and showed the same tendency toward the cyclical revival and discard of old styles; change thus proceeded not relentlessly but haltingly. Small daily struggles; turf gained, lost, and retaken—these, and not the epic losing battle of craft control against the forces of proletarianization, were the engines of history on department-store selling floors.

Chapter 1 explores the birth of American department stores between 1850 and 1890, tracing the growth of giant diversified stores which provided services as they sold merchandise, using new technology, lavish buildings, and women clerks to create a world in which middle-class women felt at home. The first forty years of American department-store retailing were a time of tremendous growth and success, but also one in which the seeds of conflicts were sown among managers, customers, and saleswomen. During the next half-century, these conflicts intensified and conditioned life on the selling floor; contained but never fully resolved, they paved the way for a major change in retailing strategy during the

1940s. Ironically, the same years were the golden age of the American department store. Developing along with the great cities, the department store expressed their spirit much as the meetinghouse embodied that of the seventeenth-century New England town. The congestion, the liveliness, the anonymity, the grand scale, the material promise, and the class divisions of the city were all distilled into the great stores. Department stores shaped cities as they were shaped by them; real estate values, urban policies, traffic patterns, and public transportation responded to the needs and demands of large retailers. Their very presence was a magnet for people and other businesses; downtown Philadelphia, to take but one example, was and still is anchored by the impressive combination of City Hall and the John Wanamaker store. The intertwined political economy of the city and the department store lies, for the most part, outside the scope of this study; I look instead at the department store as a microcosm, examining less its structural relationship to the larger world than the ways in which these relationships were reflected in contradictions within the department store.

Chapter 2 discusses department-store managers' attempts to bring order and system to their firms. Like factory managers, retail executives introduced functional organization, tried to circumscribe the power of buyers and floormen (the department-store counterparts of foremen), streamlined their shop-floor design and fixtures, and standardized their offerings. While these expedients by no means completely solved the problems of factory managers, they were even less effective for department-store managers because they only set the stage for, and did not effectively shape, the central function of selling.

Chapter 3 explores managers' attempts to bring customers under control. They provided free services and presented the department store as both a bourgeois home and a women's city club. At the same time, they developed new means of persuasion to convince the customer not just to buy discrete pieces of merchandise but also to become loyal to the store. Managers and customers differed dramatically on the results of these measures; managers felt that customers became unreasonable and demanding instead of trusting and accepting, while customers valued courtesy and accurate merchandise information above frivolous services and special favors.

Managers soon learned that saleswomen were the crucial links between themselves and customers, and Chapter 4 discusses their attempts to train saleswomen in skilled selling, to transform the "shopgirl" into a "professional" saleswoman. Managers established elaborate welfare-work programs but focused most of their effort on training. Individual stores and special school or college programs trained both saleswomen and teachers of saleswomen. The main elements in training programs were general education (ranging from etiquette to arithmetic), salesmanship classes, and education about merchandise; as a whole, these programs attempted to remake working-class saleswomen in a middle-class image. Managers backed up their training efforts with incentive-payment schemes which were the department-store equivalent of piecework in the factory.

Chapters 5 and 6 focus on the worlds of the saleswoman. Chapter 5 places department-store selling within the context of the female labor market as a whole, comparing selling to other jobs and saleswomen to other women in the labor force. Sales work had notable advantages—such as steady work and possibilities for higher pay and upward mobility—but also real disadvantages—such as unpaid overtime and long hours—in comparison to other women's occupations. In both pay and social status saleswomen were usually somewhere between factory workers and clerical workers. Even before World War II, however, the seeds of a grimmer future were already sown in Depression-era policy changes.

The final chapter focuses on the selling floor, considering saleswomen's relations to one another, to their bosses, and to their customers. While on the one hand saleswomen used many of the same techniques of restriction of output as male craftsmen, they infused them with women's culture in both a traditional and an oppositional way. A solidarity born of their gender and class as well as of their departmental work groups backed up an impressive set of unwritten rules by which saleswomen governed their daily lives. This work culture expressed the saleswoman's three identities—worker, woman, and consumer.

Seen from these different perspectives, the department store played a major cultural and economic role in late-nineteenth-century and twentieth-century American life. A new kind of public space for women, it was nonetheless a place in which gender characteristics and conduct were a matter of daily struggle. The embodiment of urban bourgeois respectability, it was simultaneously an arena for clashes of class-specific ways of behaving. Conditioned by the emergence of a service sector and of a society based on mass consumption, department stores revolved around a drama of persuasion in which social interaction replaced production as the essence of the work process.

Two matters of terminology require some comment. First, the use of the terms *manager* and *buyer*—I use the former to refer to all supervisory and managerial personnel except for department heads, whom I term buyers. While buyers were unarguably managerial personnel, they also had a peculiar relationship with their departments which justifies the difference in usage: they presided over their own little fiefdoms, protecting their merchandise and personnel from the other managers who represented the interests of the store as a whole. Second, when discussing managers and salespeople I refer to them respectively as "he" and "she." Some managers were women, although very few at the top policy-making levels, and a sizable minority of clerks were men, but the use of the generic pronoun reflects the majority composition of each group as well as the gender-based dynamic between them.

Notes

1. See Harry Braverman, *Labor and Monopoly Capital: The Degradation of Work in the Twentieth Century* (New York, 1974). The work of David Montgomery (*Workers' Control in America* [Cambridge, 1979]) was most important to me as a model study of the dialectic of the shop floor which does not lose sight of the ultimate stakes of the struggle.

2. Mintz's definition is quoted by Herbert G. Gutman, *Work, Culture, and Society in Industrializing America* (New York, 1976), 16. Gutman's work has provided labor historians with a demanding model for the study of the interaction between culture and society.

3. The preeminent works on women's culture in nineteenth-century America are Nancy F. Cott, *The Bonds of Womanhood: "Women's Sphere" in New England, 1780–1835* (New Haven, 1977) and Carroll Smith-Rosenberg, "The Female World of Love and Ritual: Relations between Women in Nineteenth-Century America," *Signs*, 1 (Autumn 1975), 1–29, reprinted in Nancy F. Cott and Elizabeth H. Pleck, eds., *A Heritage of Her Own* (New York, 1979), 311–43. For a provocative sample of the debate over women's culture, see Ellen DuBois, Mari Jo Buhle, Temma Kaplan, Gerda Lerner, and Carroll Smith-Rosenberg, "Politics and Culture in Women's History: A Symposium," *Feminist Studies*, 6 (Spring 1980), 26–64.

4. Important works on new managerial ideas and policies include Alfred D. Chandler, *Strategy and Structure: Chapters in the History of American Industrial Enterprise* (Cambridge, Mass., 1962); *The Visible Hand: The Managerial Revolution in American Business* (Cambridge, Mass., 1977); and Daniel Nelson,

Managers and Workers: Origins of the New Factory System in the United States, 1880–1920 (Madison, Wis., 1975).

5. On the definition and application of the notion of a culture of consumption, see Richard Wightman Fox and T. J. Jackson Lears, "Introduction" to Fox and Lears, eds., *The Culture of Consumption: Critical Essays in American History, 1880–1980* (New York, 1983), ix–xvii.

6. The classic treatment of the complexities of white-collar work is C. Wright Mills, *White Collar* (New York, 1951).

1

"The New Kind of Store": 1850–90

In 1840 there was no such thing as a department store; the best retail wisdom of the early nineteenth century stressed specialization as opposed to the huge assortment of merchandise that would be the hallmark of the department store. During the next half-century, the first department stores developed, flourished, and moved into the vanguard of urban merchandising where they remained for another fifty years. A new world of retailing had emerged by about 1890, created by the interaction of urban development, changing patterns of consumption, women's evolving roles, and rapid industrialization. Managers, workers, and customers all played a part in building and elaborating this new world, exciting and full of opportunity yet beset by enduring economic and cultural problems.

Much scholarly ink has been spilled in discussing the origins and definition of a department store. Some cling to the current Census Bureau definition: a firm which sells a full line of household goods and furnishings as well as clothing and dry goods. While useful for some purposes, it is far too narrow for a historical discussion concerned with business practices, everyday life, and cultural roles. Large specialty stores such as William Filene's Sons and Lord & Taylor fall outside this definition, but their managers saw themselves as part of the department-store industry and were in fact leaders in developing management strategy and a public presence for department stores. For the sake of convenience this book uses the term *department store* to refer to the large downtown stores that are its subject, department stores and large specialty stores alike. The managers of Lord & Taylor shared a common business outlook with those of Abraham & Straus across the East River in Brooklyn while shoppers in Boston's downtown thought of Filene's and Jordan Marsh as stores of the same species.

This notion of a department store emerged slowly and unevenly in the retailing world between 1850 and 1890. At mid-century, American retailing followed two patterns: the rural or small-town general store that supplied the demand of the local market and the urban shop that specialized in a narrow line of goods such as laces or umbrellas. While general stores eventually grew into department stores as small towns became cities, the pioneer department stores evolved from small shops, reacting against their key features. The typical urban shop was exclusively a retail venture, operating on the ancient principle of caveat emptor. Prices were set by haggling between customer and clerk, and adjustments on unsatisfactory or misrepresented merchandise were rare and grudging. Customers were routinely badgered to make a purchase as the price of leaving the store. Most retailers bought on credit from wholesalers and jobbers and sold on credit to the public; six months or a year would often elapse before accounts were settled.[1]

Many writers have tried to pinpoint the origins of the department store by looking for the first reversal of these practices. Alexander Turney Stewart, Rowland H. Macy, John Wanamaker, and Marshall Field—along with many unsung contemporaries—helped to move retailing into a new era by diversifying their offerings, adopting the one-price system, pledging not to misrepresent merchandise, promising refunds or exchanges for unsatisfactory goods, allowing free access to their establishments without the obligation to buy, and limiting their dependence on credit in stocking their stores. They were not, however, consciously striving toward a new type of firm, but simply making a series of tactical decisions for the immediate health of their businesses. Stewart adopted many of the new practices without fully diversifying his stock, despite his acknowledged preeminence among New York retailers; Macy edged bit by bit into the new ways as he scrambled to make his New York store succeed where his others had failed; Field insisted that his firm's retail branch remain a dry goods store, fighting Harry Selfridge's efforts to transform it into a department store every step of the way. While these men may have differed from more traditional merchants in their practices, they did not necessarily differ on basic business principles. Trade papers and individual department-store merchants alike spoke reverently of what might be called the prudential virtues. The good retailer, the argument went, was wide-awake, prudent, courteous, and honest; energy and dedication en-sured success.[2]

A broad-based shift in urban retailing was occurring, and—by about 1890—a public and industrial consensus about the nature of the new beast had crystallized. From this viewpoint, it matters little which retailing genius first adopted a new technique such as the one-price sys-tem, but rather which practices caught on and became accepted proce-dure. This line of inquiry allows us to chart a general shift in conscious-ness which transcended specific business practices. Many of the following examples are drawn from well-known stores such as those run by Stew-art, Macy, Wanamaker, and Field simply because they are among the very few well-documented firms in nineteenth-century retailing; repeated ref-erence to them should not obscure the fact that they were only the most visible parts of a pervasive reorientation of urban retailing, of the broader development of what John Wanamaker called "the New Kind of Store."[3]

The essence of the new system of retailing was its unprecedented combination of size and variety. Department stores stretched the bounds of acceptable retailing assortments, including a variety of goods that would have scandalized the early-nineteenth-century merchant specialist and spelled certain doom in his mind. This expansion of stock was often rapid and prodigious; by 1875, R. H. Macy's stock approached that of the mature department store, featuring—in addition to dry goods and ready-to-wear—home furnishing, toys and dolls, books, candy, sporting goods, china, glassware, and silver. But diversification was less a principle than a tactic employed by those who refused to be bound by traditional constraints. Rowland Macy added new departments not because he had a guiding vision of the future but because he needed to attract new custom-ers, first to establish his store at an unpromising location far from Man-hattan's retail center and later, in the 1870s, to bolster sales volume dur-ing lean times. John Wanamaker added new lines of merchandise because he foresaw economies of scale, stating on the opening of his Grand Depot store at the firm's present Philadelphia location that "with the large prop-erty we now have we can do a great deal more business with no more expense for rent, taxes, gas, and only the addition of needed clerk hire." Expansion into new merchandise lines was risky—Wanamaker's Grand Depot almost failed during its first year—but it could also bring fabulous success: Macy's sales topped one million dollars in 1870 and increased by over 80 percent during the next seven years despite falling price levels, making the store the largest retail operation in New York before it was two decades old.[4]

The increasing size of retail establishments made many earlier practices impractical or ineffective. The one-price system, while touted as a guarantee of justice and equity in pricing, was a simple necessity: for example, the 120 or so salespeople in Macy's in 1875 could not be trusted to negotiate prices. The policy of free entry arose because a diversified store relied not just on customers' quests for specific items but also on what we now call "shopping" or "impulse buying," examining wares without a prior intention to buy. As a store increased its volume and capital it could pay its obligations more rapidly, freeing itself from the constraints of long-term credit, exacting discounts from jobbers and manufacturers, and buying large lots directly from manufacturers.[5]

But more than reversing past practices, the new type of store made novel appeals to customers and developed its own peculiar internal organization. Department stores justified themselves to those who accused them of illegitimate competition by pointing to their combination of lower prices and better services to the public. They assured the former by making huge and often advantageous purchases and maintaining a rapid turnover of stock in order to maximize return on investment. Traditional retailing practice was to hold stock indefinitely until it sold; slow-moving goods could grow dusty on the shelves for more than a decade. This system gave the store an outmoded air, saddled it with the burden of long-term credit, and tied up valuable capital. Department stores, eager to avoid these problems, stressed the rapid sale of goods. The arithmetic was quite simple: if a store invested, let us say, a dollar in a dozen pairs of socks on January 1 and sold them on December 31, it realized a profit on that dollar's investment only once. But if the store sold the socks on February 28, reinvested the dollar immediately in another dozen pairs, sold them within two months, and repeated this process through the year, it would reap a profit six times on the same investment. Twentieth-century accountants would use the term "rate of stock-turn" to measure this process: in the first case, the rate of stock-turn would be one, and in the second case it would be six.

Department-store pioneers did not calculate their stock turnover precisely, but they changed the rules of the game so as to move merchandise more quickly through the store. If goods remained in the selling department longer than a specified time, they were marked down; even if they were sold at cost, the initial investment was recouped and could be turned to new and presumably more lucrative uses. Moreover, the end of each selling season was punctuated by giant clearaway sales to purge old stocks and free capital for new purchases. Along the way, retailers strove to limit the amount of merchandise they kept in stock, convinced that "lean" stocks gave them greater flexibility in responding to changes in taste and demand. These measures offered customers the appealing combination of constant novelty and attractive bargains. In their less calculating moments, retailers also engaged in price wars, ruinously undercutting competing stores in defense of their reputation for rock-bottom prices.[6]

These large and diversified stores created the department as the administrative unit for the buying and selling of a given class of goods. The department became the defining feature of this new type of store, distinguishing it on one side from the chaotic jumble of the general store and on the other from the small specialized shop. Within eleven years of the opening of his first New York store in 1858, for example, Rowland Macy had divided his store into departments, placing two or three lines of closely related merchandise under the supervision of a buyer. Store expenses were allocated proportionally to each department so that profits and losses could be pinpointed. Most stores gave buyers a free rein in running their departments; Marshall Field prided himself on having a "buyer-run" store. Coasting on the novelty of their new version of retailing, benefiting from rapidly expanding urban markets, department-store managers before 1890 gave relatively little thought to the selling of their merchandise. Buying was all; the buyer in theory was charged with both buying and selling, but the latter was widely treated as an afterthought. If the buyer had good instincts, so the assumption went, then he or she would stock the department with desirable and attractively priced merchandise which would more or less sell itself.[7]

Relatively unworried about selling, store managers before 1890 fretted instead about the fragmentation of the store created by its division into departments and compounded by the autonomy of the buyers. Their response was a plan of organization akin to but distinct from the multidivisional structure described by Alfred Chandler as the hallmark of mature industrial enterprise. The departments were analogous to the divisions in manufacturing firms except that they coexisted in the same building, and functional tasks were centralized for the whole firm. Department stores in their early stages developed separate offices to handle storewide functions such as "employment, receiving and marking, delivery, returns and adjustments, and . . . advertising." Moreover, as a counterweight to the buyers they created a corps of service personnel. Commonly known as floorwalkers and headed by the store's superintendent, they were to represent the proprietor on the selling floor, greet customers, assure that they were well served, and enforce rules evenhandedly in the face of departmental claims. Direct supervision of buyers continued to be lax, however, and in most stores amounted only to a dollar limit on buying, sporadic attention by top management, and periodic comparisons of sales volume to the department's own past performance and to the current performance of other departments. All in all, functional organization minimally constrained individual buyers and created or exacerbated tensions among them, between buyers and managers, and between buyers and floorwalkers. Jockeying for position and power within the store organization and on the selling floor became a way of life in department stores. Although they produced remarkable profits and sold prodigious quantities of merchandise, they did so with a great deal of tension and wasted motion because of their organizational confusion and divisions.[8]

As managers made a new world for themselves, they also created a new world for their customers. At every point of contact with the public, department stores worked thoroughgoing changes that testified to their new eagerness to make consumption pleasing and interesting. If managers clung to the old-fashioned prudential virtues for themselves, they urged a new therapeutic ethic upon their customers. A trade journal asserted in 1890 that merely entering a thoughtfully managed store would revive a weary and apathetic customer: "almost unconsciously the tired feeling drops away and a fresh interest awakens." Even vicarious consumption could be invigorating; an industry writer maintained that stores were "immense factors in bringing brightness and change to many who at other times pass their days in the dull monotony of a struggle to live," providing "something to think of and talk over, even if the gorgeous and beautiful trappings seen in the stores are not within the possibility of possession." In effect, shopping offered a cure for neurasthenia, an activity exciting enough to engage even the most jaded.[9]

As department stores expanded, so too did their publicity, transforming newspaper advertising in the process. Rowland Macy broke new ground by using inventive layout and typography along with interesting and often humorous copy in an era when most stores' ads looked and read like today's classified notices. John Wanamaker pioneered the full-page ad in 1879; his and other stores introduced drawings and then photographs into newspaper advertising. Stores solicited patronage with lavish descriptions of merchandise, bargain prices, and paeans to the reputation and amenities of the store. John Wanamaker's ads frequently addressed the public familiarly, using the voice of "The Founder" himself in interviews and "frank, plain, and fearless" talks which discussed store policy and principles along with merchandise. Most stores used a similar combination of merchandise and institutional advertising, seeking not just to sell individual lots of goods but to sell customers on their stores as a whole.[10]

The woman enticed by advertisements to visit a store found an unprecedented level of beauty and comfort. Windows were dressed with an artistic eye, as managers renounced the traditional practice of cramming windows with vast quantities of unrelated merchandise and instead presented smaller lots of related items in a pleasing and esthetic way. For the bored or idle, window-shopping became a welcome diversion. Parading up and down the streets, women examined the goods displayed as well as their own reflections in the plate glass windows and the mirrors cannily placed to pander to their vanity. They stopped to discuss the merchandise and the quality of the displays with their friends, their loitering in public space legitimized by its association with consumption.[11]

Store buildings were similarly designed to attract and please. Some firms grew by accretion, absorbing neighboring structures, while others built specially designed buildings. In 1880, Macy ordered the remodeling of his store's Sixth Avenue exterior, replacing the uneven array of old housefronts with an attractive cast-iron facade. Strawbridge and Clothier tripled the size of their store with an 1878 addition designed to create a symmetrical and unified whole. Marshall Field moved his retail operations into an imposing Parisian-style mansard-roofed building constructed by the Singer Company in 1879, but within nine years the firm had absorbed all but one of the neighboring buildings along a full block of State Street.[12] Whether in makeshift agglomerations or custom-designed quarters, department-store managers gave a high priority to architectural beauty.

The exteriors of these buildings presented a massive and impressive spectacle to the consumer, but contemporary writers saved their superlatives for the interiors. The Marshall Field 1879 store was painted "brilliant white" inside, the effect heightened by the daylight pouring through the windows and the giant light well in the center of the building. The floors opening onto the rotunda were lavishly embellished with "imposing columns of ornate design, beautiful railings, and bracketed cornices." Even in descriptions of John Wanamaker's relatively spartan Grand Depot store, elegance is a recurring theme; the customer entered through a grand marble arcade lighted by stained-glass skylights and chandeliers. The rotunda was a frequent feature of early department stores: the upper floors formed galleries around a central court topped at roof level with leaded or plain glass. Fine woods, gleaming marble, and luxurious carpets were staples of department-store decoration.[13]

Merchants seized upon the technological as well as the esthetic to make their stores inviting and convenient places. Elevators were common by the 1880s in smaller cities as well as large, opening upper floors for selling as department stores' demands for space grew apace with the price of central city land. Stale air was a grave problem in large stores, and forward-looking merchants such as Macy, Wanamaker, and Field installed ventilating systems in the 1880s, the one in Macy's store capable of moving one and a half million cubic feet of air per hour. Electric illumination was a boon to department stores because it was brighter than gaslight and more dependable and uniform than daylight from light wells or windows. Macy's and Wanamaker's introduced electric lights in the late 1870s, followed by Marshall Field in 1882 and then by Strawbridge and Clothier and Albany's Whitney and Co. five years later. Telephones provided reliable communication within the store, saving the cost of messengers and lessening the congestion of the store, advantages which led both Macy's and Wanamaker's to install them before 1880. Devices for conveying cash and change between selling counters and central cashiers' stations had a similar appeal, and both mechanical cash carriers and pneumatic tube systems enjoyed great popularity, the latter first used in Wanamaker's store in 1880. Stores in smaller cities with more modest standards of urban amenity adopted these improvements later and more gradually, but in all cases the message to the public was the same: that department stores embodied all that was up to date and in urban bourgeois good taste, that they were the exemplars of rising urban standards of beauty and convenience. The public's fascination with their efforts testifies to their success.[14]

While elegant and modern, department stores were also welcoming in a way that earlier retail establishments were not. The principle of free entry—the right to look around the store without the obligation to make a purchase—was axiomatic in these giant emporiums which were as much public attractions as movie palaces, theaters, or museums. A certain heady democracy obtained: the humblest daughter of the working classes could rub shoulders with the city's wealthiest grande dame—both would of course not be equally courted by managers, but there were few other places where it was possible or even likely for the two to meet. They certainly could not buy equally, the former very likely not at all, but they could look equally. Another aspect of the welcome offered by these stores was the increasing range of services they offered. As stores expanded their size and their assortment of merchandise, customers' visits naturally lengthened as they chose from more items in each category and examined the beguiling novelties at every turn. Store managers began to provide facilities to encourage the shopper to linger and, presumably, buy more: lavatories with the most modern fittings, richly appointed lounges supplied with newspapers and stationery, restaurants catering to a woman's palate. These were places where shopping women could meet and chat with their friends, comparing purchases and trading tidbits about the latest styles. Despite Macy's no-nonsense approach to retailing, the store early provided refreshment facilities for customers: a soda fountain in 1870 and the first department-store lunchroom in the United States in 1878, when the firms's ads solicited patronage on the basis of the store's "conveniences, . . . comfort, safety, and security." Field introduced food service in 1890 on a somewhat grander scale in a tearoom marked by "quiet elegance," "designed to suit a lady's taste." By the mid-1880s, stores such as Wanamaker's, Macy's, and Field's were offering other services: telephone and telegraph stations, lost and found desks, post offices, and the like.[15]

Another category of services surrounded the actual purchase of goods with new convenience. Hoping to urge their customers to purchase more merchandise on each shopping trip, stores transformed delivery service from the occasional favor to a well-known customer into a regularly scheduled service available to all. By 1875, Macy's delivered parcels not just in Manhattan but also in Brooklyn, Williamsburg, Jersey City, and Hoboken, continuing to extend its range as the spread of public transportation brought customers from farther afield. Field's delivery service was organized in the late 1870s, and Wanamaker's in the next decade. Ready and unconditional exchanges or refunds for unsatisfactory purchases were another innovation, offered by Wanamaker and Field in the late 1870s and by Macy in the late 1880s.[16]

Stores attracted patronage not just through amenities and service, but also by making themselves lively and eventful places. Seasonal clearance sales and periodic events such as white sales enlivened them, setting the shopper on the trail of the ultimate bargain, giving her the chance to prove her mettle as the family member in charge of consumption. Promotions linked shopping to the observance of holidays such as Valentine's Day, Easter, and Christmas. Seasonal openings featuring the newest fashions attracted crowds to Field's, Wanamaker's, and Macy's by the end of the 1880s. Store extravaganzas marked special occasions, suspending all sales while the public promenaded through the stores as they might through a museum; during the 1880s Wanamaker staged a "Grand Illumination" one evening and Woodward & Lothrop held a reception to inaugurate a new building. Department stores also mounted exhibitions not directly connected to their merchandise: in 1887, for example, the Wanamaker store celebrated the centennial of the Constitution with demonstrations of late-eighteenth-century crafts by people in period dress, and Macy's was host to an archery contest. These giant emporiums told their patrons in myriad ways that shopping was not just purchasing but an agreeable and leisurely diversion in luxurious surroundings, laced with exciting events to relieve daily tedium and newly linked to traditional celebrations such as Christmas.[17]

While stores such as Macy's and Marshall Field were located near opposite ends of an imaginary spectrum of which the poles were price and amenity, in fact both appealed to the consumer's frugality as well as to her desire for status and luxury. Although Macy's was never a magnet for the wealthiest of New Yorkers, it was an early if not especially opulent provider of the basic constellation of services which customers came to expect by the end of the nineteenth century—omitting only charge accounts, a Macy peculiarity. Conversely, Marshall Field, the quintessential carriage-trade store, did not scorn the more modest Chicago customers: if a woman could find $300 lace shawls there, she could also find high-style embroidered Parisian chemises for only 75¢. Store rules distributed to the firm's salespeople stipulated that they be "polite and attentive to rich and poor alike." Harry Selfridge, dynamic manager of Field's retail division from 1884 to 1904, solidified the firm's claim to the popular trade by highlighting the store's basement bargain departments and relentlessly cutting prices in each new department he opened. Macy's and Field's alike, however, neglected one class of customer: the working-class woman with little discretionary income. Department stores directed their appeals to the woman who had extra money to spend beyond her family's basic necessities, the one who could be convinced to buy three suits of specially priced underwear instead of one, who could yield to the temptation of a novelty pair of gloves. The logic was similar to Wanamaker's in justifying his store's expansion into new merchandise lines: if a customer bought three times as much, the burden of fixed expense was, all other things being equal, one third as large in relation to the size of the sale.[18]

The elaboration of department-store services was, as Ralph Hower has pointed out, fueled in an immediate way by growing competition over matters of service, but also in a more general way by the rising standards of living of an urban bourgeoisie which was enjoying greater amenity in its homes. Department stores' appeals were, in short, tied to an emerging set of class-specific manners and mores. Stores reinforced the notions of bourgeois good taste and propriety, particularly insofar as these required ever more elaborate material accompaniments: the correct clothes for each occasion, the huge assortment of china, silver, and glassware necessary for proper entertaining, the home decorated in the acme of contemporary taste. Catering to the more sophisticated consumer, the type who had "developed a larger intelligence, . . . a greater culture and a wider and more refined taste," these stores also educated those only aspiring to these heights, providing an "education in color, form, and harmony" through the display of fully decorated rooms and completely outfitted mannequins. Department stores were thus both seductive and didactic, both followers and shapers of taste, dynamic museums of a constantly changing way of life attuned to style and propriety.[19]

Yet these very class-based manners were already a source of trouble for store managers. In a very direct sense, notions of proper behavior could cost department stores money as women used stores' free services to act out their visions of socially correct behavior. Some customers, for example, used delivery services frivolously, refusing to carry parcels because of "a foolish or absurd idea that it would tend to social degradation." The trade paper condemning these women noted acidly that those who would put the store to the expense of delivering a single spool of thread often carried a poodle under their arms through a whole day of shopping. For the most part, store managers accepted these consumer peccadilloes, regarding them as an inevitable "evil incident to the retail business." To retailers in this formative period, the goal was not to reform the customer but to give in to her arbitrary demands and rude conduct, currying favor by catering to her "caprices and tastes."[20]

On a daily basis, the female salesclerks, for whom department-store

managers had created a new world of a third sort, bore the brunt of customers' misbehavior. Few stores failed to take on women as clerks between 1850 and 1890, although the proportions of women behind the
counters varied widely. Marshall Field first hired women in ready-to-wear
and lingerie, departments where the merchandise needed to be fitted and
where questions of delicacy made them preferable to salesmen. Women
moved into other departments at Field's but still comprised a minority of
the selling force by 1900. Philadelphia merchants were especially eager to
hire women; by 1887 there were so many female employees in the John
Wanamaker firm that the store opened a residence hotel for them, antici-
pating the paternalist benefits that would become so popular in department stores in the early twentieth century. Within a decade of the founding of R. H. Macy's New York store, women comprised 80 percent of its
labor force. In the country as a whole, the number of saleswomen jumped
from under 8000 to over 58,000 between 1880 and 1890. By that time,
selling was well established as a women's occupation, with a higher proportion of women in the nation's selling force than in the labor force as a
whole.[21]

The reasons for the recourse to female clerks were various and sometimes contradictory. Some argued that women's more demure standards
of conduct made them preferable: one manager told Helen Campbell in
1887, "I've been a manager thirteen years, and we never had but four dishonest girls, and we've had to discharge over forty boys in the same time.
Boys smoke and lose at cards, and do a hundred things that women don't,
and they get worse instead of better. I go in for women." Others suggested
that the saleswoman was more assertive, that "a woman behind the
counter is like a queen behind her throne" and could be relied upon to
"awe and . . . subdue" the customer into purchasing, unlike the frequently timid and less effective salesmen. Many employers appreciated
women's cheap labor, a quality some attributed simply to their gender,
others to the excess labor supply which enabled employers to instantly
replace demanding or inadequate clerks, and still others to the low
quality of the service women rendered on the job. A few managers con-
scientiously acknowledged that women equaled men in selling ability, but
still fewer voices vainly argued that they should therefore receive a salary
equal to men's. Whatever the social and cultural factors which made
women acceptable as clerks, economic factors—the large supply and low
cost of female labor—were apparently paramount in most employers'
minds.[22]

The expectations surrounding saleswomen's work were fundamentally different from those of salesmen. Men had historically worked under a kind of informal apprenticeship system, while women were hired, paid, and treated as incumbents of dead-end jobs. In this respect, sales work developed similarly to clerical work. Both were, in the early nineteenth century, the province of a comparatively small number of males, many of whom saw their jobs as stepping-stones to managerial or entrepreneurial careers. As the bureaucratic structures of business and the distribution sector of the economy expanded, employers' demands for clerical and sales workers also grew. First expanding their male staffs, managers soon turned to female labor. Department-store managers were far less selective in hiring women, assuming that they would be short-term employees and that defects in character could be offset by strict discipline and fines. The incorrigibly indifferent or insubordinate employee was ruthlessly weeded out and replaced from the growing pool of eager applicants. Like A. T. Stewart before them, department-store managers offered their saleswomen the stark choice of "diligence or discharge." [23]

From the start, though, saleswomen saw more in their jobs than their bosses were willing to acknowledge. Early saleswomen were referred to as shopgirls, an English term which conjured up visions of an inferior class position, poor taste in dress and speech, and possibly a low moral state. Some saleswomen fit the stereotype by speaking shrilly and ungrammatically, dressing flashily, and entering into the developing heterosocial culture of the urban working class. But there were other voices which managers chose to ignore: those, for example, of the New York saleswomen who scorned "shopgirl," were offended by "saleswoman," and demanded to be called "salesladies," suggesting that perhaps the American version of the shopgirl was more assertive and ambitious than her English counterparts. Annie, a saleswoman in New Holland, Illinois, wrote to the *Dry Goods Chronicle and Fancy Goods Review* in 1889, terming herself a "'WANT-TO-SUCCEED' clerk." Plucky and eager, she was nonetheless reluctant to leave the pleasant small-town circle of her family and friends for the buyer's position that might be hers in a larger city. She urged the journal not to focus exclusively on men, for "we [women] must have SOME ENCOURAGEMENT, or our hearts, as well as our hands, will fail in our attempts to do the work we are ANXIOUS TO DO." The editor responded with platitudes about hard work and persistence, sidestepping the gender issue. Annie wasn't alone in her discontent; the journal repeatedly noted women's complaints that they were being slighted, and in 1889 and 1890 ran an occasional "Our Girls" column to supplement the standard "Our Boys" feature. The contrast between the two suggests the world of difference between managers' attitudes toward the two groups. "Our Boys" columns spoke to clerks in small towns, assuming that they were on the way to bigger things—managerial or merchandising positions—in the cities. The column urged aspiring "boys" to cultivate the prudential virtues and to be ambitious for wealth and higher social position. "The rising generation of clerks," the journal assured the aspirants, "must ultimately take the place of the present merchants." The infrequent "Our Girls" columns, on the other hand, could have been directed at women in any occupation or, for that matter, to women outside the labor force. The articles lectured on proper courtship behavior, the necessity of learning to cook well, the evils of tight lacing, and the wisdom of honoring one's parents. The world of retailing is curiously absent from "Our Girls"; clearly the Annies of the world had to look elsewhere for the legitimation and encouragement of their ambitions.[24]

Had Annie migrated to a large city, she would have found more to feed her hopes for the future, but also much to shadow her working days. Macy's, for example, offered unprecedented executive opportunities for women. Margaret Getchell became the store's first superintendent, with responsibility for day-to-day operations and an important policy-making role; until 1887, all the incumbents of this position were women. A number of women became buyers at Macy's; Belle Cushman of the fancy goods department earned $25 per week in 1871, an unusually high salary for a woman. Still others were floorwalkers, commanding salaries from $10 to $16 at a time when the typical Macy saleswoman received $5 or $6 per week and the best-paid rarely made more than $10. Although women's careers in other stores are less well documented, the glamorous and responsible position of buyer was open to women from the formative years of department stores. For most, however, department-store life was far more mundane. A few firms such as Macy's and Wanamaker's granted paid vacations before 1880, but the "unpaid vacation"—the layoff, in other words—was far more common. In all stores, saleswomen were subject to harsh and arbitrary discipline. At Macy's, sitting while at work was forbidden and "unnecessary conversations" could lead to instant dismissal. Hours were inhumanly long, stretching to sixteen hours per day in the busiest seasons; employees' facilities were unsanitary and even squalid. Low wages were the scandal of the industry, and even further reduced by fines which placed "a value upon time lost that is not given to service rendered": in one store, women earning $7 per week were fined 30¢ for ten minutes' tardiness. While bad conduct was swiftly and surely punished, good performance went unrewarded or worse. A trade publication complained that virtually no department-store managers subscribed to the notion that the "well-bred or clever saleswoman is the rightful owner of a larger wage than one caring only for the stated return of her pay-day," and a reformers' pamphlet charged that one New York store regularly fired women after five years' satisfactory service in order to forestall demands for increased salaries.[25]

Believing that well-chosen merchandise would essentially sell itself, managers devoted little attention to teaching saleswomen about their merchandise or selling techniques. Instead, most of their directives to the sales force concerned the rocky interaction between saleswomen and customers. Customers appeared to prefer female over male clerks because salesmen were often discomfitingly flirtatious and less willing to tolerate customers' high-handed or disagreeable behavior. But class-based differences in demeanor disrupted sales transactions between women; the interaction across the counter took the form of a sort of duel, with the customer and the saleswoman each asserting superior knowledge about the style and quality of merchandise. Customers condemned the lack of deference in saleswomen's conduct and appearance. When a saleswoman—particularly "some inexperienced girl without a shadow of good taste"—was unbecomingly familiar or offered unsolicited advice, customers responded with an "ominous silence" or regal restraint. A lady, noted a trade journal, "could afford to let [a] snub pass unrebuked." Saleswomen who dressed in a "tawdry," "befangled," or "eccentric" fashion or who displayed an "untidy, careless toilet" offended the class-conscious or fastidious customer.[26]

Saleswomen generally ignored the chilling scorn of outraged customers, using both individual and collective methods to assert their own superiority. An individual saleswoman could turn withering disdain on a customer who asked for an unfamiliar or unfashionable item, calling into question both her taste and her marketplace acumen. Collectively, saleswomen's response to customers' "ominous silence" was animated talk among themselves, ignoring the customer and often continuing their conversation while waiting on her. They were brazenly indifferent to their customers' subtle opprobrium; in one anecdote, a woman offended by saleswomen's gum-chewing "looked her disgust and disapproval," but they persisted "perfectly undisturbed and nonchalant, in fact, rather enjoying her discomfort." In the end, of course, the customer held the higher cards; a saleswoman whom a customer reported to her superiors was treated harshly, if only to demonstrate the firm's solicitude for its clientele. The unscrupulous and touchy customers who brought un-merited rebukes down on saleswomen's heads nurtured in female clerks' hearts a "bitter sense of injustice" that assured the counter's continuing role as a line of battle in the struggle between those who sold and those who shopped. While acknowledging the often unreasonable behavior of customers, managers urged on saleswomen the same grin-and-bear-it at-titude they themselves adopted. They counseled female clerks to be "un-obtrusive" and "ladylike," to display a "quiet, unruffled demeanor" and "courteous forbearance," and to appreciate "the beauty of bending to the will of others." The first generations of department-store managers took the line of least resistance in dealing with saleswomen as with customers, urging their clerks to do little and to do it politely rather than trying to make them a more positive presence in the store.[27]

The three new worlds that department-store managers had created—for themselves, their customers, and their saleswomen—were both prom-ising and haunted by ominous problems. Their own world produced large profits and expanding sales while giving them a leading role in the culture of consumption, but it also burdened them with heavy fixed ex-penses, the coordination of a huge operation, and the management of troublesome saleswomen and customers. The customers found in depart-ment stores the delights of lower prices and lavish services but also the trials of dealing with clerks. The world of the saleswomen offered them a place in the tantalizing giant emporium, spiced by a few dazzling possi-bilities for advancement, yet it also subjected them to low wages, over-work, and persistent class-based conflict with customers. By 1890, the successes of department stores were evident: new stores were established and existing ones expanded; customers filled the stores' aisles; wage-earning women flocked to their employment offices. The nagging prob-lems beneath the surface were less obvious but held worrisome portents for the future. During the subsequent decade, they surfaced with increas-ing insistence and began to shape a department-store agenda which would absorb managers' attention through four decades of the twentieth century.

Notes

1. Ralph M. Hower, "Urban Retailing 100 Years Ago," *Bulletin of the Busi-ness Historical Society*, 12 (Dec. 1938), 91–101, and *History of Macy's of New York, 1858–1919: Chapters in the Evolution of the Department Store* (Cam-bridge, Mass., 1943), 77–88.

2. Frank M. Mayfield, *The Department Store Story* (New York, 1949), 27–45; Hrant Pasdermadjian, *The Department Store: Its Origins, Evolution and Economics* (London, 1954), 3–9; Harry E. Resseguie, "Alexander Turney Stewart and the Development of the Department Store, 1823–1876," *Business History Review*, 39 (Autumn 1965), 301–22; Tom Mahoney and Leonard Sloan, *The Great Merchants: America's Foremost Retail Institutions and the People Who Made Them Great*, 2d ed. (New York, 1966), 7–11; Hower, *Macy's*, 48–54, 98–113; Robert W. Twyman, *History of Marshall Field & Co., 1852–1906* (Philadelphia, 1954), 108–9. On the prudential virtues, see T. J. Jackson Lears, "From Salvation to Self-Realization: Advertising and the Therapeutic Roots of the Consumer Culture, 1880–1930," in Richard Wightman Fox and T. J. Jackson Lears, eds., *The Culture of Consumption: Critical Essays in American History, 1880–1980* (New York, 1983), 1–38; "Success in Retail Merchandising," *DGC & FGR*, 6 (18 Aug. 1888), 4–5; "Our Boys," *DGC & FGR*, 8 (9 Nov. 1889), 6, (23 Nov. 1889), 6–7.

3. Resseguie, "Alexander Turney Stewart"; Hower, *Macy's*; Joseph H. Appel, *The Business Biography of John Wanamaker, Founder and Builder: America's Merchant Pioneer from 1861 to 1922* (New York, 1922); *Golden Book of the Wanamaker Stores, Jubilee Year, 1861–1911* ([Philadelphia], 1911); Lloyd Wendt and Herman Kogan, *Give the Lady What She Wants! The Story of Marshall Field & Company* (Chicago, 1952); Twyman, *History of Marshall Field*. For an elegant survey of the rise of the American department store in comparative perspective, see Gunther Barth, *City People: The Rise of Modern City Culture in Nineteenth-Century America* (Oxford, 1980), 110–47. Barth surveys much the same developments as I do in this chapter, but his functionalist perspective (see esp. 133, 136) leads him to see department stores as harmonious, smoothly functioning institutions while I emphasize their built-in contradictions. Alan Trachtenberg's brief treatment of department stores (*The Incorporation of America: Culture and Society in the Gilded Age* [New York, 1982], 130–35) is more similar to mine; he sees, for example, the ways in which department stores simultaneously provided "education" and "obfuscation."

4. Hower, *Macy's*, 99–112; Appel, *Business Biography of John Wanamaker*, 81, 85–91.

5. Hower, *Macy's*, 192–95.

6. "Successful Retail Merchants," *DGC & FGR*, 4 (16 July 1887), 3; Twyman, *History of Marshall Field*, 50; Hower, *Macy's*, 168, 188, 302–3; Appel, *Business Biography of John Wanamaker*, 102–3.

7. Hower, *Macy's*, 114; Twyman, *History of Marshall Field*, 65–66; "Causes of Failures among Retailers," *DGC & FGR*, 4 (29 Oct. 1887), 5; "The Good Buyer the Successful Merchant," *DGC & FGR*, 5 (21 Jan. 1888), 4.

8. Alfred D. Chandler, Jr., *The Visible Hand: The Managerial Revolution in American Business* (Cambridge, Mass., 1977), 1–12, and *Strategy and Structure: Chapters in the History of the Industrial Enterprise* (Cambridge, Mass., 1962), 8–17; Hower, *Macy's*, 115–17, 194–95.

9. On the therapeutic ethic, see Lears, "From Salvation to Self-Realization"; "Store Attractions," *DGC & FGR*, 8 (21 Dec. 1889), 7, and 9 (15 Feb. 1890), 5.

10. Hower, *Macy's*, 54–65; Appel, *Business Biography of John Wanamaker*, 385–89.

11. "Points on Store Window Displays," *DGC & FGR*, 4 (16 July 1887), 7; "The Origin of Big Plate Glass Windows," *DGC & FGR*, 4 (24 Dec. 1887), 6; "Window Dressing," *DGC & FGR*, 5 (10 Mar. 1888), 3.

12. Hower, *Macy's*, 165–67; Alfred Lief, *Family Business: A Century in the Life and Times of Strawbridge & Clothier* (New York, 1968), 18, 33–34; Twyman, *History of Marshall Field*, 154–59.

13. Twyman, *History of Marshall Field*, 60; *Golden Book*, 51–53.

14. Hower, *Macy's*, 165–67, 450; Twyman, *History of Marshall Field*, 61; Appel, *Business Biography of John Wanamaker*, 102–5, 193; Lief, *Family Business*, 55; "The Largest Mercantile Establishment of Its Kind between New York and Chicago," *DGC & FGR*, 4 (10 Sept. 1887), 10.

15. Twyman, *History of Marshall Field*, 118, 123–25; Hower, *Macy's*, 160–67; Appel, *Business Biography of John Wanamaker*, 105–6.

16. Hower, *Macy's*, 119, 261, 282; Twyman, *History of Marshall Field*, 130–33; Appel, *Business Biography of John Wanamaker*, 81–83, 108.

17. Appel, *Business Biography of John Wanamaker*, 101–8; Hower, *Macy's*, 163, 169; Twyman, *History of Marshall Field*, 148, 228; Martha C. Guilford, ed., *From Founder to Grandsons: The Story of Woodward & Lothrop* (Washington, 1955), 52.

18. Hower, *Macy's*, 49, 118, 164–70; Twyman, *History of Marshall Field*, 24, 30, 112–14; Wendt and Kogan, *Give the Lady What She Wants*, 131–34.

19. Hower, *Macy's*, 168; "The Good Buyer the Successful Merchant," 4; "Store Attractions," *DGC & FGR*, 9 (15 Mar. 1890), 8.

20. "Ashamed to Carry Bundles," *DGC & FGR*, 10 (20 Sept. 1890), 5; "A Common Type of Dry Goods Shopper," *DGC & FGR*, 4 (9 July 1887), 1; "Buyers and Sellers," *DGC & FGR*, 7 (9 Feb. 1889), 6.

21. Twyman, *History of Marshall Field*, 69; Appel, *Business Biography of John Wanamaker*, 108; Hower, *Macy's*, 193–94; Appendix A.

22. Helen Campbell, *Prisoners of Poverty: Women Wage-Workers, Their Trades and Their Lives* (1887; rpt. Westport, Conn., 1970), 173–74; "Pity the Poor Salesman," *DGC & FGR*, 4 (15 Oct. 1887), 3; "Rudeness and Impertinence of the Sales Force in Some of Our Retail Stores," *DGC & FGR*, 5 (14 Jan. 1888), 5; "The Same Work Should Receive the Same Pay," *DGC & FGR*, 5 (28 Jan. 1888), 5; "Women's Selling Ability," *DGC & FGR*, 8 (21 Sept. 1889), 3.

23. On the development of the female office force, see Margery W. Davies, *Woman's Place Is at the Typewriter: Office Work and Office Workers, 1870–1930* (Philadelphia, 1982). "Store Attractions," *DGC & FGR*, 4 (15 Oct. 1887), 3; "Stewart, and the Dry Goods Trade of New York," *Continental Monthly*, 2 (Nov. 1863), 532.

24. "The Term 'Shop Girl,'" *DGC & FGR*, 4 (20 Aug. 1887), 1; "What Can a Girl Do, Anyway?" *DGC & FGR*, 7 (16 Mar. 1889), 6; "Our Boys," *DGC & FGR*, 8 (9 Nov. 1889), 6, and (6 July 1889), 3; "Our Girls," *DGC & FGR*, 8 (12 Oct. 1889), 3; "Suggestions to Our Girls," *DGC & FGR*, 8 (2 Nov. 1889), 3; "Talks to Girls," *DGC & FGR*, 9 (10 May 1890), 7 and (24 May 1890), 7. On the

development of heterosocial urban working-class culture, see Kathy Peiss, *Cheap Amusements: Working Women and Leisure in Turn-of-the-Century New York* (Philadelphia, 1985).

25. Hower, *Macy's*, 65–66, 115, 126, 194–96, 201–3, 303, 306; Appel, *Business Biography of John Wanamaker*, 101–3; "Store Attractions," *DGC & FGR*, 6 (14 July 1888), 7; Alice L. Woodbridge, *Report on the Condition of Working Women in New York Retail Stores* (New York, 1890), 3–7 (quotation from 5); "On Both Sides of the Counter," *DGC & FGR*, 8 (6 July 1889), 9. Sheila Rothman underestimates the promotional possibilities for women in early department stores; see her *Woman's Proper Place: A History of Changing Ideals and Practices, 1870 to the Present* (New York, 1978), 55–56.

26. "On Both Sides of the Counter," *DGC & FGR*, 7 (18 May 1889), 8, (15 June 1889), 7, (8 June 1889), 7, (29 June 1889), 7, (22 June 1889), 7.

27. "On Both Sides of the Counter," *DGC & FGR*, 7 (8 June 1889), 7, and (4 May 1889), 7; 8 (3 Aug. 1889), 8; 7 (27 Apr. 1889), 8 and (20 Apr. 1889), 10.

2

"A Homogeneous Business":
Organizing the Department Store

By the 1890s, the department store was the leading force in American retailing. Most obviously, the new type of store had a name: the term *department store* became current during that decade, an acknowledgment that forty years of innovations had coalesced into a recognizable new sort of firm. The vast majority of the big-name department stores in centers large and small were founded by the end of the 1890s; Younker Brothers in Des Moines, Rich's of Atlanta, G. Fox & Company in Hartford, J. Joske and Sons in San Antonio, and the City of Paris in San Francisco were but a few of the stores presenting the public with a merchandise mix and an appeal similar to that of pioneers like Macy's, John Wanamaker, and Marshall Field. A mere handful of major stores made their appearance after the turn of the century, among them J. B. Ivey and Company of North Carolina, Crowley-Milner and Company of Detroit, Foley Brothers of Houston, Bullock's of Los Angeles, and Neiman-Marcus. Small-business opponents of the new form of retailing had their last serious public hearing during the 1890s, and department stores were clearly vindicated; bills to limit department-store operations failed to pass in Illinois, Massachusetts, California, and Maryland, and a similar law in Missouri was declared unconstitutional by the state's Supreme Court. More important was the favorable pronouncement of the U.S. Industrial Commission, clearing department stores of charges of unfair competition, monopoly, and unusually fraudulent advertising, equivocating only on their labor policies, and concluding that they were "on the whole advantageous to the consuming public." The crowds in the aisles of the nation's department stores clearly agreed. By the turn of the century, then, the department store was both well established and pervasive.[1]

The large-scale retailers of the 1890s by no means rested on past achievements; they continued along the paths staked out by the industry's pioneers at the same time as they began to discipline and consolidate their operations. Convinced that the halcyon days of the 1880s would never return and that the future demanded more deliberate business methods, they began to experiment with new management techniques as the country recovered from the depression of the mid-1890s. Their primary goal was to weld their disparate and often warring departments into a coherent and efficient organization—"a homogeneous business," in the words of a journalist. Department-store managers joined their industrial counterparts in looking critically at management methods, agonizing over problems of size, cost, efficiency, and control. Trade journals continued to praise the prudential virtues but increasingly urged their readers to develop what might be called the managerial virtues: order and system became the watchwords of the day. Caught up in the vogue for more systematic methods, department-store and industrial managers raised their voices in criticism of past practices and eagerly embraced panaceas that promised higher productivity and tighter control over their firms.[2]

Juxtaposing department stores' version of systematic management with the more commonly studied factory experience places the peculiarities of retailers' situation in high relief. While the two sectors shared important management problems, retailing raised far more complex issues of human interaction and of the firm's social role. Plagued by expenses that were rising more quickly than those in manufacturing and yet locked into the pursuit of high-cost tactics for encouraging the culture of consumption, department-store executives persistently tried to forge a strategy that would increase both their profits and the goodwill of the consuming public. Although they achieved important gains on both fronts, a victory in one area often meant a setback in another. Management policy in department stores during the years between 1890 and 1940 tried to balance the conflicting claims of retailers' roles as cost-conscious businessmen and as cultural agents for a grandiose and often wasteful ethic of consumption.

The most striking feature of store and factory was size, both in terms of physical area and of numbers of people involved. The Marshall Field and the R. H. Macy Herald Square stores, both completed in 1902, each had over one million square feet of floor space; four factories the size of Ford's Highland Park plant would have fit comfortably inside either store.

Great size, however, meant something notably different in stores and in factories. Giant factories were more frequently built in outlying areas where land was cheap, but department stores were by definition at the center of urban life and thus had to be built on expensive and scarce land in the central business district. While the factory could build out and allocate space generously, the department store had to build up. In the department store, space was money, a scarce and hotly contested commodity.[3]

Even more important, the typical department-store executive in this period managed only one store; vertical and horizontal integration changed the nature of department-store management very little before World War II. Although some firms such as Marshall Field and Strawbridge and Clothier had important wholesale branches into the 1920s, department stores tended to supplant wholesaling by buying directly from manufacturers. A few large firms began to manufacture household goods and wearing apparel during the late nineteenth century, partly in order to cut costs and to insure high quality in an era of sweatshop production. Such efforts generally proved unprofitable or limited stores' merchandising flexibility; John Wanamaker ruefully told the U.S. Industrial Commission that he had learned "that manufacturing is quite another business, and a man had better attend to the business that he knows."[4]

Horizontal integration, whether through expansion or mergers, had little more effect on the department-store industry. Branch stores before 1940 were relatively rare; typical were Filene's college-town stores, I. Magnin's luxury-hotel shops, and Marshall Field's suburban branches. These outposts were usually quite small, sometimes seasonal, and managed as departments of the parent store. While industrial firms were experiencing a second great wave of concentration during the 1920s, department-store mergers were still in their infancy. They occasionally involved neighboring firms, such as Filene's and R. H. White or Gimbel Brothers and Saks, but more often united noncompetitive stores, as when the St. Louis firm of Scruggs-Vandervoort-Barney acquired stores in Denver and Columbus. Far more stores, however, were drawn into ownership groups such as Federated Department Stores than into outright mergers. These groups acted in effect as holding companies, standardizing the organizational structure and accounting systems of their member stores, exchanging information for research purposes, and engaging in some group buying, but they left daily operations to local managers who tried to preserve their stores' distinct personality and community appeal. Both merged stores and group stores continued to enjoy considerable autonomy and thus differed from chain stores which stressed uniformity and made few inroads into the department-store industry.[5]

To use Alfred Chandler's terms, the invisible hand of the market weighed more heavily on department stores than the visible hand of administrative coordination. Unlike steel manufacturers who dealt with a few types of raw material and a relatively limited number of customers, department stores bought from hundreds or even thousands of concerns and sold to millions, a state of affairs little affected by mergers, ownership groups, or branches. While manufacturers typically tried to corner a market by driving out competitors in a specific product line, the key strategy of large-scale retailing was diversification rather than specialization. The vast majority of department-store managers were locked into highly competitive local markets and enjoyed a high degree of local autonomy, managing their stores as independent units even when they were part of a larger firm; executives of large manufacturing firms functioned in an increasingly oligopolistic market and within a much more constricting corporate structure.[6]

Within large stores and factories alike, managers faced the challenge of coping with ever-growing numbers of people. By 1898 Macy's had three thousand employees, putting it in a class with such manufacturing giants as the Merrimack Mills in Lowell, Massachusetts, the Waltham Watch Company, and Carnegie Steel's J. Edgar Thompson plant; 60 percent of Americans lived in towns with fewer people. In 1900, Jordan Marsh, with a work force fluctuating between three and five thousand, was the fourth-largest employer in New England, surpassed only by the Amoskeag Mills, General Electric's Lynn plant, and the Pacific Mills of Lawrence.[7]

Department-store managers had to manage, in addition to their employees, the public who poured through their doors. In 1904, for example, Marshall Field's work force ranged from eight to ten thousand in a store through which as many as a quarter of a million customers passed during a day. No industrial manager had to deal with anything like this volume of humanity; by comparison, the task of supervising the Ford Highland Park plant's thirteen thousand workers in 1914 pales. Factory managers had only their workers to oversee, but department-store managers had to face an unpredictable and frequently troublesome horde of customers as well.[8]

Despite these differences, the problems of large-scale operations produced in factory and department-store executives alike an obsession with tightening the managerial reins. After 1880, American businessmen increasingly made control and efficiency their bywords, devising strategies for systematizing and regularizing their practices and for increasing the predictability of the factors with which they had to deal. By 1900, there was a new self-consciousness and determination in businessmen's efforts to rationalize both production and consumption; the conscientious manager worried over the most minute aspect of production as well as over the global question of fostering an ethic of consumption. *System* magazine, founded in 1900, expressed the breadth of these concerns and the diversity of department-store managers' interests: subjects featured ranged from an elaborate system of expense classification to a national survey of women's attitudes toward store practices.[9]

Although thoughtful executives in both stores and factories agreed on the ultimate goal of rationalization, different social realities within their firms led to differences in implementing the new ideas. For the factory executive, efforts to rationalize production and consumption were neatly compartmentalized. Within the factory, the problem was to induce workers to produce more in less time and at less cost; outside its walls, the task was to encourage people to buy more freely and with less concern for necessity. As Stuart Ewen has noted, a pivotal element in the emerging culture of consumption was the "obliteration of the factory," a bifurcation of the world into an unpleasant sphere in which goods were produced and a gratifying sphere in which they were consumed. Industrial managers could thus run their factories with a single-minded concern for productivity and leave the fabrication of demand to advertising executives and copywriters who willingly averted their eyes from the production process. Helen Woodward spoke for the latter when she said: "If you are advertising any product, never see the factory in which it was made. . . . Don't watch the people at work. . . . Because, you see, when you know the truth about anything, the real, inner truth—it is very hard to write the surface fluff which sells it."[10]

Department-store managers enjoyed no such luxury. The "real, inner truth" could not be disguised or effectively obscured when the locus of production and consumption was the same: the selling floor. Moreover, the same accounting unit, the sales transaction, measured both the salesperson's effectiveness in selling and the customer's willingness to consume. At best, the public nature of the store's operations made the retail executive's task enormously more complicated than that of the factory manager; at worst, it entangled him in a web of contradictions arising from his curious betwixt-and-between position. Retailers sought on the one hand to control and supervise their workers and their firms as closely as any of their factory counterparts: they acted like managers pure and simple. Yet they also wished to make a complex social statement that involved issues of class and gender, of psychology and aspiration, identifying consumption with a life of style, respectability, and urbanity: they acted, to use Ewen's phrase, like captains of consciousness. A measure which served one set of ends frequently conflicted with or undermined the other; wherever managers turned, they confronted unintended effects.

The widening sphere of consumption required stores to fundamentally rethink their social and economic role, but daily life in the factory was little changed. Factory managers continued to think of themselves as producers, even as the new management techniques brought changes. Retailers had traditionally emphasized the buying of their wares, considering their main chore the establishment of advantageous relations with manufacturers and suppliers, their role defined by the task of stocking stores with goods. By 1890, however, the emphasis began to shift to selling; on the eve of World War I the *Dry Goods Economist* editorialized: "[W]hile 'What to Buy and How to Sell It' has been the ECONOMIST's slogan for over a generation, of late years emphasis has been transferred from the first three words to the last four." Lew Hahn, for many years general manager of the National Retail Dry Goods Association, provided his own slogan during the 1920s to sum up the change: retailers should "act as purchasing agent for the consumer, rather than as sales agent for the manufacturer." The change was in fact even more fundamental, a later commentator noted, for the department store had become "an institution in the community; . . . it was guide, counselor and friend to the customer." The forward-looking department store would not just sell, item by item, but create an atmosphere for selling that would encourage consumption in general.[11]

The retailer's new economic stance created problems of assessment and measurement. The legendary widget manufacturer could gauge his output easily and exactly: the number of widgets conforming to specifications turned out in a given time. But for the retailer, neither qualitative nor quantitative measurement was easy. The *Dry Goods Economist* criticized those merchants who cared only for their sales totals: "[A] retail business cannot be built on the volume of sales or numerically measured trade, but must be built on the basis of one sale making another sale just like it—either of the same goods or the goods of another department." [12] Quality control had to be built into the process of selling and could be neither precise nor retroactive. The retailer was in a paradoxical position: his sense as a businessman told him that he must control and organize his business and monitor it more closely, but his position as a retailer warned him that the most critical aspects of his enterprise—those which made steady customers out of occasional purchasers—were peculiarly difficult to supervise and measure.

The endemic variability of retailing only exacerbated this dilemma. Retailing shared seasonality with certain manufacturing industries such as candy, clothing, and jewelry, but fluctuations in retail demand posed more complex and vexing problems. Unlike factories, stores could not simply close down during slow seasons, no matter how sparse the traffic during a hot August or a spring rainstorm. Seasonal fluctuations in department stores were wide, persistent, and pervasive; January sales in typical department stores in the 1920s, for example, were half those of December. Jordan Marsh's 1899 work force varied from 3000 to 5000; Macy's 1919 payroll ranged from 10,000 to 20,000; in 1927, Filene's added as many as 900 to its basic force of 3000; and in 1940 a West Virginia store increased its usual staff of 140 by 100. The peaks in trade which caused these increases in the labor force occurred not only in the Christmas season but around other holidays and special sales; the Gilchrist Company of Boston regularly brought in 500 extra people on special sale days during the 1920s. [13]

Wide fluctuations also occurred within weeks and days. Although local shopping customs varied, Saturday was usually the busiest day, Monday the next busiest, and Friday the slowest. The tide of customers began slowly in the morning and rose through the day; a vice-president of a Brooklyn store reported in 1933 that 84 percent of her store's transactions occurred during the middle six hours of the day, peaking between 1:30 and 3:45. Department-store managers could of course plan for such cycles in consumer demand, but far less effectively than industrial managers; the latter could concentrate production in one part of the day or week, but retailers had to adjust their schedules to their customers'. Further, the canniest merchant could not protect himself from whim and chance: a snowstorm during a sale of new spring fashions, a winning football team which drew away Saturday trade, or any number of personal inclinations which fostered or curbed consumption.[14]

Beset by the difficulties of standardizing and controlling retailing, stymied by the problems of balancing both sides of their identity, managers of department stores groped uncertainly toward new administrative strategies. Looking back from the vantage point of 1939, one observer saw clearly that retailers had failed to devise a unified plan of action and warned somberly against the prevailing idea "that a business can be divided into two parts—the economic aim on the one side and the social obligations on the other" when "as a matter of fact, these are merely two aspects of one whole. . . . You cannot separate them without killing both."[15]

In stores giant and modest, in the metropolis as well as in the small town, department-store managers tried to tighten their control over their firms' operations, revamping their physical plants, shifting power away from buyers, and forging new merchandising policies. These methods emerged in the decade centering on the turn of the century and spread unevenly through the industry. Few stores implemented all at the same time; few tried none. Typically, management used these methods in a cycle of enthusiasm and disillusionment. Repeatedly both individual managers and the industry as a whole embraced a tactic as a panacea, only to find that it created as well as solved problems, that in serving one end it sabotaged others; methods discredited or overused at one point tended to find favor again in later years.

Managing Department-Store Space

Reform-minded managers' efforts to rationalize store buildings and fixtures paralleled most closely those of industrialists: the planned and organized use of space brought significant benefits to factory and department store alike. In general, the physical transformation of the department store took place on three levels: as part of the urban milieu; in the non-selling sections of the store such as receiving, marking, and bookkeeping; and on the selling floor. The changes in the non-selling departments duplicated those in factories and offices and did not develop patterns specific to retailing. In the other two areas, the impact of technology was limited; department stores had far less to gain from mechanical devices than factories. Particularly in the period from 1890 to 1940, department-store technology was less a matter of new devices than of the diffusion of older ones introduced between 1850 and 1890.

Department stores had in their early years enthusiastically adopted new urban techniques in buildings and equipment, using iron, steel, and reinforced concrete construction as well as elevators, electric light, forced-air ventilation, telephones, pneumatic tubes, and modern plumbing and heating systems. After 1890, these amenities were employed more widely and with increasing calculation, as the example of electric lighting shows. Between 1911 and 1936 the intensity of illumination in the typical store tripled, with indirect lighting and accent spotlights replacing older direct lighting. One rapturous writer concluded that better lighting in one store had led to a 27 percent increase in sales, in part by making salespeople feel "more progressive."[16] Only three major new developments along these lines occurred between 1890 and 1940: floor-through construction, escalators, and air conditioning.

The rotunda design, the hallmark of the nineteenth-century department store, appeared inefficient and unsafe to twentieth-century eyes: it sacrificed valuable floor space and allowed fires to spread rapidly. Marshall Field's 1907 building and John Wanamaker's 1911 store were among the last to use the open-court form, and floor-through construction became the rule. Transportation within the store became an ever more pressing issue as selling departments spread to upper floors. Elevators had marked a significant advance over the staircase, but they could not move customers in a continuous flow and at busy times became bottlenecks. At least two New York stores—Siegel-Cooper and Simpson, Crawford, and Simpson—had turned to escalators by 1902 but they were not widely installed until the 1920s, the total number of department-store escalators increasing from seventeen to over six hundred between 1911 and 1936. The advantages of moving stairways were impressive: one could transport as many people in an hour as forty elevators. Still, many stores hesitated to install them because of the heavy investment or because they were thought to be less grand than elevators with uniformed attendants. A third change came in ventilation systems. The forced-air systems introduced by Macy's and John Wanamaker in the late 1880s became common by the 1910s, with pioneering efforts in air conditioning at Schlesinger-Mayer in Chicago in 1903 and in Filene's basement store in 1912. Like escalators, refrigerated cooling did not become a popular department-store improvement until the 1920s, and no department store was wholly air-conditioned before World War II. One new device was not widely adopted by department stores: the cash register. While the use of registers by salespeople saved cashiers' salaries and achieved marginal gains in speed over pneumatic tube systems, these advantages were offset by managers' uneasiness about decentralizing a task that could be closely supervised for honesty and efficiency in a central tube station. Some department stores did use cash registers beginning in the 1920s, most frequently in sections such as toilet goods and notions where there was a high volume of small transactions.[17]

For the most part, department-store managers had neither the opportunity nor the inclination to transform their firms through mechanical devices, which they used primarily to cope with problems of scale. Far greater changes resulted from managers' extensive efforts to redesign and rearrange the elements of their stores. While these changes were not "technological" in the usual sense of the word, they were the functional equivalent of technology in the department store: they expedited and rationalized the movement of people and materials in ways that mechanical devices did in factories. They saved labor and made larger volume and a higher stock-turn more feasible; they enhanced the disciplined, orderly, and systematic use of resources within the department store.

The first department stores had grown up in rapidly expanding urban markets; impressing the public with a combination of grand buildings and lavish merchandise selection, they had succeeded marvelously. But as the industry matured and stores began to count their costs more carefully, one of the first areas they scrutinized was the physical arrangement of the store, rearranging its elements and systematizing its functioning. They substituted for sheer quantity a reasoned principle of selection; in place of random collections of goods and departments, they introduced coordination as a touchstone. They were no longer willing to rely on the raw unadorned appeal of the merchandise but wanted to embellish its attraction and to sell a more thoroughgoing idea of consumption rather than discrete purchases. Increasingly after 1890, no physical aspect of the selling floor was immune from criticism in the name of more effective selling.

Managers began in the departments, energetically redesigning and rearranging fixtures. Their first efforts combined esthetic and practical considerations: during the 1890s and the early years of the twentieth century, stores across the country replaced high shelving and storage cabinets—often seven feet or more tall—with lower ones from five to five and a half feet in height. The new fixtures allowed customers to "take in the entire store at a glance," conveying an "idea of spaciousness." The old custom of draping and piling goods in massive displays that created "a false dividing wall between two sections of the store," of covering every bare surface with merchandise, gave way to more limited and focused displays. The lower shelving made goods more visible to customers and more accessible to saleswomen who were shorter than the men whom they replaced behind the counters of such departments as dress goods. Refurbished departments had better provisions for storing reserve stock, for sorting goods destined for the delivery department, and for disposing of rubbish. Glass showcases replaced plain wooden counters, allowing merchandise to be both displayed and protected. Excess stock was no longer piled on top of cabinets or stacked on the floor but relegated to stockrooms. The net result was a more pleasing and less congested appearance for the store and greater convenience for those who worked behind its counters. The *Dry Goods Economist* strongly encouraged these efforts, adding an occasional store-equipment supplement beginning in 1901 and fulsomely praising up-to-date store design as "the greatest money-saver, greatest time-saver, and the greatest economizer as well as the greatest attraction to customers that any investment can produce."[18]

By around 1910 department-store managers' concern with departmental design entered a new phase as they realized that the first wave of remodeling efforts had fostered convenience but not real efficiency, leaving costly bottlenecks untouched. As one of the foremost department-store planners put it, "We spend our money to get people in here with their cash, and then, because the machinery of our establishment moves so mortally slow, a lot of them go out in disgust." Rugs were stacked on the floor and laboriously turned back one by one to display color and pattern to the customer. Suits and other clothing were piled high on tables. Underwear, hosiery, and similar items were jumbled together in drawers or on troughlike tables with little regard for style or size. Small wares such as laces, ribbons, and buttons were hopelessly mixed and tangled in a welter of drawers, boxes, and bins. Heavy bolts of yard goods were stacked atop one another. Reserve stock for most departments was either thoroughly disorganized or eccentrically arranged according to the whim of a department's head of stock. The result was that the typical department was more effective at keeping the goods from the customer than at presenting them to her.[19]

Managers, eager to know the worst, performed time studies in selling areas and announced the results with horror. During one two-hour

Fig. 1. Bottlenecks in the Selling Department

"Half a dozen people were waiting, with more or less impatience, to spend their money, while the two saleswomen ransacked the shelves. 'We seem to be out of Library Bond,' observed Miss Clarkson at length."

McClure's Magazine, 40 (Dec. 1912), 233.
Original in John Hay Library, Brown University.

period, twenty-eight "prospects . . . waited from one to fifteen minutes with the apparent intention of buying, but . . . went away without being served" while only twenty-four people were helped by the clerks. The problem was that inefficient fixtures required clerks to spend more time handling goods and less time attending to customers. The investigator found that a clerk spent only thirty-nine minutes in "salesmanship at the counter" while twenty-three minutes "were devoted to removing bolts from shelves, rewinding, returning to shelves, and adjusting the stacks." The message to managers was clear: the working environment of their stores sabotaged effective selling.[20]

A second, more carefully calculated round of remodeling ensued. One manager, for example, revamped his silk goods department after losing a sale because the two desired shades were misplaced in the general chaos. His new fixtures stored the bolts in an attractive rainbow array, each in its separate compartment; the display not only enticed customers, but permitted clerks to select bolts easily and to tell instantly when one was missing. Such custom-made fixtures increasingly replaced standard shelving or tables; by providing each item with an assigned place, they enabled clerks to provide quicker service and to keep better track of stock.[21]

In apparel departments, the humble coat hanger worked a quiet revolution, saving time, decreasing wear and tear on the clothing, and displaying it more naturally and appealingly. Rugs, too, were hung so that they could be displayed with less delay and brute labor. Small wares such as collars, laces, and buttons were arrayed neatly on sample cards so that the customer could examine, for example, all the pearl buttons at once and a clerk could easily select the chosen one from a clearly labeled, neatly compartmentalized drawer. One enthusiastic writer claimed that both the number of customers served and the number of sales completed in a given time could be increased by as much as 120 percent with the introduction of new fixtures; he credited garment hangers alone with boosting a clerk's efficiency by 90 percent. Another writer calculated that moving a cash register a mere five feet could save saleswomen in a small-wares department enough time to make extra sales yielding a yearly profit of over $1000. The search for bottlenecks amounted to an industrial campaign of self-criticism: writers especially delighted in pricking the arrogance of managers who asserted that *their* stores were free of such shocking lapses from peak efficiency. One writer pointed the moral in no uncertain terms: a failing firm had been rescued but "[i]t was not a selling campaign that saved the business. A million detailed acts of management redeemed it." [22]

At about the same time as they began to redesign their departments scientifically, store managers tackled the allocation of space in the store as a whole. Delighted at being able to control one factor in a morass of unpredictable variables, they made extravagant claims for the importance of the arrangement of the selling floor:

> "Store arrangement," testified a successful retailer, "is the greatest silent force in modern merchandising. It is a pace maker for the salesman and the saleslady."
> "What portion of your total sales do you attribute to shop arrangement?"
> "Fully forty percent." [23]

In laying out selling departments, department-store managers had far more flexibility than their brethren in factories. In a textile mill, for example, there was a standard ratio of looms to spinning frames which determined the amount and location of space devoted to each. In an assembly plant, it made sense to have the basic structural elements made or stored near the beginning of the line, and the housings and trim near the end. But there was no set ratio or obvious serial arrangement in the department store. Managers had a comparatively free hand in deciding how much space should be devoted to gloves as opposed to carpets, to shoes as opposed to hairbrushes, and where each should be located.

Nonetheless, by the 1910s a conventional wisdom about the placement of the store's departments had crystallized. Commentators noted that such factors as "chance" and "architectural convenience" as determinants of store layout were on their way to a well-deserved extinction; the new watchword was "deliberation." Basements sold bargain goods, groceries, and (less often) housewares. Street floors offered cosmetics, notions, gloves, hosiery, jewelry, and other small wares—glamour and impulse items to waylay women on their way to the upper floors—and clothing and furnishings for men who were presumed too timid to venture farther into the store. Yard goods had once been a standard first-floor feature, but as their importance in comparison to ready-made goods declined they were relegated to the middle floors, which they shared with ready-to-wear clothing, shoes, millinery, and lingerie. Upper floors featured furniture, appliances, carpeting, and housewares, items that were usually the object of a special shopping trip. Within floors, there were two basic schematic plans: either segregating merchandise of a given type

Fig. 2. First Floor Plan of Saks and Company's Fifth Avenue Store, 1927

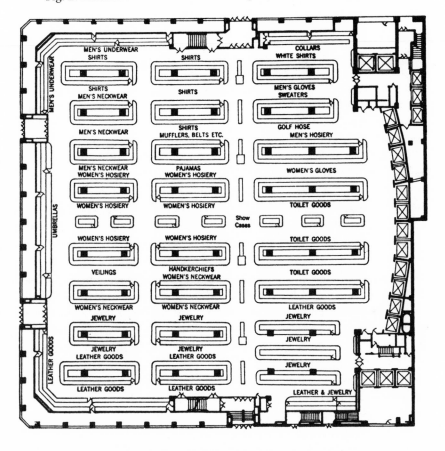

J. Russell Doubman and John R. Whitaker, *The Organization and Operation of Department Stores* (New York, 1927), 170.

into its own "shop," or grouping accessory departments around center-piece departments—draperies and linens around furniture, for example, or shirts and ties around suits.[24]

But within these general guidelines there was much room for discretion and battles over territory. The most valuable selling space went to those departments which promised the greatest "productivity" in terms of sales revenues. Diligent controllers calculated closely the revenues produced by each square foot of selling space and regularly reallocated space according to profit showings. Of course, there were questions of quality as well as quantity involved in the reckoning of space: a department at the top of an escalator or along a main-floor aisle had a great advantage over one tucked into a remote corner of an upper floor. Store managers tried both to maximize the sales potential of well-trafficked areas and to rehabilitate lost corners with irresistible merchandise. They all but auctioned off desirable turf to the buyer who promised the greatest return. The bargain basement was a common device for turning an unattractive area into a revenue producer, but some managers were more creative. A Brooklyn store president boasted that he used fashion fads to draw customers to dead corners; he was particularly proud of his music department tucked under a basement staircase—customers were drawn, as if by sirens, to the sound of music.[25]

As part of their new focus on selling, store managers began in the 1920s to draw sharper lines between selling and non-selling space, which they tellingly termed "non-productive" although a more exact term would be non-revenue-producing. Once they had made this invidious distinction, it was a short step to applying the Babbage principle to the allocation of space. Charles Babbage, an early-nineteenth-century English economist in the tradition of Adam Smith, pointed out that the division of labor—whereby only the minimum amount of skill or force necessary was hired for each job—materially cheapened the whole labor process. Like the manufacturers who used as few skilled workers as possible, department store managers used high-cost space only for those functions directly serving customers and thus demanding it. In fact, according to two experts on department-store management, the Babbage principle became the central determinant of store layout; the wise manager, they advised, should "utilize expensive selling space and expensive salesclerk's time for the most productive work; take functions off the selling floor where economical and possible to do so and centralize these in less valuable non-selling space." The space required for non-selling functions could be trimmed by designing and running these departments just as if they were in a factory, without frills and with efficiency as the prime consideration. But relegating them to cheaper locations—subbasements or upper floors—produced the most significant savings, leaving the more accessible and pleasant floors for selling departments. Many stores exiled auxiliary functions such as warehouses, shipping and receiving departments, laundries, garages, and fur storage to the fringes of the central business district or to even lower-priced land farther away. Filene's, for example, opened a service building in a warehouse district of Cambridge in 1921. This process was the equivalent in space of the division of labor applied to the work force: sections that were less "skillful" in producing sales were sent to the low-rent districts, while those more visibly and directly related to sales continued to occupy prime downtown space.[26]

A related principle was to locate those service sections most closely linked to the selling floor—wrapping desks, service desks, tube stations, and the like—so as to facilitate sales, increase customer convenience, and cut costs. One store placed these facilities near the merchandise that was more quickly sold—such as shirts—and farther from that requiring more time and deliberation—such as suits. Another arranged its service desks so that they could serve different departments as demand shifted. A lavatory near a glove department in the same store encouraged both customers and salespeople to keep their hands clean and thus avoided costly soiling of gloves. Stockrooms were placed next to fitting rooms to minimize the time it took clerks to fetch the proper sizes or styles.[27]

Departmental redesign and the more calculated use of store space produced unambiguous benefits; such efforts were unusual in not going through the cycle from panacea to false promise and back again. From the 1890s on department-store managers made their selling departments increasingly attractive and convenient places to work and shop, after 1910 applying ever-stricter standards of efficiency. At the same time, they began to juggle the demands on store space more methodically, intensifying their cost-conscious allocation of space in the 1920s and 1930s. These efforts were impressively successful, but in the streamlined and physically efficient store another less tractable problem stood out all the more clearly: that of the complex and highly personalized contest for power among top management, staff specialists, and departmental buyers. This struggle was played out through a series of changes in the store's functional organization.

Taming the Buyer through Functional Organization

In early attempts to systematize department stores, managers were often their own worst enemies. As Alfred Chandler has pointed out, the entrepreneurial mode of management persisted more strongly in the department store than in the industrial firm; store owners ran their firms "in a personal and intuitive manner," keeping both knowledge and power in their own hands as much as possible. Not surprisingly, their subordinates also proceeded on hunch and whim. These men were part of a transitional generation of managers. Bred in an era when a mixture of the old prudential virtues and a flair for the business brought success, they were nonetheless aware that the present and future demanded a more organized and impersonal approach. Often strong personalities, many became myths in their own time through their retailing acumen and prominent civic roles: men such as Oscar and Jesse Straus, John Wanamaker, Edward A. Filene, and Marshall Field made a powerful impression on urban and industrial development as well as national politics. Hundreds of others wielded more modest influence in their cities. Both inside and outside their stores, they were accustomed to power and deferential treatment. Such men found it difficult to delegate authority and failed to encourage competence and initiative in subordinates. Too frequently, these overworked executives became irritable and behaved with a surliness that suffused the store. During the three decades beginning in 1890, trade publications repeatedly admonished their readers to avoid the organizational and morale problems of one-man management, urging them to act like the train engineer at the throttle, "dictating, directing." A new generation of managers came of age in the 1920s and put large-scale retailing on a more bureaucratic basis, but an arbitrary and personalistic element persisted as a minor theme in department-store management.[28]

When the forward-looking manager dreamed of rationalizing his store, the specter of the buyer shadowed his rosy visions. The early haphazard growth of department stores had rested in large part upon the acumen of independent-minded entrepreneurial buyers whose influence reached high tide in the 1890s. Contacts among buyers became the sinews of industrial self-consciousness because they, far more often than superintendents or general managers, traveled to major wholesaling and manufacturing centers like New York and Chicago where they stayed in the same hotels and ate in the same restaurants. Retail buyers first joined the three-year-old Buyers' Association in 1900 and rapidly transformed it from a wholesalers' to a retailers' group. The association provided good fellowship, an employment bureau, conventions for the exchange of trade information and—until 1911 when the National Retail Dry Goods Association was founded—it was a key link among department stores. Industry journals also zeroed in on buyers: in 1900 the *Dry Goods Chronicle and Fancy Goods Review* changed its name to *The Buyer and Dry Goods Chronicle*, while the *Dry Goods Economist* from 1889 to 1902 used the subtitle "The Buyer's Paper." Shifts in department stores' merchandise mix further fed into buyers' prominence. During the 1890s, manufacture of ready-to-wear expanded dramatically and department stores eagerly stocked new factory-tailored items such as skirts. Wholesale buying of clothing was more difficult than purchasing yard goods, relying on highly personalized relationships with many small manufacturers and involving more complex questions of style, quality, and construction. Buyers' expertise in these novel matters gave them an edge over their superiors, many of whom had built their careers in dealing with dry goods rather than ready-to-wear.[29]

Buyers' power and influence peaked in the 1890s just as managers began to have serious misgivings about them and their departments. Top management questioned buyers' loyalty: were they working for themselves or for their stores? Disquieting evidence of the former surfaced during the 1890s when the *Dry Goods Economist* published a number of exposés about buyers who accepted manufacturers' bribes to favor their products; managers objected at least as much to the disloyalty as to the dishonesty. Stern rules about gifts and bribes brought the more egregious abuses under control by the early years of the twentieth century, but favoritism based on personal ties and minor bribes such as dinners and theater tickets persisted. Top management tried to walk a fine line between retaining buyers' allegiance and profiting from the advantageous purchases that buyers' close relationships with suppliers produced.[30]

Such ambivalence in fact pervaded managers' attitudes toward buyers. On the one hand, buyers' acumen and legendary capacity for hard work were the foundations of the firm's success; one industry writer baldly asserted that "[b]uying is really the first cause of business or no business." Buyers of course tried to convince management that good merchandise reached the store only through their irreplaceable cunning and charm. Yet buyers often overbought, snapping up special lots at attractive prices with little heed for whether or not they would sell. Through the half-century from 1890 to 1940, managers and buyers fought a war of attrition over the quantity and type of goods to be purchased, with managers arguing for lean stocks and frequent reordering—known as "hand-to-mouth" buying—and buyers pressing just as persistently for larger authorizations and more autonomy. The balance of power shifted from one to another but in the long run managers prevailed.[31]

The role of the selling departments the buyers headed was similarly ambiguous. Departments were necessary to organize inventories which by the mid-1930s included on the average a quarter of a million items, but they also fragmented the store into warring fiefdoms, each headed by a buyer concerned more with his department's own showing than with the store's overall image or profit picture. Interdepartmental competition could boost sales, particularly when quotas or contests awakened the thrill of the chase as well as buyers' fears for their careers. But competition also had its negative side. Lines of merchandise were duplicated or omitted altogether; quality and price levels varied widely among departments. Jealous of their own department's results, salespeople and buyers were unwilling to refer customers to other parts of the store or to comply with managers' entreaties to suggest specific merchandise from other departments.[32]

Frances Donovan, a sociologist who did fieldwork in department stores during the 1920s for her book, *The Saleslady*, learned about interdepartmental competition the hard way. Although her sales totals were admirably high, she was threatened with a transfer out of the Mabelle department because she sold more dresses from neighboring departments than from her own. Alerted to her error in time, she mended her ways and recited her lesson to her bemused buyer: "I thought I was selling dresses for McElroy's and it did not make any difference where they came from. Now I understand that I am selling them for the Mabelle department." The buyer who had asked to have her transferred was acting in perfect conformity to the unwritten code: that it was better to make no sale at all than to lose one to another department. Departments squabbled, often viciously, over resources—personnel, space, advertising—and the frequent result was a divided store that was unable to rise to the challenge of selling. By the end of the 1910s, interdepartmental competition was more criticized than praised, but it was easier to deplore than eliminate; managers continued to bewail its evils through the 1920s and 1930s. In 1939, a personnel manager unhappily concluded that people in the selling departments were "departmental-minded rather than store-minded."[33]

Efforts to curb the negative effects of departmentalization were doomed unless they also confronted and modified the buyer's role. Department-store buyers resembled both inside contractors and foremen in industrial corporations, supervising their sections with relative autonomy and holding enough power over the firm's functioning to retain some independence from upper management. As a rule, buyers had more limited authority over personnel than foremen or inside contractors but broader control over their materials. Few had the formal right to hire and fire, although they exerted considerable informal influence on the level of staffing in their departments and on the firing or transfer of workers who displeased them. On the other hand, while foremen and inside contractors had to tailor products to the specifications of their superiors, most buyers had quite a free hand in choosing merchandise. They often presided over their departments despotically, enlightened or not as whim dictated, treating superiors and subordinates alike to magnificent displays of artistic temperament. Marcella Burns Hahner, who established Marshall Field's book department in 1914, epitomized this type of buyer. She ruled her department like a feudal lord, dictated literary taste to Chicago's carriage trade, entertained the likes of Somerset Maugham at tea in her office, revealed a heart of gold to a select few, and turned in $750,000 in yearly sales.[34]

The traditional buyer's role was a choice one, based on the individual buyer's force of personality as well as management's definition of the job. Looking back from the vantage point of half a century, one expert painted a dramatic picture of the buyer's scope: "The buyer of [1910] was virtually a merchant in his own right. He had a free hand in merchandising; he managed his sales staff; he wrote advertising copy; spent time on the selling floor; arranged displays; and was held accountable only for the final results of his year's operation." The extent of the buyer's empire was not the only problem; equally vexing was the fact that the buyer's fixation on his own department's showing often clashed with managers' desire to maintain a reputation for low prices and accommodating service. Managers' insistence on price wars to meet competition—"one of the bitternesses of the buyer's life"—could wreck the most conscientious buyer's sales record; witness the two-day 1902 price war between Macy's and Hearn's which slashed prices on silk cloth from 41¢ per yard to eleven yards for a penny. Managers' willingness to accept returns, often under quite unreasonable conditions, similarly undercut department profits because returned goods usually had to be sold at a loss; as one buyer stormed after a member of his firm had approved the return of a coat

which had not even been bought in the store, "We are simply here to accommodate people, I suppose. Moneymaking is too plebian [sic] an occupation for people of our calibre." Managers deemphasized price wars
after World War I, but the struggles over returned merchandise if anything intensified as the percentage of returned goods skyrocketed. Buyers
were not simply vested with enormous power; their priorities often differed sharply from those of managers who were trying to frame coherent
policies for the entire store.[35]

After 1900, the bailiwicks of inside contractor, foreman, and buyer
alike came under attack because their intuitive and temperamental style
conflicted with new notions of standardization and control. Upper management whittled down the buyer's extensive and arbitrarily ruled realm
and made the buyer more accountable to others in the store hierarchy,
imposing restrictions unthinkable in the late nineteenth century. The
major developments in store organization and the elaboration of its functional structure were primarily aimed at constricting, rationalizing, or
supplanting the buyer's role. The controller, the merchandise manager,
the advertising manager, the fashion expert, the training supervisor, the
personnel manager, and the store superintendent all played a part in the
long struggle to transform the buyer's position.

By 1905, the division of labor in early department stores had begun
to crystallize into a four-part functional structure consisting of merchandising, service or store management, publicity or advertising, and control
or accounting divisions. Additional functions were usually placed within
one or another of these four basic divisions. Although personnel activities became far more important during the 1920s and 1930s, they generally remained in the service division; the first autonomous personnel division was not established until 1928 and it was nearly a decade before a
second store followed suit. The functional divisions existed in an uneasy
and shifting equilibrium, with service, publicity, and control struggling to
tame the buyers but at the same time competing with one another, while
the merchandise division was severely divided within itself. Functional
organization clarified responsibilities and supplied experts in each division, but it also left disturbing gray areas and fueled a heated race for
dominance within the store.[36]

The very creation of the merchandise division posed a challenge to
buyers' autonomy and presumptions of expertise. Its rationale included
the desire to coordinate the offerings of different selling departments; the
worry that buyers rising rapidly through the ranks required guidance to

Fig. 3. The Proletarianization of the Buyer

IS THE BUYER BEING DIVESTED OF HIS FUNCTIONS?

Journal of Retailing, 4 (Oct. 1928), 13.

compensate for their lack of experience; and the need to supplement buyers' demonstrated buying skill with managerial and selling skills. During the 1890s a number of stores delegated members of the firm to supervise groups of selling departments, but this makeshift system became increasingly impractical as men without prior retail experience joined department-store firms. In 1900, John Wanamaker became the first to appoint a merchandise manager, whose thankless task it was to coordinate and limit the activities of the buyers. This new figure's job was peculiarly difficult: he had to manage and guide the buyers, requiring conformity to certain guidelines and fiscal limitations but simultaneously nurturing initiative so that buyers sniffed out "goods that would just set the store humming." In 1924 the formation of a Merchandise Men's Group within the National Retail Dry Goods Association signaled the fact that the new position was firmly institutionalized. Buyers opposed the merchandise manager with subtle subversion and outright defiance; notably brazen was the Gimbel Brothers buyer who in 1921 held a major January sale in defiance of the merchandise manager. He placed unauthorized orders for a large quantity of merchandise, fairly smuggled it into the store and through the marking room, and staged a highly profitable sale.[37]

The next assault on the buyer's empire came from another new figure, the controller or head of the accounting department. For some, systematic management began and ended with what stores came to call "system": the collection of data about the store's buying and selling and the substitution of uniform storewide procedures for casual estimates and randomly scribbled notes. Like industrial managers, department-store managers began to use such data not just in a historical way, to assess past performance, but in a predictive way, to plan future business strategies. The controller and the system he advocated became highly influential between 1890 and 1920, a prominence underlined by the formation of the Controllers' Congress within the National Retail Dry Goods Association in 1920. Beginning in the 1890s the *Dry Goods Economist* published operating figures supplied by stores as a standard of comparison for the journal's readers. The desire to accumulate better standardized data was a powerful motivation for the formation of the NRDGA in 1911 and the primary goal behind the founding of the Retail Research Association in 1916. The major accounting advances of the prewar period were the retail inventory method, which provided reliable monthly estimates of the gross margin (the spread between the cost and the selling price of merchandise sold) and the amount of stock on hand without a time-consuming physical inventory, and a standard classification for store expenses which produced comparable industrywide data for the first time. Only after 1920, however, were these two methods widely applied. In 1921 the Harvard Bureau of Business Research began to gather and publish annually the resulting figures as *Operating Results of Department Stores.*[38]

System, because it provided quantitative data about operations long conducted on the basis of intuition and guesswork, was highly seductive to department-store managers, who accorded the controller great weight in policy matters. Before World War I, more careful accounting had helped both to provide management with a clearer picture of the firm's position and to direct store operations into well-defined channels. Buyers' long-standing monopoly of shop-floor knowledge about stock and sales was broken by the controllers' elaborate ledgers; numbers supplanted intuition. Managers' motives for expanding the control function also included self-justification. Worried about business's bad reputation during the Progressive Era, especially after Louis Brandeis's brief on the inefficiency of the railroads in the Eastern Rate Case of 1910–11, they were eager to demonstrate to a skeptical public that distribution was—unlike the railroads—efficient. Customer complaints during the inflationary period just after World War I strengthened retailers' resolve to develop a body of industrial statistics which could be used to justify rising prices.[39]

The infatuation with operating data also grew out of department-store managers' nagging sense that their firms were in fact not as efficient as they liked to think. What managers saw in their own accounts—R. H. Macy, for example, watched its gross margin edge up from 23.17 percent of net sales in 1902 to 32.74 percent in 1919—was grimly confirmed by the new industrywide figures. Absorbing costs formerly borne by wholesalers, paying higher wages and salaries, and maintaining elaborate store buildings and services all contributed to an expanding margin. The traditional retail solution to problems of high margin, championed by top management and buyers alike, was higher volume; it was a sorry buyer indeed who could not boast that the day before Christmas or the third Monday in March had a higher sales total than the comparable day in the previous year. The controller, less bound by industry custom, demonstrated that expanding volume could coexist with falling profits. Especially between 1924 and 1929, frantic efforts to increase volume led to ruinous advertising costs, thinly shaved profit margins, costly markdowns, and—not surprisingly—shrinking profits. Controllers argued that a high rate of stock-turn, and not higher volume alone, was the cer-

Fig. 4. The Dangerous Infatuation with Volume.

CHASING A WILL O' THE WISP.

Dry Goods Economist, 80 (28 Aug. 1926), 6.

tain road to lower expenses and bigger profits, noting that on the average a stock-turn of less than three led to expenses of 30.7 percent of sales and profits of 2.0 percent while a stock-turn of four or more cut expenses to 27.3 percent and boosted profits to 4.5 percent. Simply put, stock-turn maximized the productivity of variable investment in stock. Such reasoning was mathematically sound but subjectively distasteful to executives whose business culture had so long venerated volume.[40]

In fact, the controller's contribution to department stores had been ambivalently received almost from the outset. The *Dry Goods Economist* warned its readers in the early years of the twentieth century not to replace the carelessness of the past with an obsessive concern for petty detail, and no less a figure than Isaac Gimbel joined other retailers in expressing reservations about accounting procedures in a 1904 *System* symposium:

The tendency of modern retailing is to simplify every detail of the work. This means neither too much recording—red tape—nor too little recording—carelessness; it means the happy medium that gets the greatest return from the least outlay of time or money—system.

System is a necessary servant. System must be operated—it does not operate itself. System economizes time, labor, expense, and the best system is that which effects the greatest economy of all three.

System tended to proliferate wildly and to become an end in itself; accounting systems strangled initiative even as they pointed out pitfalls. Opposing those who argued in the efficiency-conscious prewar years for the primacy of system, many maintained that there was still a place for the intuitive style in a tightly run store: "[T]he source of increased efficiency is not what so many believe it is, viz., labyrinthian routine—falsely termed 'system'—but the steady application and use of common 'horse-sense' methods."[41]

During the 1920s and 1930s industry leaders questioned the scientific validity of controllers' figures, the high cost of maintaining elaborate figures of doubtful utility, and the tendency of controllers to focus on minutiae while losing sight of larger trends. That these criticisms coexisted with great admiration for the controller is illustrated in the National Retail Dry Goods Association's twenty-fifth anniversary publication. In a poll about the nature of retail progress since the association's founding in 1911, one quarter of all the members responding—far more than named any other factor—cited retail accounting and control procedures as the foremost advance. The association's managers were chagrined at this response, stating that "[i]f there has been no more vital progress in a quarter of a century than improved accounting it would appear as though the retail business has not progressed as it should." They went on to compare these accounting systems to plumbing in a home, noting acerbically that: "no one ever makes the mistake of holding that the most important thing which has happened in his house over a long period of years has been that the plumbing has worked satisfactorily, or even that the plumbing facilities have been modernized." They acknowledged the prodigious development of accounting systems but warned that many stores had gone too far and "enmeshed themselves in a dangerous web of system." [42]

The economic collapse of the 1930s lent new appeal to the intuitive style of retailing; since system availed little in the face of the Depression, perhaps merchandising genius could help. Faced with stiff opposition, individual controllers as well as the Controller's Congress energetically defended their methods. The strength of the intuitive tradition in retailing, the inability of statistics to consider issues of service and culture, and the rigidity of accounting procedures reversed the trend toward mathematical control which controllers had set in motion during the prewar years. No store reverted to the catch-as-catch-can methods of the late nineteenth century, but most redressed the imbalance caused by the eager hope that the controller had a cure-all for the industry. Having swung too far toward the pure-businessman side of his personality, the department-store manager swung back. Arthur Lazarus, one of the most respected authorities on department-store organization and a member of the Columbus merchant dynasty, summed up the situation in an exasperated tale of his long wait to buy a pair of boots in an overcrowded, understaffed department while a snowstorm raged outside and salespeople in other departments stood idle. Railing at the impossibility of transferring personnel from the empty to the busy department because it would "interfere with the accounting control," he sputtered, "It is a sorry day when the selling department shall be subservient to accounting convenience." [43]

Changes in the department store's focus and appeal also altered the buyer's position. While the early department store was a congeries of departments, each more or less going its own way and presenting its own line of merchandise to greatest advantage, the drive to tighten the reins of central power and to present a unified vision of fashion and service limited departmental autonomy. Worries about articulating the store as a unified entity appeared in the 1890s and concrete steps in that direction began after the turn of the century. The merchandise manager was of course one harbinger of this new emphasis on a coherent store image, but in a broader sense buyers were increasingly treated as members of a group rather than individual geniuses. They had the novel experience of being summoned to coordinating meetings where they had to account for their merchandise choices. The growing elaboration of fashion, with its emphasis on the latest in style and the coordinated ensemble, made merchandise choice a matter of store policy rather than of individual conviction. In 1915, for example, Macy's sent each of its buyers a subscription to *Vogue* and instructed them in detail about how to apply the magazine's information to their departments. A new expert, the stylist, began to appear in merchandise or publicity divisions during the 1920s, setting fashion policy for the store and coaxing or bullying buyers into following a prevailing idea of style. No longer could buyers expound idiosyncratic ideas of fashion; handbags now had to harmonize in style and color with shoes, underwear with outer garments. Paralleling industrial efforts to train foremen, department stores began in the mid-1920s to train buyers, stressing their need to fit into the store image and to comply with store policies.[44]

Buyers were also required to conform more closely to storewide notions of service. Once monarchs of all that transpired in their departments, after the turn of the century they increasingly had to share power with members of the store's service division. Variously termed floorwalkers, floor managers, aisle managers, or floor superintendents, these officials were the representatives on the selling floor of storewide interests, a counterweight to the buyer's narrow view: "In dealing with the public the floorman has the advantage over the merchandise department head that a floorman is not biased by personal considerations; he is not worried about sales volume, markdowns, beating the record of the same day last year, and other considerations which may influence the buyer when he deals with a customer who proves irritable or unreasonable. That fact in itself is one of the cardinal reasons for the floorman's presence in the store."[45]

The nineteenth-century floorwalker had been a "mere figurehead," limited to "answering queries, rubbing his hands, and looking pretty," while his twentieth-century counterpart supervised salespeople, service to customers, and transactions such as returns and exchanges. The upgrading of the floorwalker did not bring with it autonomy; managers asked of them not initiative but evenhanded enforcement of store rules, a requirement impressed on them beginning in the 1920s through training courses. What floorwalkers lacked in autonomy they gained in power, marshaling the full force of store policy behind them in a persistent and growing challenge to the buyer's reign over the selling floor.[46]

More generally, the challenges posed to the buyer by storewide notions of fashion and service evidenced the department store's new emphasis on selling. The reoriented store relegated the buyer to the position of procurer of goods and charged other store executives with selling them. It was a commonplace by the early 1920s that "[n]o GOOD buyer is also a good seller," and sound business sense dictated the separation of the two. Some stores began to employ sales managers within the service division to oversee selling just as the merchandise manager supervised buying. The traditional buyer would, for instance, buy merchandise at what he thought was a decent wholesale price and then set its retail price at what the traffic would bear, sometimes charging different prices for the same item in different colors. Under the stern eye of a sales manager, however, buyers were ordered to buy goods to sell at a certain price based on the store's markup, regardless of whether they were "good buys" at wholesale in the absolute sense.[47]

Upper management began to urge buyers to devote more time and attention to the selling floor, a demand that implied lower status. First, it assumed that buyers were going to be more accountable for their day-to-day conduct and not just for their departmental showings at the end of the month or the quarter. Second, it went along with new duties for buyers, particularly the job of training the sales force according to storewide definitions of store service. Third, it directed buyers to seek salespeople's advice about merchandise, making it policy for them to heed those on a lower rung of the department-store prestige ladder. Finally, it led to a fundamental reorientation of the buyer's world: no longer were contacts with merchandise sources the basis of power and prestige in the store, but rather contacts with customers on the selling floor. The lament of a Filene's buyer expressed the frustration of coping with these new demands: "Most any fool can buy enough / But who in h—— can sell the stuff?"[48]

Within the general trend toward the restriction of buyers' independence, top management's vision of buyers' role varied cyclically. After the advent of the merchandise manager in the early 1900s there was a rush to cut buyers' salaries and to give them responsibility for an increasing number of departments, to proletarianize and speed them up. Such tactics tended to backfire, highlighting managers' dilemma in dealing with their subordinates, customers, and saleswomen alike: how could they secure both loyalty and acquiescence on the one hand and initiative and enterprise on the other? Most who tried to cheapen the buying function soon reversed field, convinced that high-quality buyers had to be highly paid and that their intelligence and experience were well worth the price. The 1920s emphasis on storewide uniformity in fashion, service, and training again led to lower salaries and increased work loads for buyers.

During the economic crisis of the 1930s some stores relaxed restrictions on buyers, returning staff prerogatives to them in the hopes of saving the salaries of staff personnel and stimulating them to bolster sagging sales. Even so, the buyers never regained the freedom of action and the central role which they had enjoyed during the late nineteenth century: a *Department Store Economist* editorial in the late 1930s grudgingly allowed that "the occasional prima donna is a tasty tang of paprika who snaps up the works" but that the tang palled and the store floundered when there were too many.[49]

On the whole, appreciation of the buyer's special acumen varied inversely with admiration of elaborate functional organization. Fred Lazarus, Jr., another member of the Columbus department-store family, argued in the late 1930s that functional structure had been hammered out in a period when the goal was to make the department store more rational and to bring it under closer control; that goal having been accomplished, functional organization had outlived its usefulness and begun to choke initiative instead of checking foolhardiness. Complaints that functional organization hampered effective selling built to a crescendo during the 1930s; in the words of one management consultant, "When a buyer has three or more bosses and a salesperson has as many as seven, it is little wonder they settle down to a plodding gait and just try to keep out of trouble." In 1937, four stores followed the lead of the Namm store of Brooklyn in establishing autonomous personnel departments, and retailers' plans for the post–World War II era invariably gave a high priority to placing personnel on an equal level with the other divisions. Managers attacked the problem of selling from another direction by advocating the creation of a sixth division, sales promotion, to oversee and coordinate all aspects of selling and to develop a storewide selling policy.[50]

Despite the best efforts of department-store managers and consultants, department-store organization posed as well as solved problems. On the positive side, the functional organization had enabled stores to tackle the problems arising from great size and had allowed each division to develop its own strengths. On the negative side, it had encouraged the proliferation of red tape, created an imbalance by giving coordinate status to functions that were properly subordinate to the main one of merchandising, and failed to focus attention clearly on the central problem of selling. The resulting confusion, delay, and duplication of effort gave the department store a bit of the air of an elephant executing a ballet. The buyer, although diminished, remained a figure to contend with and repeatedly bounced back after attacks on his domain.

Blueprints for Buying

The combined effect of redesigned selling departments, functional organization's uniform storewide policies, the emphasis on high rates of stockturn, and the shift from buying to selling was to show the need not just for restrictions on the buying of merchandise but for a positive and carefully calculated blueprint for it. Two warring tendencies had contributed mightily to department stores' success from their earliest days. The first was the effort to dazzle customers with broad assortments, to fill the most unusual request, and to cater to a wide range of tastes. The second was the reliance on lean stocks and "hand-to-mouth" buying. In fact, the first had won most of the battles; the injunction to maintain lean stocks was—except as a brief response to crises such as the Panic of 1907 and the post–World War I recession—honored more in the breach than in the observance.

Once the stock of selling departments was methodically arranged, the flaws in buying policy became painfully clear; one merchandise writer lamented that "overbuying" was "the greatest curse in the retail business." By the early 1920s, industry observers pointed again and again to ridiculous situations in which stores maintained absurdly large stocks. One exasperated writer, noting the astounding variety of men's collars on the market, grumbled that "[i]t would be indeed a peculiar race of men that required 150 styles of collar to cover their necks." Moreover, buyers had tended to purchase merchandise haphazardly, a special job lot here and an interesting closeout there; large inventories were by no means comprehensive. The result was huge but spotty stocks filled with buyers' coups but sellers' nightmares, instead of well-rounded assortments of highly saleable items.[51]

The merchandise manager, the controller, the advertising head, the

Fig. 5. The Absurdity of Unlimited Assortments

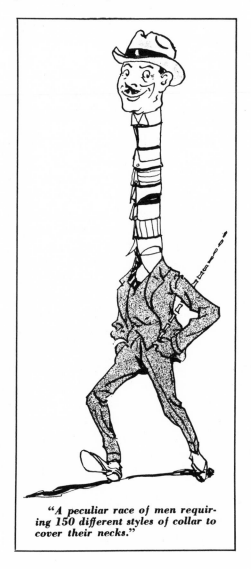

"*A peculiar race of men requiring 150 different styles of collar to cover their necks.*"

Dry Goods Economist, 77 (6 Oct. 1923), 43.

stylist, and the service manager all agreed on the need for a more focused buying policy that would specify not just "how much" but also "what." Enormous inventories inevitably led to lower rates of stock-turn and conveyed a confusing impression rather than a focused fashion statement. Assortments that were incomplete in size, color, and style led to lost sales and customer complaints.

Merchandise control was the retailer's solution to the problem of large but incomplete stocks. Also termed simplification and the model stock system, merchandise control referred to a variety of schemes to key stocks to a given department's clientele. This movement was the retailing correlate of similar campaigns in manufacturing. The drive to simplify manufactured goods, eliminate duplication, and generally rationalize each industry was directly encouraged by Herbert Hoover through the Department of Commerce from 1921 to 1929. In fields with relatively few firms and strong trade associations, simplification could be accomplished at the level of the factory, but the industries from which department stores purchased most of their stock were characterized by a large number of small firms; the clothing industry is a case in point. Retailers, through the NRDGA, encouraged manufacturers to produce clothing in standardized sizes; they had some success with knit underwear manufacturers by 1923, but sizing for the most part remained eccentric. Still, retailers influenced manufacturers by purchasing from those whose size ranges were more reliable and stocking fewer variants of any given item. Planned buying was the key to the standardization of retail stocks. The aftermath of World War I powerfully impressed on department-store managers the wisdom of merchandise control. Many stores benefited handsomely from wartime inflation and built up large stocks as a hedge against rising prices. During the drastic deflation of 1920–21 their losses, not surprisingly, were ruinous. Chastened by the sad results of their orgy of hog-wild buying, retailers were ready for the gospel of merchandise control as preached by Edward Filene. The fact that Filene's, operating under the new buying principles, had easily weathered the postwar dislocations notably increased their attentiveness.[52]

Filene's scheme for "scientific" retailing, the model stock plan, began with an assessment of the store's sales patterns. What were the most popular prices for each item? Filene maintained that purchases tended to cluster at low, medium, and high price ranges for each type of merchandise, and that the store which concentrated 85 percent of its stock at these preferred prices would be able to meet the overwhelming bulk of the demand with smaller inventories. In addition, Filene urged merchants to supply both a "best buy"—an item carefully selected for high quality and good price—and a "more profitable item"—one with fashion appeal—for each line of goods, thereby catering to customers inclined toward value as well as toward style. Stock selected by these methods would, Filene claimed, sell more quickly and more easily and thus increase stores' all-important rate of stock turnover. Many advantages followed: with a streamlined stock, stores could respond sensitively to consumer demand, finance purchases of new stock on a revolving basis, and avoid the losses that came from marking down unsold goods. Equally important, merchandise control promised to decrease the unpredictability which had long plagued retailing; narrower stocks circumscribed both clerks and customers, the one with fewer wares to offer, the other with fewer from which to choose. Finally, leaner stocks were easier to police, permitting prompt reorders and the maintenance of full assortments.[53]

The model stock plan as outlined by Filene was fairly rigid and more than most buyers could be made to swallow, but his general principle was widely applied. Department stores of all sizes moved toward smaller and more carefully selected stocks. Some stores eliminated all but one best model in each category; others narrowed their price ranges—one department, for example, offered shirts at four prices where there had once been twenty. The advantages of the new method were apparent to all concerned: no longer need a clerk concoct a tortuous and largely fictitious explanation as to why one shirt was priced at $2.50 and another at $2.55; no longer need a customer be confounded by fifteen lines of underwear when the retailer had preselected the three he deemed best.[54]

Merchants enthusiastically reported their success with smaller stocks. One euphorically if not poetically titled his testimonial "133% on Invested Capital; 7 Turns, through the 'Flyer' Plan," and made the startling suggestion that merchants keep no more than three weeks' stock on hand. Although results varied from firm to firm and from year to year, there is no doubt that merchandise control enabled department stores to increase their stock turnover markedly during the 1920s and 1930s. An especially relentless application of merchandise control during the 1930s decreased the percentage of markdowns to total sales in department stores from about 8 percent in 1930 to as low as 6 percent by 1940. Such a decrease taken by itself may not seem startling, but when combined with other gains from tighter management of the store, it enabled American department stores to equal their 1929 profits by 1940 despite lower overall sales and higher expenses.[55]

Like other rationalization techniques, merchandise control had its perils for the merchant who used it too rigidly. Retailing literature repeatedly warned department-store executives not to succumb to the temptation to "starve their stocks" or cut back to the point where they were unable to satisfy the bulk of the demand. In addition, the model stock plan too rigorously applied conflicted with the department store's ideal of service and indeed undermined its traditional attraction of a broad selection of goods. These problems were particularly troublesome in carriage-trade stores which put relatively more emphasis on service than on the balance sheet. James Simpson, president of Marshall Field, cited the example of a toilet soap which was infrequently but steadily purchased by a handful of customers: a cost-conscious model stock plan would have eliminated it, but Marshall Field kept it on the shelves as a testimony to its concern for the exceptional customer.[56]

Beginning in the early years of the twentieth century, department-store managers made mighty efforts to adapt to four factors. The first was the dramatically increased scale of their operations. Second, they sensed that their initial flush of success was behind them and that department-store productivity was lagging in comparison to other sectors of the economy. Third, they took seriously the era's focus on increased efficiency and predictability, and found their firms deficient in both respects. Finally, and perhaps most important of all, they tried to reconcile their operations with their new orientation toward the customer rather than toward the manufacturer.

The spatial arrangement of the department store was the most amenable to managers' campaigns for systematic management. The redesign of departments and fixtures eased and speeded the process of selling; the more calculated placement of departments maximized the return on expensive real estate. These were in themselves unambiguous improvements, but together they were only a necessary first step in reforming the irregular practices of department stores—comparable to tidying up a slovenly house only to find that the furniture was in shambles and the inhabitants diseased. Far more resistant to management initiatives was the functional organization of the store; here the abiding problem was to mold a miscellaneous collection of selling departments and highly individualistic buyers into a well-coordinated store in which uniform policies would be framed by staff executives such as merchandise managers, controllers, store superintendents, advertising managers, and stylists. Buyers persisted in competing rather than cooperating, struggling with the staff executives and one another. The controller, an equally troublesome figure, swamped the store with paperwork, asserting that only the numbers mattered and slighting the service and cultural roles of department stores. Designed to unify the store, functional organization in practice fragmented authority and did little to produce more effective selling. Merchandise control was a further step in rationalizing both the functioning of the selling departments and the role of the buyer, imposing stern limits on the amount and type of merchandise offered. While such schemes assured full assortments, they also risked cutting stocks to an absurd degree and undermining the department store's traditional ability to satisfy the unusual as well as the typical taste.

In sum, the advances brought by systematic management were partial and problematic. Problematic, because they too often heeded the balance sheet instead of the service role of the department store. Partial, because they dealt with sales transactions as discrete events instead of as part of a comprehensive plan to woo the whole customer—and indeed the whole society—to a way of life that placed a high value on gratification through consumption. Managers' own discontent with the new methods found expression both in their repeated warnings that systematic management had gone too far and in their recurring advocacy of more intuitive business methods. Systematic management made the store easier to move around in, imposed some order on its anarchic and personalistic structure, and presented merchandise more rationally. Similar gains might have satisfied factory managers, but the department-store executive had to devote special efforts to the social aspects of selling, to managing the human interaction that was at the heart of the store's success. In the theater metaphor that was a staple of retail writers' vocabulary, systematic management could only set the stage in the department store; it overlooked the need to manage the actors in the drama of consumption—the customers and the salespeople. Managers' efforts to deal with these two groups are the subject of the next two chapters.

Notes

1. The best encyclopedic guide to American department stores is Robert Hendrickson, *The Grand Emporiums: The Illustrated History of America's Great Department Stores* (New York, 1979). Although not without errors, the book provides thumbnail sketches of major stores. On the public debate about department stores, see "The Big Stores Win," *DGE*, 51 (12 June 1897), 16; William Matthews Handy, "The Department Store in the West: The Struggle in Chicago,"

Arena, 22 (Sept. 1899), 321–24; Eva A. Carlin, "The Department Store in the West: 'America's Grandest' in California," *Arena*, 22 (Sept. 1899), 333; "The Bubble Pricked," *B & DGC*, 29 (3 Mar. 1900), 5; *Report of the Industrial Commission on the Relations and Conditions of Capital and Labor*, 19 (Washington, 1902), 547–49.

2. "Recognizing the New Era," *DGE*, 51 (15 May 1897), 15; John S. Steele, "The Department Store in the East: General Storekeeping in New York," *Arena*, 22 (Aug. 1899), 174; on the new managerial virtues see, for example, "Order and System in Business," *DGC & FGR*, 6 (28 July 1888), 4–5; "Truth and Honesty in Business," *DGC & FGR*, 6 (11 Aug. 1888), 4; "Wide-Awake Retailing," *DGE*, 49 (19 Jan. 1895), 117.

3. J. Russell Doubman and John R. Whitaker, *The Organization and Operation of Department Stores* (New York, 1927), 156; Ralph M. Hower, *History of Macy's of New York, 1858–1919* (Cambridge, Mass., 1943), 323; Robert W. Twyman, *History of Marshall Field & Co., 1852–1906* (Philadelphia, 1954), 43; Daniel Nelson, *Managers and Workers: Origins of the New Factory System in the United States, 1880–1920* (Madison, Wis., 1975), 16, 24.

4. *Report of the Industrial Commission*, 7 (Washington, 1901), 455–56, 696, 736; Lloyd Wendt and Herman Kogan, *Give the Lady What She Wants! The Story of Marshall Field & Company* (Chicago, 1952), 308–12; Alfred Lief, *Family Business: A Century in the Life and Times of Strawbridge & Clothier* (New York, 1968), 168; "Department Methods," *DGE*, 53 (14 Jan. 1899), 17; Hower, *Macy's*, 111–12, 248–49.

5. Hendrickson, *Grand Emporiums*, 164; Tom Mahoney, *The Great Merchants: The Stories of Twenty Famous Retail Operations and the People Who Made Them Great* (New York, 1955), 77, 80, 127; "Marketing and Selling," *Magazine of Business*, 55 (Jan. 1929), 58; "Growth of Department Store Chains," *DGE*, 78 (4 Oct. 1924), 11; "Department Store Consolidation and Association," *JR*, 2 (Apr. 1926), 14–15; W. D. Darby, "Story of the Chain Store," *DGE*, 82 (21 Apr. 1928), 13–14; U.S. Department of Commerce, Bureau of the Census, *Fifteenth Census of the U.S., Census of Distribution, Retail Distribution, Retail Chains* (Washington, 1933), 43–44, 55–56; *Census of American Business: 1933, Retail Distribution, United States Summary: 1933* (Washington, 1935), 15; John William Ferry, *A History of the Department Store* (New York, 1960), 120.

6. Alfred Chandler, *The Visible Hand: The Managerial Revolution in American Business* (Cambridge, Mass., 1977), 1.

7. Nelson, *Managers and Workers*, 7–8; Hower, *Macy's*, 305; John Livingston Wright, "The Department Store in the East: Confusion from Cheapness in Boston," *Arena*, 22 (Aug. 1899), 168–69. Wright wrongly claims that Jordan Marsh was New England's largest employer.

8. Nelson, *Managers and Workers*, 9; Clowry Chapman, "A Great Retail Store and Its System," *System*, 5 (Mar. 1904), 158.

9. C. Bertrand Thompson, "Scientific Management in a Retail Store," *System*, 27 (Jan. 1915), 66–71; "Ninety-Four Housewives Tell Why They Buy," *System*, 28 (Nov. 1915), 481–89.

10. Stuart Ewen, *Captains of Consciousness: Advertising and the Social Roots of the Consumer Culture* (New York, 1976), 77–80; Ewen quotes Woodward, 80.

11. "Seventy-One Years—and After," *DGE*, 71 (18 Nov. 1916), 27; *DGE*, 76 (19 Nov. 1921), 287; Beatrice Judelle, "The Changing Customer," *Stores*, 42 (Nov. 1960), 14; see also John W. Wingate, "Editorial," *JR*, 3 (July 1927), 33–34.

12. "Sales, or Customers?" *DGE*, 72 (29 Dec. 1917), 353.

13. Philip J. Reilly, "Reduction of Waste in Operating Departments of Large Retail Stores," *Bulletin of the Taylor Society*, 8 (Feb. 1923), 31; John Livingston Wright, "Confusion from Cheapness," 168–69; Hower, *Macy's*, 491; *Echo*, 18 (28 Oct. 1927); George Plant, "Store Personnel Divisions Build Christmas Staffs," *BNRDGA*, 22 (Oct. 1940), 20; T. G. Goodwin, "Rush Seasons Don't Find Us with 'Green' Help," *System*, 42 (Nov. 1922), 561.

14. Reilly, "Reduction of Waste," 32; B. Eugenia Lies, "Improving Department-Store Technique," *Bulletin of the Taylor Society*, 10 (Aug. 1925), 186; Bess Bloodworth, "Store Hours and the Five-Day Week," *BNRDGA*, 15 (June 1933), 51.

15. Philip Cabot, "Leaders of the Past and Leaders of the Future," in NRDGA, *Management Conference Proceedings, May 1939* (New York, 1939), 66–67.

16. NRDGA, *Twenty-Five Years of Retailing, 1911–1936* (New York, 1936), 26, 92–93; Hrant Pasdermadjian, *The Department Store—Its Origins, Evolution, and Economics* (London, 1954), 25; Bert A. Teeters, "Light Made the Sale 'Go,'" *System*, 45 (June 1924), 863–64; Walter S. Brown, "Utilizing Light to Make More Sales," *System*, 48 (Mar. 1925), 214–18; Clotilde Grunsky, "What Improved Lighting Arrangements Have Done for Two Stores," *System*, 56 (Sept. 1929), 40–41.

17. On the rotunda, see "The Modern Dry Goods Store," *DGE*, 56 (21 June 1902), fixtures supplement, 5; "Valuable Space Lost," *DGE*, 58 (14 May 1904), 19; Twyman, *History of Marshall Field*, 159; *Golden Book of the Wanamaker Stores* ([Philadelphia], 1911), 283–84. Discussions of the escalator are "A Welcome Innovation," *B & DGC*, 30 (27 Oct. 1900), 13; "Interior Appointments," *DGE*, 56 (11 Jan. 1902), 59; "Make Upper Floors Pay," *DGE*, 66 (27 Jan. 1912), 87–89. There were no escalators in Saks Fifth Avenue's New York store until 1979 (Paul Goldberger, "Redesigning a Department Store's Space," *New York Times*, 15 Nov. 1979, C10). On air conditioning, see "Type of Modern Store," *DGE*, 57 (31 Jan. 1903), 53; Hendrickson, *Grand Emporiums*, 131, 135; NRDGA, *Twenty-Five Years*, 109–10. The unsuitability of cash registers for department stores is noted in Store Managers' Division, NRDGA, *Convention Reports—2d Annual Convention, 1925* (New York, 1925), 7; Elizabeth Beardsley Butler, *Saleswomen in Mercantile Stores: Baltimore, 1909* (New York, 1912), 107–10; J. Julian Osserman, "They Can Always Make Change," *System*, 47 (Jan. 1925), 102–4; "Manufacturer's Demonstrators," *JR*, 4 (Oct. 1928), 3; Frances R. Donovan, *The Saleslady* (1929; rpt. New York, 1974), 60–70.

18. "Decorating the Store," *DGE*, 53 (22 Apr. 1899), 5; "The Modern Fix-

ture," *DGE*, 56 (23 Aug. 1902), 21; "Wide-Awake Retailing," *DGE*, 56 (22 Mar. 1902), 81; "Arrangement of Stores," *DGE*, 53 (8 Apr. 1899), 14; "The American Store," *DGE*, 56 (21 June 1902), 45; "Ways of Attracting Trade," *DGE*, 60 (2 Dec. 1905), 5.

19. Edward Mott Woolley, "A Short Cut to Salvation," *McClure's Magazine*, 40 (Dec. 1912), 231; Edward Mott Woolley, "'Lost Motions' in Retail Selling," *System*, 21 (May 1912), 469.

20. Edward Mott Woolley, "'Lost Motions' in Retail Selling," *System*, 21 (Apr. 1912), 371–72.

21. Marshall Jewell Bailey, "When Fixtures Sell Goods—II," *System*, 23 (June 1913), 571–72.

22. Woolley, "'Lost Motions,'" (May 1912), 465–72 and (April 1912), 366–76; Edward Mott Woolley, "Speeding Up the Sales Machine," *System*, 22 (July 1912), 33–41; Marshall Jewell Bailey, "Helping the Customer to Buy," *System*, 24 (Nov. 1913), 489–95; Bailey, "When Fixtures Sell," 571–79; Melvin W. Cassmore, "Steps Wasted Mean Lost Efficiency in Small Wares Department," *DGE*, 76 (26 Aug. 1922), 67–71; Woolley, "Short Cut," 227–36.

23. C. E. Cake, "Arranging Goods to Make the Shopper Buy," *System*, 18 (Dec. 1910), 590.

24. Cake, "Arranging Goods," 591; "Arrangement of Stores," 14; "Interior Appointments," 59; "Dress Goods on Main Floor," *DGE*, 58 (6 Feb. 1904), 19; "Piece Goods Upstairs," *DGE*, 59 (23 Sept. 1905), 31.

25. R. A. Sprouse, "Making Store Space Pay Bigger Dividends," *System*, 58 (Oct. 1930), 286–88; Benjamin H. Namm, "Increased Volume: 48% Last Year," *System*, 41 (May 1922), 534–35, 633.

26. Harry Braverman, *Labor and Monopoly Capital: The Degradation of Work in the Twentieth Century* (New York, 1974), 79–82; B. Eugenia Lies and Marie P. Sealy, "Planning a Department-Store Layout," *JR*, 4 (Apr. 1928), 26; "An Efficient Central Wrap System," *DGE*, 73 (19 Apr. 1919), 77, 83; Merrill W. Osgood, "Mail Sorting That Gives Us an Early Start Daily," *System*, 45 (Mar. 1924), 329–31; A. Lauritano, "Scientific Layout: Reduces Expense and Aids Operations in Receiving, Marking, and Reserve Division," *BNRDGA*, 14 (Aug. 1932), 563–64, 593; *Echo*, 17 (17 Feb. 1921).

27. Leroy Nowlin, "Saving the Frequent Steps," *System*, 44 (Sept. 1923), 387; "I Like to Trade at Parker's," *System*, 44 (Aug. 1923), 174–75; "Saving Clerk's Time," *DGE*, 64 (14 May 1910), 85.

28. Chandler, *Visible Hand*, 238; "Wide-Awake Retailing," *DGE*, 49 (2 Mar. 1895), 71; "Wide-Awake Retailing," *DGE*, 55 (2 Mar. 1901), 79; "Teamwork in Management," *DGE*, 67 (3 May 1913), 27; "The Efficient Employer," *DGE*, 69 (31 July 1915), 27; "Self-Handicapped Merchants," *DGE*, 69 (7 Aug. 1915), 24–25; "Train an Understudy," *DGE*, 71 (11 Aug. 1917), 107; "Foster Initiative," *DGE*, 73 (31 May 1919), 7–8; "Give Them a Chance to Make the Team!" *DGE*, 74 (30 Oct. 1920), 13–14; Twyman, *History of Marshall Field*, 83–88; Appel, *Business Biography of John Wanamaker*, 308–21; Leon Harris, *Merchant Princes* (New York, 1980), 24, 45–46, 51; "Wide-Awake Retailing," *DGE*, 56 (8 Feb. 1902), 95.

29. "The Buyers' Annual Convention," *B & DGC*, 30 (18 Aug. 1900), 9; "Buyers Meet in Convention," *B & DGC*, 30 (18 Aug. 1900), 11; "What Is It For?", *B & DGC*, 30 (18 Aug. 1900), 14; "The Age of the Ready Made," *DGE*, 49 (9 Mar. 1895), 29; "Importance of Ready-Made Wear," *B & DGC*, 29 (17 Feb. 1900), 7.

30. "The Bribing of Buyers," *DGE*, 48 (4 Feb. 1893), 9; "The Bribing of Buyers," *DGE*, 51 (2 Jan. 1897), 14–15; "Gifts to Salesclerks," *DGE*, 57 (27 June 1903), 17; "Full Confidence or None," *DGE*, 57 (8 Aug. 1903), 21; "Buyers and Salesmen," *DGE*, 59 (8 Apr. 1905), 41; "Buyers and Salesmen," *DGE*, 59 (2 Sept. 1905), 23.

31. "Wide-Awake Retailing," *DGE*, 55 (26 Jan. 1901), 61; "Department Methods," *DGE*, 53 (14 Jan. 1899), 17; "Merchandise Man's Talk to Buyers," *DGE*, 64 (1 Oct. 1910), 55; "The Hand-to-Mouth Buying Policy," *DGE*, 66 (3 Feb. 1912), 41.

32. NRDGA, *Twenty-Five Years*, 124; Samuel Hopkins Adams, "The Department Store," *Scribner's Magazine*, 21 (Jan. 1897), 7; "Department Methods," *DGE*, 53 (7 Jan. 1899), 14; "A Thing to Avoid—or Rectify," *DGE*, 68 (18 Apr. 1914), 31; Namm, "Increased Volume," 633.

33. Donovan, *Saleslady*, 69–70; "A Good Scheme," *DGE*, 56 (13 Sept. 1902), 17; "Similar Lines in Two Departments," *DGE*, 64 (12 Feb. 1910), 53; Arthur Lazarus, "Fresh Viewpoints on Store Problems That Should Start You Thinking," *DGE*, 79 (31 Jan. 1925), 23; Gertrude H. Sykes, "Employment Policy and Practice Which Takes Advantage of Experience Rating," in NRDGA, *Management Conference Proceedings, May 1939* (New York, 1939), 114.

34. For discussions of foremen, see Nelson, *Managers and Workers*, chap. 3, and Dan Clawson, *Bureaucracy and the Labor Process: The Transformation of U.S. Industry, 1860–1920* (New York, 1980), 126–32 and passim; on inside contracting, see Clawson, *Bureaucracy and the Labor Process*, chap. 3. Emily Kimbrough, *Through Charley's Door* (New York, 1952), and Wendt and Kogan, *Give the Lady What She Wants*, 303–4, describe Hahner.

35. Beatrice Judelle, "The Techniques of Buying and Merchandising," *Stores*, 42 (June 1960), 11–12; Charles E. Cake, "The Organization of a Retail Store," *System*, 8 (Dec. 1905), 577; "Department Methods," *DGE*, 53 (28 Jan. 1899), 15; "Battle of the Prices," *DGE*, 56 (18 Jan. 1902), 17; "Department Methods," *DGE*, 53 (11 Feb. 1899), 16.

36. On the development of functional structure in American industry, see Alfred Chandler, *Strategy and Structure* (Cambridge, Mass., 1962). On department-store functional organization, see Cake, "Organization," 577; Earl W. Elhart, "Modernizing Store Organization to Improve Employee Relations," *BNRDGA*, 20 (Mar. 1938), 83.

37. "The Buying Manager," *DGE*, 56 (25 Jan. 1902), 13; "An Audience Assured," *DGE*, 56 (29 Nov. 1902), 13; "The Merchandise Manager," *DGE*, 57 (4 Apr. 1903), 27; "The Buyer of To-Day," 58 (28 May 1904), 15; "A Notable Change," 59 (14 Jan. 1905), 17; "The Buyer's Salary," *DGE*, 60 (23 Dec. 1905), 3; Hartley Davis, "The Department Store at Close Range," *Everybody's Magazine*, 17 (Sept. 1907), 322–23; "Merchandise Management," *DGE*, 63 (16 Jan.

1909), 4; "Merchandise Man's Broad Field," *DGE*, 68 (6 June 1914), 23; "Merchant, or Figurehead?" *DGE*, 70 (29 July 1916), 27–28; J. J. Halsey, "Merchandise Office along Bank Lines Makes Turnover Swift and Sure," *DGE*, 74 (21 Aug. 1920), 23–25; John Mench, "The Merchandise Division—Why It Exists, and Its Job," *JR*, 1 (July 1925), 5–6; NRDGA, *Twenty-Five Years*, 27; "Forum for Stores' Merchandise Managers," *DGE*, 78 (29 Dec. 1923), 14; "Merchandise Men's Group," *DGE*, 78 (16 Feb. 1924), 15–16; "A Leader, or a Watchdog?" *DGE*, 67 (14 Dec. 1912), 27; Raymond Edwin Bell, "Gimbel Investigation: Report on Industrial Relations, June 1921," Part I, 104–5, in folder 1610, box 105, Mary Van Kleeck Papers, Sophia Smith Collection, Smith College.

38. Pasdermadjian, *Department Store*, 38–39, 66–69.

39. "For Greater Efficiency," *DGE*, 65 (25 Feb. 1911), 28; NRDGA, *Twenty-Five Years*, 44, 74–79; Arthur Lazarus, *Department Store Organization* (New York, 1926), I, v.

40. Hower, *Macy's*, 390–91; "Department Methods," *DGE*, 53 (7 Jan. 1899), 14; Malcolm P. McNair and Eleanor G. May, *The American Department Store, 1920–1960*, Bulletin No. 166 of the Bureau of Business Research (Boston, 1963), 22–23; "Volume Froth vs. Net Solids," *DGE*, 80 (13 Feb. 1926), 17–18; Malcolm P. McNair, "What Can a Retailer Do to Reduce His Costs of Doing Business?" *DGE*, 78 (24 Nov. 1923), 16–17; "Little Peterkin Asks a Question," *DGE*, 81 (18 June 1927), 7–8. Retailers also worried that their gains in efficiency lagged behind those of manufacturers; figures gathered by Harold Barger during the 1950s proved that they were quite correct. Output per man-hour increased somewhat more rapidly in manufacturing than in retailing from 1879 to 1919, but in the next decade the former took a quantum leap of 60.9 percent, far outdistancing the latter's gain of 10.7 percent. Barger further showed that department-store margin increased far more rapidly than margin in other branches of retailing. Even without access to such figures, department-store managers sensed their comparatively poor showing and tried to better it. See Harold Barger, *Distribution's Place in the American Economy since 1869* (Princeton, 1955), 38–39, 81.

41. "Value of System," *DGE*, 58 (6 Feb. 1904), 19; "From Scrap Paper to System," *DGE*, 58 (21 May 1904), 17; "Successful through System," *System*, 6 (July 1904), 62 (see also 58–63); "Adopt the Right Methods!" *DGE*, 69 (27 Mar. 1915), 28. See also "Errors in System," *DGE* 67 (14 Dec. 1912), 11; "May Go Too Far," *DGE*, 67 (1 Mar. 1913), 44.

42. Lazarus, "Fresh Viewpoints," 23; Harold B. Wess, "Merchandise Control," *DGE*, 79 (11 Apr. 1925), 19; Norris H. Brisco, "Research and the *Journal of Retailing*," *JR*, 1 (Apr. 1925), 4; A. H. Klubock, "Getting the Most from Statistics," *BNRDGA*, 13 (May 1931), 301–2, 325; "Controlling the Controller," *JR*, 8 (Apr. 1932), 15–18; B. Earl Puckett, "Eliminating Waste from Merchandising and Sales Promotion," *BNRDGA*, 14 (July 1932), 481; NRDGA, *Twenty-Five Years*, 22–24.

43. Lazarus, "Fresh Viewpoints," 23.

44. "Buyer's Meetings," *DGE*, 67 (12 Apr. 1913), 28; "A Documentary History of the R. H. Macy Company," Manuscript Division, Baker Library, Harvard Graduate School of Business Administration, 152, 157; "Is the Buyer Being Di-

vested of His Functions?" *JR*, 4 (Oct. 1928), 13–14; Otho J. Hicks, "Sales Promotion and Training," *BNRDGA*, 15 (Apr. 1933), 56; Estelle Hamburger, *It's a Woman's Business* (New York, 1939), 69–74, 174–76; Bernice M. Cannon, "The Importance of Training Assistant Buyers," *BNRDGA*, 8 (Apr. 1926), 38–40; Channing E. Sweitzer, "Report of the Managing Director," in NRDGA, *The Work of the NRDGA in 1931* (New York, 1931), 56–57.

45. "Respect for Self and for Job First Things to Teach the Floorman," *DGE*, 77 (14 Apr. 1923), 24.

46. "Aisle-Manager's Work," *DGE*, 56 (15 Feb. 1902), 36; "Floorman Holds Mighty Power for Service: Do You Get It?" *DGE*, 74 (3 Apr. 1920), 35–36; "Finding Your Plane of Educational Work," *DGE*, 74 (24 July 1920), 15–16; "More Than Sales Count in Fixing Standing of Hamburger Employees," *DGE*, 76 (4 Mar. 1922), 77; "Consider the Floorwalker, How He Works." *Literary Digest*, 76 (24 Mar. 1923), 52–57; A. E. Simmons, "That Isn't in This Department," *System*, 44 (Oct. 1923), 464–66.

47. Ernest J. Hastings, "Sales Manager of the Future Will Show Up Present Crop as Raw Recruits," *DGE*, 75 (12 Feb. 1921), 32; Ernest J. Hastings, "Just One Job for Manager: Pushing Out What Buyers Take In," *DGE*, 76 (18 Feb. 1922), 31; A. E. Simmons, "A Policy That Simplifies Store Management," *System*, 43 (June 1923), 753–54.

48. "A Notions Buyer Fable," *DGE*, 55 (2 Feb. 1901), 39; "Get Next to Your Help," *DGE*, 55 (12 Oct. 1901), 13; Edward A. Filene, "How a Buyer Can Answer: When? How Much? What?" *System*, 44 (Dec. 1923), 817; "Seller, As Well As Buyer," *DGE*, 67 (14 Dec. 1912), 27; "'It's a·Gamble,' but Use Your Head," *DGE*, 77 (18 Aug. 1923), 24; *Echo*, 26 (29 July 1927).

49. "Costly Cheese-Paring," *DGE*, 56 (8 Mar. 1902), 51; "Salary and Commission," *DGE*, 58 (6 Feb. 1904), 19; "New Buying System," *DGE*, 58 (24 Sept. 1904), 41; "One Section or Many?" *DGE*, 59 (3 June 1905), 22; "The Buyer's Salary," 3; "The New Buyer," *JR*, 4 (Apr. 1928), 9; "Sets Buyers Thinking," *DGE*, 78 (3 Aug. 1924), 19–20; Emily Mills Hopson, "The Training and Development of Buyers," *BNRDGA*, 15 (Mar. 1933), 40–42; Kenneth Collins, *Retail Selling and the New Order* (New York, 1934), 20–21; "Editorial," *DSE*, 1 (10 Oct. 1938), 32.

50. Otho J. Hicks, "Have You Streamlined Your Organization Set-Up for Selling?" *BNRDGA*, 20 (Nov. 1938), 16, 51–52; "Merchandise Men Talk Organization from the Buyer's Viewpoint," *BNRDGA*, 21 (Feb. 1939), 25; Elhart, "Modernizing Store Organization," 83; "Retailing Needs Top-to-Bottom Overhaul to Meet Demands of Postwar Selling," *BNRDGA*, 27 (Apr. 1945), 19–20, 58.

51. "Merchandise Man's Talk to Buyers," 55; "Saving Simplicity vs. Costly Complexity Is the Next Fight on the Program," *DGE*, 77 (6 Oct. 1923), 43.

52. "Bigger Profits through Simplification," *DGE*, 77 (14 Apr. 1923), 21; "How Long Are 38s to Be Only 36s?" *DGE*, 79 (21 Mar. 1925), 23–24; "Standardization of Sizes," *DGE*, 79 (14 Nov. 1925), 24; Claudia B. Kidwell and Margaret C. Christman, *Suiting Everyone* (Washington, 1974), 107–11; H. P. Dalzell, "Simplified Practice as an Aid to the Merchandiser," *BNRDGA*, 13 (Feb. 1931), 93–94, 104–5; Edward A. Filene, "More Sales; More Satisfied Custom-

ers—but Smaller Stocks," *System*, 44 (Sept. 1923), 270, 273, 350; Edward A. Filene, "The Three Price Levels That Move Stocks," *System*, 44 (Oct. 1923), 431–34, 478–84; Edward A. Filene, "What Is Back of a Fast Rate of Turnover?" *System*, 44 (Nov. 1923), 583–86, 658–65; Pasdermadjian, *Department Store*, 41–42.

53. F. Altergott, Jr., "How We Applied Simplification in a Retail Store," *System*, 43 (Jan. 1923), 35–37, 115; George M. Gales, "How We Sell Twice As Much on Half the Stock," *System*, 43 (May 1923), 583–87, 632–36; Tom B. Stedman, "Buy Little and Often," *System*, 45 (Feb. 1924), 250–51; Charles S. Miller, Jr., "133% on Invested Capital; 7 Turns, through the 'Flyer' Plan," *System*, 46 (Dec. 1924), 786; Walter Hammitt, "A Plan That Synchronized Fashions, Stocks, and Profits," *System*, 58 (July 1930), 33–34, 62; William O. Jelleme, "Hand to Mouth Buying: An Appraisal of Current Buying Practice," *Bulletin of the Taylor Society*, 12 (Feb. 1927), 294–302; Paul W. Mazur, *Principles of Organization Applied to Modern Retailing* (New York, 1927), 2; Edward A. Filene, *The Model Stock Plan* (New York, 1930); R. P. Connally, "How Can the Retailer Lower the Present Cost of Distribution?" *BNRDGA*, 13 (Aug. 1931), 465–67, 515.

54. Altergott, "How We Applied Simplification," 35–37; "Bigger Profits through Simplification," 11; Ray E. Bigelow, "Simplification in a Retail Store," *System*, 49 (Mar. 1926), 372.

55. Miller, "133% on Invested Capital," 786; NRDGA, *Twenty-Five Years*, 45; Pasdermadjian, *Department Store*, 68–69, 167; McNair and May, *American Department Store*, 22–24.

56. "Bigger Profits through Simplification," 11; James Simpson, "What Is More Important Than Fast Turnover?" *System*, 44 (July 1923), 21–22, 24; "The Safe Way," *DGE*, 67 (2 Nov. 1912), 31.

3

"An Adamless Eden":
Managing Department-Store Customers

Relations with customers placed in the highest relief the central issue facing department-store executives: how to make the store a haven of luxury and amenity at the same time as they made it an efficient business. Managers wished to appeal to and indulge customers as well as to manipulate, educate, and discipline them. The task was not simply to sell individual pieces of merchandise but to build a following of loyal and reliable customers who would visit the store repeatedly, speak well of it in the community, purchase goods readily and frequently, and pay their bills promptly. Just as managers became more self-conscious and deliberate in administering their stores, so they developed more systematic and calculated ways of dealing with customers. Their methods included fashion propaganda as well as lavish store facilities, consumer credit as well as solicitous service, appeals based on quality as well as on price—all designed to teach the customer an acceptable way of consuming. These tactics frequently had contradictory effects, furthering one of the retailer's aims at the expense of the other and leaving both managers and customers dissatisfied with their interaction.

The vexed quality of the manager-customer relationship grew not just out of the retailer's ambitious agenda but also out of larger issues. The two groups struggled to define the ground rules for a consumption-oriented society and confronted powerful issues of class and gender. The department-store customer was still a novel type in the late nineteenth century, a result of one of the most profound changes in recent history: the shift from a production-oriented society to one that centered on consumption. Although there had long been women whose families lived well above subsistence, only with the growth of the urban middle classes and the expansion of mass production did they become numerous and their margin of prosperity significant. For more and more people, consumption ceased to be a matter of barely satisfying urgent basic needs and became a matter of choice—very broad for some, narrower for others.

For women, the change was a trade-off, offering new delights and conveniences while devaluing old skills; as one writer put it, "the expression 'homemade,' which was once an encomium, is become a reproach." From the retailer's point of view, the woman with choices to make in the marketplace was a mixed blessing; her purchases were larger and more profitable yet far less predictable than those of a woman whose purchases were dictated by the cruel pinch of want. Between 1890 and 1940, managers and customers were adjusting to this deep and disruptive change in Americans' lives; they were the first generations to be faced with integrating the new world of mass consumption into their personal and business lives.[1]

This task was enormously complicated by its relationship to gender and class. While virtually all department-store managers at policy-making levels were men, the vast majority—eight or nine of every ten—of their customers were women. A journalist gave this dizzying description of the department store in 1910:

Buying and selling, serving and being served—women. On every floor, in every aisle, at every counter, women. . . . Behind most of the counters on all the floors, . . . women. At every cashier's desk, at the wrappers' desks, running back and forth with parcels and change, short-skirted women. Filling the aisles, passing and repassing, a constantly arriving and departing throng of shoppers, women. Simply a moving, seeking, hurrying, mass of femininity, in the midst of which the occasional man shopper, man clerk, and man supervisor, looks lost and out of place.

Edward A. Filene, surveying his Boston store, wryly called it "an Adamless Eden." The store was female territory: socially determined gender roles cast women as consumers, and store practices encouraged and intensified this tendency. The ironic result was that the male executives who made the major decisions in the department store were in fact "out of place": eager to appeal to women, they created an atmosphere which female customers could manipulate in unexpected ways.[2]

More specifically, the department store tailored its appeal to women of the middle and upper classes. While some stores used the appeal of low prices more than others, all prized most those customers with family incomes large enough to permit discretionary and impulse buying; controllers argued convincingly that larger transactions and multiple sales were an important key to higher profits. A generous family budget provided not only consumer goods to fit styles of life that demanded ever more elaborate commodities, but also comparative leisure for the housewife through the provision of laborsaving devices and services and the hiring of domestic servants. By the 1890s, the comfortable middle-class urban family enjoyed electric lighting, central heating, a full bathroom, and an icebox, all of which lightened the physical burden of housekeeping. Steam laundries relieved women in these families of the staggering burdens of washday. High quality, stylish ready-made clothing could be purchased for all members of the family. Servants performed the work unaffected by technology or commercial services. A growing concern for what Faye Dudden has termed "status pursuit and status maintenance" kept the servants busy meeting ever-higher standards of cleanliness and propriety. Even as the ratio of servants to population declined and as the basis of domestic service shifted from "live-in" to "day-work"—changes well advanced by 1920—such boons as electric washing machines, gas and electric stoves, refrigerators, electric irons, and vacuum cleaners made more efficient use of the servant's time and relieved the servantless woman of physical drudgery. The time freed by servants and household appliances was readily absorbed in fulfilling socially and esthetically expanded notions of good housekeeping—in large part through consumption.[3]

While many working-class people could afford occasional department-store purchases, particularly at sale prices, their budgets excluded luxury goods and items such as clothing which could be more economically made at home. But even the more prosperous among the working class lacked the time to browse with their middle-class sisters among department-store wares: work in mills and factories, wage-earning in the home, and household chores made working-class women anything but creatures of leisure.

The class bias of department stores went beyond working people's lack of time and money. Unlike many of the other palatial buildings of growing urban centers, which were either private residences or forbidding public institutions such as libraries or museums, the department store was both open and inviting to all comers. But this accessibility and evenhandedness were undermined by department stores' appeal to bourgeois manners, styles, and pretensions. Eager for the more lucrative trade of the middle and upper classes, store managers created an atmosphere which could alienate as well as attract working-class people. Although they did not scorn poorer families' dollars, they solicited them in bargain or low-priced departments inferior in merchandise and decoration to the rest of the store. Not surprisingly, working-class people frequently chose to shop in the neighborhoods where they lived and worked, where store-keepers were often kin or friends, where they could (if immigrants) speak a familiar tongue and expect their requests to be treated with respect, and where they might obtain the credit which department stores denied to those of modest means.

Scholars are only now beginning to study this new world of consumption and its links to class and gender. Some, such as Daniel Boorstin, celebrate the shift and see it as an essentially unmixed blessing, part of the rich promise of American life. Others, such as Stuart Ewen, argue that it produced a deceptive and manipulative culture orchestrated by the advertising industry and its patrons. Neither model fits the world of the department store. It was not merely the site of useful and satisfying purchases, but also the scene of a subtle and complex interplay of power and influence, of suspicion and dependence, as managers and customers pursued their own ends. Nor, as Ewen would have it, was it a place where managers' ideas about consumption inexorably displaced older or oppositional ideas; the battle was far more evenly matched. Managers supplied customers with merchandise and service that could give them pleasure and comfort as well as enhance their stature in their own eyes and in those of their peers. But customers exerted a fearsome power over managers' balance sheets; they controlled the dollars for which stores vied and could in the process of spending them disrupt store operations, sabotage their procedures, and sap their profits. As a general social rule, women— the majority of customers—were subordinate to men—the majority of managers. But the microcosm of the department store created a more nearly equal balance of power, one that exploited the contradictions in the social construction of gender.[4]

Recent work suggests the complexity of the world of consumption, particularly as it was intertwined with women's lives. Ann Douglas has found in nineteenth-century novels written by women a decline in characters displaying female "faculty," the ability to cope practically and resourcefully yet gracefully with the demands of daily life—in short, to be producers—and the rise of those like Harriet Beecher Stowe's Eva Van Arsdel, a charming though parasitic woman, "dependent if decorative"—

a consumer and not a maker of things. Van Arsdel was one model of the woman consumer, enshrined in popular culture as the type who solves all problems by buying something for herself or her home. But women did not learn the art of consumption from novels alone. Writers on the domestic sphere sternly advised women to manage their homes in an organized fashion. From 1840 to 1873, Catherine Beecher's domestic manuals bluntly asserted that "There is no one thing, more necessary to a housekeeper, in performing her varied duties, than *a habit of system and order.*" The home economics movement spread a similar message through land grant colleges, urban cooking schools, and public schools, introducing the notion of scientific and businesslike home management. Bertha June Richardson Lucas urged women to manage their consumption through "wise spending of time, effort, and money." The "housekeeper of *today,*" maintained Christine Frederick, must become a *"trained consumer"* and an "efficient 'purchasing agent.'" The National Federation of Women's Clubs made the encouragement of such self-conscious consumption a priority in the early twentieth century. Advertisers intensified their efforts to manage women's consumer behavior, making more insistent claims about the virtues of their products and touting brand names as tokens of dependability. By the late 1920s, manufacturers began to link consumption with social anxieties, suggesting that nightly "Luxing" of underwear would save a shaky romance. Popular and women's magazines such as the *Ladies' Home Journal* highlighted advertising in both their editorial content and layout, advocating "domestic efficiency and civic activity" and "system in shopping."[5]

Many teachers, many messages; the department-store manager's pleas for store loyalty and inducements to impulse buying competed with many different consumption ethics. Most important of all, they vied with women's ways of filtering these messages through personal inclination and experience. Consumption was an enduring theme in women's interactions with one another. The *Dry Goods Economist* noted in the late 1890s that "the relation between visiting [among women] and the demand for dry goods is too clear to *Economist* readers to need further comment," while a Minneapolis department-store executive maintained in 1930 that "stores are probably women's most widely discussed institution." Women individually and collectively forged their own ethics of consumption, behaving whether by accident or design in ways that conflicted with the retailer's interests. Lillian Gilbreth, a woman with a foot in each camp as the widowed mother of a large family and a management consultant, cautioned retailers in 1932 that they were "dealing here not with an 'Unclassified moron,' but with a thoughtful, reasonable, and reasoning person." Department-store managers had earned her blunt words. Blinded by social images of women and by confidence in their own powers of manipulation, they had great difficulty in understanding customers' behavior and persisted in viewing the woman consumer as childish, willful and capricious instead of independent-minded and discerning.[6]

In selling his wares, the retailer faced different constraints than the manufacturer. First, the latter sold to a comparatively small number of clients, while department stores appealed to the public in general. They dared alienate no one; all were potential sources of revenue and goodwill. Second, manufacturers' operations were more or less insulated from public scrutiny. Industry gossip of course traveled in businessmen's circles, but factories were rarely as closely examined by their customers as retail stores were by the consuming public. Third, manufacturers increasingly operated in a national market while department-store managers had to function simultaneously within a highly competitive local context and a developing nationwide culture of consumption.

At the local level, there was a major tension between competition and cooperation among merchants in dealing with customers. Usually stores favored collective action in the matter of services—returns, exchanges, deliveries, and the like—in order to impose new practices or restraints on the consuming public. They preferred to avoid interstore competition on costly matters such as complimentary services. On other issues, such as price and style, they remained keenly competitive. In both cases, however, retailers far more than manufacturers had to be public relations experts, to give a favorable impression of the individual establishment as well as of the industry as a whole. Retail operations were a public spectacle in a way that manufacturing plants simply were not.

Moreover, while factory managers were by and large content merely to sell their goods, retailers wanted to do more. They wanted each transaction, and for that matter each visit to the store, to build in consumers' minds a positive image of the store in particular and of the delights of consumption in general. Seen from this point of view, making a purchase was not just an economic exchange, but also an incident in socialization. As Lillian Gilbreth told the 1927 convention of the National Retail Dry Goods Association: "The customer must not only like the goods she has bought, the surroundings in which she has done the buying, and the people from whom she has done the buying, but she must like herself better at the end of the transaction." Although manufacturers could hardly ignore their customers' sensibilities, they dealt primarily with measurable needs rather than matters of individual psychology. In the words of T. J. Jackson Lears, retailers encouraged the development of a "therapeutic ethic" composed in part of a "need to construct a pleasing 'self' by purchasing consumer goods." [7]

Manufacturers appealed directly to the consumer on the relatively narrow basis of the product alone, usually relying on a trademark or a slogan to convey their message. But the newly self-conscious department-store manager spoke lyrically of developing a store image—presenting the store as a coordinated whole, harmonizing all its aspects, standardizing the quality of service and merchandise in all departments, and doing so with a special twist that would distinguish the store in the mind of the public. Some firms adopted a certain pattern or color scheme, with decor, supplies, and wrappings all in "a common motif." Delivery fleets often mirrored the store's trademark or color scheme, the typical driver no longer of "uncouth appearance" but now a "better type" fitted out in a "distinctive uniform." A woman carrying a package wrapped in the well-known manner of the city's most prestigious store, or in front of whose house that store's truck often stopped, gained in the estimation of those who calculated status by patterns of consumption. [8]

For the half-century between 1890 and 1940, the department store channeled the interaction between managers and customers into two main arenas unified by their goal of creating not just devotees of consumption in general but also loyal customers for the individual store. The first, the world of bourgeois gentility and lavish service that I call the palace of consumption, was in many ways the more important. Using an elaborate array of services to create an ethic of consumption that transcended individual sales, the palace of consumption was the department store's peculiar contribution to the consumer society. In the second—the more specific merchandise appeals involved in advertising, fashion propaganda, and focused sales campaigns—the department store shared the stage with other types of retailing, manufacturers, advertising agencies, and the mass media. Accordingly, the primary focus of this chapter is on the first arena. But in both realms, the structural relationship between managers and customers fostered mistrust. Managers were convinced that customers were constantly scheming to take unfair advantage of them, while customers looked at retailers with age-old fears of being cheated in the marketplace.

The Palace of Consumption: The Lure of Service

Retailers most obviously attempted to impress customers with the delights of consumption through the design of store buildings and the provision of various services. This activity was the province of the store's service or store management division. Managers wanted not only to make their stores efficient, to make them machines for selling; they wanted also to make them beautiful, to make them palaces of consumption. In some ways, the two goals dovetailed nicely: the new custom-made fixtures designed to increase selling efficiency were frequently handsome pieces of furniture, made of rich woods and pleasingly designed. In other instances, the goals clashed sharply: the cost-conscious drive to make every accessible square foot produce revenue directly conflicted with the service-oriented impulse to use valuable space for reading rooms, lounges, and the like.

After the depression of the 1890s lifted, retailers began to remodel existing stores and build new ones with a double interest in luxury and efficiency. To the average customer, the former was by far the more obvious; the *Dry Goods Economist* approvingly noted "the large amount of money invested in forms not calculated to bring direct returns." The new buildings opened by R. H. Macy and Marshall Field in 1902 show the pervasive concern for grand conception and decoration. Although the Macy Herald Square store was hardly a match for the Marshall Field palace, the difference between the level of amenity in the popular and in the carriage-trade store was one of degree rather than of kind. Macy's boasted of its price policy, vowing to undersell competitors, but still treated customers to a range of services and touches of luxury as they shopped: the main floor columns of the store were made of marble, the escalators framed in "burnished wood." Marshall Field displayed greater opulence, the galleries of the store's rotunda being supported by "parallel rows of classic white Grecian columns," the floors covered with red marble, "thick pile carpeting or Oriental rugs," lighted by Tiffany chandeliers, the merchandise "encased in polished mahogany and French glass counters."[9]

The combination of great size and luxurious appointments conveyed a powerful message: that consumption was not just a matter of keeping one's person decently clothed or one's linen press well-stocked, but also a way of behaving that had links to class, particularly to urban gentility. The palace of consumption elevated prosaic goods and touched them with the aura of elegance while fostering a taste for luxury and encouraging the sale of finer goods. The store could become an object of civic pride, an attraction in itself and a validation of the city's stature and cosmopolitanism. Marshall Field reported on the progress of its new store "as it might a civic celebration," and Filene's attracted in just two months visitors from Buffalo, Minneapolis, New Jersey, California, Mexico, Japan, and China, plus some South Carolinians interested only in Filene's and the Bunker Hill monument in all of Boston. Many of the store's amenities could be enjoyed free, and the make-believe of a shopping trip with no intention of buying was within the reach of all.[10]

Department-store managers modeled the store along two complementary lines: as a home and as a downtown club. In the first case, the customer was treated not just as a potential spender, but also as a guest, catered to and coddled. The store, as one observer put it, became "a supplement to the home." Hortense Odlum, president of Bonwit Teller, used this tactic to help rescue her store from the torpor into which it had fallen in the late 1920s and early 1930s. "From the beginning," she later wrote, "I tried to have the policy of the store reflect as nearly as it was possible in the commercial world, those standards of comfort and grace which are apparent in a lovely home." Odlum, secure in her position as the appointee of her husband's firm and unconstrained by prior retail experience, carried the policy to extremes: she was always "at home" to customers, greeting even those in a complaining humor "pleasantly and casually as though it were a social call," dedicating herself "to make a friend of every customer." The male majority among managers was less actively involved in store hospitality, but attempted through the palace of consumption to disarm the customer by replicating the ambience of a bourgeois home where "the atmosphere of trade is removed and with it the defensive fortifications of the buyer."[11]

Pursuing a second model, stores spared no effort to relieve "patrons of every arduous and disagreeable accompaniment of shopping" and created the women's equivalent of the men's downtown club. The department store provided both accommodations and service to ease the rigors of consumption for females much as men's clubs eased the burdens of paid employment for men. An early-twentieth-century writer noted the utility of such a technique:

[Department stores] induce men and women to visit their establishments for purposes wholly apart from buying. They spend thousands of dollars yearly for a
purpose that has no apparent connection with the selling of goods. Their object is
to get the people in the store and surround them with subtle influences which will
metamorphose visitors into customers. . . . For the shopping, bargaining instinct
is substituted a friendly confidence more valuable to the store than if all visitors
had come with a definite purpose of purchasing.

Whether as home or downtown club, department stores created new public space for women, providing a socially acceptable way for them to enjoy the excitement of urban downtowns and a woman-oriented center of
comfort and amenity.[12]

Managers did not inflict this type of store on an indifferent public,
for department stores were one aspect of larger social forces inspiring
customers to expect more than merchandise alone for their consumption
dollar. Customers had long objected to needless delays and inconveniences while shopping, but by the 1890s they had begun to demand
"pleasure in buying" as well. They were making an esthetic demand for
"beautiful and even artistic surroundings" in which to make their purchases as well as a sociological statement of distaste for the effects of
"dinginess, dirt, and unsanitary conditions" on both shoppers and employees. The store as home and downtown club exerted a powerful pull
on customers. The superintendent of Chicago's Carson, Pirie, Scott &
Co. maintained, "We draw people to our store through *conveniences* and
accommodations. Newspaper advertising, in my judgment, attracts only
about two in ten visitors to the store." Industry writers agreed that investment in store amenities paid off more handsomely than money spent on
newspaper advertising. Aware of the effect of amenity and graciousness
on their customers, managers went to great lengths to preserve such an
atmosphere.[13]

Department stores provided an impressive range of services. Some
had no direct relation to shopping itself, while others were designed to
aid the customer in buying. Not all stores offered the full range of services; the whim of managers, the size and profitability of the store, and
keen local competition shaped each store's array of services. In general,
however, the higher a store's gross income, the higher the proportion of
its gross income spent on services. The Emporium in San Francisco provided a typical range of services at the turn of the century: "a parlor with
papers, periodicals, and writing materials; a children's nursery; an emergency hospital, with a trained nurse in attendance; a Post Office station;

a Western Union telegraph office; a theater-ticket office; a manicuring and hair-dressing parlor and a barber shop; public telephones; a lunch room; an information bureau; [and] always some free exhibition in the art rooms,—all of these under one roof, and most of them free." Such services proliferated wildly during the first three decades of the twentieth century. In 1929 a nationwide survey of ninety-one stores, large and small, revealed that over half offered the following services: public telephones, parcel checkrooms, lost and found services, shopping assistance, free delivery, waiting rooms, gift suggestion departments, mail-order departments, telephone order departments, accommodation bureaus, barber shops, restaurants, post offices, hospitals, radio departments, bus service, and shoe-shining stands. Over a fifth provided nurseries for shoppers' children, and a few offered Saturday afternoon children's theaters. One or more stores offered forty-eight other services; the array was, apparently, limited only by the scope of managers' imaginations.[14]

The woman shopper could easily pass the whole day in her favorite store, socializing with her friends. Doormen bowed customers into the store while uniformed chauffeurs whisked their cars off to the garage and attendants received their wraps and packages. When shopping became too wearing, they could relax in a restaurant to the music of live musicians, refresh themselves with a hot bath, or distract themselves by attending a lecture, viewing an art exhibition, or planning a vacation at the travel bureau. Indoor playgrounds amused their children with such distractions as miniature zoos and fish ponds with mechanical boats. The simple rest room became "an elaborate lounging place, extravagantly furnished, equipped with expensive stationery, with uniformed maids in attendance, and a rental charge equal to that of an average store." Taking the idea of a women's city club to its logical conclusion, a number of stores provided free meeting rooms for women's organizations, and a Providence store set aside a space for organizations' food sales.[15]

Sometimes non-selling service verged on the ludicrous, but two extreme examples help to show the double motive behind such services. An Oklahoma City store held a baby week during which it offered nine babies for adoption; six of the lucky tykes found new homes, and the store sold a complete layette with each, earning profits as well as a good reputation. Some stores maintained nurse registries for the use of their customers. The *Dry Goods Economist* strongly endorsed this practice because it would please customers and at the same time "win the good will of the nurses, who are frequently intrusted with the purchasing of

Fig. 6. The Women's City Club

THE GREAT AMERICAN PUBLIC-SERVICE INSTITUTION

Journal of Retailing, 5 (Oct. 1929), 25.

supplies for cases on which they are called, and who will, naturally, give preference to the store aiding them." This assumption, that goodwill would lead to good profits, guided managers who devoted precious space and funds to these non-selling services.[16]

Managers were even more eagerly accommodating when addressing the problem of shopping itself. Stores began in the 1890s to provide hostesses or special guides who did not actually sell merchandise but shepherded customers about the store and pointed out items of particular interest. Hostess service developed into the personal-service bureau, the refuge of any customer with a difficult or unusual shopping task; among other things, personal-service staffs planned weddings and funerals, provided interpreters for those who could not speak English, advised on the proper attire for special occasions, and tracked down bizarre items. Customers came to regard these bureaus as all-purpose sources of information and assistance. Filene's personal-service department provided the dates for Civil Service examinations in Philadelphia and the schedule for the Seattle-to-Nome boat; Marshall Field's reunited long lost friends and arranged for diapers and baby formula to be delivered to a New York-bound mother as her train paused in South Bend. Customers uncertain of their taste or tormented by indecision could consult an interior decorating service about anything from drapery fabric to the furnishings for a whole house. Those too feeble or sensitive to face the ordeal of walking about the store could retire to a special room and recline in regal privacy while goods were brought in for consideration. When style and size did not coincide, stores would willingly alter garments, sometimes practically remaking them; increasingly after World War I, though, customers had to pay for this service. Concerned that no customer depart unsatisfied, department stores filled special orders; although some firms discouraged them because of the extra expense involved, others turned a nuisance into a money-maker. By the mid-1920s, Jordan Marsh boasted that its special-order department filled 2000 requests per week, giving satisfaction in nineteen out of twenty cases. Filene's, Jordan's competitor across the street, provided instant gratification by sending someone out to purchase the desired item elsewhere while the customer waited. Should a customer wish to defer payment for her purchases, most stores offered the privilege of a charge account, and virtually all sent packages COD. Stores made every effort to speed the customer's purchase, shaving the time spent in wrapping packages and making change. Transfer systems spared the

shopper the nuisance of carrying packages from department to department; all her purchases were sent to a central desk and wrapped together.
Alternatively, there was no need to carry even the smallest parcel when
stores offered free and frequent deliveries within a wide area. For those
who came from outside the delivery area, some stores offered free deliveries to railroad stations and fare rebates if purchases totaled a certain
amount. Retail managers campaigned for low transit fares, provided direct entrances from subways into their stores, and—in Bridgeport in
1920—intervened in a dispute between transit companies to return to service the trolleys favored by their wealthy customers. A customer who
changed her mind about an item had virtually unlimited privileges of returning it, and most stores would send a delivery truck to call for it.[17]

Shoppers did not in fact need to leave their homes. Department stores
began mail-order service in the late nineteenth century in order to meet
the competition of the large mail-order houses such as Sears, Roebuck,
and added telephone service in the early twentieth century. But they went
beyond catalog houses' promises to fill orders swiftly and efficiently. They
acted as "personal shoppers," fulfilling ambiguous requests and suggesting additional merchandise. Sears could send out five size-38 union suits
as promptly, and probably more cheaply, than John Wanamaker, but only
Wanamaker's would try to select a waist suitable for an elderly, dark-
haired woman. Some customers placed themselves entirely in the hands of
their favorite store: for five years, Filene's Personal Service Bureau chose
every garment—except for three dresses bought in Paris—in an Illinois
woman's wardrobe. Stores such as Wanamaker, Filene's, Abraham &
Straus, and Mandel Brothers of Chicago excelled in providing such careful personalized service. Mandel had a corps of thirty-five order buyers
who "represent[ed] the customer alone."[18]

Telephone selling worked in a similar way. Even before World War I, a
large New York department store maintained telephone service between
the store's closing hours and midnight, thereby "facilitating purchases at
the moment when the buying impulse makes itself felt." Even more extreme was a competitor's offer to telephone customers daily to take their
orders. Other stores paid the toll charges on out-of-town orders. The
quality as well as the convenience of the service mattered; one store
manager wrote of his efforts to train personnel so that they no longer answered calls "with all the grace and politeness of a hyena." Telephones
could be especially useful in a crisis: during a transit strike one firm organized salespeople to follow the example of one enterprising saleswoman

who had called customers for orders. Even in normal times, the telephone had important advantages. Retailers who worried that telephone selling service discouraged customers from coming to the store where they might succumb to impulse purchases were shouted down by those who pointed out that small sales could be handled more quickly and cheaply over the telephone than over the counter, that merchandise purchased by telephone was rarely returned, and that most customers telephoned orders during the early morning hours when salespeople were often idle.[19]

The palace of consumption, with its myriad services, appeared to be a relatively democratic institution; the free-entry and one-price policies in theory guaranteed the same reception and treatment for all. Managers rarely imposed limits on the use of store accommodations, but when they did it was usually to protect the sensibilities of their well-heeled customers. Siegel-Cooper barred noisy and unkempt East Side children from the lounge, another New York store distributed tickets for free afternoon tea only to "regular customers and prosperous looking visitors," and a Boston store closed its women's smoking room when rowdy young women made it their headquarters. Their concerns reached even beyond the doors of their stores: in 1916, the *Dry Goods Economist* complained that customers of New York's Fifth Avenue stores were offended by apparel-industry operatives loitering on the sidewalks and seriously suggested that measures be taken to bar the intruders.[20]

Department stores eagerly accepted all dollars, whether proffered by the rough red hand of a charwoman or the kid-gloved hand of a millionaire's daughter. Separate articles in the same 1899 issue of the *Dry Goods Economist* warned retailers on the one hand not to scorn the "wealthy and conservative trade" for the "mass trade" yet on the other not to give up bargain tables simply because the well-to-do complained that they attracted "too much of a cheap class of trade." Managers gracefully accommodated both groups through sorting mechanisms which segregated the more affluent customers—the "carriage trade"—from the poorer—the "shawl trade." Each group, they argued, was uncomfortable associating with the other. One commentator noted that "unduly handsome fixtures" created an "idea of costliness" which led "*the masses* to conclude that the CUSTOMERS HAVE TO PAY for the concern's lavish expenditures in the shape of abnormally high prices." Conversely, noted another writer, "People of culture and refinement dislike crowds and crushes in stores. Your true 'swell' likes to trade at a store where there is plenty of room and an abundance of air, with surroundings of an elegant, not to say esthetic, charac-

ter. Shawl-crowned people wearing market baskets on their tawny arms
are not the sort that frequent such stores, and it is their company to
which elegance and refinement are especially adverse." [21]

The solution was clear: to provide bargain-price departments which
sold lower-quality goods in spartan settings, usually in store basements.
Beginning just after the turn of the century, this "double stock" idea
spread rapidly; expanding markets with minimal investment, the plan
was heralded for having "few or no disadvantages." The bargain-section
strategy allowed department stores to pursue simultaneously their strategy of "trading up," or seeking an even wealthier clientele, and their goal
of increasing sales volume. A corollary was to divide the stock in the main
store by price; by the mid-1920s, for example, Filene's sold women's
dresses, ranging from one-of-a-kind designer models to basement markdowns, in at least five departments. [22]

Department stores gave special consideration to the freest spenders.
One method of doing so was to encourage salespeople, floor managers,
and doormen to greet customers by name. Managers urged saleswomen
to build up clienteles, to learn steady customers' names and preferences
and give them special treatment. A customer might be flattered if "her"
saleswoman called to tell of a new handbag in her favorite color or to
remind her that it was time to choose a winter coat. Department-store
managers continued to believe that the personal touch was crucial, even
when difficult to maintain in the face of stores' increasing size and
bureaucracy. [23]

A second method of identifying the select was the charge account.
Until World War II, most stores maintained such tight requirements for
granting credit that only the wives of "substantial citizens" and not those
of working-class families had the privilege of a charge account. By the
early twentieth century the typical department store had abandoned
long-term credit, offering only the open charge account payable in full each
month as a convenience for those who disdained paying for each purchase
individually. Few department stores offered installment-payment plans before World War II. [24]

Charge customers were particularly valuable to department stores
for a variety of reasons. First, "charge sales fluctuate[d] less than the total
store volume" because credit was available only to the solidly prosperous
who could maintain their levels of spending in difficult times. For example,
during the recession of the later 1930s, installment sales fell 15 percent,
cash sales dropped 8 percent, and charge sales shrank by only 5 percent.

Second, charge customers made, on the average, larger purchases than cash customers. A 1928 Department of Commerce study vividly demonstrated this point. In one department, charge sales were only 3 percent of total transactions but accounted for 18 percent of total sales volume; in another, 1 percent of the transactions but 5 percent of total sales were charges. Third, charge sales used salespeople's time more productively than cash transactions. The Department of Commerce study found that charge sales took up to twice as long as cash sales, but that the payoff in sales revenue per minute was nearly three times greater for charge sales.[25]

For these reasons, department-store managers prized their charge customers and cultivated their loyalty. They accepted their returns more graciously, filled their special requests more solicitously, and reserved special shopping days and selected lots of merchandise for them. Salespeople frequently served them before unfamiliar customers. Before consumer credit expanded after World War II, the possession of the token or address plate identifying one as a charge customer was a mark of distinction. Managers and salespeople alike regarded charge customers as, in the words of Hortense Odlum, the "bread and butter" of a store but tended to see cash customers as transients. Their attitudes were reflected in notably different behavior toward the two groups.[26]

Even as they redoubled their efforts to attract everyone in general and a core of devoted customers in particular with lavish and accommodating service, department-store managers understood that this was a perilous course. The complimentary services they offered cost them a great deal indeed and frequently failed to produce the necessary results. As one writer put it: "The worst of the whole business is that what is offered as a luxury today is demanded as a necessity tomorrow, and instead of a special inducement we have a permanent addition to our overhead which does not do any one of us any particular service."[27] The expense hurt all the more because managers were convinced that customers were responding in inappropriate ways.

The Perils of Service

Once services had become accepted features of department stores, certain customers demanded special individual attention. To some women of the middle and upper classes, the emphasis on amenity and luxury in the store was not just an invitation to consume in style, but also a blank check for the exercise of their class prerogatives. Pampered and treated as

Fig. 7. A Customer Trained to Be Unreasonable

"My husband did not like me in this hat"

Woman Citizen, 11 (May 1927), 10.

guests, customers sometimes became imperious, pressing minor or fabricated complaints, taking for granted and abusing privileges which stores considered favors. To many a customer, the message conveyed by the service-oriented store was that she could act as if she were the mistress and the store her servant.

Department stores fully realized that they had played a lamentable part in producing this attitude. John Wanamaker had coined the slogan "the customer is always right," and it haunted department-store managers and employees ever afterward. On the one hand, it inspired confidence and gave the assurance of good service, but it also suggested to the temperamental or unscrupulous customer that she could take advantage of store policies. Even before World War I, store managers worried about "mis-educating" customers to demand yet more profit-eating services; throughout the 1920s, writers lamented that stores who accepted customers' claims and demands uncritically were "[t]rain[ing] [u]nreasonable [c]ustomers"; and during the Depression they asserted firmly that it was time to eliminate the "frills" of more prosperous times.[28]

Lore about the extremes to which misguided customers would go was a staple of the trade literature; writers seemed to compete perversely to top one another's outrageous stories. One of their most frequent causes of complaint was returns of merchandise. Undecided customers routinely sent home a number of garments, planning to choose among them at leisure and return the rejects; a variation on this practice was to buy the same item at many different stores, have them all sent home, and then keep only the best of the lot. Another source of irritation was the looker: department stores, by granting free entry and encouraging browsing, had created the shopper who had no real intention of buying but demanded service all the same. Rheta Childe Dorr wrote bitterly of the "empty-minded, idle and foolish" customers who looked at goods ad nauseam, acting as if they intended to buy although they were clearly just passing time. Frequently a looker would make a COD purchase to maintain her credibility, sending it to a false address or refusing it when it was delivered. Even more extreme was a woman who sent thousands of dollars worth of goods to various fictitious addresses, and when caught explained to a stunned manager that "[s]he was teaching her daughter how to shop!" Managers also alleged that customers regularly wore garments and then returned them.[29]

Many of these anecdotes show the ability of customers to browbeat managers. The tale of Mrs. Allen of Cleveland is instructive: she tried to return a monogrammed set of six dozen pieces of silver flatware, inventing an excuse to conceal the fact that she had bought the same silver more cheaply at a receiver's sale just after she had ordered it at the first store. She remained adamant despite the store's offers of a compromise and in the end had her way with the ominous threat: "I'll withdraw my account." Tea-room customers plagued a Baltimore department store by insisting that their bones be wrapped and delivered, free of charge, for their dogs' delectation. The executive who complained of this practice admitted that she was unable to resist the customers' demands. It was a rare manager who told of standing up to an implacable customer, but Hortense Odlum triumphantly reported that she gave a firm "no" to at least one wildly unreasonable woman. The customer had bought a suit on sale, specified extensive alterations, and then demanded that the suit be delivered a week earlier than promised so that she could wear it to a special engagement. Two months later, she appeared at Bonwit Teller to claim full credit for the suit because "I asked you to deliver it at one, and it didn't come until one-thirty, and I was late for my appointment. It ruined my day and I'll never be happy in the suit again." This literature pictured the woman customer as a spoiled overgrown child who would not be denied her whims and would resort to transparent lies or nasty tantrums in her determination to have her own way.[30]

In fact, managers were probably more at fault than they acknowledged. Desperate to garner extra business by giving extra service, unwilling to trust to the reasonableness of the bulk of customers, they knuckled under when they knew better. The gender dynamics of the department store probably played a part in this state of affairs: any complaint or request which was out of the ordinary was customarily referred by the selling department or the adjustment desk to a higher executive who was almost invariably male. The male managers treated the female customers with a contemptuous indulgence that spoke both of paternalism and of the sexual conflict built into an "Adamless Eden" managed by men. Women as consumers in department stores had a power out of all proportion to their power in the society as a whole, and managers told of customer demands in a tone which suggests their resentment at having to bow within the store to those whom they could dominate outside it. Male managers, however they might joke about gossiping women, knew well that those women had the power to make or break their trade. A delighted customer who urged her friends to patronize her favorite store was a priceless asset; one who broadcast tales of real or imagined insults damaged a firm's reputation and sales; those who learned of a special favor accorded to one woman would demand the same consideration themselves. Managers trod carefully in the world of women, a milieu which they dimly understood and were unable to control. More often than not, they played it safe and took the line of least resistance when confronting a customer. One female executive clearly understood the dynamics of this process: "It has seemed to me that through the generations it has been the province of men to humor the foolish ideas of women. When customers have come in with their complaints and have criticized the things which stores have done it has been the attitude of the management to pacify those complaints rather than see what actual facts caused them."[31]

Customers, when questioned in marketing surveys, had a notably different view of the situation. Instead of perceiving department stores as indulgent and accommodating, women emphasized the degree to which they wanted—and did not find—"human warmth" and "natural friendly . . . information in the department store." The emphasis on organization and system which was so problematic in the internal management of the store subtly infected relations with consumers as well; bureaucracy tended to make members of the organization think more of their own places in the system than of those whom it was designed to serve. Complaining about this impersonal and instrumental tendency, Christine Frederick framed her solution in exactly the terms that store managers would have used. Noting that "Mrs. Consumer is often regarded as so much coal in a chute, passive and stupid, and shunted about the store as if she were an inanimate object with no feelings, and all the time in the world," Frederick counseled retailers to concentrate on *"making a customer"* rather than *"making a sale."*[32]

Consumers had a sounder view of retail services than managers' anecdotes would lead one to believe. Mrs. Roye Fleming of Hot Springs, Arkansas, brought to the 1940 National Retail Dry Goods Association as "Mrs. Typical Customer 1940," delighted the gathering by affirming that she never returned goods, taking the responsibility for incorrect choices upon herself. While Mrs. Fleming may have been playing to her audience, the rudimentary data available on consumer preferences before World War II indicate that she was not alone in her attitudes. In 1915 *System* magazine questioned ninety-four women's club presidents about which department store "service, courtesy, or favor" had made the strongest impression on them in the previous year. Fewer than one-third mentioned services such as credit or the return privilege. None mentioned the more frivolous services and one blamed the high cost of living on "the fact that the public accepts (I do not believe it demands) unnecessary luxuries provided by large department stores." Nearly 60 percent of these women felt that at least one of the services commonly offered by retailers could easily be discontinued. A survey conducted in the late 1920s showed that shoppers' sensible outlook still prevailed. The women questioned appreciated most the basic services such as delivery, telephone booths, and rest rooms, rather than the more outlandish frills, and were willing to have even these cut back if it meant lower prices. Finally, a 1940 survey showed that, far from blithely returning anything that didn't perfectly suit their fancy, 38 percent of the customers interviewed actually did not try to return "unsatisfactory purchases."[33]

Still, managers persisted in emphasizing customers' demands for services. In 1939, a member of the Filene firm stated emphatically that the contemporary customer was very different from her forebear in the 1890s: "She wants a lot of things her mother and grandmother never thought of in their wildest dreams—goods and services of all kinds, shapes, and forms." Department-store managers who considered cutting expenses by reducing or charging for services were wary and tentative for two reasons. First, having spent so much effort developing the palace of consumption and educating customers to expect the finest service, they were reluctant to reverse field, particularly in a locally competitive industry where their rivals might not follow suit. Second, they had formed exaggerated fears of customers' touchiness; their anecdotes showed a preoccupation with the unreasonable few which blinded them to the more reassuring evidence of the surveys.[34]

Stores first tried to pinpoint and control nuisances within their own clienteles. During the 1900s, one resourceful store manager established a "Jay Club," membership in which was distinctly not an honor. When a customer complained unnecessarily and excessively, took up an unconscionable amount of clerks' time, returned a large number of items, or abused services, her name and description circulated through the store. The next time she made a nuisance of herself, the clerk alerted a special worker, known as the diplomat, who laid out store policy pleasantly but firmly. If the Jay persisted, each successive talk was blunter until she was simply advised to take her patronage elsewhere. The scheme worked beautifully: the clerks later claimed that eliminating the Jays gave them one-quarter more time to devote to more reasonable customers.[35]

As a rule, however, merchants' associations rather than individual stores launched the campaigns against unreasonable customers. Only through a united front could they assure that one store's Jay wouldn't move on to terrorize another and that costly service competition among stores could be eliminated or limited. The first concerted public drive against "super-service" came during World War I. With the excuse of wartime shortages of gasoline and rubber, stores used methods including friendly persuasion, fees, and outright refusal to cut down deliveries. They also tried to limit deliveries by improving service in the store, cutting the time it took to wrap merchandise. Some stores instituted charges for credit accounts during the war, assuming that customers beset by shortages of consumer goods would willingly pay for amenities. A third wartime retail campaign was against the wearing of full mourning. The *DGE* asked rhetorically, "Shall [w]e [b]e [p]atriots or [c]onventionalists?" But along with the fervent note of patriotism went the more practical consideration that catering to mourning customers often involved opening the store at odd hours and making emergency alterations, both of which were costly and disruptive to the store.[36]

Despite their hard-line stance during the war, most stores once again fell into old habits during the 1920s; there was no general limitation of services in that decade, and laments about their costs continued. During the Depression, there were some cutbacks of services, but moderate reduction and not radical elimination was the rule. Stores reduced the number of service personnel or consolidated services that were formerly administered separately, such as mail and telephone orders. Through these years, some individual stores and some store groups tried to cut services or make customers pay for them directly, but there was no broad consensus on most issues.[37]

The exception to this rule was the matter of returned goods. Of all customers' deplorable habits, managers regarded merchandise returns as the most common and most damaging. When a purchase was returned, the store's expenditures in marking, selling, wrapping, delivering, and bookkeeping had essentially been wasted, and it was unlikely that the store would be able to resell the item at the full retail price—particularly if, as was often the case, it was out of season or worn by its travels. Returns also caused friction within the store, especially between the selling department and the general management. Most stores had a policy of generously accepting returns, but everyone in the selling departments from buyer on down to stockperson disliked the practice since returned goods meant extra work and deductions from personal and departmental sales totals. Store figures showed that returns increased alarmingly after 1890, in part because of the growing importance of ready-to-wear. Returns as a percentage of net sales increased at Macy's from .82 percent to 4.38 percent between 1891 and 1917 and at Marshall Field from 12.20 percent in 1890 to 16.66 percent in 1906. During the 1910s and 1920s, stores reported returns of 15 to 28 percent of total charge sales, 5 to 7.5 percent of total cash sales, and 12 to 20 percent of COD sales. Most disquieting was the fact that charge customers were the worst offenders; in 1904, Marshall Field refunded one of every four dollars spent on charge purchases but only one of every twenty spent on cash sales. The spread was, of course, exaggerated by stores' greater willingness to take back goods that had been charged.[38]

The battle against "unreasonable" returns was joined in the mid-1900s when the *Dry Goods Economist* launched a tirade of criticism at customers who returned merchandise as well as at retailers who allowed them to do so. The latter, the weekly charged, offered the "wildest concessions . . . voluntarily," even accepting pieces of yard goods sold two years previously. Moreover, department-store managers faced with unfounded demands tended to delay and vacillate, allowing customers to wheedle them into grudging compliance; the proper course was "prompt, decisive and courteous" treatment. Merchants deluged the *Economist* with approving letters. Stores waged three campaigns against excessive returns: they tried to correct, just as they had with deliveries, internal practices which encouraged returns; individual stores confronted the worst offenders; and credit bureaus or boards of trade set citywide policies and maintained lists of chronic offenders. The first of these will be treated in the next chapter since it is primarily a matter of managers' discipline of salespeople. The other two used a variety of means in addition to confronting individual offenders: among them were time limits after which merchandise was not accepted for return; requirements that sales checks accompany the goods; seals to prevent the merchandise from being worn; and advertising campaigns and lectures to female students and women's groups about the high costs of returns. Managers reported good results from these efforts, estimating that returns fell by from 10 to 30 percent. The success of the campaigns against returns provided ample evidence that the woman customer was willing to be reasonable when presented with clear procedures.[39]

Managers' enduring if unjustified conviction that their women customers were too demanding led them to seek increased male trade and to attempt to train future female patrons from an early age. Attracting male shoppers was an enduring concern of department-store executives; they regarded men as an untapped market holding out the promise of increased sales volume, particularly when they felt that they had fully exploited the female market. But more frequently managers longed for male customers because they perceived them as personally preferable to women. They characterized women as capricious and unpredictable, too caught up in their role as consumers. As one manager mused, criticizing women for precisely the qualities retailers had encouraged in them: "The difficulty in keeping a woman's trade is that sooner or later her personality becomes involved, often in most unexpected ways. . . . freshness, flippancy, or indifference to her wishes are discourtesies she can hardly forgive. For shopping is serious with her, not only because it is a recreation, and possibly an adventure, but likewise because it calls for the exercise of the best judgment in spending whatever money she has in her possession." They portrayed men, by contrast, as more instrumental and businesslike in their approach to consumption: "They do not 'shop' in the sense that a woman does. A man goes into a store usually with a specific purchase in mind, which he makes as expeditiously as possible and then gets out." The irony was considerable: while they were trying to create a female style of shopping, they found a male style of making discrete purchases personally more appealing and less disruptive of store operations.[40]

Retail writers argued that department stores failed to attract male trade because they did not sufficiently appreciate this difference; they did not realize that for men, unlike women, time was money. Inadequate store directories left the male customer to wander in search of the right department; tedious waiting for change and packages tried his patience. Stores therefore tried to cut through red tape to save men's valuable time and to arrange their departments to minimize contact between male and female customers—as one writer put it, "the busy business man finds no enjoyment in elbowing his way through crowds of women." Some stores moved toward the logical extreme of complete segregation: Marshall Field devoted its annex entirely to men's wear, serving "hearty food" in its Men's Grill; by the early 1920s, a number of firms had established special Christmas-season shops where men could make their holiday purchases in an all-male environment. Managers also assumed that the busier, more deliberate male customer would be less prone to demand extra services—and hence less likely to increase stores' expenses. As a general rule, this was probably the case, but men were by no means immune to the service orientation. For example, the *Echo* told of a fireman who had brought his baby along on a Christmas shopping trip, assuming that he could leave her at a store nursery. Upon being told that Filene's maintained no such service, he complained, "What, no place to hock a kid? This is a hell of a store."[41]

Department stores attempted to socialize girls and young women into more acceptable ways of shopping and to teach them womanly skills, taking over that function from older women and families. A Cincinnati store executive urged his fellow retailers to appeal to "thousands upon thousands of possible buyers when they are at the most impressionable age—at a time when their regard may be secured with less effort than will be possible when other stores compete for their attention." Stores appealed to young shoppers with playgrounds, free favors, and holiday parties, treating them "with as much respect and consideration as [they] would an adult." Most self-consciously didactic of all was the Iowa department store which encouraged mothers to send their children to the store alone with shopping lists: "[A]s salespeople fill the orders, they train the child in shopping, explaining why a certain thing is selected or why and how a substitute is provided, breeding their own generation of intelligent and discriminating shoppers." Some children indeed learned early; one precocious child surprised Edward Filene: "One afternoon he presented a handsome doll to a little girl with whom he had struck a conversation [in Filene's toy department], and waited, beaming, to see what she would say. The child's mother waited, too. 'What are you going to say to the gentleman?' she urged. The dear looked at Mr. Filene firmly. 'Charge it,' she said." Department-store classes also taught young women the skills of housewifery and motherhood: Rich's of Atlanta ran popular embroidery classes, Filene's held a series of lectures on child care, and Marshall Field conducted cooking classes.[42]

In response to the relative prosperity and the youth-oriented culture of the 1920s, stores opened new departments to attract both youthful and male customers: camping and year-round toy departments, as well as sporting goods, motor accessories, and radios, all became accepted features of department stores. Responding to the vogue for short hair, Filene's opened a second hairdressing salon named, inexcusably, The Bobber Shop as part of its "specialization for young women." During the mid-1920s, the same store boasted of providing twenty-five distinct services in its Men's Store, and in 1928 topped off its offerings with an indoor putting green. Even in trying to appeal to new types of customers, department-store managers fell into the old patterns; service appeals remained a staple of their tactics.[43]

The department store's presentation of itself to the public as a palace of consumption had major costs and built-in disadvantages as well as real virtues. On the one hand, this image differentiated department stores from other types of retailing establishments; the smaller store could not afford the capital investment or high overhead of providing a broad array of services and accommodations. Only the department store, thanks to its size and varied appeal, could claim so much of the shopper's time and attention. On the other hand, it was difficult for any individual department store to set itself apart from its competitors on the basis of service. Intense competition among stores over special treatment to the public tended to homogenize service offerings in a given area. Always lurking behind these facts was the balance sheet, which indicted the palace of consumption because of its cost and its tendency to encourage a troublesome minority of customers to abuse services. Having charted their course toward elaborate services rather than stripped-down convenience, however, department-store managers hesitated to deviate. At least until World War II, they maintained their allegiance to the palace of consumption as a bulwark of their strategy.

The Powers of Persuasion

The department-store manager's campaign of service and amenity was but half of his effort to attract customers; he also devoted a great deal of energy and expense to urging merchandise upon them. Merchandise appeals incorporated the same issues of class and gender as service appeals but differed in two critical respects. First, merchandise appeals revolved around the ever-changing concepts of stylishness, unlike service appeals which rested on relatively enduring ideas about gentility. Second, while the palace of consumption was peculiar to department stores, other types of business and the mass media joined them in advertising and fashion appeals. The central theme in department-store publicity was the effort to drown out the others' messages and to secure the customer's loyalty to one store.

By the 1890s managers no longer simply tried to respond to their customers' demands and cater to their tastes; stores actively sought to influence the public's notions of what was stylish and appropriate. At first trying only to be "a little ahead of [their] customers," department stores during the first two decades of the new century elaborated and intensified their efforts to guide customers in the proper channels. A small-town Ohio retailer expressed the industry's confidence in its powers of persuasion: "Create in the mind of the customer a desire for other things she sees, as well as the article she asks for. People used to buy what they needed, now it's what they want; and that want is created by store display or advertisement." That confidence ebbed after World War I as customers became less predictable; the consumer of the 1920s, a speaker warned a convention of the National Retail Dry Goods Association, was no longer "a searcher but a chooser," more prone to exercise independent judgment than simply to accept what stores featured. Department-store managers became more sensitive to customers' preferences and dissatisfactions and began to see their relationship with their customers as one of mutual accommodation.[44]

Department stores stimulated patronage in various ways: they advertised in all available media and decorated their windows and departments with attractive merchandise, convincing customers to buy their wares on the basis of fashion, quality, or price. Advertising, like other store functions, became increasingly systematic and self-conscious. Changes in window display illustrate the key components of the new approach. By the 1910s, display managers began to show merchandise in the settings in which it would be used and devised the ensemble technique—displaying whole outfits of clothing down to the last accessory, or rooms fully decorated from carpets to ash trays. They more carefully aimed their messages at their firm's clientele. Carriage-trade stores often decorated their windows thematically, highlighting an artistic motif or timely issue along with related merchandise, while popular-priced stores focused more directly on merchandise itself. Sometimes different windows appealed to different segments of the store's trade; front windows, for example, might show "prestige goods" while side windows contained sale merchandise. Bloomingdale's in New York took this approach to its logical extreme: one set of windows showed style merchandise for the Park Avenue crowd; another, top-quality merchandise for the Long Island suburbanites; and the third, medium-priced merchandise for upper-East-Siders with modest budgets. Window and interior display, like other aspects of store publicity, had become a matter for specialists. The International Association of Display Men flourished as display technique matured. Founded in

1898, by the end of World War I it attracted one thousand members to its annual meetings.[45]

The largest share of a store's publicity budget went for newspaper advertising, following R. H. Macy's lead toward ever larger and more attractive ads. The high-quality graphics, arresting design, and lively text of department-store ads frequently eclipsed other copy in the newspaper. Most department-store advertisements featured merchandise but an important minority were institutional messages designed to convince customers to shop loyally at a given store because of its general features—honesty, civic responsibility, up-to-date fashions, or commitment to high quality—rather than because of any individual piece of merchandise. The customary form for the institutional advertisement was the editorial, sometimes signed by the owner or manager, laying out the store's policies and appeal. In 1905, for example, a Marshall Field ad promised Chicago women "style supremacy" enhanced by "Individuality—Exclusiveness—Refinement"; during the 1920s, Atlantans read this comforting credo: "Who! You! Who built your store? You! . . . Abstract theories of merchandising are nothing to us. *You want* something. We train events to produce it. Rich's is built on the very *human* wishes of its consumers." Department stores exploited other media as well, advertising on the radio and featuring merchandise, particularly clothing and home furnishings, which customers had seen in theaters and films.[46]

Most department stores shied away from nationally advertised brands before World War II. They often yielded lower profits than non-branded goods, but managers were primarily concerned that the customer's loyalty be to the firm rather than to a brand which might be purchased any number of places. In addition, their emphasis on selling a distinctive selection of merchandise rather than standard items led them to favor non-branded goods. A few stores, such as the Hecht Company of Washington, D.C., anticipated the post-World War II dependence on national brands with an aggressive brand-name campaign in the later 1920s, but they were exceptions. Many stores, in fact, resented the intrusion of the nationally advertising manufacturer into their relations with the customer, refusing to handle branded goods or taking on selected lines—especially in toiletries and major appliances—only when customer demand was irresistible. Managers tried to secure exclusive local rights to sell nationally advertised goods or, that failing, established private brands. The latter flourished beginning in the 1890s; R. H. Macy sold a wide variety of items under the "Macy" and "Red Star" brands, claiming by the 1910s to furnish quality equivalent to national brands for as little as half the price. Filene's proudly offered $39.50 Barbara Lee dresses which they alone sold in Boston, urging saleswomen to point out that they were advertised in *Vogue* and *Harper's Bazaar* and doing little to dispel customers' notion that Barbara Lee was Filene's own private brand.[47]

Department-store publicity of all types tended toward the grandiose; "showmanship" and "dramatization" became advertising-department watchwords. Stores often mounted elaborate multimedia campaigns: during the 1930s a number of retailers joined manufacturers of yarn, piece goods, and dresses in a campaign that featured a special dance taught by instructors and featured at a New York hotel floor show, and music played by big-name bands and sold as a phonograph record. Even institutional advertising aimed for the big splash. Two New York stores, Bloomingdale's and James A. Hearn and Son, established awards for the best essays on retailing by high school students and in preparation for the competition guided some 12,000 students through their stores.[48]

Not surprisingly, these elaborate publicity campaigns were a significant factor in the rising cost of doing business. In fact, the variety of advertising activities "share[d] [with customer service] the main responsibility for the increase of the expense percentage of department stores" from 1880 to 1920 and the advertising burden continued to edge up during the 1920s and early 1930s, falling slightly by the end of that decade. This orgy of spending on advertising, suggested an international authority on department stores, resulted from the fact that they lost ground after 1900 to smaller stores which imitated the unique combination of lower prices, variety, novelty, and class appeal that had brought department stores their early successes.[49]

While the huge sums spent on publicity were by no means wasted, department-store managers became convinced that a number of factors were undermining the impact of their advertising. First, as Chapter 2 showed, many stores were unable to satisfy efficiently the demand that advertising created. Second, advertising was not well coordinated with sales efforts within the store. Managers complained bitterly that salespeople refused to inform themselves about advertised merchandise, and many a customer who went looking for an item she had seen in an ad or display window received little help from the sales staff. Third, effective though it was in awakening demand, advertising could target only a tiny proportion—from 1.5 to 5 percent—of the quarter-million items in the average department store. Customers would decide to buy other items out of need or on impulse, but even the most carefully designed displays presented only about 60 percent of the store's stock to the public. Managers nursed hopes of overcoming these problems but found other difficulties less within their control far more vexing.[50]

While store managers were changing and elaborating their publicity tactics, the object of these tactics was also changing: the customer was developing new habits and characteristics. Shopping changed from a straightforward matter of supplying the family's needs into a complex activity involving amusement, diversion, a widening sphere of choice, and class-based standards of taste. One of the great ironies of the department-store manager's life was that as the services provided by the palace of consumption competed for the customer's attention, the actual purchasing on a given shopping trip decreased. One observer looked back nostalgically to the 1890s when, he recalled, customers "spent on one shopping trip the seventy-five dollars they today divide over fifteen or twenty." The balance of power between retailer and customer had shifted in a most disturbing way; another writer noted that the customer was no longer "the goat" of "take-it-or-leave-it" retailers, but was now the one "with a favor to bestow."[51]

Advertising messages had the power to attract as well as repel this "much more discerning" customer. The tendency of advertisements to become "bombastic" and "sensational" had troubling implications; such ads might attract the "less fortunate" but, the *Dry Goods Economist* warned, the wealthier customers found them "repugnant." Moreover, these ads tended to rely heavily on "extravagant and often ridiculous claims and assertions," reinforcing the prevailing skepticism toward advertising. Customers saw ads as useful guides to shopping, but they also viewed them with an abiding and understandable distrust since a minority of retailers did indeed engage in deceptive advertising, particularly of bargains. Retailers earnestly cooperated in campaigns to increase public trust of advertising messages, yet they shared consumers' cynicism. When Cecile Powell, the NRDGA's Mrs. Typical Consumer for 1939, told that year's convention that she believed the ads she read, the audience responded with "audible snickers." The rest of her comments, though, should have given the merchants food for thought rather than merriment, for she showed that she was no passive recipient of the advertising message, but adapted it to her needs and way of life:

Yes, I do [believe advertising]. Because I read the whole body of the ad. I don't let trick headlines mislead me. . . . You ask whether headlines, pictures, or the copy attracts my attention. The headlines first. The pictures are often very far-fetched. Pictures of beautiful, sylph-like women, although most of us aren't that type at all! So that I have to wonder whether the thing advertised will be suitable for me. If the ad is well written, it carries much more weight with me than does the picture.

She went on to say that most of all she wanted more information in ads, having repeatedly been led to think that a piece of merchandise had certain features only to find at the store that such was not the case: "'Of course that can't be called an untruth, but . . . .' (Punctuation by the audience, which here supplied laughter and prolonged applause.)" If retailers themselves put little trust in the advertising messages they sent out, it was small wonder that consumers were wary.[52]

Managers devoted special attention to comforting mistrustful customers during the late 1920s and 1930s. Their favorite tactic was the testing laboratory, which set minimum standards and tested merchandise so that the store could make well-founded claims about the properties and durability of its wares. Montgomery Ward, Filene's, and Marshall Field pioneered testing laboratories but they remained alone in the field until 1928, when individual stores, ownership groups, and the NRDGA all established testing programs. While these efforts were part of what Stuart Ewen has termed the advertising industry's construction of a new realm of "facts" and "truth" to legitimate the consumption process and narrow the range of consumer initiative, testing bureaus were also a response to the specific conditions of the relationship between managers and customers in the department store. First, managers saw merchandise testing as one more way to cement customers' store loyalty by "prevailing upon customers to depend for good quality on the store's expertness in buying rather than upon their own skill or upon national brands." Second, managers were responding to individual customers' demands for more reliable information about merchandise and to the growth of independent consumer groups with their own testing programs. The emphasis on "facts" and "truth" about merchandise was not simply, as Ewen would have it, a management initiative to control the process of consumption, but rather the result of a struggle between managers and customers—the one seeking to tell as little as possible, the other always demanding more.[53]

But most dramatic of all the changes in consumer behavior was the response to fashion. Department-store managers had at first welcomed

Fig. 8. Gaining the Public's Trust

the notion, asserting as early as 1899 that "the chief underlying feature of the dry goods trade, the stratum on which the very substructure of the business rests, is fashion." Stores prided themselves on being in touch with the latest French styles; in 1880 John Wanamaker was the first retailer to establish a permanent Paris office and the *Dry Good Economist* sent correspondents there beginning in the 1890s. Changing fashions held the doubly happy prospect of higher sales volume—because "when the impression is forced on consumers of all classes that the last season's coat, costume or hat is irretrievably out of date, demand is created that cannot but result happily for those whose business is to cater thereto"— and of fatter profits—because "fashion gives an artificial value to merchandise and in this artificial value lies profit for the retailer." [54]

Department stores, worried that fashion could grow into an independent force outside their control, mounted elaborate efforts to persuade customers to follow their lead. Advertisements and catalogs urged women to dress in the mode of the store, stressing the importance of coordinating garments and accessories. Individual firms published magazines, usually issued free to their customers. Marshall Field, for example, began in 1914 to publish *Fashions of the Hour* every other month. The magazine firmly excluded all explicit advertising, although the idea of fashion that it purveyed was the same that informed Field's buyers as they stocked the store. Photographs of prominent society women in Field's gowns also had a powerful persuasive effect. *Fashions of the Hour* tried to give an overall impression of luxury and style; its literary offerings included works by Christopher Morley and Emily Kimbrough. Even a relatively small store such as Gladding's of Providence had its magazine, *Fashions & Home*, published eight times a year. Along with notes on society, the arts, entertaining, and nutrition, *Fashions & Home* contained frank advertising of both merchandise and services offered by the store. Easily the most ambitious project of this type was Bamberger's *Charm;* introduced in 1924, it was less a house organ than a general circulation magazine dedicated to encouraging ideas of style and consumption favorable to the department-store industry. At about the same time, the *Dry Goods Economist* introduced a monthly fashion supplement which was published by five general-interest magazines and simultaneously distributed to retailers so that they could prepare for the resulting demand. [55]

Activities in the store reinforced the fashion message of the print media. Fashion shows and special seasonal openings were an early staple of department-store life, and in some cities stores pooled resources to mount fashion extravaganzas. During the 1920s, the fashion campaigns became more elaborate and self-consciously didactic: an Ohio department store conducted a buying school which gave information about style and quality, and Jordan Marsh established a speakers' bureau which provided women's clubs with fashion lectures. Bamberger's launched a major campaign to capture the trade of women who had their clothing custom-made, providing lectures, fashion shows, a cutting and fitting service, and a consulting dressmaker. Through one method or another, these stores and hundreds of others tried to establish themselves as arbiters of fashion. At the same time, they taught customers about the quality and care of department-store merchandise, hoping to replace folk wisdom and gossip as the sources of consumer information. In all cases, the ultimate aim was the same: to suggest a common set of standards in the hope that a uniformly educated consumer public would be more predictable.[56]

Fashion, though profitable, injected a new note of uncertainty and unpredictability into the already volatile retail environment, as retailers began to complain early in the 1910s: "Few of our citizens now lay in a stock of anything—though such was formerly the custom, especially in connection with staples. To-day . . . the chief factor of desirability and of value in the majority of dry goods lines is the approximation of the merchandise to the current fashion standard." The customer relied on the retailer as one of a number of sources of fashion information, yet she became—particularly after World War I—increasingly independent as ideas about fashion diffused throughout society and as she developed her own sense of style. Fashion-conscious women structured their wardrobes in new ways, upsetting the long-standing calculations of department-store executives. They bought for a season, not for a decade, and were less willing than they had been to spend large amounts on any one garment. The *Dry Goods Economist* consoled those distressed at the brevity and simplicity of flappers' garments: "We think that there is no question that there was never a time when the feminine wardrobes of America were more abundant or the demand for constant variety and change larger." The woman who had once been content with two or three dresses per season now considered herself well turned out only if she had a dozen frocks, each with a set of matching accessories. Fashion invaded even the most tradition-bound departments of the store: lingerie and underwear by the mid-1920s, domestics and linens during the next decade.[57]

A second disquieting aspect of fashion was its uneasy relationship to the three other pillars of department stores' merchandise appeals: quality, price, and large stocks. As ready-made clothing accounted for a growing proportion of their sales, managers fretted about the tendency for the latest styles to appear in cheap and often tawdry copies. Would their clients follow their fashion advice when the same style was sold as a polo turban in the "most exclusive millinery shops" and as "what some are pleased to call the pill-box" in cheaper departments, wholesaling at $9 per dozen? Would democratized fashions undermine the appeal to the class prejudice of wealthy customers? In some ways, the fashion prophets had succeeded too well; by the mid-1900s the editor of the *Dry Goods Economist* could assert that "practically every woman in this country is interested in the dictates of fashion." Once awakened, the desire for stylish clothes could not easily be crushed nor could its leveling tendencies be reversed. Department-store managers first turned to quality as a selling point when style failed to distinguish adequately among classes of merchandise. Industry writers noted approvingly that ready-to-wear was becoming more "dressy and elegant," using fine fabrics and elaborate linings and interlinings which could not be duplicated with coarser materials and cheaper construction techniques. "Those whose credit is of the best, who are expert judges of quality as well as style, and who are willing to pay for these" provided a ready and expanding market for such fine garments which set them off from those who purchased the clumsy lower-priced copies. In the years before World War I, quality was the factor which mediated the conflict between high styles and low prices.[58]

Two factors disrupted that equilibrium in the 1920s. First was the increasing simplicity of prevailing fashion: loosely cut, less elaborate styles were more convincingly duplicated at low prices. Second was the broadening of the department-store clientele to include "wives of skilled labor and young women in white-collar occupations"—people with enough money to afford more department-store merchandise than ever before but still not enough to merit charge-account privileges, comfortable enough to seek fashion and quality but not to ignore price. Although department stores had achieved much of their early success by offering lower prices than their competitors, their managers had less insistently touted low prices since the end of the depression of the 1890s. By the mid-1910s, retail writers agreed that a strident and exclusive emphasis on price was self-defeating because it devalued the public image of the whole enterprise and undermined retailers' other efforts to educate their clientele about fashion, quality, and value. The 1920s brought a revival of price-conscious promotions, causing one writer to grumble that "price is always the 'fairheaded boy.' Quality, durability—yes, even style in many cases—is a stepchild." [59]

Yet when used with finesse, price appeals were extremely effective and a necessary adaptation to the near-universal appeal of style, to a broadened clientele, and to gains in manufacturing productivity. As A. Lincoln Filene put it, "Once upon a time, it was only the grand lady who demanded style in her clothes and in her home. Today the humblest person, economically speaking, imitates the style adopted by people of means. Fortunately for the wage-earner's wife, the lower manufacturing costs of many commodities have brought such gratifications within the reach of limited pocketbooks." Moreover, even the wealthy customer was bound to give more thought to price when she was buying a larger and larger number of garments and accessories. The demand for modestly priced fashionable merchandise during the 1920s led merchants at both ends of the department-store spectrum to rethink their traditional stances. The venerable carriage-trade store of Marshall Field, for example, departed dramatically from time-honored practice by featuring stylish dresses at the unheard-of (for Field's) bargain price of $15. At the other extreme, Macy's of New York and Rich's of Atlanta, both seasoned veterans of low-price campaigns, asserted themselves as style stores as well. Rich's, late in the 1920s, declared Tuesday "Fashion Day" and each week staged special fashion events. The cartoon accompanying the *Dry Goods Economist* article on Rich's made the point eloquently: customers ignored a dowdy dress offered at half price, while they worshipped at a pedestal on which a stylish number stood. During the Depression of the 1930s, of course, even the crudest price appeal had a new relevance. Still, some retailers took the long view and worried about the effect of cheap but shoddy merchandise on their reputation. They organized, with the blessing and assistance of the National Retail Dry Goods Association, the Quality Movement in Merchandise, a campaign to urge retailers to shun the inferior goods flooding the market and to persuade customers that a bit more money spent on quality goods in the short run was a good investment in the long run. [60]

Fashion, finally, threatened department stores' reputation for stocking full assortments of staple merchandise—items relatively immune from style changes. Staples were in some ways less attractive to department-store managers than fashion items. They generally had a lower rate of stock turn and their stolid dullness contrasted jarringly with the dominant emphasis on the novel and modish. Moreover, customers were even

Fig. 9. Style Eclipses Price

more independent-minded in buying staples than they were in buying stylish goods; as one writer ruefully noted, "Every woman knows what Fruit of the Loom is worth, and what women do not know about qualities and values of every home staple is not worth knowing. Frequently they can give the store people points, and still beat them." Because consumers could more easily gauge their value, staples were notably less profitable than fashion items. Many stores consequently went overboard on novelty or fashionable items which sold more quickly and profitably. This policy disappointed the customer who was in search of staples and discouraged steady year-round trade in favor of seasonal, special occasion, or impulse buying. Whereas a good balanced stock of staples could be an anchor to windward against the storms of fashion, too heavy a reliance on fads put the store at the mercy of the slightest fashion squall, alienating part of the store's clientele as well as defeating the controllers' goal of stabilizing the store's business.[61]

The retailer's uncertainty in choosing among appeals to price, quality, fashion, or staple reliability led him to try to be all things to all people. Too often, he found that he thereby weakened his ability to reach any one group. By the 1920s, many of the better-managed stores were reconciled to attracting only a segment of the total retail demand in their areas. One major multiunit store simply gave up on the wealthiest one-eighth of trade and focused on the other seven-eighths. Such policies did not, however, become the rule, as the NRDGA lamented in its twenty-fifth anniversary survey of the industry. In 1939 a "high executive in a well-known department store" complained anonymously in the *Department Store Economist* that "the average big department store is striving to satisfy Mrs. Gotrocks from the swanky suburb as well as Mrs. Gotrocks' washwoman from the seething south side."[62]

Most retailers probably clung to a scattershot approach because they had only the foggiest and most impressionistic sense of who their best customers were and what they wanted of the store. They were, as a Filene's vice-president sneered, "merchandis[ing] on opinions, not on facts." Filene's got its facts by maintaining elaborate daily inventories and by requiring saleswomen to note the reasons why they lost sales, but a more common method was for stores simply to ask customers what they wanted. Although marketing research did not come into its own until the 1930s, merchants conducted customer surveys long before that. In 1917, one store had its employees question each customer about her expenditures for housedresses, and two years later the manager of another store

testified in *System* that demographic data gathered by his store staff had
helped him to improve his business notably. By the 1920s, stores were becoming more active in the field, collecting a wide range of information
from their customers; typical was the eager-beaver advertising manager
who made his own door-to-door survey.[63]

Beginning in 1936—perhaps as a response to the growing consum-
erism of the Depression era—some managers recruited customers as advisors on a variety of issues concerning service and merchandise. The pioneer in this area was Hortense Odlum of Bonwit Teller. Worried that her
store would lose touch with customers' wishes, she finally hit upon a solution: "It was as obvious as that. I would have Bonwit Teller friends to
lunch. Over the luncheon table we'd be able to talk frankly and pleasantly
about the things that concerned us all. Through such meetings we would
learn customer reaction and also, perhaps, acquaint our customers with
the store's viewpoint." Odlum was serious about heeding customers'
guidance and implemented several suggestions ranging from posting
signs about special events to designing a whole new line of clothing for
the mature woman. But perhaps the most extreme of all the attempts to
sound out customers was the 1932 study in which a New York University
professor wired customers up to a "psychogalvanograph"—presumably
an ancestor of the polygraph—to gauge their responses to sales talks. Although clearly quixotic, the scheme was seriously and favorably discussed
in the staid *Journal of Retailing*, clearly indicating department-store
managers' intense new interest in learning what the customer wanted.[64]

Department-store managers' efforts to appeal to and direct customers had locked them into an expensive and not very reliable system. While
the industry as a whole flourished from 1890 to 1940, given the fluctuations in the business cycle, managers were persistently uneasy with the
palace of consumption and their merchandise appeals, beset by a nagging
feeling that they could be selling more effectively to their customers. Part
of their problem was that they had chosen methods which carried high
fixed costs, but more important was the fact that they were trying to
channel and control a complex form of behavior by people over whom
they had influence but not power. Basing much of their appeal on class
and gender, they found that these forces could work as much against
them as for them. Making shopping into an elaborate ritual in which social categories such as class and gender intersected with personal preferences and experiences, they hoped to touch the customer's sense of herself

in a way that sparked that elusive quantity, store loyalty. The managers' divided consciousness, which made them at once businessmen and arbiters of culture, led them to give their customers more than they really wanted to and to hope for more than they could logically expect in return.

Despite their best efforts to use service and merchandise appeals to breed loyalty to a consumer-oriented way of life and to individual stores, managers signally failed to create the docile and predictable customer of their dreams. The women who shopped in their stores continued to display what managers regarded as unwonted initiative and independence. Store executives bitterly complained, for example, that customers persisted in shopping in only one or two of their departments, seeking other items elsewhere. Clearly, store loyalty was difficult to inculcate, particularly when it clashed with female customers' notions about independent-minded shopping skill. Even store managers' successes were bitter. A woman customer who adopted the new style of service-oriented shopping cost the stores extra time, trouble, and expense, making managers yearn for "businesslike" male customers. A charge customer who ran up sizable bills also held the fearsome power to withdraw her account—and to tell her friends of any injury done to her. A customer who succumbed to the gospel of fashion developed her own ideas of style; one who diligently followed the ads became a discerning critic of them.[65]

Managers' efforts to sell goods through both services and merchandise appeals of course had considerable effect, but they contributed to rather than assured sales. Some merchandise was sold by advertisements; some because store services put the customer into the right mood; some because of the stylishness, price, or quality of the item. Some was sold because the customer had a genuine need for it, or because she was bored, or because she was elated. The factors under the control of department-store managers by no means outweighed those over which they exerted only the most accidental influence. Customers, unlike store fixtures or accounting systems, were enduringly resistant to rationalization. Managers' relatively remote influence on them was not sufficient to persuade them to buy an item they were uncertain about, or to sell them an item in which they had no initial interest, or to convince them to buy merchandise in quantities or ensembles. Only the salesperson could accomplish these profit-boosting tasks. As managers tried to increase their sales, they became ever more thoroughly convinced of the centrality of the salesperson in their profit pictures.

Customers shared this recognition. In virtually every survey reported in the trade journals from the first one in 1915 until 1940, customers named salespeople as the preeminent influence on their shopping behavior. In 1915, over half of the women questioned by *System* stated that the quality of clerks' service was the most important factor in determining their opinion of a store. A 1940 study showed that a similar proportion placed the blame for unsatisfactory purchases and returned merchandise on salespeople's behavior. For good or for ill, the role of the salesperson, as managers learned to their dismay, was a controlling one. Too often that role was negative. For example, a 1917 survey by a New York store revealed that customers blamed well over half of lost sales on salespeople's behavior, and a 1938 survey of 50,000 customers in sixteen cities showed that 36.4 percent of customers' grievances had to do with clerks' bad conduct, while good salespeople were mentioned as factors in choosing a department store only 1.6 percent of the time.[66]

The lesson was clear: salespeople could do incalculable harm to the store. One customer, complaining of saleswomen's "deliberate rudeness" and "disdain for the mere customer," put the matter in terms to chill a department-store manager's heart: "It is a great waste for the employer to spend thousands of dollars to create goodwill by advertising only to have this hard won impression ruined the minute a customer enters a store." Taking their cue from their own observations, as well as from their customers', managers undertook a third campaign: to rationalize the behavior of the saleswoman just as they had tried to rationalize the conduct of the customer and the functioning of the store.[67]

Notes

1. "The Age of the Ready Made," *DGE*, 49 (9 Mar. 1895), 29. William R. Leach's work on department stores vividly discusses the "imaginative reconception" which the culture of consumption provoked in women who experienced it, stressing the liberating quality of early consumer capitalism. Our work overlaps at a number of points, but my perspective differs from his in seeking to understand the day-to-day dynamic of department-store shopping. See Leach, "Transformations in a Culture of Consumption: Women and Department Stores, 1890–1925," *Journal of American History*, 71 (Sept. 1984), 319–42.

2. C. E. Cake, "Arranging Goods to Make the Shopper Buy," *System*, 18 (Dec. 1910), 593; "Making Shoppers into Buyers," *Magazine of Business*, 52 (Sept. 1927), 284; Rheta Childe Dorr, *What Eight Million Women Want* (Boston, 1910), 115–16; *Echo*, 26 (4 Nov. 1927).

3. Susan Strasser, *Never Done: A History of American Housework* (New York, 1982); Faye E. Dudden, *Serving Women: Household Service in Nineteenth-Century America* (Middletown, Conn., 1983), 112–26 (the quotation appears on 112); David M. Katzman, *Seven Days a Week: Women and Domestic Servants in Industrializing America* (Urbana, 1981), 286, 297; Ruth Schwartz Cowan, *More Work for Mother: The Ironies of Household Technology from the Open Hearth to the Microwave* (New York, 1983).

4. Daniel Boorstin, *The Americans: The Democratic Experience* (New York, 1973); Stuart Ewen, *Captains of Consciousness: Advertising and the Social Roots of the Consumer Culture* (New York, 1976).

5. Ann Douglas, *The Feminization of American Culture* (New York, 1978), 75–77; Catherine Beecher, *A Treatise on Domestic Economy*, intro. Kathryn Kish Sklar (New York, 1977), 144; Strasser, *Never Done*, 202–23; Bertha June Richardson Lucas, *The Woman Who Spends: A Study of Her Economic Function* (Boston, 1910), 24–25; Christine Frederick, *Household Engineering: Scientific Management in the Home* (Chicago, 1920), 315–17; Christopher P. Wilson, "The Rhetoric of Consumption: Mass-Market Magazines and the Demise of the Gentle Reader, 1880–1920," in Richard Wightman Fox and T. J. Jackson Lears, eds., *Culture of Consumption: Critical Essays in American History, 1880–1980* (New York, 1983), 54, 59–60.

6. "The Roads and Business," *DGE*, 51 (17 Apr. 1897), 13; Lois B. Hunter, quoted in Store Managers' Division, NRDGA, *Proceedings, Seventh Annual Convention* (New York, 1930), 26; Lillian M. Gilbreth, "What Does the Customer Want?" *BNRDGA*, 14 (Mar. 1932), 155.

7. "What Was Said and Who Said It at the NRDGA Convention," *DGE*, 81 (19 Feb. 1927), 14; T. J. Jackson Lears, "From Salvation to Self-Realization: Advertising and the Therapeutic Roots of the Consumer Culture, 1880–1930," in Fox and Lears, *Culture of Consumption*, 4, 27.

8. "The Inside of Store Service," *DGE*, 73 (23 Aug. 1919), 281; "Right Kind of Supplies," *DGE*, 65 (16 Sept. 1911), 56; Robert F. Jenista, "Development of Retail Delivery," *JR*, 3 (Apr. 1927), 21.

9. "The Modern Store," *DGE*, 56 (11 Oct. 1902), 29; Ralph M. Hower, *History of Macy's of New York, 1858–1919* (Cambridge, Mass., 1943), 333–34; Jesse Kornbluth, "The Department Store as Theater," *New York Times Magazine*, 29 Apr. 1979, 66; Robert W. Twyman, *History of Marshall Field & Co., 1852–1906* (Philadelphia, 1954), 156–57. An interior view of the Marshall Field store appears in *System*, 5 (Mar. 1904), 159.

10. "Cost of Doing Business," *DGE*, 59 (4 Mar. 1905), 41; Twyman, *History of Marshall Field*, 157; *Echo*, 33 (31 Aug. and 7 Sept. 1934).

11. G. W. Stoddard, "Giving a Store Home Surroundings," *System*, 15 (June 1909), 666; Hortense Odlum, *A Woman's Place* (New York, 1939), 111, 122, 124; George Louis, "The Gentle Art of Subtle Selling," *System*, 20 (Aug. 1911), 154.

12. Daniel Vincent Casey, "Team Work for Wider Retail Trade," *System*, 14 (Nov. 1908), 461; Louis, "Gentle Art of Subtle Selling," 154.

13. W. Cooke Daniels, *The Department Store System* (Denver, 1900), 28–29; Wheeler Sammons, "Keeping Up with Rising Costs," *System*, 25 (Apr. 1914),

377; Benjamin F. Schlesinger, "How to Bring Visitors into the Store," *System*, 9 (Mar. 1906), 292; "A Good Investment," *DGE*, 56 (15 Mar. 1902), 17–18.

14. L. D. H. Weld, "What Size Store Is Most Profitable?" *System*, 44 (Nov. 1923), 571; Eva V. Carlin, "'America's Grandest' in California," *Arena*, 22 (Sept. 1899), 335; "Evaluation of Services to Customers," *JR*, 5 (Oct. 1929), 25–26.

15. Lloyd Wendt and Herman Kogan, *Give the Lady What She Wants! The Story of Marshall Field & Company* (Chicago, 1952), 313; "Children's Park in Retail Store," *DGE*, 56 (21 June 1902), 48; untitled note, *DGE*, 59 (20 May 1905), 13; "The Store Entertainment," *DGE*, 57 (18 Apr. 1903), 33; Schlesinger, "How to Bring Visitors," 292; "Extravagant 'Service' Expenditure Takes Deadly Toll of Profits," *DGE*, 79 (7 Mar. 1925), 23; A. Pickernell, "What about Customer Services?" *BNRDGA*, 13 (Aug. 1931), 481–82; *Echo*, 22 (3 Oct. 1924); *System*, 39 (Feb. 1921), 238; "Courtesy to Club-Women," *DGE*, 64 (21 May 1910), 39; "What the Other Fellow Is Doing," *DGE*, 82 (2 June 1928), 15.

16. "Store Gets Nine Babies Adopted," *DGE*, 78 (24 May 1924), 41 (the title is incorrect, as only six were adopted). "Various Merchandising Aids," *DGE*, 66 (17 Feb. 1912), 109.

17. "New Kind of Employee," *DGE*, 53 (25 Mar. 1899), 15; "Special Care of Customers," *DGE*, 58 (16 Jan. 1904), 21; *Echo*, 14 (13 Aug. 1926); Wendt and Kogan, *Give the Lady What She Wants*, 353–54; "Making Shoppers into Buyers," 284; Bert Teeters, "You Don't Have to Walk," *System*, 46 (Nov. 1924), 614; "Charging for Alterations," *DGE*, 73 (8 Nov. 1919), 38, 74; Merrill W. Osgood, "Keeping 2,000 Promises a Week," *System*, 45 (June 1924), 872–74; "Two Thousand Promises a Week Made and Kept Cement Customers' Friendship," *DGE*, 79 (3 Jan. 1925), 14; *Echo*, 22 (22 Sept. 1922), 29 (21 Nov. 1930); "Retail Development," *DGE*, 58 (23 Apr. 1904), 19; "Saving the Shopper's Time," *DGE*, 57 (11 July 1903), 17; Casey, "Team Work," 452–61; "Grapple with This Problem," *DGE*, 69 (23 Oct. 1915), 35–36; "Stores Cutting Down the Percentage of Returns," *DGE*, 70 (12 Feb. 1916), 35–36; "Exchanges and Refunds Can Be Cut Down," *DGE*, 70 (19 Feb. 1916), 33–34; "High Time to Grapple with Returns Problem," *DGE*, 77 (20 Oct. 1923), 11; Gladys G. Miller, "Reducing Returns," *JR*, 1 (July 1925), 21–23; Paul R. Ladd, "Keeping Goods Sold," *DSE*, 1 (25 Oct. 1938), 2; "Stores Limit Returns," *Business Week*, no. 423 (9 Oct. 1937), 17; "Ran a Special Excursion," *DGE*, 59 (14 Jan. 1905), 17; Alfred Lief, *Family Business: A Century in the Life and Times of Strawbridge & Clothier* (New York, 1968), 119–20; *Golden Book of the Wanamaker Stores* ([Philadelphia], 1911), 113.

18. *Echo*, 23 (19 Mar. 1926); "The Handling of Mail Orders," *System*, 2 (Nov. 1902), n. pag.

19. John David Newman, "Telephone Short-Cuts to Results," *System*, 24 (July 1913), 46–51; "Store Telephones Made Productive," *DGE*, 66 (6 Jan. 1912), 33–35; Lawton Mackall, "Switchboard Selling," *Magazine of Business*, 53 (May 1928), 619; Edith Grimm, "Plus Business from the Telephone Order Board," in NRDGA, *Joint Management Proceedings—1940* (New York, 1940), 30–31; Tyson Cook, "Taming the Store Telephone," *System*, 23 (Feb. 1913), 123–30; H. F. Ettinger, "The Telephone in Modern Merchandising," in Store

Managers' Division, NRDGA, *Convention Reports—2d Annual Convention, 1925* (New York, 1925), 3.

20. "Conveniences for Shoppers," *DGE*, 53 (3 June 1899), 5; untitled note, *DGE*, 60 (3 Mar. 1906), 3; "Ladies' Smoking Room Closed—Too Popular," *RCIA*, 32 (Nov. 1925), 25; "Saving Fifth Avenue," *DGE*, 70 (8 Apr. 1916), 39–40.

21. "An Object Lesson," *DGE*, 53 (29 Apr. 1899), 13; "The Bargain Counter," *DGE*, 53 (29 Apr. 1899), 18; "Building and Equipment," *DGE*, 66 (17 July 1912), 31; "Wide-Awake Retailing," *DGE*, 56 (10 May 1902), 59; "Wide-Awake Retailing," *DGE*, 56 (17 May 1902), 59.

22. "The Bargain Section," *DGE*, 57 (11 Apr. 1903), 25; "Basement Business," *DGE*, 70 (29 Apr. 1916), 433; "Under-Price Sections," *DGE*, 63 (3 Apr. 1909), 31; "Under-Price Section," *DGE*, 66 (11 May 1912), 37–38; Winthrop Seelye, "An 'All-American' Basement Store," *JR*, 7 (Apr. 1931), 6–7; "Special Sportswear Feature," *DGE*, 75 (14 May 1921), 39–57; "A Stout Department That Gets Turnover," *DGE*, 77 (24 Nov. 1923), 45, 51; Macy Documentary History, Baker Library, 169–71, 258, 886.

23. Emily Kimbrough, *Through Charley's Door* (New York, 1952), 10–20; see Chap. 4, 150, below.

24. Beatrice Judelle, "The Changing Customer," *Stores*, 42 (Nov. 1960), 7–8, 14, 17; "Modern Credit System," *DGE*, 56 (26 Apr. 1902), 18.

25. Malcolm L. Merriam, "Consumer Credit Trends and the Relation of Store Collections to National Income," in J. Anton Hagios, comp., *Credit Management Year Book, 1938–1939* (New York, 1939), 62; George E. Bittner, *Analyzing Retail Selling Time: Cost of Selling Commodities over the Retail Counter*, U.S. Department of Commerce, Bureau of Foreign and Domestic Commerce, Domestic Commerce Division, Distribution Cost Studies No. 2 (Washington, 1928), 9–12. For more detailed data on department-store credit sales, see Susan Porter Benson, "'A Great Theater': Saleswomen, Customers, and Managers in American Department Stores" (Ph.D. diss., Boston Univ., 1983), 130–31.

26. Odlum, *Woman's Place*, 129–32 (quotation appears on 130); Zelie Leigh, "Shopping Around," *Atlantic Monthly*, 138 (Aug. 1926), 200; "Special Privileges to Charge Customers," *JR*, 4 (Apr. 1928), 14–15. A number of stores had long used tokens bearing a customer's account number, but Filene's was the first to introduce, in 1930, the small metal charge plate which became the standard charge-account identification until the advent of plastic credit cards. See "'Firsts' in American Retailing," *DSE*, 24 (Jan. 1961), 194; "Identifying Charge Trade," *DGE*, 58 (1 Oct. 1904), 15.

27. "Extravagant 'Service' Expenditure Takes Deadly Toll of Profits," 23.

28. "Mis-Educating Customers," *DGE*, 70 (9 Sept. 1916), 31; "Do Stores Train 'Unreasonable' Customers?" *DGE*, 77 (7 July 1923), 14; Harry W. Schacter, "Profitable Store Management in 1931," *BNRDGA*, 13 (May 1931), 306, 322.

29. W. H. Leffingwell, "Sizing Up Customers from behind the Counter," *American Magazine*, 94 (July 1922), 152; Rheta Childe Dorr, "Christmas from behind the Counter," *Independent*, 63 (5 Dec. 1907), 1343; "The C.O.D. Privilege," *DGE*, 56 (22 Feb. 1902), 37; Hartley Davis, "The Department Store at

Close Range," *Everybody's Magazine*, 17 (Sept. 1907), 323; Anne O'Hagan, "The Customer Is Always Right," *Woman Citizen*, 11 (May 1927), 43. It is noteworthy that the anecdotes about customers virtually never mentioned shoplifting. While clearly a persistent and costly problem, theft by customers highlighted the dilemma faced by department-store managers; they deplored theft and tried to curb it with store detectives and careful procedures but they also feared alienating the well-off woman customer who was the typical nonprofessional shoplifter. See Elaine S. Abelson, "'When Ladies Go A-Thieving': The Middle-Class Woman in the Department Store, 1870–1914," paper delivered at the Berkshire Conference on the History of Women, June 1984, and part of a 1985 New York Univ. diss. "'When Ladies Go A-Thieving': Shoplifting, Social Change, and the City, 1870–1914."

30. O'Hagan, "Customer Is Always Right," 43–44; Odlum, *Woman's Place*, 134–35.

31. Ruth Chapin, quoted in Store Managers' Division, NRDGA, *Proceedings, Seventh Annual Convention* (New York, 1930), 170.

32. Alice Hughes, "A Customer's Idea of Good Store Service," *BNRDGA*, 17 (Feb. 1935), 75; Christine Frederick, *Selling Mrs. Consumer* (New York, 1929), 295–96.

33. "Mrs. Fleming of Arkansas Meets the Retail Trade," *BNRDGA*, 22 (Feb. 1940), 29; "Why Women Buy," *System*, 28 (Dec. 1915), 584–85; "Ninety-Four Housewives Tell Why They Buy," *System*, 28 (Nov. 1915), 485, 487; "Department-Store Services to Customers," *JR*, 3 (Jan. 1928), 30–32; Lawrence G. Nordstrom, "How Customers Explain Their Unsatisfactory Purchases," *JR*, 16 (Feb. 1940), 22.

34. "Superfluous or Necessary? Retail Services Defined by Kirstein," *BNRDGA*, 21 (Feb. 1939), 35.

35. "The Pest Eradicator," *System*, 15 (Mar. 1909), 315; a similar scheme is described in "Is the Customer Always Right?" *System*, 37 (Feb. 1920), 33.

36. "Solving Delivery Reeducation Problem," *DGE*, 71 (1 Sept. 1917), 8; "Looking Ahead," *DGE*, 71 (27 Oct. 1917), 5; "Seeking a Solution," *DGE*, 74 (4 Aug. 1917), 43; "Fall in Line," *DGE*, 71 (28 July 1917), 3; "Shall We Be Patriots or Conventionalists?" *DGE*, 71 (1 Sept. 1917), 8–9, 17; *Echo*, 31 (9 Sept. 1932).

37. Pickernell, "What about Customer Services," 481–82, 504, 514.

38. "Retail Imposition," *DGE*, 30 (3 Nov. 1900), 7; "Exchanges and Refunds," *DGE*, 57 (28 Mar. 1903), 31; "Policy Must Govern," *DGE*, 62 (29 Aug. 1908), 27; Hower, *Macy's*, 291, 296; Twyman, *History of Marshall Field*, 130; Leffingwell, "Sizing Up Customers," 152; "Grapple with This Problem," 35; "Percentage of Returns in Ten Boston Stores," *DGE*, 77 (1 Sept. 1923), 18; Odlum, *Woman's Place*, 129.

39. "All Goods on Approval," *DGE*, 58 (27 Aug. 1904), 14; "Reasonable Returns," *DGE*, 59 (5 Aug. 1905), 17; "As to Unfair Returns," *DGE*, 59 (26 Aug. 1905), 16; "Grapple with This Problem," 35–36; *Echo*, 13 (18 Nov. 1915); "Stores Cutting Down the Percentage of Returns," 35–36; "Exchanges and Refunds Can Be Cut Down," 33–34; "Stores Individually Have Cut Down Returns," *DGE*, 70 (4 Mar. 1916), 39; "Training Salespeople to Sell Silverware,"

DGE, 70 (16 Sept. 1916), 51; "High Time to Grapple with Returns Problem," 11; "Stores Again Strive to Lessen Returns," *DGE*, 78 (20 Sept. 1924), 15–16; Gladys G. Miller, "Reducing Returns," 21–23; M. J. Phillips, "Handling the Returned Goods Problem" *System*, 58 (Aug. 1930), 126–27; M. J. Phillips, "Detroit Fights the Returned Goods Evil," *System*, 59 (Jan. 1931), 34–35; Ladd, "Keeping Goods Sold," 2; "Stores Limit Returns," 17.

40. "Department Store Managers Have Their Troubles," *DGE*, 71 (3 Feb. 1917), 47, 49; Archer Wall Douglas, "Why Don't More Women Trade with Me?" *System*, 32 (Dec. 1917), 906; Kendall Banning, "Catching the Male Trade," *System* 15 (May 1909), 486; see also L. W. Libby, "Selling Men's Wear—If Ever," *BNRDGA*, 15 (Mar. 1933), 35.

41. Banning, "Catching the Male Trade," 487–91; Cake, "Arranging Goods," 591; "Drill! Drill! Drill!" *DGE*, 63 (3 July 1909), 28; "Bigger Profits through Simplification," *DGE*, 77 (21 Apr. 1923), 11; Wendt and Kogan, *Give the Lady What She Wants*, 297; "Men Jump at the Chance to Get Away from the Eternal Feminine," *DGE*, 79 (14 Feb. 1925), 16; Odlum, *Woman's Place*, 223; *Echo*, 30 (23 Dec. 1931).

42. "What Was Said and Who Said It at the NRDGA Convention," 16; "School-Time Soon," *DGE*, 70 (5 Aug. 1916), 89; "Selling to the Young Girl," *DGE*, 73 (9 Aug. 1919), 45; *Echo*, 24 (31 Dec. 1926); "Encourages Child to Do Mother's Errands," *DGE*, 75 (8 May 1920), 24; *Echo*, 33 (31 Aug. 1934); Henry Givens Baker, *Rich's of Atlanta: The Story of a Store Since 1867* (Atlanta, 1953), 122–23, 162; *Echo*, 12 (26 Feb. 1915); Wendt and Kogan, *Give the Lady What She Wants*, 306.

43. "A New Department," *DGE*, 71 (3 Mar. 1917), 3–4; "Toys and Sporting Goods Team Up Ideally in Los Angeles Store," *DGE* 74 (2 Oct. 1920), 319, 321; "Profits and Pitfalls in Radio," *DGE*, 79 (27 June 1925), 13–14; *Echo*, 31 (11 May 1923), 20 (5 May 1922), 24 (2 July 1926), 26 (13 Apr. 1928).

44. Sidney S. Wilson, "How Retailer Keeps Trade at Home," *DGE*, 67 (1 Mar. 1913), 47.

45. NRDGA, *Twenty-Five Years of Retailing, 1911–1936* (New York, 1936), 27–28, 124; O. C. MacLeod, "Merchandising through the Windows," *JR*, 5 (Oct. 1929), 15–18; "Window Display Policies," *JR*, 4 (July 1928), 13–14; "Display Men 1,000 Strong at Detroit," *DGE*, 74 (17 July 1920), 18; "Hands across the Counter," *Printer's Ink*, 184 (28 July 1938), 218.

46. Wendt and Kogan, *Give the Lady What She Wants*, 239; Henry Givens Baker, *Rich's of Atlanta*, 192; "Indirect Results," *DGE*, 59 (3 June 1905), 21; NRDGA, *Twenty-Five Years*, 122–24; Kimbrough, *Through Charley's Door*, 170–71; "Fashions on the Stage," *DGE*, 57 (23 May 1903), 23.

47. "A Department Store Features Nationally Advertised Brands," *JR*, 4 (July 1928), 14; Hower, *Macy's*, 252, 258–59; *Echo*, 20 (13 Oct. 1922), 23 (8 May 1925).

48. NRDGA, *Twenty-Five Years*, 127; Charles M. Smith, "Educating the Public to Changing Conditions in Retailing," *JR*, 4 (Oct. 1928), 3–5.

49. Hrant Pasdermadjian, *The Department Store: Its Origin, Evolution and Economics* (London, 1954), 29–61 (the quotation appears on 40); Paul H.

Nystrom, *The Economics of Retailing* (New York, 1917), 212; Malcolm P. McNair, "What Can a Retailer Do to Reduce His Costs of Doing Business?" *DGE*, 78 (24 Nov. 1923), 17, and "Will Retail Distribution Costs Drop?" *BNRDGA*, 26 (Sept. 1944), 50; Malcolm P. McNair and Eleanor G. May, *The American Department Store, 1920–1960*, Bulletin No. 166 of the Bureau of Business Research (Boston, 1963), 22–25.

50. Edward Mott Woolley, "A Short Cut to Salvation," *McClure's Magazine*, 40 (Dec. 1912), 231; Carroll D. Murphy, "The Blind Side of the Show Window," *System*, 16 (Aug. 1909), 139–41; NRDGA, *Twenty-Five Years*, 124.

51. Sammons, "Keeping Up with Rising Costs," 377; "Attending to Business," *DGE*, 66 (9 Nov. 1912), 41.

52. "Bombast in Ads," *DGE*, 59 (6 May 1905), 17–18; "The Advertising Problem," *DGE*, 60 (14 July 1906), 3, 44; NRDGA, *Twenty-Five Years*, 72–74, 122–23; "For Truth in Advertising," *DGE*, 69 (30 Jan. 1915), 30; Ewen, *Captains of Consciousness*, 71; "Mrs. Powell Has Her Say," *BNRDGA*, 21 (Feb. 1939), 29–30.

53. "Protecting the Customer," *JR*, 4 (Apr. 1928), 13–14; John W. Wingate and Elmer O. Schaller, "Merchandise Testing in Retail Organizations," *JR*, 4 (Jan. 1929), 8–13; Ewen, *Captains of Consciousness*, 56–71; Wingate and Schaller, "Merchandise Testing," 11; Melville C. Dearing, "Technical Testing of Merchandise a Foundation Stone in Building Customer Confidence," *DGE*, 76 (1 Apr. 1922), 143, 183; "Protecting the Customer," 13–14; "Two Customers Look at Sales Training," *BNRDGA*, 19 (Nov. 1937), 17–18, 51; Lew Hahn, "The Great Consumer Movement—Watch It!" *BNRDGA*, 20 (Jan. 1938), 15–16, 94.

54. "The Essence of Dry Goods," *DGE*, 53 (18 Feb. 1899), 13; *Golden Book*, 68; "New Lamps for Old," *DGE*, 57 (15 Aug. 1903), 51; "Meaning of This Number," *DGE*, 56 (30 Aug. 1902), 39.

55. Wendt and Kogan, *Give the Lady What She Wants*, 293–94. Scattered copies of *Fashions & Home* are in the Rhode Island Historical Society Library. "February Introduces First Issue of 'Charm,' New Bamberger Magazine," *DGE*, 78 (2 Feb. 1924), 23; John E. O'Connor and Charles F. Cummings, "Bamberger's Department Store, *Charm* Magazine, and the Culture of Consumption in New Jersey, 1924–1932," *New Jersey History*, 102 (Fall/Winter 1984), 1–33; "We Are Fashion Editors for Five Magazines," *DGE*, 78 (1 Mar. 1924), 14; "Benefits Retailers and Consumers, *DGE*, 78 (5 Apr. 1924), 16.

56. "Fashion Shows in Which Retailers Cooperate," *DGE*, 68 (4 Apr. 1914), 147; Ernest S. Jaros, "Working Up a Cooperative Style Show," *DGE*, 68 (10 Oct. 1914), 34–46; *System*, 39 (Jan. 1921), 151; *Fellow Worker*, 11 (Feb.-Mar. 1928); Edward F. Roberts, "Training Customer Vital Factor in Success of Bamberger Fabric Promotion Scheme," *DGE*, 81 (16 Apr. 1927), 13–15.

57. "The Hand-to-Mouth Buying Policy," *DGE*, 66 (3 Feb. 1912), 41; "Why Hand-to-Mouth Buying?" *DGE*, 79 (18 July 1925), 12; "The Old Order Changeth," *DGE*, 74 (27 Dec. 1919), 22; "Woman of To-Day Defies Style Creators with Ideas of Her Own," *DGE*, 74 (7 Feb. 1920), 47, 49; "The Flapper's Wardrobe," *DGE*, 79 (31 Oct. 1925), 10.

58. "It's Style and Quality That Count," *DGE*, 59 (8 Apr. 1905), 47; "The

Fall Fashions," *DGE*, 59 (19 Aug. 1905), 63; "For Garment Buyers," *DGE*, 56 (12 July 1902), 59.

59. Judelle, "Changing Customer," 14; "Low-Priced Goods," *DGE*, 70 (3 June 1916), 51; "The Retailer's Most Pressing Problem: Diminution of Profit," *DGE*, 68 (23 May 1914), 35; "Radical Change Needed," *DGE*, 79 (14 Feb. 1925), 14.

60. A. Lincoln Filene, "A Merchant Looks at Stabilization," *Survey*, 65 (1 Feb. 1931), 490–91; "Can a Store Be Too Exclusive?" *DGE*, 82 (22 Sept. 1928), 9; "Style vs. Price," *DGE*, 82 (21 Apr. 1928), 7; John Guernsey, "Retailng in 1932," *BNRDGA*, 14 (Feb. 1932), 76; "The Quality Movement in Merchandise," *BNRDGA*, 14 (Apr. 1932), 227, 234–37; "Special Bulletin on Quality," *BNRDGA*, 14 (Nov. 1932), 861–76; "Editorial," *BNRDGA*, 17 (Oct. 1935), 732.

61. "Wide-Awake Retailing," *DGE*, 56 (16 Aug. 1902), 79; "Profits in Fashion," *DGE*, 57 (28 Mar. 1903), 29; "Enlightened Advertising," *DGE*, 57 (15 Aug. 1903), 51; "Why It Pays to Push Staples," *DGE*, 79 (24 Jan. 1925), 21–22.

62. E. S. Kinnear, "20 Plans That Boost Our Volume and Hammer Down Overhead," *System*, 50 (Nov. 1926), 614; NRDGA, *Twenty-Five Years*, 127; "Hidebound by Habit," *DSE*, 2 (25 Aug. 1939), 1, 21.

63. Louis E. Kirstein, "Why We Know 'What the Public Wants,'" *System*, 42 (Aug. 1922), 155–57, 182–84 (the quotation appears on 155); *System*, 31 (Aug. 1917), 188; A. C. Torgeson, "Taking a Census: How It Helped Our Business," *System*, 36 (Dec. 1919), 1076–78, 1162–69; "What, Why, and How of Community Analysis," *DGE*, 76 (1 Apr. 1922), 19–20; O. E. Klingaman, "Rich Mine of Info in Survey When Properly Made and Used," *DGE*, 76 (1 Apr. 1922), 21–22; Guy Hubbert, "Community 'Sales Analysis' Has Saved the Day for Volume More Than Once," *DGE*, 79 (1 Apr. 1922), 23, 183; Frank H. Williams, "When the Lady of the House Speaks, What She Says Is Worth Listening To," *DGE*, 77 (2 Dec. 1922), 13, 84; "Do You Know Your Customers," *DGE*, 78 (8 Dec. 1923), 15; "Long, my dear, and solid colors," *Management Methods*, 61 (Feb. 1932), 83.

64. Odlum, *Woman's Place*, 160; O. Preston Robinson, "Customers' Reactions to Organized and Unorganized Sales Talks," *JR*, 8 (Oct. 1932), 90–92.

65. *Echo*, 21 (5 July 1923); J. R. Ozanne, "What Do You Know about Your Own Employees?" in Store Managers' Division, NRDGA, *Convention Proceedings, Fourth Annual Convention* (New York, 1927), 124.

66. "Why Women Buy," 584; Nordstrom, "How Customers Explain Their Unsatisfactory Purchases," 21; *Echo*, 13 (18 Oct. 1917); "Pin-Pricks and Preferences," *DSE*, 1 (10 Jan. 1939), 6. For similar findings, see also Richard Steed, "Is the Salesforce Neglected?" *DGE*, 79 (7 Nov. 1925), 23; "Your Greatest Leak," *DGE*, 80 (19 June 1926), 15; and Arthur Lazarus, "Store Organization," *DGE*, 80 (20 Mar. 1926), 20.

67. "Thoughts of a Plain, Everyday Woman on Things the Customer Sees," *DGE*, 77 (16 Dec. 1922), 13.

4

Made, Not Born:
From the Shopgirl to the Skilled Saleswoman

The control of selling and of the people who did it was by far the most persistent and troubling problem of department-store managers. As their orientation changed from buying to selling, managers realized that salespeople had formidable influence over the success of their stores. The people behind the counters could enhance or doom management efforts to make the store efficient, profitable, and an effective agent of the culture of consumption. Managers could devise policies to improve their profit positions or their standing with the public, but the salespeople determined the success of such policies by the way in which they implemented them and through their own interactions with the store's clientele. Managers might advertise lavishly, but their expenditures were for naught if salespeople failed to follow up the interest they awakened in customers. Managers might frame stern policies to cut the costs of customer service, but if salespeople informed customers of these rules in a tactless way, they might turn out to be false economies. Managers might streamline their stock and choose assortments cannily, but merchandise would sell only if salespeople presented it convincingly to customers.

The task of devising a labor-management policy that would consistently and dependably turn the balance in their favor was an enduring preoccupation of department-store managers. They were, of course, not alone in feeling anxious and dissatisfied about their relations with their employees; labor militancy and changes in the organization of production had made labor management a nationwide preoccupation of businessmen, workers, and interested citizens by the 1890s. Department-store executives' tactics were in some ways similar to those of their factory counterparts, with whom they shared a desire for an efficient and

124

tractable labor force. Both experimented with more humane and re-spectful treatment of workers, the paternalistic benefits known as welfare work, and money incentives, although department stores adapted each of these to the special conditions of large-scale retailing. In one respect, however, department-store and factory practice diverged dramatically. The unique element in department-store labor policy was the encouragement of skilled selling: the use of trained salesclerks to increase the size and number of sales transactions through merchandise information and sales psychology. It contrasted with self-service schemes, which department stores shunned before World War II, in that salespeople controlled the customer's access to the merchandise and actively influenced the course of a sales transaction. Department-store managers placed great faith in this hybrid strategy, asserting that it would enhance their public image and increase productivity while creating a contented, loyal, and re-spectful sales force.[1]

In fact, the problems associated with selling were far less tractable, grounded in an emerging world of service work. Just as department-store managers and customers clashed over ground rules for a new world of mass consumption, so managers and salespeople struggled to define the terms of service work. Department-store selling was not only one of the first of these new occupations—distinguished by their remove from pro-duction—to emerge but it also displayed the characteristics of service work in uncommonly high relief: the addition of the client to the usual worker-employer dyad was always implicit in service work, but the client was directly and emphatically present on the selling floor as he or she was not, for example, in a steam laundry. Social relations played an important part in every work situation, but in department-store selling they became the essence of the work itself. Department-store managers were in the vanguard of the still-continuing effort to forge labor-management poli-cies appropriate to the new situation.

The desires for control, predictability, and efficiency which guided managers in their efforts to rationalize the organization of their firms and to shape customers' behavior also informed their dealings with their salespeople. Once again, they had a divided view of their role, embracing both the new managerial virtues and the service orientation of their in-dustry. Recent writing on labor-management policy during the late nine-teenth and twentieth centuries has been sparked in part by Harry Braver-man's *Labor and Monopoly Capital*. Braverman's major thesis is that, over the course of the twentieth century, Americans' work has been degraded, or deskilled, as managers increasingly separated the conception of work from its execution. Central to this process was scientific management, which gave precision and rigor to the far older method of the division of labor. Richard Edwards and Dan Clawson have offered important refinements of Braverman's framework. Edwards, in *Contested Terrain*, maintains that not one but three systems of control have been used during the twentieth century to enforce workplace discipline. First was simple control with direct and personal discipline; the second, technical control, emerged in large firms where machinery replaced skill and paced the work. Finally, since 1945 a system of bureaucratic control has developed, emphasizing conformity to rules rather than gross output, stressing the "good" worker as its ideal product. All three continue to exist today in different types of firms. Clawson's *Bureaucracy and the Labor Process* contends that managers' primary goal was to keep workers from thinking and to deprive them of knowledge.[2]

All three focus on manufacturing, the primary employing sector through the first half of the twentieth century. Braverman and Edwards comment briefly on retailing: the former argues that "the 'skills' of store operations have long since been disassembled and in all decisive respects vested in management," while the latter maintains that systems of simple control prevail in retail selling. Both, understandably trying to fit retailing into their models, overlook the peculiar characteristics of department-store operation. Whatever the successes of self-service since World War II, at least until then department-store managers wanted to enhance rather than dismantle skill, trying to root out the practices of simple control and to forge a system of bureaucratic control which would produce a loyal salesperson. Far from, as Clawson would have it, seeking unthinking and uninformed workers, they encouraged the saleswoman to be resourceful in her sales techniques and an expert on her merchandise.[3]

Department-store managers were going against the grain of prevailing labor-management trends in the twentieth century. They hoped to foster skill when the central tendency was to undermine it. They undertook to monitor that skill with the supervisory and accounting methods developed elsewhere to deskill and regiment workers. Even more, they attempted to harness skill in social interaction, a most unmanageable quality and one even harder to control than manual skill. In the factory, manual skill could ultimately if not easily be taken into the hands of management, mental and manual work divorced, and skill separated from the social relations of the workplace. In the store, however, the skill of selling was intimately and organically bound up with the social relations of the selling floor and the work group; only in the hands of the workers could it have the desired effect on sales. Ultimately, store managers had an apples-and-oranges problem: they were trying to combine elements that grew out of fundamentally different systems.

Equally troublesome were the problems of assessing and measuring the productivity of selling personnel. Those features of retailing which had limited department-store managers' efforts to systematize the store's organization had an even more dramatic effect on their attempts to mold the sales force. The central problem, wrote an industry observer in 1913, was that "[t]he best salesperson . . . is *not necessarily* the one that *has the largest book*"—book being selling-floor slang for the day's sales totals. High productivity, measured by sales alone, was not a reliable indicator of a salesperson's effectiveness. If an item was not sold properly, with due consideration for the customer's sensibilities, the store stood to suffer in the short run through the return of the merchandise and in the long run through the loss of the customer's goodwill. High production in a factory was, by contrast, a virtually unmixed blessing. On the selling floor, manner was at least as important as cumulative result: it mattered little if a worker stamped out a widget while in a high temper, but it made a great difference if a saleswoman sold a pair of stockings while in a grouchy mood. Moreover, a department could not function smoothly unless salespeople gave due attention to such non-selling tasks as stock work and display. Department-store managers never successfully integrated these intangibles into a clear measure of productivity.[4]

Monitoring performance was as difficult as monitoring output. The complex social dynamics of selling were not easily reduced to clear directives; even had they been so, the close supervision necessary to enforce them would have jeopardized sales by annoying customer and salesperson alike. The core of scientific management in the factory—dividing and regularizing the work process—simply was not applicable to selling as it was defined in the palace of consumption. Non-selling workers often made change and wrapped packages, but the interaction between customer and salesperson could be neither subdivided nor standardized. Store executives had little choice but to allow salespeople broad latitude in dealing with the public.

The flow of work in retailing remained intractably irregular. Daily, weekly, and seasonal fluctuations were compounded by departmental variations, changes in fashion, the weather, and the moods of countless customers. Planning and staffing became monumentally difficult in the face of this endemic variability. Unlike factory managers, department-store managers could not regulate the flow of work, shift it from one department to another, or simply require overtime work to cope with a rush. Customers demanded to be served when and where they presented themselves; assuring service without astronomical personnel expenses was an enduring problem of the department-store executive. Unable to smooth out work load fluctuations, managers shifted the onus to their salespeople and demanded more intensive sales efforts to compensate for slow periods.

A fourth stumbling block on the road to tighter control of the work force was the public nature of the store. Labor policies were open for all to see, and concerned observers could easily question workers about the terms of their employment. The conditions under which goods were manufactured were not normally visible to the public, while the conditions under which they were sold were a public spectacle. Both organized and unorganized women shoppers were outraged at seeing overworked, underpaid women toil long hours in unhealthy surroundings; almost invariably, the same middle- and upper-class women who made up the backbone of the store's clientele spearheaded the campaigns for better conditions for working women.

The Shopgirl: Class, Gender, and Selling

The selling staff of the typical department store by the 1890s was overwhelmingly working-class and overwhelmingly female, and these facts powerfully shaped labor policy. Class and gender in selling interacted in extremely complex ways, sometimes complementary and sometimes contradictory. Executives set out to change the class-based characteristics of their salespeople and to co-opt their gender-based characteristics, unwittingly entering a maze of difficulties from which they never extricated themselves.

Mid-nineteenth-century policies had built into department stores a class tension which bedeviled managers well into the middle of the twentieth century. Their methods of attracting customers and their policies toward the sales force conflicted sharply and sometimes explosively. The cultural demands of the growing urban middle and upper classes set the tone for the store, but department-store selling did not attract those of the same backgrounds. The comparatively low pay, long hours, and difficult working conditions as well as the popular image of the blowzy shop-

Fig. 10. The Sins of the Shop-Girl

*"You annoy him to distraction. You are untidy. And
you ask a customer how much she wants to pay"*

Collier's, 51 (23 Aug. 1913), 20. Original in John Hay Library, Brown University.

girl usually drove middle-class working women into other employment such as clerical work. Working-class saleswomen behaved in ways that were grounded in their own cultural background but grated on their employers and their customers. Contemporary accounts of saleswomen frequently recall *Pygmalion:* some raved at the ingratitude of those who dared to be different from themselves; others winced at saleswomen's demeanor, language, and dress. Ungrammatical colloquialisms and familiar forms of address appalled employers; one observer noted censoriously, "[T]he salespeople have become so forward as to call customers 'Dearie.' The use of such terms is a liberty which the woman of finer sensibilities quickly resents." Dress also conveyed a powerful class-laden message: customers were displeased when "approached by an employee who is overdressed and who bears on her person marks of opulence which apparently do not accord with her position." The social conflict that electrified relations between saleswomen and customers was fundamentally of the store manager's own making: eager for the cheap labor of uneducated women, viewing selling as semi-automatic, setting his sights on an affluent clientele, he had created the problem of lackluster selling for which he blamed his saleswomen.[5]

While managers condemned clerks' class attributes out of hand, they found much to recommend in their gender characteristics. Certain aspects of women's culture dovetailed with managers' developing conceptions of skilled selling. If class was a divisive factor in the clerk-customer relationship, gender was a unifying one. Qualities which had for a century been encouraged in women—adeptness at manipulating people, sympathetic ways of responding to the needs of others, and familiarity with things domestic—fit nicely into a new view of selling. Managers urged saleswomen to transfer skills from their domestic to their work lives; during the early 1920s, Filene's tested aspiring coat, suit, and dress saleswomen on their knowledge of style and fabrics and their ability to choose "the correct style" for different types of customer. Making the store more and more like a home, executives encouraged saleswomen to act more and more like hostesses, to treat their customers as guests. Empathy and responsiveness constituted the irreducible core of selling skill. A writer in 1911 urged, "Shop *with* the customer, not *at* her"; Macy's training director affirmed in 1940 that "interest in the customer's problems" was the key to selling success. Twentieth-century selling centered on the salesperson as a lay psychoanalyst of the counter, the evangelist of the therapeutic ethic of the culture of consumption.[6]

Managers praised "womanly" personal characteristics, but their emphasis on interaction also resonated with the collective aspects of women's culture. Recent research in women's history has called attention to the existence of affective and supportive female networks over the last century or so. From Italian and Jewish women in Providence immigrant communities to middle-class women dispersed around the country, female networks valued cooperation over competition, stressed the commonalities of female experience, and provided channels for the exchange of services and emotional support. As dimly as retail managers understood women's culture and its modes of functioning, in some unexamined way their definition of selling skills rewarded women for being women, gave exchange value to their culture.[7]

In department stores' formative years women's cheapness and cultural characteristics dovetailed nicely. But as executives pursued their goal of skilled selling more energetically, a contradiction between women's position in the labor market and their role as skilled saleswomen emerged. Saleswomen constantly heard their supervisors emphasize the critical importance of skilled selling, and understood from their daily experience their ability to make or break a sale, but as women workers they remained low-paid and low-valued in the labor-market hierarchy.

Department-store managers' attempts to co-opt women's culture were less explicit and self-conscious than their efforts to eradicate working-class culture. As Joan Kelly has pointed out, the sex-gender aspects of a society are often less easily and less clearly discerned than the class aspects, but the social configuration of department stores added a power dimension to this tendency. The men who dominated the upper levels of department-store management were at home with urban gentility; asserting its hegemony in the store consolidated their power by making working-class saleswomen act in a way that was less disruptive to social relations within the store. By contrast, they were on alien ground when they tried to manipulate gender-based culture, which divided them from both customers and saleswomen.[8]

Defining the Problem: Pressures from Within and Without

While building, organizing, decorating, and systematizing the store, executives had slighted the critical area of selling—the interaction across the counter. Convinced on the one hand that selling as men had practiced it was an inborn talent, and on the other that attractive goods presented in a luxurious environment would practically sell themselves, managers between 1850 and 1890 had believed that the ideal sales force was composed of neatly dressed, polite women who would sell mechanically and inoffensively. Certain that they needed only cogs on their wheels, department-store managers had wasted little time and energy on the development of their sales forces. They encouraged a passive style of selling in their employees, as described by a turn-of-the-century writer: "Complaint is made by many that the [department] store had stifled the art of selling. This is admitted by the New York [department] store manager. His salespersons do not urge the customer to buy, and dilate upon the beauties of his wares. They simply hand the customer what he or she wants, and make a record of the sale. It is not his desire, the merchant says, to sell the customer what he does not want." Another observer noted that clerks' behavior varied in different grades of store: at the cheaper end of the spectrum, managers tolerated "rudeness, stupidity, and indifference," while in carriage-trade firms they demanded "intelligence, cheerfulness, and courtesy." But neither type of store expected energetic selling effort.[9]

In small ways in the 1890s and more intensely during subsequent decades, a disturbing conjunction of forces impelled managers to revise their views of their clerks. They began to realize that their irresistible ads, dazzling merchandise, and sumptuous stores had solved one set of problems—the attraction of crowds to the store—only by creating another— that of high overhead. The public spectacle of the department store was commercially viable only if customers spent more than they would from simple need or random impulse. Managers convinced themselves that only skilled selling could accomplish this; the executive secretary of the NRDGA estimated that the salesperson's powers of persuasion clinched nearly two-thirds of all sales. Cost-cutting in the non-selling departments made only a fractional difference in overhead costs, but the sale of a tie with a shirt or of three pairs of stockings instead of one dramatically decreased the proportion of fixed costs to selling price. In one notions department, for example, a 2 percent increase in the size of a sale produced a 14 percent increase in the net profit; notions were notoriously low-profit items, and the profit increases in other departments were yet more impressive. Managers concluded that selling was the bellwether that would lead the way to more profitable and efficient operations: "The selling force is the best place to start at when a general speeding up of the entire organization is necessary or desired. And in view of the position of the salesforce as a motive power, increase of salesforce efficiency will stimu-

Fig. 11. Skilled Selling: The Source of the Store's Power

Why the Car Stopped.

Dry Goods Economist, 80 (19 June 1926), 16.

late all the other parts of the machinery." As the buyers' store changed into the sellers' store, the selling function took center stage.[10]

As department-store managers began to feel the internal pressure of increased costs, they also faced two new sets of demands from the consuming public. First, customers wanted more than ever before from those who served them. They expected more deferential service as new standards of gentility became more firmly entrenched:

> This closer contact with Old World manners has created in our opulent citizens a relish for subserviency on the part of those who attend upon them; and this tendency on the part of the newly rich is spreading even to those who do not possess the golden talisman which crooks so many knees.
>
> This expectation of and demand for polite, quiet, high-class service is further spread by the foreign air which our better hotels all over the country have assumed. . . . Even the farmer, the once rough, unlettered tiller of the soil, now has his daily paper, goes frequently to town and has his auto—that symbol of wealth and creator of class distinctions.
>
> More consideration for the customer on the part of the clerk will be insisted on. The "take-it-or-leave-it" attitude on the part of the clerk will be less and less tolerated. There will be a greater recognition of those assistants who make sales in a quiet, dignified, respectful manner and with a minimum of friction.

But they were also increasingly fashion- and quality-conscious and required a salesperson with information and poise, a person "of intelligence, whose pleasure as well as duty will be to show and describe goods in a pleasing and comprehensible manner." Second, the public demanded that department stores treat their employees more humanely, inspired by the socially concerned investigators who swarmed through the American world of work from the 1880s to the 1920s. As participant observers, journalists, or social investigators, often in cooperation with women's reform organizations such as the National Consumers' League, the Women's Trade Union League, and the Young Women's Christian Association, they closely scrutinized the department store. Their conclusions were frequently damaging to the reputations of saleswomen, of department stores as places of employment, and of department-store managers. Some of their complaints focused on the physical aspects of the store: bad lighting, inadequate ventilation, a lack of seats, squalid toilet and lunchroom facilities. Others concerned worker-manager relations, such as long hours, extremely low pay, brutal and humiliating discipline, fines for infractions of rules, and prohibitions on the use of seats even where they were provided. A third class of complaint considered the effect of working conditions on women's lives, stressing ill health, exhaustion, an impoverished social life, and prostitution.[11]

The critique of the department store became so widespread and was so easily verified by the concerned public that even relatively favorable articles included the Consumer League's indictment of department-store practices. Other observers, particularly those who had tried life behind the counter, painted far more lurid pictures. Annie Marion MacLean, a Chicago sociologist, worked in two department stores during the pre-Christmas rush season. Gloom, filth, and weariness pervaded the first store, which paid its women employees so little as to force them to choose between "starvation and shame." The second store had a more wholesome atmosphere, but still the hours there were long and the wages "woefully insufficient." Another investigator found that even in one of New York's best stores, low wages doomed saleswomen to "a life stripped of humanity, robbed of most that makes life beautiful, and spent in one ceaseless, perpetual grind—simply *to live*." Perhaps most bitter of all was Rheta Childe Dorr, whose experience selling handkerchiefs during the holiday season convinced her that she could never again bear to give Christmas presents. Describing vividly the physical strain and nervous exhaustion afflicting the women behind the counters, she concluded that the whole spectacle was "sordid and hateful."[12]

Perhaps the most damaging, and certainly the most sensational, charge was that department-store saleswomen were in special peril of prostitution, whether professional or occasional. The public nature of the store, its sumptuous atmosphere, and its low wages combined, so the argument went, to make the transition from the counter to the bordello all too easy. As the Vice Commission of Chicago put it: "Some of the girls who are most tempted, and enter lives of prostitution, work in the big department stores, surrounded by luxuries, which all of them crave, and sell large quantities of those luxuries for a wage compensation of about $7.00 or $8.00 a week, and even less." Such writers argued that the saleswoman was in perpetual danger, whether from madams, pimps, and lecherous men who entered the store as freely as respectable matrons or from bosses who were given to sexual harassment. The department-store manager who hinted to his employees that they would have to supplement their low wages through prostitution was a stock character in this literature, which blamed immorality not on the women who yielded to "temptation" but on the employers who refused to pay a living wage.[13]

Department-store managers counterattacked, most notably through a 1913 investigation of New York stores by the National Civic Federation's Welfare Department. The report denied that the department store was a breeding ground for prostitution, citing studies showing that few saleswomen became prostitutes and praising store managers for trying to protect their saleswomen from the apostles of vice. Mary Van Kleeck, Elizabeth Dutcher, and other champions of wage-earning women damned the report as a "whitewash," condemning stores' low wages and oppressive policies in the pages of *The Survey*.[14]

Department stores came off little better in government investigations. In Illinois hearings on a proposed state minimum wage in 1913, executives of such nationally known stores as Marshall Field, Carson Pirie Scott, and The Hub testified that they could afford a minimum wage of $12 per week—as much as twice the prevailing wage—and still make respectable profits. The store managers' frankness earned them the withering sarcasm of their enemies. The New York State Retail Dry Goods Association somewhat more diplomatically testified against a proposed state minimum wage, stressing opportunities for efficient saleswomen to better themselves as well as the benefits received by the general run of employees. Still, their description of department-store selling as "light, not onerous" work was but a feeble counter to exposés of store life. Bluntly declaring that they would pay only what the market would bear unless the law dictated otherwise, all but a handful of store managers refused, like their brethren in factories, to pay a living wage.[15]

The combination of financial pressures within the store and external pressures from customers and social reformers pushed the department-store executive to frame a new role for his employees and new policies to deal with them. His balance sheets suggested that only skilled selling could reduce the impact of high fixed costs and maximize the effect of expensive advertising and service schemes. Aware of his image as an exploiter of women workers, he undertook to upgrade both the image and the actual experience of his saleswomen. On the one hand, he wanted to reap the goodwill benefits of broad-minded policies; as a writer in *Munsey's Magazine* put it, "The public resents the worn out, famished type of clerk, and its feelings are hurt by seeing women faint behind the counter." On the other, he hoped that a fully trained, decently treated, and more refined type of clerk would be a more loyal and effective saleswoman. Whatever methods he used—simple kindness, welfare work, training, or financial incentives—the goal was the same: the development of skilled selling. A perturbed industry observer summed up the difference between the old and new views on the subject:

> As a rule, the salesforce grows up like Topsy. It is neither born nor made. No sensible attention is given to its creation nor to its training. The result speaks for itself more eloquently than any tongue can express.
>
> Every merchant should remember that his clerks are his personal representatives and that the public only know him, and pass their judgment upon him, from their CONTACT WITH HIS SALESFORCE.

The idea that the salesperson was the merchant's emissary to the public was the foundation of the emerging retail personnel wisdom, although it was a difficult lesson for many managers to learn. Even in the late 1920s, industry writers still felt it necessary to remind department store executives of the pivotal place of salespeople in their store: "A manager has only one pair of eyes and only one pair of ears, but he needs more. So he must train his salespeople to keep their eyes and ears open for customers' sympathetic reactions. . . . To the public, our corporation is the girl behind the counter." There was respect for the salesperson in the new view, but there was also fear—and both were aspects of the retailer's uneasy recognition of the alarming power of a group which he had once considered no more than a passive adjunct to his elaborate store systems.[16]

Retailers began to explore their own contribution to the sorry state of the sales force. The trade journals sternly warned that bosses who misrepresented their wares to the public undermined employees' respect for their supervisors and sometimes turned employees into outright adversaries. The *Dry Goods Economist* pointed the danger with a rhetorical question: "[I]sn't it queer that a man should expect people to misrepresent for him, but not to him?" The conclusion was obvious: only the man whose own conduct was above reproach could expect his employees to be loyal. Other writers criticized the prevailing mode of discipline—known in the trade as "driving," with bosses acting "cold and dictatorial," like "Simon Legree." Even worse, many executives publicly dressed down their employees, not only humiliating the worker but also offending customers who witnessed the rebuke. Managers' obsequiousness toward customers made their high-handed treatment of salespeople seem even worse by comparison. "It is," marveled the editors of the *Dry Goods Economist*, "astonishing that houses which adopt the most broadminded and liberal methods in the treatment of customers do not see the advisability of extending this policy to their employees." The problem was compounded by the fact that authority over salespeople was both divided and unclear, causing a Boston store manager to complain: "The salesperson is sent to the Training Department for further instruction regarding dress regulations, as her costume is not businesslike. She is then routed to the Superintendent's Office for a gentle reprimand because her dress is not clean. She is next sent to the Health Department for a less gentle reprimand because her neck is much soiled. And she is finally sent to the Store Manager's Office for a pass so that she can stay and work the rest of the day, just as she is." Anyone and everyone above her in the store hierarchy could—and did—give orders to the saleswoman.[17]

Too often, discipline on the selling floor was all stick and no carrot, with harsh words underlined by elaborate systems of fines and penalties. Many stores appeared to assume their employees had criminal tendencies. Store detectives, spying floor managers, undercover agents, and cumbersome procedures for employees' purchases and for the removal of their personal property from the store kept them under constant and intrusive surveillance. Tardiness, small errors in filling out sales checks, and faults in procedure led to fines or some form of infantilizing public exposure and confession. Some stores required employees to sign a slip acknowledging the error; others demanded confessional interviews with supervisors; still others posted the names of the most frequent offenders. Leslie Woodcock Tentler has correctly pointed out that wage-earning women in all occupations endured fines and petty discipline, but fines could be particularly ruinous to saleswomen because they handled money. The clerk who had to repay her employer the five dollars extra change she gave to a customer lost not just a few cents, but most of her week's salary. Such penalties alienated customers as well as workers. One customer, enraged when a clerk was fined for some accidental breakage, paid the saleswoman's fine and vowed never to return to the offending store. Complaints about such practices were a staple of trade-journal editorials from the early 1910s to into the 1930s, showing that managers did not easily learn the lesson of more respectful conduct toward their employees.[18]

Still, the need to cultivate a cheerful, satisfied, and cooperative sales force led many retailers to moderate the harsher aspects of store discipline and to favor the carrot over the stick. As early as the mid-1890s, retail writers urged managers to "enforce justice and fairness." The hallmarks of the new approach were an appeal to the good nature of the clerk, "rewards for accuracy" rather than "fines for mistakes," and showing "the employee how he will *gain* if he endeavors to advance himself, rather than how he will *lose* if he does not." The enlightened approach curiously combined repentance for past injustices, a concern for public image, a consciousness of the importance of the salesperson, and a conviction that arbitrary treatment backfired. One observer smugly noted that an abusive employer might as well save his breath: "In rough tones, not unaccompanied by opprobrious language, he scolded the help, while they listened to him with sullen glances or cynical smiles. It was also noticeable that on his departure one or two employees began at once to do the very thing for which he had just blamed them, and which he had just forbidden." Warning that authoritarian pressure frequently sparked rebellion, another grimly noted that "if this is true of men, it must be even more true of the twentieth century woman." [19]

Industry writers counseled managers to instill the spirit of cooperation in their employees, to change their terms as well as their tone. Many stores proscribed the old standby term of "clerk," supplanting it with "saleswoman" or more rhetorical terms such as "associate," "co-worker" or member of the "business family" or "store family." Some firms experimented with inspirational meetings in which managers delivered "little family chats" designed to whip up store spirit. Store newspapers, beginning in the 1900s, helped to "build up a spirit of harmony and loyalty and to promote team work." By 1920 the *Dry Goods Economist* reported that it regularly received fifty, and a 1937 survey of "leading retail stores" found that over two-thirds either currently had employee newspapers or had been forced by the Depression to curtail publication. The typical paper combined store news, words of instruction or reproof, and employee gossip.[20]

Perhaps the most common method of avoiding capricious management practices was the rule book. Around the turn of the century, many retailers had begun to spell out both expected conduct and the penalty for violations. Rule books were a response to the growing size of department stores, a recognition of the need to end arbitrary practices, and a means of exacting genteel behavior from the sales force. One of the most pervasive and enduring of the new rules was that regarding dress; appearing first during the late 1890s, dress regulations were accepted practice by the 1920s. In 1929, for example, a survey of twenty-two stores in the New York metropolitan area showed that every store but one specified the color of saleswomen's clothing. Some managers required dark, inconspicuous clothing because they liked the uniformity it gave to the store's appearance. Others hoped that drab colors would minimize the "danger of display of poor taste and lack of background on the part of the employees," a hope they underlined by displaying clothing acceptable in style and color near employees' lunch rooms. But they also saw semi-uniform clothing as a subtle way of controlling employees' behavior. They worried that an overdressed saleswoman would behave in a high-handed way: "because she 'sports' good clothes and an exaggerated coiffure, [she] thinks she can lord it over all with whom she comes into contact, be it customer or fellow-employee." Conversely, dress codes enforced "a defined and appropriate 'class distinction' between the customer and the assistant, which is . . . very pleasant to the lady shopper." [21]

Managers' kinder and less arbitrary treatment might improve the morale of the salespeople and brighten the atmosphere of the store, but it could also produce lackluster employees. In 1903, a buyer pointed out the perils of the rule-bound store: "It is responsibility that brings out character, that gives force and initiative, that puts man (or woman) 'on his mettle.' Good help is impossible where employees are treated like slaves or children." Two decades later, the *Dry Goods Economist* echoed his warning, telling retailers that they still tended to "crush ambition and stifle initiative." Moreover, managerial whim continued to weigh heavily on the saleswoman. The move toward more humane and evenhanded treatment was spotty and inconsistent, as managers' attitudes toward seats for saleswomen show. [22]

Early-twentieth-century reformers secured the passage of many state laws requiring the provision of seats for saleswomen, but it was another question entirely whether saleswomen would actually be permitted to use the seats. Managers early realized the wisdom of allowing idle saleswomen to sit down: it was "absurd to expect continual interest and civility" from someone who was on her feet nine hours or more and "the sight of unoccupied saleswomen seated, instead of standing, at their counters redounds to the reputation as well as to the pecuniary benefit of the store proprietor." Women's Bureau investigators during the 1920s, however, found widely varying management policies on this issue. In Oklahoma, for example, one saleswoman reported that she was treated as if she "were committing a crime" when she sat down; in a second store, managers instructed saleswomen "not to tire themselves by constant standing"; and in a third firm women were forbidden to sit by the first-floor manager but permitted to do so by the second-floor manager. [23]

Managers adjusted their own behavior and attitudes in limited ways but planned thoroughgoing changes in the sales force. They found sales-women a ready scapegoat for and a potential solution to all their prob-lems. The "shopgirl," as she was popularly dubbed with a mixture of scorn, condescension, and pity, suited neither her employers nor her cus-tomers; as an overworked, underpaid toiler in the great stores she was cast as both victim and offender.

Department-store managers rejected both the older ideal of the natu-rally gifted salesman and the late-nineteenth-century model of the pas-sive, unskilled, order-taking saleswoman. They undertook to shape a whole new breed of clerks, no longer taking salespeople as they found them. Selling skill, twentieth-century style, could be codified and taught; in the words of a Chicago department store manager in 1910:

> There is no mystery in the art of salesmanship. The qualities required are born in every one, and only a reasonable amount of training is needed to bring these qualities to the surface and make them serviceable. . . .
>
> As I say, good salespeople are made. They make themselves. . . . The expres-sion, "He is a born salesman" may have meant something twenty years ago before modern experience had analyzed all the little secrets of the art, but to-day no one with common sense, industry and a real desire to learn need fear to tackle the task of soon becoming a leader in the ranks of truly good salespeople.

Most observers were more careful to specify that managers should con-trol the new skill, that salespeople should be made by their superiors rather than by themselves. Even a small-town retailer in 1913 understood the importance of this point: "The success of salespeople is entirely the result of training, dependent entirely upon the opportunity for develop-ment and the result of the right working conditions. It lies within the power of every proprietor of every store, large or small, to re-create, re-construct, and re-organize the potential selling ability of his salespeople." The tacit assumption was that unskilled women were putty in the hands of their managers, blank slates on which the new selling wisdom could be writ large—one more element in the store to be rationalized and systematized.[24]

Convinced that the customary agents of early socialization—the home and the school—had failed, managers began to transform depart-ment stores into educational institutions. They blamed "unpropitious home surroundings and . . . defects in our educational system" for the fact that so many salespeople "frequently [spoke] and act[ed] in ways which [did] not commend them to people of refinement." Working-class and immigrant children were simply not being assimilated into the respectable middle-class mainstream fast enough to fill the places behind the counters of department stores. The schools, moreover, were falling short in their methods as well as in the ideology they taught: they did not encourage thinking, provided only *"admonition"* and not "EXPLANA-TION," failed to teach students to "ANALYZE, rather than *memorize.*" These complaints are a measure of the distance between department stores' and manufacturers' labor requirements. Most of the latter would have been content had the schools inculcated the traditional virtues of hard work and obedience through admonition and memorization, while department-store managers wanted initiative and independent judgment grafted on as well.[25]

In order to transform those who became saleswomen, department stores undertook to "furnish the definitive, formative influences that the home and our educational facilities lack under present-day conditions." The school-and-family imagery pervaded the retail literature: a 1916 discussion of Marshall Field's personnel department described it both as "Dean of Women" and as "a conscientious mother." The theme was played out explicitly in the store as well. At Filene's, for example, the store manager and a counselor were known to the female employees as "Dad" and "Mother" through the 1910s and 1920s.[26]

Managers were confident that the benevolent guidance of the store would transform the dismal product of an unfortunate home and a misguided school. Samuel Reyburn, president of Lord & Taylor and a key figure in department-store management circles in the 1920s and 1930s, spoke glowingly of the impact of the store environment on such a girl: "Constant contact with the woman who is in charge of her department will have an influence on her. Daily contact with other girls who have been subjected to influences in business will have an influence on her. Daily observations of customers in the building will influence her, and slowly she will change because of these influences. She will lower the tone of her voice, grow quiet in her manner, exhibit better taste in the selection of her clothes, become more considerate of others." But, Reyburn continued, this "natural" process was too slow and haphazard; the enlightened store would hurry it along in an organized, deliberate socialization campaign.[27]

Welfare Work

There were two major strands in this effort. The first, commonly known as welfare work, flourished during the first two decades of the twentieth century and merged into the personnel management movement of the 1920s. Training, the second, began in the early 1900s, was firmly established in the 1910s, and became widespread after 1920. Welfare work included store facilities and social service programs for workers, activities that were implicitly rather than directly didactic, while training taught everything from arithmetic to modern art to sales psychology to the proper way to fill in a sales check. Welfare work and training shared the goal of inculcating salespeople with a new outlook that would make them more effective at skilled selling. They frequently overlapped in execution, particularly in trying to modify the class and cultural perspective of the salesperson. Both offered certain benefits to workers at the same time as they demanded in return more compliant and efficient behavior. Finally, class and gender were central issues in both efforts.

Managers devoted most of their attention to remodeling the people whom they hired and relatively little to reforming their own hiring practices, paralleling management practices in other industries. But retail executives were especially indifferent to new recruiting methods; they were convinced that their labor pool was alarmingly deficient and that only training would produce better selling. Not until the 1920s did department-store executives systematically address the problem of hiring, and even then it continued to take second place to the primary issue of training. For the most part, they continued to hire those who fit their prejudices about what types of people should sell certain types of merchandise. As a rule, stores adopted the psychological and intelligence tests so popular in personnel circles during the 1930s only to evaluate applicants for non-selling jobs, despairing of measuring "the less tangible qualities inherent in good salesmanship." When managers did succeed in attracting "salespeople who ha[d] the best possible native qualities," it was less a consequence of deliberate hiring practices than of their efforts to make the store and the job of selling more attractive through welfare work and training.[28]

Welfare work combined workers' services and facilities—rest rooms, lounges, dining rooms, gymnasiums, infirmaries, libraries, vacation retreats, and savings banks—with some rudimentary education along the lines of personal hygiene, etiquette, and grammar classes. Some of the new facilities were spartan—a lunchroom might amount to some rickety benches and a table in a basement room—but others rivaled those provided for customers. Lord & Taylor's Fifth Avenue store, opened in 1914, had luxurious rest and recreation facilities for the store's employees, while in 1916 San Francisco's Emporium bought a thirty-two-acre resort

Fig. 12. Employees' Facilities in the Lord & Taylor Store, Opened 1914

Employees' Gymnasium

Employees' Promenade, Roof

The New Store of Lord & Taylor (New York, 1914).

and opened the lavish facilities to its workers for a nominal fee. Following the lead of Providence's Shepard Company, a number of department stores during the 1900s and 1910s employed welfare secretaries to oversee these programs and to dispense advice and counseling to troubled employees. Some stores, notably Filene's, encouraged the formation of store organizations which functioned as company unions.[29]

Welfare work in the store as in the factory had many meanings: it provided a much-improved work environment; it secured more efficient performance either directly or indirectly; and it enhanced the firm's public image. A store lunchroom, for example, served healthful, cheap lunches, gave workers quick service so that they could return punctually to the selling floor, and looked good in store publicity. Outings similarly provided good advertising and pleasant diversion along with an opportunity to build the store spirit which produced eager and efficient workers.[30]

The goals of welfare and efficiency coincided not only in the store but also in the careers of welfare work's most enthusiastic practitioners. Diana Hirschler, who became the welfare director at Filene's in 1905, left in 1912 because she had "outgrown the scope of welfare work" and had "become interested in the larger problem of raising saleswomanship efficiency." Mary Van Kleeck, long a dedicated advocate of saleswomen, had embraced efficiency by the mid-1920s. Not only was she a frequent contributor to the *Bulletin of the Taylor Society*, but she was also one of the society's three delegates, along with Josephine Goldmark and Lillian Gilbreth, to the Women's Industrial Conference in 1926. Edith Wyatt, who with Sue Ainslie Clark had damned department-store working conditions as an embarrassment to a democracy, also converted to scientific management. While remaining sympathetic toward the saleswoman, they all became convinced that she must supply her employer with efficient labor in order to merit decent treatment and adequate earnings.[31]

Welfare work in department stores assumed the added burden of dampening the class conflict across the counter. One enthusiastic writer likened Jordan Marsh's employee facilities to a "high-class hotel," asking rhetorically: "If a girl, say, reared in humble surroundings, spends some part of her day amid pictures and cheerful furniture and tasteful rugs and books and sunlight, will she not insensibly acquire a clearer insight into the ideas and needs of the majority of the store's customers? Will she not, then, be better able to wait upon her trade deftly, sympathetically, and understandingly?" Some aspects of welfare programs served all four ends. Clinics, for example, increased efficiency, in one store reducing absenteeism so much that the work force could be cut by fifty-four people. Free or low-cost medical care was no small boon to the clerk who earned barely enough for the day-to-day necessities; suitably publicized, it created goodwill for the store. Finally, medical care could eradicate health problems related to class status and thus eliminate a jarring note in the palace of consumption: in the words of a journalist, "A customer is attracted to a person of wholesome appearance who will promptly and quite excusably shrink from a clerk whose hair shows the presence of vermin, or who is careless in controlling a cough." In the end, welfare work promised not only to mollify the customer and transform the working-class saleswoman—it held the hope of attracting the elusive "better class" of salesperson to an increasingly attractive and respectable workplace.[32]

Managers worried that welfare work, while decreasing class conflict between saleswoman and customer, might increase it between saleswoman and the firm. Like workers in other industries, retail workers resented welfare work when it was too obviously tinged with noblesse oblige or paternalism. Canny observers realized that the best way to circumvent employee resentment was to acknowledge frankly the employer's self-interest in welfare work:

> The more he [the employer] emphasizes among his employees the idea that in doing welfare work he does not regard it as a charity or philanthropy, but that it is due to his recognition of the broader principles on which a business organization should be based and run, the better will be the results obtained. In a word, spread the tidings among the employees that the benefits derived from the store's welfare work are mutual.
>
> Such a course will tend to greater self-respect on the part of all concerned, and the more independent among the help will more readily accept and have greater regard for the advantages extended to them.

By 1920, the term "welfare work" had become indelibly marked with paternalism and many concerns had substituted the more neutral label of personnel work. By whatever name, however, welfare work persisted as a feature of department-store life. The programs and facilities established in the years before World War I virtually always continued and often expanded in the succeeding decades. If the managers spoke less frequently about welfare work as such, it was not because they had abandoned it as a tactic but because it had become axiomatic, an accepted feature of department store life and one that required relatively little energy and attention to maintain.[33]

The Varieties and Scope of Training Programs

Welfare work helped to change the popular image of the shopgirl by improving her working conditions and beginning to attack her class-based characteristics. Still, it provided no clear vision of what the new skilled salesperson would be like; clean towels, hot meals, and edifying literature could set the stage for skilled selling, but they could not write the script. This task fell to training programs. Tremendously varied in their specifics, these programs attempted to build upon the educational aspects of welfare work but focused more directly on the demands of department-store selling. Training sought both to increase immediate, quantifiable efficiency—for example, to teach saleswomen punctilious accuracy in filling out sales checks—and to develop the ability to cope creatively with situations requiring discretion instead of cut-and-dried compliance with rules. The second aim is most important because it defined and, insofar as possible, transmitted selling skill. Advocates of training assumed that their programs would have broad institutional benefits as well as positive effects on individuals; one writer argued, for example, that training programs would break down institutional barriers by bringing together people from different departments.[34]

Training consisted of general education, merchandise training, and salesmanship training; all three were recognized by the mid-1900s. General education, building on welfare work's foundation, sought to fill the gaps left by inadequate family and school training. Courses ranged from grammar-school work for younger employees to university-level offerings for adults. Although this aspect of training did not speak explicitly to better selling performance, it grew out of the conviction that a better education would give an air of polish and efficient competence to the sales force. Attempting to convey middle-class values and behavior, arithmetic classes included Franklinesque exercises in personal budgeting, and English instruction prescribed a drawing-room version of standard English.[35]

Merchandise training surveyed the historical development of a product, its manufacturing process, its properties, and its uses. It was a curious amalgam of high culture (in, for example, visits to museums), traditional womanly wisdom about homemaking and dress, new "scientific" information about the care of various fabrics and articles, and the dictates of fashion. The combination conveyed to the saleswoman a uniform notion of respectable "good taste." In the words of Helen Rich Norton, an important figure in retail training circles, "the broadest and most important of the aims" of retail training was to impress upon the students "[i]mproved standards of living, better habits of thought, higher interpretations, and ideals." Some attempts to reach this goal verged on the absurd: both the NRDGA and the *Dry Goods Economist* circulated films showing life in Palm Beach and Miami so that salespeople could develop the "mental 'atmosphere'" to advise resort-bound customers properly. Norton's textbook, *Retail Selling*, included five pages of essential French terms, suggesting that stores retain a French teacher to teach proper pronunciation to the sales force. Whether programs tried to apply a veneer of middle-class trappings or to remake the saleswoman's "inner consciousness," the target was the same: the saleswoman's class identity.[36]

By contrast, salesmanship training built on the saleswoman's gender identity. Women had been trained to be consumers even before they were trained to be saleswomen; for example, their socialization encouraged them to pay attention to the style and construction of clothing. Such a consciousness became selling skill when saleswomen could guess a customer's size at a glance or estimate her budget by assessing the clothes she wore. Similarly, saleswomen had as women learned to deal with affect, to sense and meet people's needs. Once behind the counter, they had only to apply their interpersonal talents to dealing with their customers.[37]

Training programs encouraged saleswomen to develop their social skills as well, so that they could create sales where there would have been none. Trainers counseled saleswomen to expand the individual sales transaction through suggestion selling and to set the stage for future sales by building up a clientele of customers. Suggestion selling was by far the most popular tactic urged upon salespeople; the literature is filled with inspirational pieces touting, quite correctly, its powers to expand profits and cut costs. Bosses exhorted saleswomen to size up each customer's budget and preferences in order to maximize her purchases each time she visited the store, suggesting a tie to go with a shirt—a second pair of hose—a handbag to match shoes—a good buy on dish towels. Suggestion selling could also serve as a form of speedup. Sanger Brothers of Dallas, for example, launched a major campaign for suggested sales in September 1921. The firm promised to maintain salaries despite the sharp postwar deflation if salespeople kept sales up to the old dollar levels, a task requiring them to increase the number of sales by from one-third to one-half.[38]

Skilled selling tested the mettle of the saleswoman: if she were uninspired, too aggressive, or too timid, her suggestions could at best fail and at worst alienate the customer. But suggestion selling prescribed collective effort as well, inculcating "the spirit of the hive." It countered the rigidity of departmental separations without sacrificing the clarity of store organization. During the late nineteenth century, clerks had frequently breached department barriers to move freely about the store with their customers. A dress saleswoman, for example, often accompanied her customer to purchase harmonizing gloves, shoes, and hats. This method maximized the individual sale but was wasteful and even counterproductive from the point of view of selling service in the store as a whole. It caused a maldistribution of selling personnel through the store, made it difficult to allot selling expenses to a given department, and gave saleswomen more freedom than managers could tolerate. Increasingly rigid departmental divisions had inexorably led to more compartmentalized selling. By 1910 a handful of stores still had a few crack salespeople who sold throughout the store, but industry writers urged an early end to this practice in order to foster specialized selling within each department and keep tighter control of the salespeople. Despite the control and accounting problems it presented, however, this practice—known as interselling—continued to appeal to managers as a way of dealing with the customer as a whole person. As late as 1940, a number of managers at the NRDGA convention advocated the revival of interselling in a form acceptable to salespeople, buyers, customers, and controllers alike.[39]

Suggestion selling provided a middle ground between interselling and overspecialization. Each time a salesperson suggested the merchandise of another department or referred her customer to a clerk in another department, she undermined the barriers that balkanized the store and lowered the store's profits. Some stores devised specific plans for increasing interdepartmental suggestions. One firm developed a buddy system in which pairs of "sales pals" referred customers to each other; others required salespeople to suggest items featured in the firm's advertisements, sometimes assigning certain salespeople to specialize in suggesting another department's goods. As one writer put it, "The adman only snapped the camera and left the plate in the customer's mind. The saleswoman develops it. She is the ruby room of advertised goods." Filene's devised one of the most elaborate systems, supplying salespeople with referral cards which introduced a customer to a salesperson in another department.

Collection and tabulation of the cards showed that in 1924 suggestion sales between departments accounted for an impressive 11 percent of total sales. Suggestion selling in this context bolstered profits but also broadened the outlook of the store's personnel. As an industry observer noted, it encouraged salespeople to "talk as part of the organization, not as clerks apart from it." [40]

Developing a clientele, the other major technique of skilled selling, required a long-term rapport between saleswoman and customer and once again a delicate balance between increasing sales and avoiding offense. Training programs urged saleswomen to maintain files of their customers' names, addresses, sizes, and buying habits. The expectation was that clerks would write or phone their clientele when merchandise of special interest arrived and consult the files when a customer visited the department. In order to deal successfully with her clientele, a saleswoman had to develop empathy with a varied group of comparative strangers, to learn to anticipate their merchandise wishes, and to develop a way to approach each individual. [41]

Department stores embraced training enthusiastically, progressing from vague ideas about educating salespeople in the 1890s to full-scale programs in the early twentieth century. Virtually the only argument against training was that expert employees would seek better opportunities elsewhere, a quibble that was shouted down as hopelessly narrow-minded. Filene's led the way with a formal training program in 1902, followed by Los Angeles's Broadway the next year; Macy's took a pioneering step with the establishment of the nation's first autonomous training department in 1915. Training programs were pervasive by the late 1920s. In 1926, all but twelve small stores among thirty-two surveyed in Pennsylvania had organized training for salespeople. In 1918, only one Pittsburgh department store had a training program; by 1927, all did. Still, training programs fluctuated with the business cycle and were one of the first store activities to be cut back in straitened times. Training expanded "until the depression of 1920–1922 when it was drastically curtailed; it expanded again until 1929, when with the depression it was again curtailed, reorganized, or completely abandoned; it again came into prominence between 1935 and 1937." A general trend from centralized to decentralized training accompanied this mixed history. Decentralization not only fit in with the growing conviction that selling could best be learned on the shop floor, but it was also less expensive since it relied on sponsors and buyers more than on specially hired training personnel. Even more revealing of the cost-conscious manager's attitude toward training was the long-term trend to speed it up by packing more and more information into less and less time.[42]

While the in-store program continued to be the most prevalent form of training, a number of other organizations trained both saleswomen and teachers of saleswomen. The prototype of modern store training was the school founded by Lucinda Wyman Prince, a veteran of the college settlement movement, at the Women's Educational and Industrial Union in Boston. Sharing other social workers' conviction that women workers had to become more efficient if they were to be better paid and more respected by their employers, Prince decided to put her theories into practice in training saleswomen. In seeking the cooperation of Boston department stores, she encountered the vestiges of a nineteenth-century attitude: that salesmanship, if it could be taught at all, could be taught only by those with experience. Undaunted, Prince proved that selling was not an arcane science by working briefly at a bargain counter and dramatically outselling the more experienced saleswomen. Store executives and prospective students were interested but skeptical, the former reluctant to make a financial commitment to Prince and many of the latter unable to sacrifice earnings to attend Prince's classes. Prince persevered and conducted her first class in 1905, combining general education and demonstration sales with information about merchandise and retail practices.[43]

The graduates performed so well that within two years sixteen Boston stores had agreed to accept the school's students for part-time work and its graduates for full-time jobs after a month's probation. Prince accurately presented her project to department-store managers as a good business proposition. Under the leadership of George Mitton of Jordan Marsh, Boston merchants contributed to the rent and maintenance of the Prince School's building. In exchange, they committed themselves to little, retaining the right to refuse or discharge a Prince woman, and received dependable, high-quality labor on Mondays and the other five afternoons when they most needed it. Prince and her associates, on the other hand, took a maternal interest in the women. The teachers and members of the WEIU did "friendly visiting" with students and graduates at home and on the job, urging good conduct on saleswomen and employers alike. In order to meet the growing demand for Prince-trained women, the school shifted its emphasis to training teachers of saleswomen in 1912 and became affiliated with Simmons College the next year. Prince graduates fanned out through the country and figured prominently in all aspects of retail training. Prince herself became a celebrity in retailing. Her 1915 speech to the NRDGA national convention inspired the association to appoint her the head of a new department of education (later the Personnel Group) and to support her school handsomely. She worked closely with the NRDGA for twenty years until her death in 1935; no one did more than she to shape the course of retail training.[44]

A similar effort began in New York in 1908, under the sponsorship of Anna Garlin Spencer and with teaching by Diana Hirschler, former welfare-work supervisor at Filene's. Beginning as a night school for those already working as saleswomen, it followed the Boston pattern and expanded into teacher training. Textbooks written by teachers at these schools further broadened their impact: Hirschler produced the widely used *Art of Retail Selling*, rivaled in popularity only by *A Textbook on Retail Selling* by Helen Rich Norton, associate director of the Prince School. The Spencer-Hirschler effort affiliated with the New York public schools, a feature which gave it a certain permanency as well as the luxury of not charging tuition. Other cities such as Detroit followed suit, but Providence public schools refused to absorb a retailing program established by the city's merchants. Public school programs in retailing expanded somewhat when the Smith-Hughes Act of 1918 provided federal matching funds for state vocational programs, but retail vocational education came of age only in 1936 when the George-Deen Act allotted federal matching funds specifically for part-time or evening vocational programs in retailing or other aspects of distribution. Department-store managers, once skeptical of public schools' ability to train retail personnel, eagerly embraced programs which absorbed part of their training costs and supplied them with free or low-cost labor during peak hours. The Retail Clerks International Protective Association, the major clerks' union, hailed the idea of public vocational education because it acknowledged selling as skilled work deserving higher wages, but condemned the actual programs because they were merchant-dominated. The union complained that schools provided stores with a steady supply of students "of superior ability and skill" who received the same low wages as their untrained co-workers and undercut experienced workers' demands for raises.[45]

Universities eagerly leaped on the bandwagon. By the late 1920s, there were retailing programs at Simmons, New York University, the University of Pittsburgh, Ohio State University, and the University of Southern California; at least one more, Northwestern University, joined their ranks during the next decade. Most received major financial support from local merchants; the New York University program was sustained by six New York department stores led by Percy Straus of Macy's. Post-secondary retailing programs typically focused on training retail teachers and combined classroom work with field work in stores. Next to the Prince School at Simmons, probably the most influential was the University of Pittsburgh's Research Bureau for Retail Training, later absorbed into the School of Business. A major research institution as well as a teaching program, the RBRT received one million dollars from Pittsburgh stores by the 1930s.[46]

The NRDGA and the major retail periodicals also supported training activities. The *Journal of Retailing*, the organ of the NYU School of Retailing, focused on training because of NYU's specialization in preparing retailing teachers. The *Dry Goods Economist* staunchly advocated training of all kinds, and began during the 1920s to publish a yearly education issue. The NRDGA, in addition to its commitment to training in general and to Prince in particular, began in 1928 to operate a consulting service which established or improved store training programs around the country.[47]

The Contradictions in Training

Despite managers' high hopes, training programs in fact ran into many obstacles which offset or negated their benefits. The great paradox in training saleswomen was that it succeeded best on the selling floor where store managers had the least reliable control. General education and store system could easily be taught in a traditional classroom setting, but the most critical part of training—that involving merchandise and interaction with customers—was more effectively learned through experience and participation. One writer maintained that fully 85 percent of training time should be spent in the selling department. The training director of R. H. Macy & Co. was adamant on the point: "The great laboratory in which to learn selling *is the selling floor.* Just as theory without practice is cold and dry, so practice without stimulation seldom progresses. Skill flourishes through practice."[48] Yet training on the sales floor was usually conducted by the buyer and the sponsor, both of whom had a primary loyalty to their department and different ideas about selling skill than did upper management. Buyers were frequently and necessarily absent from the departments and, even when they were present, tended to emphasize the speedy sale of current stock more than the development of a sound selling staff for the future. Finally, they often imposed their idiosyncracies on their training efforts, conveying their own idea of selling skill rather than a uniform, storewide version.[49]

The sponsor, a saleswoman assigned the duty of greeting, indoctrinating, and training newcomers to her department, appeared on the scene at the turn of the century. Her position was anomalous: her role as sponsor gave her authority over those who were technically her equals. Financial incentive reinforced the contradiction; if the sponsor spent too much time in training, her own sales totals and thus her reputation with her superiors would suffer. A sponsor was rarely well trained for her role, and her immediate superiors begrudged any time she spent away from selling. But most disquieting of all was sponsors' great latitude in training; managers rarely knew precisely what they told new employees. Sponsors were dangerous because potentially subversive, but approximately half of the nation's department stores continued to use them between 1910 and 1940 because they provided a convenient and economical means of training.[50]

Just as selling skill was best transmitted on the selling floor, so there it was forged. Management wisdom competed with on-the-job wisdom developed by saleswomen. Sometimes the two versions clashed, as Chapter 6 will demonstrate, but even when they coincided managers were eager to gain control of the transmission of knowledge. One of the signs of managers' new fearful respect for their salespeople was their desperate eagerness to solicit advice and suggestions, not just because it earned employees' goodwill but also because it was an important source of good ideas. Salespeople developed resourceful tactics for dealing with customers and had the best up-to-the-minute reading of demand, and managers were eager to appropriate that knowledge so that they could recycle it in training programs. One of the most widely used textbooks on salesmanship, *How to Sell at Retail*, was mainly a compendium of the "practical methods" used by "three hundred expert salespeople." The use of sponsors was a similar attempt to harness shop-floor wisdom. Managers encouraged salespeople to turn in suggestions for better selling service and required them to fill out "call slips" whenever a customer requested an item that was out of stock and sometimes whenever they lost a sale. Such campaigns were potentially useful ways for upper management to learn what was happening on the sales floor; they served as a check on the performance of buyers and salespeople alike and spotlighted areas for special training efforts.[51]

Managers also tried to simulate the flavor of real selling away from the selling floor, primarily through demonstration sales and playlets. The demonstration sale was an extemporaneous enactment of a sale, with a student as the salesperson and a student or teacher playing the customer. Criticism and discussion followed the demonstration. Playlets often focused on service problems as well as selling challenges, relying on the comedy of outrageously bad conduct in contrast to demonstration sales which were supposed to display the participant's best talents. Both sought to teach by example the quality and content of skilled selling, using relatively controlled situations rather than the difficult-to-supervise atmosphere of the selling floor.[52]

A second built-in contradiction in sales training was that between managers' lofty goals for training programs and their practical scorn for selling as a function and for those who did the work. Managers hoped to induce their saleswomen to forget the mixed reputation of department-store selling and to think of it as a profession, a vocation conferring dignity on those who practiced it. John Wanamaker refused to have employees called "shopgirls" or "help," and asserted that "[w]e are men and women, living our lives, doing our share, doing it with dignity, doing it in the most respectable way." The Filene *Echo* somewhat more grandly likened the art of selling to the work of ministers and lawyers. Lucinda Wyman Prince pointed to the change in self-image that training in skilled selling would bring about: "The change in the individual is a new conception of the dignity of work in general and of the chosen occupation in particular. There is a satisfaction that comes with mastery of certain of the forces of one's environment, and a pride inseparable from acquired skill and the achievements it makes possible." Managers wanted to develop saleswomen personally as well as professionally. The *Dry Goods Economist* urged teaching rather than training: "Nor can the human being who is *trained* go anything like as far as the one who has been taught. The latter is able to apply the instruction he has received to conditions which are new and widely different from those to which the teaching itself immediately related."[53]

Countering this rhetoric were the actual position of selling in the stores and the reality of training programs. The retail literature constantly urged executives to spend more time on the selling floor, teaching by example and proving management's respect for selling, yet department store executives from buyers to general managers were notorious for fleeing to their offices at the first opportunity. Most retail executives in fact concentrated on merchandising, disdaining selling and assuming it would somehow be fostered by others. Scorn for selling went hand in hand with a low opinion of those who sold. One early-twentieth-century writer sneered, "The average salesgirl or clerk is neither a Chesterfield nor a Macchiavelli. Reared in a limited sphere, she has no knowledge of human nature." A training director in the mid-1920s bewailed the typical salesperson's indifference to information about her wares as well as her inability to assimilate materials unless presented graphically. A decade and a half later, a writer denounced saleswomen, noting that they required "pre-digestion of anything which [they were] to absorb" because they were "incapable, first, of boiling down copious information about even a single line to usable dimensions; second, of remembering the extracted nuggets of wisdom; and third, of making a selling application when face to face with the customer." This sort of complaint may have revealed more about saleswomen's active resistance to training than about their intellectual limitations, but it also showed managers' impatience for quick and dramatic results.[54]

Training specialists responded by drilling salespeople in various canned schemes for selling. These devices—including "standardized selling sentences" and taxonomies of customer "types"—were especially popular during the 1930s, when any cheap route to better selling was attractive. Some of the schemes did contain helpful information about merchandise, while others were childish or laughable, such as those which divided adjectives into the proscribed (those beginning in "gr" or "sn") and the approved ("irresistible," "girlish," and "distinctive"). This sort of training did little to give the saleswoman a feeling for the dignity of her work or pride in her accomplishments.[55]

The major method of assessing sales performance also belied managers' rhetoric about the professional nature of skilled selling. Sales force performance was evaluated by sales totals, through direct ratings by superiors, and through the reports of service shoppers. The first, as noted earlier, dangerously emphasized quantity at the expense of quality and the second was as subjective and arbitrary in the store as in other settings. Service shopping was the peculiar department-store form of evaluation, providing a comprehensive shop-floor view of selling through the use of undercover employees who posed as customers and reported on the ser-

Fig. 13. Training Programs Had Unintended Effects

Dry Goods Economist, 77 (16 Dec. 1922), 13.

vice they received from salespeople. The shoppers were recruited by individual stores, supplied by schools of retailing, or hired from commercial shopping services such as the Willmark Service System. The women chosen as shoppers came from the same general social and economic strata as the department-store clientele as a whole; service shopping was thus doubly useful since it revealed the typical customer's standards for store service along with her assessment of the degree to which the sales force met those standards. Managers asked shoppers to rate salespeople on everything from "[e]vidence of taste and judgment" to honesty to whether they had a salesbook and pencil handy. Shoppings ranged from the completely secret, with no warning whatever to employees, to the relatively open, in which case employees were told what the shoppers were looking for as well as the week or month in which the shopping would take place; in all cases, of course, the individual shoppers remained unknown to the sales force. Managers almost always told the salespeople the results of the shopping reports and targeted low-rated areas for special training efforts, usually followed by repeated shoppings. A form of industrial espionage, service shopping impressed workers with their subordinate status and their bosses' distrust of them.[56]

A related contradiction was built into skilled selling by the disparity between managers' rhetoric about the importance of training and its actual position within the industry and store hierarchy. Lucinda Wyman Prince and other nationally known training experts accused the NRDGA of treating the Personnel Group "as the step-child of the organization" and of labeling it a relative "nonessential" because most of its practitioners were women. They feared that other functional groups within the NRDGA, notably the Store Managers' Group, were trying to absorb and control their activities. Within individual stores, women in charge of training complained that their activities were not taken seriously, that their departments were the first to be cut when business was bad, and that they were underpaid compared to other store executives. Training directors surveyed by the Bureau of Vocational Information in 1920 commented on the clash between their ideals and the conduct of their stores. A Minneapolis educational director spoke of her difficulty in adjusting to the fact that "present day business is more *competitive* than *altruistic*," and even the training supervisor at the progressive Filene store grumbled about "limitations which may be put upon a person by a management which is lacking vision or social consciousness." The responses of these women showed that they were as imbued with a social-work orientation as welfare directors were with an efficiency point of view. As a personnel manager for an upstate New York store put it, department-store educational work was "the best kind of social service work in the world." While managers reinforced welfare directors' preoccupation with efficiency, they scorned the social-service outlook of training specialists, belittling an activity that failed to have "definite results . . . as when a column of figures may be shown." Many trainers complained that buyers and other executives were obstructionist or contemptuous; the second-class status of training personnel and programs contrasted all too obviously with managers' glowing sermons about the importance of an educated sales force.[57]

The relationship between salespeople and their customers produced a final contradiction in skilled selling. Customers and managers wanted salespeople to be both deferential and authoritative, but the two characteristics clashed rather than complemented each other. The more managers urged their saleswomen to become experts on their merchandise and fashion, the more likely clerks were to resist the demand for deference. At the same time, managers zealously tried to prevent their salespeople from assuming terms of familiarity or equality with their customers, and retail periodicals were filled with outraged accounts of saleswomen who presumed that customers would share their tastes. Typical of the genre was a tale about a saleswoman who offered a collar to a "smart-looking business woman with an air of authority":

> "Here's one that we are selling lots of to stenographers and typewriters, and lots of us girls have bought 'em, too," the girl explained.
> Harriet saw a shade of resentment pass over the woman's face, as she set her lips firmly, dropped the collar and started to turn away.[58]

Incentives for Skilled Selling

Department-store managers bolstered their rhetoric about the joys of professional selling with financial incentives. The notion of incentive was integral to welfare work: while medical care supplied by the store might well lead to greater loyalty and efficiency, it was also a reward in itself. Not so with training, which—especially in its more simplistic forms—offered no inherent benefit to the salesperson. Department-store managers therefore introduced a variety of incentives for skilled selling, borrowing schemes from their brothers in manufacturing.[59]

Predictably, managers disagreed about the appropriate wage for saleswomen. Many wanted only to pay the lowest possible wage; as one retailer testily put it, "Who will dare tell you and me what a green, un-disciplined untrained stubborn girl is worth; and can any thinking person claim that the merchants of this country owe her a living wage?" A sizable minority of merchants continued to feel that cheap help, cheaply paid, was the best basis for a sales force. Those of this school typically hired women because they could pay them less than men, both in absolute terms and as a percentage of the worker's average sales.[60]

In opposition were those who felt that such economies were false in-deed. Warnings that inept selling would persist as long as "merchants and managers continue to select their salesforce by the standard of cheapness instead of efficiency" began in the 1890s. A writer in 1910 saw "unques-tionably a great future before the merchants . . . who will not only train their help, but pay a salary large enough to attract people of ability, of intelligence, and of some breeding." Champions of welfare work and effi-ciency both advocated higher wages, pointing out on the one hand that a decent wage meant being able to live in "moral safety" and on the other that scientific management meant proper training and not wholesale wage-cutting. The managers of Gladding's in Providence testified in 1913 that their $8.00 minimum wage for saleswomen had earned "the confi-dence and goodwill of the women of Southern New England which, by increasing the firm's trade, cut down the relative cost of doing business," while the "far more than ordinary intelligence, interest, and efficiency" of the saleswomen they attracted produced sales "not only actually, but pro-portionately greater than those made by less skilled saleswomen." Such arguments convinced only an enlightened few among department-store managers. In the end, most chose incentive forms of payment rather than a higher overall wage, linking a higher standard of living inextricably to higher productivity.[61]

In fact, all forms of payment for department-store selling were ulti-mately based on productivity. The question was not, therefore, whether selling would be paid on an incentive basis, but how explicit the connec-tion between compensation and sales levels would be. Individual salaries were based on selling cost: a salesperson's net weekly salary as a percent-age of expected weekly sales. The figure varied according to the size of the store—with larger stores usually having lower selling costs—and accord-ing to department—those with high average sales, such as coats and suits, having a lower selling cost than those with low average sales, such as no-tions. Selling costs after the early 1920s—earlier figures are not available—ranged from about 3 percent to about 12 percent, with a storewide average of 6 to 7 percent.[62]

All four of the major types of department-store selling salaries were linked to the store's target selling cost. A clerk on straight salary generally received the selling-cost percentage of her expected or past sales. For example, the new clerk's salary in a department with a selling cost of 5 percent, in which the average employee sold $300 worth of goods in a week, would have been $15. When salespeople were paid solely on commission, the rate was customarily the same as the target selling cost so that selling costs would never be exceeded. In a commission-plus-salary system, the base salary was the selling-cost percentage of the expected minimum sales in the department; commission was paid on all sales at a low rate of perhaps .5 percent. The conservative calculation of the base salary combined with the low commission rate kept salaries at or below the selling cost. In the quota-bonus system the base salary was the same as it would be under the straight salary plan, but salespeople earned a bonus on all sales made above the quota, or expected level of sales. The bonus rate was lower than the target selling cost, although higher than commission rates, assuring that total compensation would remain within the selling cost limits. An executive of Jordan Marsh admirably summed up the common goal of all four plans in describing his store's quota-bonus system in the mid-1920s: "We started it at a time when wages were on the increase and, while we were willing to increase wages, the plan was primarily intended to stimulate sales."[63] Incentive plans in department stores worked much the same as piecework schemes in factories.

Although selling on commission had a long history, the use of all forms of incentive payment became much more widespread during the 1910s. In 1919, well over two-thirds of stores responding to an NRDGA survey had some sort of bonus or commission system, but less than half of those had used it for as long as three years. The association made more systematic studies in 1929 and 1936, and found that in both years 41 percent of reporting stores used a straight salary system. In the 1929 study, salary-plus-commission was the next most frequent method of payment, in 30 percent of all stores, as opposed to quota-bonus, in only half as many stores. In the later study, the ranking was reversed, with 38 percent of all stores using the quota-bonus system and only about a third as many using salary-plus-commission. Straight commission stores were only 4 and 5 percent of the total respectively in each year. What is most interesting, though, is stores' frequent changes in payment methods—the 41 percent paying straight salary in 1929 were by no means the same stores using salary in 1936. The later report concluded that there was no clear trend and that "retail management as a whole is still experimenting with salary methods in a somewhat hit-or-miss fashion."[64]

Store managers endlessly tinkered with salary systems because they worried that incentive payments overemphasized sales totals. Factory managers could simply pay incentives for each item that passed quality control, while retailers had no way of knowing if a sale was satisfactorily conducted. Managers feared that incentives would lead salespeople to slight those who were "just looking," indecisive, or small spenders. In their eagerness to boost their book, salespeople might oversell merchandise, thus increasing the store's proportion of costly returned goods. Moreover, incentive plans rewarded neither the intangibles involved in a sale (such as attitude, demeanor, and helpfulness) nor the performance of other sales floor duties (such as stock work, merchandise display, and cooperation with fellow workers). A writer in the *Dry Goods Economist* spoke for many of his colleagues when he stressed the connection between incentive payments and training: "it is a mistake to introduce the bonus on sales system in a store without educating the sales force to GIVE THE CUSTOMER WHAT HE WANTS."[65]

Both industrial and retail managers were hard put to provide a flow of work steady enough to encourage workers on incentive payment to increase their output, but for retailers the problem was the especially intractable one of assuring a steady flow of customers rather than a flow of materials. Moreover, opportunities to earn incentive pay were unequally distributed throughout the store. Departments along the major lines of traffic flow in the store, those such as toys which had sharp seasonal peaks, and those whose merchandise was especially amenable to suggestion sales offered better-than-average opportunities for incentive earnings. Managers tried to moderate these effects by pegging each incentive system to the variations in trade, but uneven opportunities remained and caused jealousies and discouragement in the sales force.[66]

As early as 1920, department-store managers began to realize that the overall quality of the store management and the degree of the employee's loyalty to the firm increased sales more than either the mechanics or the size of the financial incentive. Still, despite the disadvantages of incentive pay schemes, the majority of department stores studied by the NRDGA in 1929 and 1936 continued to use one form or another. Perhaps part of the explanation for the continued popularity of these plans was the hope that they would spur Depression-era employees to extra effort in the face of declining business.[67]

Retailers supplemented individual incentive pay with special events and contests with prizes for collective rather than individual achievement. Sometimes, the goal was simply to beat a previous record. In 1913, one store awarded weekly banners to the department making the highest percentage increase over its previous year's sales and at the end of the contest period awarded $25 to each salesperson in the department with the best overall record, a substantial prize that was as much as three times the normal weekly salary. One resourceful buyer sold her saleswomen shares in $5000 worth of special merchandise; the company helpfully advanced a week's pay to those who would otherwise have been unable to buy. Profits were distributed in proportion to stock ownership with individuals receiving from $1.25 to $10. The saleswomen eagerly and enthusiastically sold as a group.[68]

An older form of incentive was the premium, dating back at least to the mid-nineteenth century. The premium (abbreviated PM) was a small payment, usually from about five to fifty cents, paid for selling a particular item of old or slow-moving merchandise. Sometimes, especially in the case of small wares and notions, the manufacturer supplied the premium directly to salespeople as a bribe to favor his brand. This practice was particularly prevalent in the late 1900s and 1910s and universally condemned by retailers. Many of the more progressive retailers regarded in-store premiums as equally pernicious; as one writer put it, a salesperson dazzled by the prospect of the reward "could sell a stick of dynamite if a PM were on it." Despite their bad press, premiums persisted, because of the weight of tradition, because buyers strongly supported them, and because managers were convinced that they were indeed an effective if expensive way of selling targeted merchandise. By the late 1930s the debate was not over the elimination of premiums but over how to keep them from turning "into a bribe against the customer's interest, . . . a stimulus to morally dishonest selling." In using premiums instead of outright markdowns in the selling price, the manager gave the salesperson instead of the customer the benefit of the store's bad fortune. In any case, the premium was a last resort where sales training and other more subtle systems of incentive payments failed.[69]

A less immediate but ultimately more consequential incentive was promotion. In general, department stores offered, particularly for women, remarkable opportunities for advancement. The idea of individual advancement was inherent in training: the more training emphasized the general development of selling skill and the less it stressed narrow compliance with rules, the more promotion became its logical consequence. In fact, the admonition to "promote from within" became accepted retail wisdom early in the twentieth century at about the same time as training programs and other incentive systems became entrenched. Stores which provided basic general education along with specific retail training built in opportunities for their sales force that were rare in other American industries. Bamberger's of New Jersey, for example, began in 1920 to pay half of employees' tuition for university courses.[70]

When seen from the top down, the possibilities for promotion looked very good indeed. The Bamberger's tuition assistance plan bore fruit for those who took advantage of it: after eight years, half of them had won promotions. In 1927, one researcher claimed that the average buyer had started as a stock girl or in some other "junior" job at about age sixteen, had moved up to selling within two years, was head of stock the next year, an assistant buyer at twenty-two, and a full-fledged buyer at twenty-seven. The seasonal variations in retailing gave salespeople a special opportunity to prove their mettle as they moved into temporary positions supervising the extras hired for rush periods.[71]

From the point of view of those at the bottom trying to move up, however, the picture at first looks somewhat grimmer. As one writer pointed out, the bundle-wrapper's dream of becoming an assistant buyer or buyer was thwarted by the fact that these jobs were only a bit over 1 percent of the total department-store labor force. In reality the individual's chances of moving up were dramatically increased by the high rate of turnover in stores. Department-store managers were eager to reduce the rate of employee turnover, and indeed one purpose of training and promotion programs was to do just that. Store managers shared with factory managers a worry about the cost of turnover: estimates of the cost of hiring and training a new salesperson ran from $38 to $45 and rose to $100 when other costs such as the lowered efficiency of a new employee were added in. These figures in themselves appear relatively inconsequential, but they totaled a staggering $152,000 for one unfortunate store which hired 4,000 employees in a single year. In addition, department-store managers had to worry about indirect costs of turnover to which their factory counterparts could be relatively indifferent. A salesperson who stayed only briefly could not build up a personal clientele; one who did have a following could take it with her to another store. Store turnover was far more obvious to the public than factory turnover, and customers would suspect a store whose employees moved on too rapidly of harsh or unscrupulous policies.[72]

Studies of department-store labor turnover in 1925 and 1930—again earlier data are lacking—found rates from 67 percent to over 250 percent per year. The author of the later study, far from being appalled, suggested that these rates were surprisingly low for the industry as a whole. Later in the 1930s, however, a shortage of jobs led to dramatically lowered rates of turnover. One major store, the J. L. Hudson Co. of Detroit, found that even junior employees, usually the most transient, held onto their jobs so long that the average age of those in stock and marking positions had risen from seventeen or eighteen to twenty-one or twenty-three. Too little turnover turned out to be as problematic as too much. During the Depression, department-store managers realized how much they had counted on turnover to enable them to infuse departments with fresh blood, avoid stagnation, and satisfy ambitious employees with promotions.[73]

Some stores set up formal channels for promotion. During the 1920s both Filene's and Jordan Marsh ran classes to prepare employees to move up. Between 1929 and 1934, nearly nine of every ten people appointed buyers and assistant buyers at Filene's were products of the promotional course. At Chicago's Wieboldt store, nearly half of the promotions in 1927–28 moved salespeople up to higher positions. J. L. Hudson began a College Training Course in 1929, preparing college-educated people for executive positions. When Depression conditions made it impossible to actually place the trainees in suitable positions, the course was abolished and in 1935 its successor, the Executive Training Squad, was established. This program included half college and half noncollege personnel and was a direct response to in-store resentment toward the threat of an outsiders' monopoly on executive-level positions.[74]

In the end, kinder and more equitable treatment, welfare work, training, and incentives through wages, premiums, and promotion failed to replace the shopgirl with a skilled saleswoman who met department-store managers' complex and contradictory specifications. Four decades of effort to produce a skilled selling force left retail managers nearly as unsatisfied with the performance of the women behind their counters as they had been in 1900. One despairing writer complained that, "In spite of the efforts of training departments, the standard of service remains mediocre. . . . [F]ew clerks can be depended upon really to facilitate an intelligent choice."[75]

Each of the methods for remodeling saleswomen had serious flaws as well as strengths. Attempts to moderate and regularize discipline produced clear rules which governed both managers and workers, but often at the price of thwarting salespeople's initiative. Some managers treated their subordinates in a newly respectful manner, but others persisted in the old retailing pattern of quirky and personalistic supervision. Welfare work could awaken loyalty and help to decrease class-based tensions, but it could also arouse resentment against its paternalism; it could set the mood for efficient selling, but it did little to translate that mood into effective action. Training programs attempted to prescribe selling skill, but that skill flourished on the sales floor where managers' power was limited. They tried to convey an idea of the dignity and professional nature of selling, but too often resorted to cut-rate methods that demeaned the message of skilled selling. Financial incentives might produce higher sales tallies or speed the sale of slow-moving merchandise, but they could also reward overbearing selling tactics that ran roughshod over the customers. Promotion opportunities could raise the quality of saleswomen's performance, but only if the opportunities were numerous enough and only if women were interested in a long-term career.

But the failure of efforts to remake saleswomen went beyond flaws in tactics; the crusade was doomed by more general features of department-store life. First, managers' conduct often belied their rhetoric about selling. While they argued in theory that they must reorient themselves from buying merchandise to selling it, in fact they clung to the buying role because it was more comfortable and more controllable. Selling, and the people who did it, remained solidly on the bottom rungs of the store's prestige ladder. The development of true selling skill would have demanded a transformation in the roles of manager and salesperson alike, a thoroughgoing revision of the store's prestige and reward system. In fact, most managers shied away from the disruptive possibilities of such a change and were satisfied with limited measures to mollify their critics and marginally improve their balance sheets. The price of skilled selling was too high in two senses: wage, training, and welfare-work costs would have been prohibitive, and skilled workers had a dangerously subversive potential.

Second, managers had set themselves a virtually impossible task. They were trying to systematize and rationalize a highly variable type of human interaction, to teach their saleswomen initiative and independence and yet to control the exercise of these characteristics. Saleswomen were to be thinking but also obedient employees; they were to follow store procedure to the last rigorous detail and yet respond creatively to the special opportunities to sell each customer; they were to develop independent judgment but still display unquestioning loyalty to the store; they were to try very hard to sell but not *too* hard. These contradictions are a measure of the difficulties of managing service workers. The endemic variability of retailing was nowhere more troubling: the infinite possibilities of the exchange between salesperson and customer defied standardization and control.

Third, managers were tinkering with two fundamental social categories: class and gender. They tried to modify the class-related personal characteristics of their employees, to narrow the gap between saleswomen on the one hand and managers and customers on the other. But they did so without offering saleswomen either the social or economic power of members of the class they were urged to emulate. They tried to exploit their saleswomen's gender-based personal characteristics, but only dimly understood the difficulties of integrating women's culture with business culture. The women who ran the welfare work and training programs were in a curious halfway position, demanding that women workers render their employers higher-quality service yet urging top management to incorporate altruistic "womanly" values into their competitive, profit-oriented outlook. Department store managers' effort to manipulate class and gender produced enduring tensions in their stores.

Finally, and perhaps most important of all, department store managers took too little account of the fact that their saleswomen had a different agenda than they did. Store executives persisted in underestimating and misunderstanding their saleswomen just as they did their customers. While the changes described in this chapter and in Chapter 2 improved saleswomen's working conditions in many ways, they were also partial and contradictory and thus failed to inspire saleswomen to do their utmost for the firm. In large part, this was because these management practices had little impact on two worlds in which saleswomen but not their bosses participated. The first, the world of women's work, is the subject of the next chapter; the other, the realm of saleswomen's work culture, is the theme of Chapter 6.

Notes

1. Useful perspectives on labor-management relations in this period are: Daniel Nelson, *Managers and Workers: Origins of the New Factory System in the United States, 1880–1920* (Madison, Wis., 1975); Dan Clawson, *Bureaucracy*

and the Labor Process: The Transformation of U.S. Industry, 1860–1920 (New York, 1980); Foster Rhea Dulles and Melvyn Dubofsky, *Labor in America: A History*, 4th ed. (Arlington Heights, Ill., 1984).

2. Harry Braverman, *Labor and Monopoly Capital: The Degradation of Work in the Twentieth Century* (New York, 1974); Richard Edwards, *Contested Terrain: The Transformation of the Workplace in the Twentieth Century* (New York, 1979); Clawson, *Bureaucracy and Labor Process*.

3. Braverman, *Labor and Monopoly Capital*, 371; Edwards, *Contested Terrain*, 179; Clawson, *Bureaucracy and Labor Process*, 229–32.

4. The quotation appears in "Breeds Disloyalty," *DGE*, 67 (22 Mar. 1913), 31; see also "Courtesy an Important Factor," *DGE*, 60 (7 July 1906), 3; "Employee Rating System Maintains White House Personnel's Reputation," *DGE*, 79 (23 May 1925), 13; *Echo*, 45 (3 May 1929).

5. *DGE*, 64 (19 Mar. 1910), 48; "Saleswomen's Appearance," *DGE*, 64 (20 Nov. 1909), 44.

6. "Keeping Store Forces Intact," *Garment Weekly*, 24 Sept. 1921, in Folder 1590, Box 103, Mary Van Kleeck Papers, Sophia Smith Collection, Smith College. G. W. Stoddard, "Giving a Store Home Surroundings," *System*, 15 (June 1909), 666; "A Creed," *DGE*, 68 (31 Jan. 1914), 69; Eva Bassingwaite, "An Analysis of the Women's Coat Department in a Specialty Store" (M.A. thesis, Univ. of Pittsburgh, 1932), 65, 73; Florence L. Luman, "An Analysis of the China and Glassware Department in a Department Store" (M.A. thesis, Univ. of Pittsburgh, 1932), 154; "Help the Customer Buy," *DGE*, 66 (9 Dec. 1911), 43; Orie W. Sherer, "Can Salesmanship Be Taught?" *BNRDGA*, 22 (Feb. 1940), 34. Sarah Smith Malino has noted the congruence between womanly characteristics and the characteristics of a good saleswoman; see her thoughtful discussion in "Faces across the Counter: A Social History of Female Department Store Employees, 1870–1920" (Ph.D. diss., Columbia Univ., 1982), 196–223.

7. Carroll Smith-Rosenberg, "The Female World of Love and Ritual: Relations between Women in Nineteenth-Century America," *Signs*, 1 (Autumn 1975), 1–29; Judith E. Smith, *Family Connections: A History of Italian and Jewish Immigrant Lives in Providence, 1900–1940* (Albany, 1985). By the first decade of the twentieth century, managers had already had an impressive demonstration of the functioning of these networks in the campaigns of the Women's Trade Union League and the National Consumers' League.

8. Joan Kelly, "The Doubled Vision of Feminist Theory: A Postscript to the 'Women and Power' Conference," *Feminist Studies*, 5 (Spring 1979), 216–27.

9. John S. Steele, "General Storekeeping in New York," *Arena*, 22 (Aug. 1899), 179; Anne O'Hagan, "Behind the Scenes in the Big Stores," *Munsey's Magazine*, 22 (Jan. 1900), 533.

10. Lew Hahn, "Salesmanship—The Art of Making Compromise Easy," *BNRDGA*, 21 (July 1939), 25; Melvin W. Cassmore, "Steps Wasted Mean Lost Efficiency in Small Wares Departments," *DGE*, 76 (26 Aug. 1922), 67; "Training in Sales by Suggestion Builds Efficiency," *DGE*, 69 (31 July 1915), 31.

11. "Retail Store Manners", *DGE*, 64 (8 Jan. 1910), 43–44; "In the Next Century," *DGE*, 51 (3 Apr. 1897), 13. There is no comprehensive survey of these

social reform efforts, but Meredith Tax, *The Rising of the Women: Feminist Solidarity and Class Conflict, 1880–1917* (New York, 1980), places them in the context of feminism and working-class struggles.

12. Samuel Hopkins Adams, "The Department Store," *Scribner's Magazine*, 21 (Jan. 1897), 25–27; Steele, "General Storekeeping," 176–77; Eva V. Carlin, "'America's Grandest' in California," *Arena* (22 Sept. 1899), 334; Annie Marion MacLean, "Two Weeks in Department Stores," *American Journal of Sociology*, 4 (May 1899), 729, 735; Mary K. Maule, "What Is a Shop-Girl's Life?" *World's Work*, 14 (Sept. 1907), 9316; Rheta Childe Dorr, "Christmas from behind the Counter," *Independent*, 63 (5 Dec. 1907), 1345.

13. Vice Commission of Chicago, *The Social Evil in Chicago* (Chicago, 1911), 202, 209; John Livingston Wright, "Confusion from Cheapness in Boston," *Arena*, 22 (Aug. 1899), 169–71; Louise DeKoven Bowen, *The Department Store Girl* (Chicago, 1911), 13. W. I. Thomas stressed the increasing importance of short-term or part-time prostitution in connection with sales work; see his *Unadjusted Girl* (1923; rpt. New York, 1967), 119–25.

14. *National Civic Federation Review*, 4 (15 July 1913), 2, 28–31; Mary Van Kleeck, "Working Conditions in New York Department Stores," *Survey*, 31 (11 Oct. 1913), 50–51; "Editorial," *Survey*, 31 (11 Oct. 1913), 185–86; Elizabeth Dutcher, "Department Store Clerks," *Survey*, 31 (20 Dec. 1913), 336–39; S. Nicoll Schwartz, "Civic Federation Report," *Survey*, 31 (17 Jan. 1914), 478–79.

15. Thomas H. Russell, *The Girl's Fight for a Living* (Chicago, 1913), 68–71; State of New York, *Fourth Report of the Factory Investigating Committee* (Albany, 1915), Part 3, 814–15; Mary LaDame, *The Filene Store* (New York, 1930), 148–49.

16. O'Hagan, "Behind the Scenes," 535; "Train the Salespeople," *DGE*, 65 (3 Dec. 1910), 45; A. N. McFadyen, "The Chain Store Learns What Makes a Merchant," *Magazine of Business*, 55 (Mar. 1929), 274.

17. "Merchant May Be at Fault," *DGE*, 76 (9 Sept. 1922), 17; "Breeds Disloyalty," 31; "Service-Value Factor," *DGE*, 66 (2 Mar. 1912), 105; "Courtesy and Quietude," *DGE*, 63 (6 Mar. 1909), 27; "Grouch and Gain," *DGE*, 66 (24 Feb. 1912), 59; "Increase Your Business!" *DGE*, 71 (10 Mar. 1917), 3–4; "When the Boss Sells," *DGE*, 71 (12 May 1917), 61; "Why I Was Fired," *DGE*, 77 (9 Dec. 1922), 13; "Get Your Salespeople to Increase Their Sales," *DGE*, 77 (21 July 1923), 30; "The Best Safeguard," *DGE*, 56 (13 Sept. 1902), 17; H. E. Lovett, "Changes in Store Organization," in Store Managers' Division, NRDGA, *Analysis of Current Management Problems* (New York, 1932), 13; see also "Loss by Lack of Harmony," *DGE*, 60 (24 Feb. 1906), 3.

18. "Robbery in Our Department Stores," *B & DGC*, 29 (31 Mar. 1900), 7–8; "If Caught Pilfering," *DGE*, 59 (1 Apr. 1905), 56; Leslie Woodcock Tentler, *Wage-Earning Women: Industrial Work and Family Life in the United States, 1900–1930* (New York, 1979), 49–50; *Echo*, 1 (Dec. 1902); "Liberality Pays," *DGE*, 58 (17 Sept. 1904), 45.

19. "Wide-Awake Retailing," *DGE*, 49 (19 Jan. 1895), 117; "The Discipline of Freedom," *DGE*, 70 (18 Mar. 1916), 40; "The Boost, Rather than the Knock," *DGE*, 68 (30 May 1914), 37; "Cooperative Spirit," *DGE*, 68 (30 May 1914), 55;

"What San Francisco Store Does for Employees," *DGE*, 69 (28 Aug. 1915), 31; "Waste Is Costly," *DGE*, 60 (3 Feb. 1906), 31; "Encouragement Where Due," *DGE*, 69 (20 Feb. 1915), 48.

20. "'Store Family' Paper Creates Team-Work," *DGE*, 69 (23 Oct. 1915), 47; "No Longer 'Employees,'" *DGE*, 72 (24 Nov. 1917), 5; P. J. Minzesheimer, "'All for One—One for All' Motto of This Store Is Lived Up To," *DGE*, 76 (1 Apr. 1922), 123; J. DeWitt Kreps, "Cash Return from 'Introductory' Selling Proves Its Value," *DGE*, 76 (9 Sept. 1922), 17; "Wide-Awake Retailing," *DGE*, 55 (7 Sept. 1901), 63; "Wide-Awake Retailing," *DGE*, 56 (26 July 1902), 175; "Importance of Good Help," *DGE*, 60 (28 Oct. 1905), 29; "Running a Store Paper," *DGE*, 56 (15 Mar. 1902), 19; James W. Fisk, "The News of the Store," *System*, 22 (Sept. 1912), 294; "American Department Stores Well Represented by Store Papers," *DGE*, 74 (7 Aug. 1920), 99–101; LaVahn Overmyer, "The House Organ as a Tool of Management," *JR*, 13 (Oct. 1937), 84.

21. "The Handling of Help," *DGE*, 57 (6 June 1903), 32; "Instructions to Employees," *DGE*, 57 (13 June 1903), 5; "Built Successful Business," *DGE*, 59 (8 July 1905), 19; "Saleswomen's Appearance," 44; Gertrude H. Sykes, "Dress Regulations in New York Metropolitan Stores," *JR*, 4 (Jan. 1929), 28; *Echo*, 29 (27 June, 11 July, 18 July, 26 Sept., and 3 Oct. 1930 and 27 Mar. 1931); "Employees' Dress Regulations," *BNRDGA*, 10 (Oct. 1928), 457; "Store Instructs High School Students," *DGE*, 69 (13 Mar. 1915), 33; "Uniforms for Employees," *DGE*, 53 (11 Mar. 1899), 17.

22. "Nickel-in-the-Slot Help," *DGE*, 57 (14 Mar. 1903), 43; "Merchant May Be at Fault," 17.

23. "Seats for Female Employees," *DGE*, 60 (21 Apr. 1906), 3; *Women in Oklahoma Industries*, U.S. Department of Labor, Women's Bureau, Bull. No. 48 (Washington, 1926), 62.

24. "To Be Good Salesmen," *DGE*, 64 (26 Feb. 1910), 37; Sidney S. Wilson, "How Retailer Keeps Trade at Home," *DGE*, 67 (1 Mar. 1913), 47.

25. "Where the Schools Fail," *DGE*, 67 (10 May 1913), 27–28.

26. *National Civic Federation Review*, 4 (15 July 1913), 24; "Creating Efficiency among Store Employees," *DGE*, 70 (1 Jan. 1916), 45; "Looking After the Needs of Employees," *DGE*, 70 (8 Jan. 1916), 47; *Echo*, 7 (Jan. 1910), 14 (6 Dec. 1918), 15 (5 Dec. 1919), 21 (25 Jan. 1924), Memorial to T. K. Cory, special issue (25 Aug. 1925), 25 (6 May 1927), 33 (7 Sept. 1934).

27. Samuel Reyburn, "Training for Selling," in Store Managers' Division, NRDGA, *Convention Proceedings, Fourth Annual Convention* (New York, 1927), 102.

28. Nelson, *Managers and Workers*, 79–100; "Discussion: The Consulting Engineer's Point of View," *Bulletin of the Taylor Society*, 8 (Feb. 1923), 36; B. Eugenia Lies, "Improving Department Store Technique," *Bulletin of the Taylor Society*, 10 (Aug. 1925), 187; *Report on Current Store Experience with Employee Testing*, vol. 4 of NRDGA, *Management and Personnel Proceedings—1941* (New York, 1941), 21; Stanley Roth, "The Selection and Placement of Salespeople," in NRDGA, *Confidential Bulletin*, 7 (Mar. 1925), 40. See also Chap. 6.

29. *The New Store of Lord & Taylor* (New York, 1914); "Better Work, Better Play Foster Emporium Spirit," *DGE*, 80 (24 Apr. 1926), 72; "Comfort of Store Employees," *DGE*, 53 (13 May 1899), 4–5; "Share Employees' Troubles," *DGE*, 58 (11 June 1904), 17; "Cosier the Clerk," *DGE*, 59 (27 May 1905), 13; "Store Organizations," *DGE*, 58 (2 Apr. 1904), 20.

30. "Lunchrooms for Clerks," *DGE*, 63 (20 Mar. 1909), 41; "Prepare for Heated Spell," *DGE*, 64 (16 Apr. 1910), 36; "Helping the Employees," *DGE*, 66 (1 June 1912), 27–28.

31. "Teaching the Girl behind the Counter," *Technical World Magazine*, 17 (June 1912), 391; Mary Van Kleeck, "The Social Meaning of Good Management," *Bulletin of the Taylor Society*, 9 (Dec. 1924), 242; Mary Van Kleeck, "Discussion of *Financial Incentives*," *Bulletin of the Taylor Society*, 12 (June 1927), 440–41; Mary Van Kleeck, "Discussion of *Notes on Economic and Social Surveys*," *Bulletin of the Taylor Society*, 13 (Feb. 1928), 34–35; Mary Van Kleeck, "Discussion of *The Work-Week or the Work-Life?*" *Bulletin of the Taylor Society*, 13 (Dec. 1928), 244–45; Samuel Haber, *Efficiency and Uplift* (Chicago, 1964), 61, 69n.

32. "Jordan Marsh Ninth Floor Heralds New Era in Personnel Work," *DGE*, 74 (13 Mar. 1920), 73; Arthur B. Emmons, *Health Control in Mercantile Life* (New York, 1926), 222–24; "Hygiene behind the Counter," *Survey*, 36 (22 July 1916), 434; "Training the Help," *DGE*, 65 (30 Sept. 1911), 41; Budgett Meakin, *Model Factories and Villages* (Philadelphia, n.d.), 59.

33. "Good Work and Practical," *DGE*, 63 (10 July 1909), 39; "Welfare Work's Progress," *DGE*, 65 (11 Feb. 1911), 27; "Jordan Marsh Ninth Floor," 77.

34. Personnel Group, NRDGA, *The Scope of Training for Retail Store Service*, Federal Board for Vocational Education, Trade and Industrial Education Service (Washington, 1929), 4; "Training the Help," *DGE*, 60 (10 Feb. 1906), 3.

35. "Training of Salespeople," *DGE*, 56 (4 Jan. 1902), 17; "School the Salespeople," *DGE*, 59 (7 Jan. 1905), 13; "Instruction for Clerks," *DGE*, 60 (23 June 1906), 24; Helen Rich Norton, *Department-Store Education*, U.S. Department of the Interior, Bureau of Education, Bull. No. 9 (Washington, 1917), 13–35; "Sales Training," *BNRDGA*, 22 (Mar. 1940), 67.

36. Norton, *Department-Store Education*, 12; "Fashion Training for Salespeople of Ready-to-Wear," *JR*, 4 (Apr. 1928), 29; Helen Rich Norton, *A Textbook on Retail Selling* (Boston, 1919), 272–76; Personnel Group, NRDGA, *The World of Fashion* (New York, 1931), I, 9–45; II, 47–61; "Expose Employees to Knowledge," *DSE*, 1 (10 Aug. 1938), 35.

37. Felix Koch, "Making the Customer Happy with Her Purchase, Is Mabley's Selling Keystone," *DGE*, 78 (5 Jan. 1924), 33; Martha Elliott, "The Buyer's Share in Training," *BNRDGA*, 16 (July 1934), 39.

38. George Louis, "The Gentle Art of Subtle Selling," *System*, 20 (Aug. 1911), 149–54; "Two Sales to Each Customer," *System*, 31 (Feb. 1917), 203; Research Bureau for Retail Training, *Personnel Research in Department Stores* (Lancaster, Pa., 1927), 29–31; H. F. Twomey, "How to Raise the Average Sales Check through Productive Advertising and Display," *BNRDGA*, 14 (July 1932),

492; Virginia Thatcher, "Organizing Suggested Sales," *BNRDGA*, 14 (Sept. 1932), 667–70; Mary Curtis, "How Does a Good Saleswoman Sell?" *BNRDGA*, 17 (Aug. 1935), 17–18; A. Grace Walton, "Charting Suggested Sales Awoke Salespeople to Real Chances They'd Overlooked," *DGE*, 76 (20 May 1922), 23.

39. "Only Well-Planned 'Suggestive Selling' Will Do," *DGE*, 74 (2 Jan. 1920), 21; "The Broader Influence of Sales by Suggestion," *DGE*, 69 (7 Aug. 1915), 25; "Training in Sales," 31; "Hints on Store Departmentization," *DGE*, 66 (25 May 1912), 29; "A Thing to Avoid—or Rectify," *DGE*, 68 (18 April 1914), 31–32; "Improved Service," *DGE*, 70 (15 July 1916), 175; Arthur W. Einstein, "Interselling versus Specialization of Sales Efforts," in NRDGA, *Joint Management Proceedings—1940* (New York, 1940), 89–95; Arthur L. Manchee, "Better Service through Selling Flexibility," *BNRDGA*, 23 (Mar. 1941), 66–67.

40. "To Stimulate Selling by Suggestion," *DGE*, 78 (2 Aug. 1924), 9–10; "Post Clerks as to Advertised Specials," *DGE*, 62 (5 Sept. 1908), 24; "Ads and Salespeople," *DGE*, 72 (5 Jan. 1918), 29; George Louis, "What's the Matter with Distribution?" *System*, 21 (Feb. 1912), 160.

41. Lynn Sumner, "Retailing by Wire," *System*, 15 (Mar. 1909), 280–81; Henry A. Breithaupt, "Putting Personality into a Store," *System*, 48 (Aug. 1925), 222–24; Julius Goldman, "Salespeople Today Should Have a Clientele," *DGE*, 82 (12 May 1928), 15, 29; "Hello,—Mrs. Jones?" *DGE*, 82 (12 May 1928), 14, 29; Caroline Spalding, "Case Studies in Training," *BNRDGA*, 18 (Feb. 1936), 87.

42. "Wide-Awake Retailing," *DGE*, 48 (27 Apr. 1893), 47; "Training of Salespeople," 17; "Help Should Be Trained," *DGE*, 65 (12 Aug. 1911), 32; "Let Employees Advance," *DGE*, 66 (16 Mar. 1912), 60; LaDame, *Filene Store*, 390–91; "One Cause of Success," *DGE*, 57 (23 May 1903), 26; Ralph M. Hower, *History of Macy's of New York, 1858–1919* (Cambridge, Mass., 1943), 379; Margaret L. Lovell, *The Personnel Policies of Pennsylvania Department Stores*, Pennsylvania Department of Labor and Industry, Bureau of Women and Children, Spec. Bull. No. 13 (Harrisburg, 1926), 6, 29; Research Bureau for Retail Training, *Personnel Research*, 1–2, 16; Josephine Boyle, "Trend in Retail Training," *JR*, 14 (Oct. 1938), 86–90 (quotation on 86); O. Preston Robinson and James C. Edwards, "The Current Status of Retail Training," *JR*, 15 (Oct. 1939), 69–74.

43. Norton, *Department-Store Education*, 8. This attitude persisted; see Personnel Group, NRDGA, *Scope of Training for Retail Store Service*, 2.

44. Lucinda Wyman Prince to Ruth Fagundus, 12 Mar. 1931, Records of the Prince School, Simmons College, Box V, File 74; Elizabeth B. Butler, "Training for Salesmanship," in Academy of Political Science in the City of New York, *The Economic Position of Women* (New York, 1910), 57–58; Norton, *Department-Store Education*, 7–47, 65–66; Samuel H. Halle to Lucinda Wyman Prince, 9 Apr. 1926, Records of the Prince School, Simmons College, Box V, File 67; Files "Finance—Simmons Affiliation" and "Agreement between NRDGA and Simmons College concerning the Prince School," Records of the Prince School, Simmons College, Box I; NRDGA, *Twenty-Five Years of Retailing, 1911–1936* (New York, 1936), 58–59.

45. "City Takes a Hand," *DGE*, 62 (10 Oct. 1908), 39; Butler, "Training for Salesmanship," 58–60; "Retail Salesmanship," *DGE*, 63 (28 Aug. 1909), 25; "Stores and the Schools," *DGE*, 67 (5 Apr. 1913), 2; "Salesmanship Instruction in Public Schools," *DGE*, 68 (10 Jan. 1914), 27–28; "Salesmanship School," *DGE*, 64 (22 Jan. 1910), 43; "Salesmanship School," *DGE*, 64 (9 July 1910), 45; "For Vocational Training," *DGE*, 72 (20 July 1918), 3–4; Jay D. Runkle, "Get Due Benefit of Public Schools," *DGE*, 73 (6 Sept. 1919), 81, 85; "School for Store Help," *DGE*, 56 (27 Sept. 1902), 44; "Training the Help," *DGE*, 60 (10 Feb. 1906), 3; Paul A. Nystrom, "With the Help of Our Government," *BNRDGA*, 19 (Feb. 1937), 110–12; Paul A. Mertz, "Retailers Prepare to Meet the Call for Assistance in Vocational Training," *BNRDGA*, 19 (Aug. 1937), 14–16, 69–71; C. C. Coulter, "Salesmanship Taught in Public Schools," *RCIA*, 34 (Feb. 1927), 3–7 (quotation appears on 4); C. C. Coulter, "More about Salesmanship and the Public Schools," *RCIA*, 34 (Sept. 1927), 1–4.

46. "Retailing in the Universities," *JR*, 3 (Oct. 1929), 27–28; "Stores and Universities Cooperate on Trial Training Projects," *BNRDGA*, 19 (May 1937), 64; "Retail Selling Teachers' Class," *DGE*, 73 (9 Aug. 1919), 57; Lucinda Wyman Prince to Lew Hahn, 5 Mar. 1926, Records of the Prince School, Simmons College, Box V, File 67; Research Bureau for Retail Training, *Personnel Research*, 1–2.

47. "NRDGA Launches a Broader Personnel Service," *BNRDGA*, 10 (Mar. 1928), 98.

48. James H. Greene, "Are You Using the Department Store Training Department?" *Printer's Ink*, 138 (27 Jan. 1927), 17–20; "Sales Training," 68.

49. "Tell Your Salespeople," *DGE*, 65 (26 Aug. 1911), 53; Elliott, "Buyer's Share," 39–40.

50. "Wide-Awake Retailing," *DGE*, 55 (5 Oct. 1901), 63.

51. "Wide-Awake Retailing," *DGE*, 48 (18 Mar. 1893), 55; "Suggestions by Clerks," *DGE*, 58 (16 Apr. 1904), 19; Werrett Wallace Charters, *How to Sell at Retail* (Boston, 1922), vii; "Goods Not in Stock," *DGE*, 56 (1 Mar. 1902), 17; "A Reminder to Clerks," *DGE*, 63 (9 Oct. 1909), 109; *Echo*, 1 (Oct. 1902), 5 (June 1907), 15 (17 July 1919); "Knowing the 'Why' of Each Sale Lost Will Help to Increase the Number of Satisfied Customers," *DGE*, 76 (11 Mar. 1922), 109; "Want Slip System Will Repay Effort," *DGE*, 78 (26 July 1924), 11; "What Happens to the Want Slips in Your Store?" *DGE*, 79 (5 Sept. 1925), 18; Margaret Holbrook Titcomb, "Selling to the Selling Force," *DGE*, 80 (19 Dec. 1925), 13.

52. Lucinda Wyman Prince to Ruth Fagundus, 12 Mar. 1931, Records of the Prince School, Simmons College, Box V, File 74; *Echo*, 4 (Dec. 1906); "Store Employees as Actors," *DGE*, 70 (18 Dec. 1915), 7; *Echo*, 23 (8 May 1925); Julia Houston Railey, *Retail and Romance* (Boston, 1926), 29; Helen R. Norton, "Summaries of Convention Personnel Sessions," *BNRDGA*, 17 (July 1935), 40, 84.

53. "General Type of Employee Must Be Raised, Charters Asserts," *DGE*, 74 (28 Feb. 1920), 17; "The Merchant and His Employees," *DGE*, 63 (21 Nov. 1908), 49; *Echo*, 1 (Aug. 1902); *Report of the United States Commissioner of Education, 1916* (Washington, 1917), I, 173 (I am indebted to Janice Weiss for

this quotation from Prince); "Teaching, and Training," *DGE*, 71 (10 Feb. 1917), 4.

54. "On Deck, There!" *DGE*, 58 (26 Nov. 1904), 15; Mary C. Clendenin, "Know Your Merchandise and Stop Losing Sales," *BNRDGA*, 11 (Oct. 1925), 10; and "Self-Training for Vivid Selling," *DSE*, 2 (10 May 1939), 1. See also Edward A. Filene, "How a Buyer Can Answer: When? How Much? What?" *System*, 44 (Dec. 1923), 817; Louis Kirstein, "A Problem in Management," *System*, 43 (June 1923), 754; Hahn, "Salesmanship," 25; Richard E. Steed, "An Answer to the Problem of Better Personnel," *BNRDGA*, 7 (July 1925), 24; "Training of Salespeople," 17.

55. Agnes S. Cronin, "Ready-Made Responses for Salespeople," *BNRDGA*, 15 (Aug. 1933), 68–70; O. Preston Robinson, "Customer Types in the Teaching of Salesmanship," *JR*, 13 (Dec. 1937), 125–27; "What Selling Service Means," *BNRDGA*, 16 (June 1934), 27–28, 80; "Magic Words That Sell," *DSE*, 1 (25 July 1938), 6; William Robins, "Choose Your Words," *DSE*, 1 (10 Aug. 1938), 2 and (25 Aug. 1938), 3; O. Preston Robinson, "The Challenge of Over-the-Counter Salesmanship," *JR*, 15 (Feb. 1939), 8–9; Alice Resch, "Open to Buy—That's Your Customer,' *DSE*, 2 (10 Sept. 1939), 2.

56. Helen R. Norton, "Service Shopping in the Light of Today," *BNRDGA*, 15 (Jan. 1933), 96, 124; Georgia Wittich, "Constructive Uses of the Shopping Report," in NRDGA, *Joint Management Proceedings—Concurrent Conventions* (New York, 1934), 15; Nancy L. Larson, "Service Shopping and How It Is Done," *Retail Bureau Bulletin*, 9 (Jan. 1936), 24.

57. Katherine J. Dennis to Lucinda Wyman Prince, 3 June 1929, Records of the Prince School, Simmons College, Box V, File 73; Bess Bloodworth to Lucinda Wyman Prince, 4 May 1933, Lucinda Wyman Prince to Bess Bloodworth, 5 May 1933, Records of the Prince School, Simmons College, Box V, File 71; Lucinda Wyman Prince to Genevieve Gordon, 21 Nov. 1932, Records of the Prince School, Simmons College, Box V, File 76; Bureau of Vocational Information questionnaires, Schlesinger Library, Box 5, File 72, Questionnaires 6, 37, 40, 158; File 73, Questionnaires 6, 12, 19, 24, 25, 32, 33, 45, 47, 55, 59, 63, 69, 89, 109, 120, and 125. The quotations appear in questionnaires 59, 33, 125, and 12.

58. "Told to the Salespeople," *DGE*, 67 (8 Mar. 1913), 95.

59. On the use of incentive payments in manufacturing, see Nelson, *Managers and Workers*, 51–54, 72–78.

60. *Survey*, 29 (15 Mar. 1913), 842; *BNRDGA*, 2 (July 1913), 3; Alphonsus P. Haire, "The Deadline of Retail Profit," *System*, 19 (Mar. 1911), 244–51; Philip J. Reilly, "Reduction of Waste in Operating Departments of Large Retail Stores," *Bulletin of the Taylor Society*, 8 (Feb. 1923), 32.

61. "Parrot Talk," *DGE*, 49 (6 Apr. 1895), 65; "The Salesforce Payroll," *DGE*, 64 (3 Sept. 1910), 35; "Discussion," 35–37; "Store's Minimum Wage," *DGE*, 67 (15 Mar. 1913), 57. See also "Does Cheap Help Pay?" *B & DGC*, 29 (13 Jan. 1900), 11; "Salaries," *DGE*, 64 (24 Sept. 1910), 79; "The Clerk's Difficulties," *DGE*, 64 (22 Oct. 1910), 61; LaDame, *Filene Store*, 148–52, 159–60; Ernest C. Hastings, "Employee Shares New Responsibility in the Wage Problem Now," *DGE*, 75 (12 Mar. 1921), 157; "As to Voluntary 'Raises,'" *DGE*, 63

(1 May 1909), 27; "The Salary Problem," *DGE*, 70 (11 Nov. 1916), 39–40; "Wage Cuts Should Be Last Resort," *DGE*, 79 (17 Jan. 1925), 9–10; "How Well Known Department Store Figures View Salespeople's Status," *DGE*, 80 (20 Mar. 1926), 20–21.

62. Malcolm P. McNair, "What Can a Retailer Do to Reduce His Costs of Doing Business?" *DGE*, 78 (24 Nov. 1923), 17; Philip J. Reilly, "The Bases Used by Department Stores in Establishing Wage Rates," *Annals of the American Academy*, 100 (Mar. 1922), 31; NRDGA, *Report of the Commission for the Study of Wage Problems* (New York, 1920), 29.

63. H. D. Gillis, "What Our Quota Bonus Plan Does for Us," *System*, 45 (Jan. 1924), 84.

64. "Spread of Bonus Plans," *DGE*, 74 (6 Dec. 1919) 6; NRDGA, *Report of Commission for Study of Wage Problems*, 3–4, 42; Store Management Group, NRDGA, *Trends in Compensating Salespeople* (New York, 1938), 21–23.

65. "Does the Sales Bonus Pay?" *DGE*, 80 (27 Feb. 1926), 86. See also "Salaries or Commissions," *DGE*, 58 (9 July 1904), 47; "Help on Commission," *DGE*, 59 (1 Apr. 1905), 53; "The Percentage Stimulus," *DGE*, 60 (2 June 1906), 28; "Holiday-Period Bonuses," *DGE*, 72 (21 Sept. 1918), 3–4: NRDGA, *Report of Commission for Study of Wage Problems*, 43–46; Frank H. Neely, "Special Incentives for Increasing Production," *BNRDGA*, 13 (June 1931), 358–59, 377; Benjamin H. Bonnar, "A Quota-Bonus System for Salespeople," *BNRDGA*, 18 (July 1936), 44; B. S. White, "Effect of Compensation Methods on Management Operation and Employee Production," in Store Management Division, NRDGA, *Compensation Methods and Selling Costs*, Report No. 3 of *Store Management Convention Proceedings* (New York, 1936), 14; Store Management Group, *Trends in Compensating Salespeople*, 9–15.

66. A. E. Simmons, "A Bonus Plan That Encourages Year-Round Work," *System*, 45 (Apr. 1924), 490–91.

67. Store Management Group, *Trends in Compensating Salespeople*, 16, 19; NRDGA, *Report of Commission for Study of Wage Problems*, 43, 46; Anne Bezanson and Miriam Hussey, *Wage Methods and Selling Costs* (Philadelphia, 1930), 346–49; Robert W. Pogue, "A Bonus Plan That Cuts Costs," *System*, 37 (Jan. 1920), 61; Bonnar, "Quota-Bonus System," 44.

68. "Timely Welfare-Work Hint," *DGE*, 65 (19 Nov. 1910), 35; George Louis, "Paying More than Wages," *System*, 25 (June 1914), 604; "For Increasing Sales," *DGE*, 67 (25 Jan. 1913), 35; "Buyer's Novel Scheme," *DGE*, 63 (27 Feb. 1909), 59.

69. "Subsidizing the Clerk," *DGE*, 64 (4 Dec. 1909), 27; "Testimony of Four Hundred Retailers," *DGE*, 66 (11 May 1912), 39, 41; "Would Replace PMs with Bonuses on Sales," *DGE*, 69 (29 May 1915), 29; "Wide-Awake Retailing," *DGE*, 56 (26 July 1902), 175; "About the PM Policy," *DGE*, 58 (6 Aug. 1904), 45; "Department Management," *DGE*, 55 (9 Mar. 1901), 15; "Do PMs Really Pay?" *DGE*, 53 (10 June 1899), 18; "The Essence of a Good PM," *DSE*, 1 (10 Nov. 1938), 31.

70. "For Better Service," *DGE*, 64 (25 June 1910), 31; Clarice Young, "Bring-

ing the University into the Store," *BNRDGA*, 10 (May 1928), 228, 238; "Promotion for Merit," *DGE*, 60 (14 July 1906), 44; "Promote the Deserving," *DGE*, 62 (12 Sept. 1908), 40: "Don't Stifle Ambition," *DGE*, 67 (8 Nov. 1913), 34.

71. Young, "Bringing the University into the Store," 238; Henry Kitson, "Developing a New Interviewing Technique," *BNRDGA*, 9 (Oct. 1927), 206; "Holiday Extras," *DGE*, 76 (2 Sept. 1922), 14.

72. Anna E. Nicholes, "Wage-Earning Women in Stores and Factories," *Survey*, 26 (30 Sept. 1911), 907–9; "High Cost of Hiring," *DGE*, 70 (23 Sept. 1916), 47; O. Preston Robinson, "Labor Turnover in New York Metropolitan Stores," *JR*, 6 (Oct. 1930), 88; "Wide-Awake Retailing," *DGE*, 55 (28 Sept. 1901), 63; "Wide-Awake Retailing," *DGE*, 55 (5 Oct. 1901), 63.

73. O. E. Klingaman, "The Need for Better Control of Labor Turnover," *BNRDGA*, 7 (Apr. 1925), 36–37; Robinson, "Labor Turnover," 89; Betty Berkebile, "Today's Problem of Employee Promotion," *BNRDGA*, 17 (July 1935), 41.

74. George D. Halsey, "Personnel Work in Retail Stores," in *Proceedings of the National Conference of Social Work* (Chicago, 1923), 124; Mary L. Collins, "When Day Is Done—The Evening Class," *BNRDGA*, 16 (Jan. 1934), 52–53; Gladys Tobin, "The Promotion Plan," *BNRDGA*, 11 (June 1929), 337–38; Berkebile, "Today's Problem," 42.

75. Collins, "When Day Is Done," 99.

5

"The Cinderella of Occupations": Department-Store Saleswomen and the World of Women's Work

In 1905, having left school to support her ailing parents and six siblings, sixteen-year old Bessie Harrison became a $4-a-week duster in the china department of a San Francisco department store. Five months later she began selling for $8 per week. Ambition, acumen, and good luck brought her, within a decade, a buyer's position at twenty times her starting salary. Harrison's career embraced the diverse possibilities of department-store life; the people inhabiting this world were no less varied. Immigrant daughters and a sprinkling of society women, grammar-school dropouts and college graduates, middle-aged widows and teenage girls, Christmas extras and lifelong saleswomen, part-timers and full-timers, all had a place in the department store selling force, which in turn was a microcosm of the increasingly varied and complex arena of women's paid work.[1]

Between 1890 and 1940, dramatic population increases, changes in industrial organization and technology, and the growth of cities created new types of jobs while increasing the demand for women in more traditional occupations. The shift from home to factory production accelerated during this half-century, drawing more and more women into assembly and machine-tending jobs. The growing size and more complex organization of business firms produced a demand for legions of clerical workers. A burgeoning commercial sector mobilized armies of saleswomen and stock people. A service sector—in which workers were divorced from the production of goods—was born and almost from the beginning sought the relatively cheap and supposedly docile labor of women. Simultaneously, women at the other end of the economic spectrum flocked to colleges and universities in search of education and training for professional careers. Domestic service, while still the single most numerous women's occupation through 1940, engaged a declining number and proportion of working women. While the dominant cultural prescription during this period demanded that women work for wages outside the home only when unmarried and childless, more and more married women entered the labor force. Economic necessity pushed most of them to seek jobs, sometimes as a result of a changing calculus within the family economy: the older pattern of mothers staying in the home while their children went out to work was being replaced by one in which mothers earned wages so that their children might remain in school. "Working women" or "working mothers" were hardly new during this period, but they were certainly more numerous and their paid labor was visible in new ways as it moved out of the home and into the industrial/commercial economy of the nation's large cities.[2]

At least two features linked the working lives of these women, from the millions of factory workers to the handful of women professionals. First, their work took place for the most part in a sex-segregated atmosphere. As Valerie Kincade Oppenheimer and Alice Kessler-Harris have noted, women have consistently been concentrated in certain occupations rather than being spread evenly or randomly throughout the labor force. In 1930, for example, nine out of ten women workers were in occupations in which they were overrepresented—that is, in which their proportion was greater than women's proportion in the total labor force. Sex segregation was as much a part of the lives of candymakers as it was of social workers. Second, women were paid less than men. The exact ratio of women's earnings to men's has varied according to region, occupation, and time, but the rule has been virtually invariable: women earned less, both when women and men did identical jobs and when they performed separate but comparable work. The sex-based wage differential weighed heavily on the woman college professor, the female government clerk, and the cash girl alike.[3]

Department-store selling was no exception to these generalizations about women's paid work. First, the field expanded dramatically. Until 1930, the categories of saleswomen and female clerks in stores grew even more rapidly than the female labor force as a whole. In 1890, fewer than one in fifty working women was a saleswoman; in 1940, one in every sixteen was. Second, selling in general was a highly feminized occupation. Women were already overrepresented among salespeople in 1880, with a

Fig. 14. The Sex-Based Wage Differential

"But sister and I reckon that our salaries together
are equal to one man's"

Collier's, 48 (16 Mar. 1912), 16. Original in John Hay Library, Brown University.

share in the occupation half again as large as their proportions in the total labor force; a similar degree of overrepresentation persisted through the next sixty years. In 1890, two in every nine salespeople were women; in 1940, two in every five were. Within department stores, the preponderance of women was even greater: they made up from half to almost nine-tenths of total employees and a similar proportion of the sales force. Department-store saleswomen's immediate work groups were even more sex-segregated than either their occupation or their industry. Men were generally confined to men's clothing, sporting goods, rug, and appliance departments, while women sold most other items; among the few departments in which men and women sold together were silks, shoes, and men's furnishings. Third, women earned less than their male counterparts. The departments staffed by men, particularly the "big ticket" ones, paid higher base rates and often added a hefty commission. Saleswomen's earnings ranged from 42 to 63 percent of salesmen's. The disparity between men's and women's earnings in stores was even greater than that in many other industries; evidence from the 1920s and 1930s suggests that in clerical work and various branches of the textile and apparel industries the sex-based wage differential was narrower than in selling. The sex-segregation of selling departments may have dulled saleswomen's resentment at this wage gap, but one woman who sold shoes alongside men vented her anger to an Iowa labor department investigator in 1886: "I don't get the salary the men clerks do, although this day I am six hundred sales ahead! Call this justice? But I have to grin and bear it, because I am so unfortunate as to be a woman." [4]

Beyond these common features lay the peculiar characteristics of department-store selling: its relation to other women's occupations in pay, hours, and working conditions; its social status; and the types of people who chose and were chosen to sell. The three were obviously connected, but they must be approached from different directions, each with its peculiar perils. The ranking of sales work on quantitative measures and the demographics of those who did it can be compiled from investigations of state and federal officials and of socially concerned writers and activists. Primarily statistical, this material may be used with caution to construct a profile of selling and saleswomen. Unfortunately, these studies rarely provide strictly comparable information; even the very useful Women's Bureau state reports of the 1920s and 1930s are not exactly parallel. Yet more troublesome is the problem of classification: department-store saleswomen often fall within a larger category. "Women in trade," for example, includes those in tiny shops and in five-and-ten-cent stores along with those in department stores. "Saleswomen," unless otherwise qualified, poses the same problems. "General mercantile," the category used most frequently by the Women's Bureau, excluded small shops and five-and-ten-cent stores but included workers of all kinds—workroom, office, and other non-selling employees—along with saleswomen. In most studies, department-store saleswomen were the most numerous group within any of these categories and thus the averages are weighted toward their experience. The social status of department-store selling, on the other hand, is a qualitative matter and bits of relevant evidence come from a variety of sources including films and novels as well as studies and articles directly focused on women's work or department stores. They present a vivid if highly unsystematic view of saleswomen's conception of their place in the world and rarely allow them to speak directly as their employers did through the management literature.

The evidence, both qualitative and quantitative, suggests that the occupation of department-store saleswoman was an intricate patchwork of the best and the worst, the most deadening and the most challenging, the worst-paid and the most lucrative to be found in the world of women's paid employment. The experiences of most saleswomen fell between these extremes: their advantages over other workers were marginal rather than dramatic and were to some degree offset by the peculiar disadvantages of their occupation. The extremes, however, gave a distinctive flavor to department-store selling; the director of the Research Bureau for Retail Training unwittingly captured this duality when he complained that department-store selling was regarded as "the Cinderella of occupations." At one pole, toil, tedium, and poverty; at the other, glamour, fulfillment, and financial security.[5]

A profile of department-store selling which places it, however imperfectly, in the world of women's paid labor can illuminate the extraordinarily complex process by which the department-store selling force was shaped. The process began as some decided to apply for certain jobs and not for others; the second phase took place as managers chose from the pool of applicants. The two were, of course, not completely separate, for workers chose to apply to department stores partly on the basis of what they knew about managers' past hiring patterns, and managers selected their saleswomen knowing what sorts of people they could expect to find in their employment offices. Workers and managers carry in their heads a cultural map of the work world which balkanizes it into enclaves according to sex, age, ethnicity, race, and class. But this map cannot predict what any individual will do for a living. Virtually no woman job-seeker between 1890 and 1940 had a statistician's grasp of the opportunities nor, even if she had, would she have based her decision on quantifiable variables alone. Her personal needs and inclinations guided her along with gossip about good jobs, good bosses, good workplaces, and available openings that circulated in family, neighborhood, and peer networks. Still, the profile gets us beyond both managerial prescriptions and popular stereotypes, helping us to understand who saleswomen were and what their working lives were like and to assess the impact of managers' concern for skilled selling on the conditions of sales work.

Earnings: Snapshots

Virtually all wage-earning women in the years between 1880 and 1940 shared the grim sisterhood of a low return for their labor. As Leslie Woodcock Tentler has pointed out, women's low wages were in no way accidental, but the result of close calculation by employers determined to minimize their labor costs. Yet, despite the popular image of the exploited shopgirl, saleswomen in fact had relatively good financial prospects in comparison to other women workers. The simplest method of illustrating this point is through comparisons at different points in time. Appendix C summarizes these snapshot views, presenting forty-six opportunities to compare saleswomen's earnings with those either of all women workers or of women workers in specific sectors. In over two-thirds, or thirty-one, of the studies women in stores earned more than women in manufacturing or all women workers. Saleswomen measured up so well partly because few of the studies included the most highly paid women's occupations in the clerical and professional categories. Approximately half of the studies done before 1920 and during the 1930s and over three quarters of the 1920s investigations found saleswomen to be better paid than other women studied. Department-store managers during the 1920s apparently backed up training for skilled selling with more generous wages; although their concern for selling remained high during the 1930s, economic conditions required payroll cutbacks, as we shall see later.[6]

Wages in all fields varied widely from time to time and place to place, but the patterns of variation in retailing were in two respects distinct from those in other fields. Nationally, women's earnings in retailing varied less than those in manufacturing. Women's Bureau studies of women's earnings in thirteen states showed, for example, that the highest state median in general mercantile stores was less than 50 percent above the lowest, while in manufacturing the highest median was about 130 percent above the lowest. Because women's earnings in retailing were more uniform throughout the country than those in manufacturing, the relative position of saleswomen depended in large part on the local mix of industries and the prevailing level of manufacturing wages. Saleswomen in the South benefited most from this situation: twelve of the thirteen states in which general mercantile stores paid better than any other industry were southern or border states. On the other hand, the earnings gap between urban and rural stores was greater than that between country and city factories, reflecting the fact that shirt factories in a southern village and a northern city were more similar than the small-town general store and the urban palace of consumption. Comparatively speaking, then, saleswomen in the South and those who migrated to cities benefited the most from the prevailing patterns of variation in women's earnings.[7]

Certain industries generally offered higher earnings than stores provided. Beauty shops, various branches of the needle trades, tobacco processing, and printing and publishing almost always paid better than stores; firms manufacturing metal and electrical products, shoes, chemicals and drugs, optical goods and scientific instruments, glass bottles and containers, and pottery sometimes did. Laundries and five-and-ten-cent stores virtually always paid lower wages than department stores. Some of these differences appear to be random, but others have clear causes. Laundry workers suffered from a race differential in pay; this was one of the few industries that employed large numbers of Black women. Five-and-ten-cent store workers were penalized for their youth, usually being the youngest and the shortest-term workers of all. Women in printing and publishing and in the needle trades were probably more highly unionized than any other group of women during the 1920s and 1930s, and their wages reflected this fact.[8]

Within the realm of white-collar work, clerical workers consistently earned more than saleswomen, and the gap apparently widened over time. In 1914, Ohio clerical workers earned about one-quarter more than store workers; in 1922–23 they earned half again as much. If this pattern prevailed elsewhere, perhaps selling lost cachet among white-collar workers even as it stood in greatest advantage to manufacturing occupations. Clerical work had long enjoyed greater prestige than selling because it paid more, required more education, and involved less contact with the public, but selling had provided a more readily available white-collar job for the untrained woman. By 1930, the working class in at least one city had attuned its family strategies to the greater rewards of clerical work. Explaining why so few saleswomen appeared in a study of South Bend, Indiana, the Women's Bureau noted: "the canvass was concentrated in sections where industrial workers predominated. In the families in these sections many factory employees were interviewed and also many young clerical workers, daughters who had the advantage of a business education; but there were few saleswomen." These families invested in their daughters' education with the hope of a higher return in earnings and—possibly—prestige than if they had sent uneducated daughters to work in the city's stores.[9]

Steady Work: Department Stores' Two-Track System

Saleswomen's long-term earning possibilities far overshadowed their short-term advantages over other women workers. Most important of all, women in retailing enjoyed steady, full-time work. They experienced the nagging fear of seasonal layoffs and short time far less intensely than their sisters in manufacturing and no more frequently than women in clerical work. As early as 1885, Massachusetts saleswomen were only one-half as likely as all gainfully employed women to have been out of work at some time during the year; during the 1920s, Women's Bureau studies showed that eight or nine of every ten women in general mercantile stores worked a full year, compared to between four and eight in every ten in laundries and between one-quarter and one-half in manufacturing. Other studies showed similar results.[10]

Steady work in department stores was, however, maintained only at the expense of a corps of part-timers; managers had created a two-track system. One group of employees worked all or most of every day that the store was open. Another, called extras or contingents, worked either a fixed part-time schedule or came in for special sales and rush seasons. The former were the full-time employees of whom the studies speak, the core staff who could count on steady work because the latter were locked into part-time slots. A wage differential underlined the difference between part-timers and full-timers: part-time saleswomen usually earned about 10 percent less for the same amount of work. The combination of short hours and lower rates of pay meant that part-timers earned a meager wage indeed. In 1916, for example, more than half the extras in

Boston earned less than $3 per week while better than eight in ten of the regular saleswomen earned $8 or more; a group of studies in the 1930s found that part-timers earned from one-eighth to four-tenths of full-timers' median salaries.[11]

Department-store managers had created the two-track system as a way of adjusting their operations to the changing rhythms of retailing. They began in the early years of the century to recruit a corps of contingents who could provide reasonably high quality part-time and peak-season labor. Stores trained extras, kept careful records of their sales performance and deportment, and rewarded the more efficient with longer working hours. Firms apparently had little trouble developing a reliable force of extras and some maintained waiting lists of eager applicants. The arrangement seemed to appeal to two types of women. The first included those for whom part-time store work, ill-paid though it was, provided a welcome supplement to family income or income from other sources. Some of these were piecing together a living from bits of part-time or temporary work; some were moonlighting; others pooled earnings with their families. The second group wanted full-time store work and hung on as extras in the hope of breaking into the regular selling staff. Harriet A. Byrne, writer of the Women's Bureau report on West Virginia, suggested that the latter was the more numerous group, noting that "these workers desire full-time employment and are eking out a meager existence on what they earn for part time." Meager indeed, at $2.75 per week. But department-store managers preferred those who were content with their lot as extras and not likely to make troublesome demands for full-time positions. Some stores, Lord & Taylor among them, had a firm policy of hiring only those for whom wage-earning was not a necessity.[12]

By the 1920s, managers had focused their recruitment efforts on two groups—students and married women—who could provide respectability and high-quality service. The manager of a Fort Wayne, Indiana, department store explained in a trade periodical his store's method of recruiting students. The firm's original dragnet method of hiring had brought in "a pretty bad bunch" who sold only $50 on a Saturday and caused trouble with "petty thieving, rough talking, and all that sort of thing." The store then sought out high school students, but soon found that not all of them were suitable. One group generally sold $100 on a Saturday, came from large families "of the same general class as retail salespeople," and needed their salaries badly. The less successful sold only $25–50, came from affluent families, considered themselves "above the work," and had taken the job for a lark or to earn money for some special treat. The canny manager devised a questionnaire about family background and personal values to separate the latter from the more reliable sorts. Numerous other stores sought out students, whether for Saturdays, year-round, or for holiday seasons.[13]

While students offered a plentiful but transient source of labor, married women were a more stable group and fit managers' ideal of a "high type" of employee who would content herself with earning pin money during her idle afternoons. Students were ideal Saturday and vacation-replacement workers, well-suited to departments not requiring particular skill or maturity. Married women worked the busiest mid-day hours and often turned in impressive sales totals in the more prestigious departments. Managers assumed that both were docile employees: their primary identities lay elsewhere, and they had limited financial requirements. The scant evidence about the pool of part-timers suggests that managers were indeed successful in recruiting workers who could afford to—or who had no choice but to—content themselves with part-time work. A 1915 survey of Boston extra saleswomen showed that nearly three-quarters were students, married women, or women who for some reason could not accept full-time work; a Milwaukee store reported a similar distribution during the late 1930s. Many of the Milwaukee women had worked as contingents in the same store for as long as twenty years.[14]

The proportion of part-time jobs in retailing increased from 1900 to 1940, although the degree of reliance on part-timers varied significantly from time to time and firm to firm. A 1912 study of Massachusetts saleswomen showed that from less than a tenth to over half of a store's total female employees worked short time, while a study of Ohio working women from 1914 to 1924 found that no more than two-thirds to three-quarters of saleswomen could hope to find year-round employment. During the Depression-era drive to cut costs, the number of part-timers soared—according to one estimate increasing from 8 to 20 percent between 1930 and 1932. Even then, individual stores differed in their approaches. In Ohrbach's Newark store, the regular sales force stayed almost exactly the same from 1931 to 1932, but the number of female extras dropped by one-third. At Bamberger's in the same city, by contrast, the regular force dropped by over a third while the number of part-time workers increased dramatically.[15]

These disparate responses reflected the two logical but opposing arguments on the subject. The first held that managers should stand by the full-time employees who were the heart of the firm, the best-trained and most valuable workers. The second maintained that cost-cutting through the use of part-timers was the paramount consideration. History was on the side of those who took the second position, even though it was the one least likely to foster the skilled selling which was so dear to managers' hearts. Although many resisted the temptation to use cheaper part-timers, the trend toward part-time work that is today the bane of women's service employment was firmly established in department stores well before World War II. One of the major advantages of department-store selling—stable, full-time work—rested on the exploitation of part-time workers, a practice which in time eroded the core of steady jobs.

The Long Run: Earnings, Employment, and Economic Crisis

Full-time store workers not only had steadier work than women in factories; the trends in their earning and employment prospects were also more favorable. Only two studies offer reliable information on wage changes over time, but they suggest that—at least until the late 1930s—the earnings of women in stores increased more rapidly than those of women in other industries. In New York between 1913 and 1923 the increase in women's earnings in stores was proportionally greater than in three of the four manufacturing industries with which they were compared, including the better-paid shirt and collar and tobacco industries. In Ohio from 1918 to 1929 the real earnings of salespeople rose by 56.3 percent, only one percentage point less than the clerical workers' gains, and dramatically more than the average increase of only 33.7 percent for all wage earners. Once again the 1920s emerges as a particularly favorable period for saleswomen, a time in which their earnings bore some relation to their bosses' rhetoric about their jobs.[16]

Even more impressive was the tendency of store workers' earnings to hold up better than the average, and certainly better than those of factory workers, during economic crises. Many scholars have noted that disproportionately female occupations were less prone to unemployment than predominantly male fields during periods of recession and depression, but in selling there was a particular incentive to maintain wage as well as staffing levels. As one writer warned darkly, "A happy, easy-minded staff is one thing on which you dare not take a markdown." Fearful, resentful, or distracted employees would not sell effectively; humanitarianism and wise management coincided. Still, many employers were not temperamentally inclined or financially able to spare their employees in times of severe economic dislocation, and trade journals persistently exhorted readers to trim costs in other ways and to cut jobs and salaries only as a last resort.[17]

No data are available for the depression of the 1890s, but the panic of 1907 intensified factory women's tendency to work irregular hours and short time without significantly affecting department-store conditions. The more severe depression of 1920–22 similarly spared women in retailing. In four states studied by the Women's Bureau, women in general mercantile stores had wage gains ranging from .1 percent to 11.7 percent, while those in manufacturing suffered proportional wage losses up to three times as great; in a fifth state, the experience of women in stores and factories was quite similar. In Ohio, women's sales employment fell less in the early phases of the economic slump than did men's. Both in comparison to other women workers and to men, women working in stores fared quite well during the depression of the early 1920s.[18]

The picture for the Great Depression is considerably more mixed. Between 1931 and 1932, the earnings of women in Texas department stores dropped by only half as great a percentage as those of women in factories, but in Tennessee between 1934 and 1935 the earnings of women in department stores fell at a rate eight times that of women in manufacturing. Among a group of professional and business women, saleswomen's salary losses were greater than all but one of nineteen occupations studied. During the 1930s, saleswomen in Arkansas and South Bend had lower unemployment rates than other women workers, but those in Boston were more likely to be out of work than the average woman worker. Store women's earlier decisive advantage over other women workers in times of economic crisis had by the 1930s been replaced by a contradictory and overall less favorable set of possibilities. The use of part-timers may have been part of the problem: the stability of wages in Texas department stores probably was related to the State's unusually low proportion of part-time saleswomen.[19]

Although less well situated during the Depression in comparison to other women, saleswomen continued to fare better than their male co-workers. In seven of eleven major department stores in New Jersey, California, and Denver, saleswomen were laid off at a lower rate than salesmen. From one point of view this made good economic sense, since women customarily commanded lower wages. Yet other data from Illinois and Ohio suggest that salesmen's earnings dropped earlier and more dramatically than saleswomen's and that the gap between the two narrowed between 1929 and the mid-1930s. All in all, saleswomen were hardly immune to economic crises but they were less affected than most other women workers and salesmen; this is, however, yet another instance in which their edge diminished during the 1930s.[20]

The Long Run: The Individual Career

Even though the relative fortunes of saleswomen as a group declined during the Depression, the possibilities for the individual saleswoman remained better than those open to other women workers. The gap between starting and maximum salaries was notably larger in stores than in factories, as Appendix D shows. Women in retailing could hope eventually to earn from about half again as much to twice as much as beginners, while women in factories could hope only for more modest advances of about one-third to four-tenths above starters' earnings. In addition, women in stores almost always continued to increase their earnings over a longer period than did their sisters in factories, who usually attained their maximum earnings after only three years on the job. These figures reflect the fact that there was a fundamentally different dynamic at work in determining factory as opposed to store earnings. In the factory, women attained their maximum efficiency at relatively routine tasks rather quickly. In the store, saleswomen continued to hone their selling skills over many years; greater personal maturity, broader selling experience and frequently the opportunity to move up to more highly paid departments or positions enabled them to advance their salaries more than women in manufacturing. And, because managers pegged sales salaries to past or projected sales, we know that the higher salaries in the stores reflected higher productivity.[21]

Long-run earnings, of course, mattered to an individual only if she stayed on the job long enough to reap some of the benefits of longevity. By the early twentieth century, as Appendix E shows, women in department stores increasingly tended to remain with their firm or occupation longer than did women in other lines of work. During the 1920s, for example, Rhode Island women in retailing were nearly twice as likely, and Texas department-store women one and a half times as likely, to remain in their occupations for at least a decade as all working women in their states.

Saleswomen appear to have been more committed to the retail sector than other workers were to their industries. This was probably related to the better long-term financial possibilities of selling, but two other factors were involved. Selling, first of all, differed more from clerical work and manufacturing work, for example, than factory operatives' work in different industries. To move from assembly work in one industry to a similar job in another industry meant very little change in the work one did, while to move from selling to factory or office meant a far more dramatic change. Second, there was a broad range of possibilities within retailing.[22]

Within the Industry: Range and Hierarchy

Within retailing, women had a variety of opportunities with significant implications for their earnings. First of all, selling salaries in most cities varied from store to store. Susan Carter and Michael Carter, analyzing payroll data collected by the New York State Factory Investigating Commission in 1913, have shown that saleswomen at Lord & Taylor earned on the average 40 percent more than their counterparts at Hearn's. Women's Bureau studies of five "comparable" New Jersey stores twenty years later found a similar gap between saleswomen's median earnings in the highest-paying and lowest-paying stores. The difference in salaries corresponded in part to a difference in social status and clientele: Hearn's catered to "the emerging mass of middle class bargain hunters" while Lord & Taylor aimed for the top of the market. Larger specialty stores, such as Lord & Taylor and Filene's, frequently hired more selectively than true department stores, employing only experienced saleswomen who had proven themselves elsewhere and paying them handsomely—at up to one-fifth more than the going salary. Other firms paid premium salaries as a matter of policy, assuming that fatter pay envelopes inspired more efficient work and enhanced a store's humanitarian reputation. In the years before World War I, a number of stores established voluntary minimum wages ranging from $7 at a Michigan store to $8 at Gladding's in Providence and Filene's and $9 at a Spokane store. Some cities, similarly, offered saleswomen better relative salaries than others. The 1909 federal study of woman and child wage earners showed that a woman working in a Chicago store had a nearly even chance of earning a "living wage" of $8, while one in New York had less than a one-in-four chance. Women in Atlanta stores in 1920 and in New York City stores in 1923 earned nearly half again as much as their counterparts in Georgia and New York stores outside these cities.[23]

From one point of view, these variations in saleswomen's earnings were arbitrary and even irrational: saleswomen in New York and Chicago, at Hearn's and Lord & Taylor, needed their meager salaries equally badly, and differences in skill and salary did not always coincide. Yet from another perspective these variations meant that ambitious saleswomen could advance themselves by a horizontal move into another store or—for the more adventurous—a move to another city or from a small town into a large city. Saleswomen did their best to exploit this wage differential, often making or threatening moves at the busiest seasons when harassed managers were more openhanded about salaries; stores tried to foil this practice by refusing to hire a woman without proof that she had resigned from her present position.[24]

Within the department store, and the larger specialty stores as well, saleswomen had a place in hierarchies of sex, age, function, and department. However ill-paid they were, there were always some below them in pay and rank—younger men and women who worked as cash, bundle, and message carriers, as wrappers, inspectors, and stock people. Although salespeople were not technically their superiors, in fact they often exercised an informal authority over these younger folk. Before World War I, saleswomen's weekly earnings were about double those of the "junior" workers, as they were called in store parlance. After the war, these youngsters were replaced by slightly older workers who were expected to move up the ladder to become cashiers, salespeople, or office workers. As the younger group became less a caste apart, the saleswoman's salary advantage over it shrunk to the point where she earned only 25 to 50 percent more.[25]

Saleswomen customarily earned less than the women in store workrooms who did alterations, pressing, and millinery work. Although they were usually on completely separate tracks—it was rare for a worker to move from the sales to the workroom staff or vice versa—workroom personnel could be useful allies for the saleswoman. Called in on a difficult sale, the alterations woman could clinch the sale by offering to do drastic alterations or convince the customer to buy another garment by arguing that the necessary alterations were impossible. And, of course, she could intentionally or inadvertently sabotage a saleswoman's strategy by ignoring her signals about what to tell the customer. Workroom women's earnings reflected both their ability to influence store profits and the high wages skilled needleworkers could command. Before World War I, they earned from about 12 percent to about 80 percent more than saleswomen. The spotty data for the postwar era indicate that cost-cutting campaigns had trimmed the workroom employees' advantage to only about 2 percent more than saleswomen's earnings. This relative decline reflects managers' attempts to save money on a particularly labor-intensive part of non-selling operations as well as an intensification of the long-term trend toward more standardized garments and less custom work. The net effect was to improve saleswomen's relative financial position within the store.[26]

Saleswomen's salaries compared more favorably to those of store clericals than to those of office workers in general. In five cases out of twelve, all before World War I, saleswomen earned more than the office workers in their stores. The cases in which store clericals earned more were scattered throughout the period, although office workers' salary advantage over their co-workers was greater up through the 1920s (from about 14 percent to about 36 percent more than others) than it was in the 1930s (when it ranged from 4 to 6 percent). Again the earnings differentials among occupations leveled off. Saleswomen's earnings, then, reflected with increasing accuracy the store manager's rhetorical appreciation of their critical role in the store's profits; in relation to their better-paid co-workers in the store, if not to an absolute standard of a decent wage, saleswomen's financial rewards improved.[27]

As noted earlier, salesmen earned more than saleswomen, a differential underlined by the sex-segregation of selling departments; women's selling salaries always averaged less than two thirds of men's. Even among the female-staffed departments, there was a wage hierarchy that reflected management's ideas about the prestige and profitability of different types of merchandise. Moves up or down the hierarchy could materially change saleswomen's financial prospects. Selling behind a counter was more lucrative than selling at bargain tables set up in the aisles. Women in Indiana department stores before World War I earned more than twice as much selling coats, suits, and skirts as selling notions. In the largest stores of the big cities, the starting salary for women selling millinery and cloaks and suits was the maximum to which saleswomen in the other departments could aspire. There is some evidence that time, particularly in combination with labor unions, went a long way toward smoothing out the differences between departments. The Retail Clerks' 1940 contract with Gimbel Brothers stipulated beginning salaries of $15 or $16 in most female-staffed departments, with maxima varying from $17.50 to $20.00. Saleswomen of women's and misses' coats and suits stood out in being paid on straight commission rather than salary-plus-commission as was the case in other departments. The contract still included sex differentials. When men and women worked in the same department, women's salaries ranged from 70 to 90 percent of men's, and men working wholly on commission were guaranteed a minimum weekly wage unlike the women selling coats and suits.[28]

Saleswomen were neither a particularly badly paid lot nor a privileged elite among women workers. While they often earned somewhat more than the average woman worker or woman factory worker in their locale, they stood at the top of women's salary scale only in the South. Saleswomen's real economic advantage lay in their greater ability to find steady, full-time work and in their industry's tendency to weather economic crises comparatively well. The two-track system in department stores meant, however, that the favorable position of the full-timer was possible only at the expense of the part-time force. Whether because of the marginally better pay or because of the prospect of steady work, saleswomen tended to stay with their industry longer than other workers. Within the realm of women's white-collar work, however, saleswomen came out a distinct economic second to clerical workers.

In some respects, time was on the side of the saleswoman; her salary increased at a faster rate than that of women in other industries, particularly through the 1920s. During the 1930s saleswomen notably bettered their position in respect to men in their field although the picture is more mixed in relation to other women workers. Perhaps most important of all, saleswomen gained more handsomely from seniority and experience than did their sisters in other industries. In other respects saleswomen's position deteriorated, particularly as part-time employment chipped away at the core of full-time jobs. Within the store, the wage hierarchy flattened out, leaving saleswomen with a narrowed but still significant advantage over junior employees and more nearly on a par with clerical and workroom employees.

Hidden Costs and Hidden Benefits

Certain peculiarities of department-store life both augmented and diminished saleswomen's salaries. Fines levied a toll on pay envelopes; many a saleswoman learned only on payday that an offense of which she had been unaware had cut into her small salary. Fines for procedural errors were already falling out of favor in the early 1910s, but those for tardiness persisted into the 1930s. A quarter of New York City women surveyed in 1913 reported fines (usually for lateness) ranging from a tenth to a half of their salaries. Another hidden cost borne by saleswomen was the expense of being impeccably dressed on the job. Providing a clean white waist every day was no trivial matter, and saleswomen had an unhappy choice between the after-work drudgery of rubbing, boiling, blueing, starching, and ironing and the staggering expense—as much as half what they spent for lodging—of commercial laundry services. Looking well also required substantial expenditures for clothing, and the limited evidence suggests that saleswomen probably spent a higher proportion of their salary on clothing than did other working women. The combination of a need to be well dressed and a limited income could force a saleswoman into ruinous expenditures: Lucy Cleaver spent $23.52 for twenty-four tawdry waists in one year because she could never save enough money to buy a better one, whereas the women in a working-girls' club estimated that six higher-quality waists, at a total cost of only $8.50, would have been adequate for "comfort and a presentable appearance."[29]

Numerous fringe benefits helped to offset fines and work-related expenses. Discounts on purchases within the store were nearly universal, ranging from 10 to 25 percent and sometimes graduated according to the type of merchandise purchased. The value of the discount, depending on the individual saleswoman's family budget, could be considerable indeed and constituted a decisive advantage of store workers over those in other industries. Commissions probably added only marginally to saleswomen's earnings since they were combined with low base salaries, but occasional bonuses and premiums sweetened their pay envelopes.[30]

Some aspects of welfare work provided free services for which employees would otherwise have had to pay. Stores had, for example, particularly good medical facilities, and were far more likely than the average company in both 1918 and 1936 surveys to provide some type of health care. Their services were either free or provided below the going rate. Store workers had greater access to education and training than the average worker; to the extent that these paved the way to better-paying positions or provided free services for which workers might otherwise have paid, they supplemented the pay envelope. Stores also provided more and better dining and recreation rooms than firms in other industries, but the dollars-and-cents value of these facilities was undercut by the social cost of them. On the one hand, they supplied food at cost and offered free alternatives to other more expensive forms of entertainment, but they sometimes bore the mark of management's heavy hand: exhortations to sell advertised merchandise intruded on lunch-hour relaxation and social events had to conform to store policies and manager's whims. More generally, welfare work did not guarantee a humane working atmosphere and often coexisted with the "marked injustice" of low wages, long hours, and arbitrary treatment.[31]

The most valuable and unambiguous welfare-work benefit was the paid vacation. Stores began to give paid vacations earlier and more frequently than factories. In Boston in 1884, for instance, one in eight women working in stores but only one in fifty working in factories enjoyed paid vacations. Other studies between the turn of the century and 1928 showed that about one-half either of stores or of store workers had paid time off, while no more than one-fifth of factory workers were so favored. By the mid-1920s, the vast majority of major department stores gave time off with pay, and the once-common mandatory unpaid vacation was a vanishing phenomenon. In 1936, one study found that retail workers were more likely than those in any other industry to have both paid holidays and paid vacations. A few firms offered vacation plans of a generosity unequaled by many firms a half-century later. J. L. Hudson of Detroit and R. H. Macy provided four paid weeks after, respectively, ten and twenty-five years of service, and after ten years Hudson's added cash bonuses over and above regular vacation pay.[32]

Paid or unpaid, vacations helped store managers deal with the problem of excess staff in slack times and were of course better fitted to retailers' needs than the blanket layoff since they could be staggered. While most managers assumed that paid vacations benefited the store as well as the worker, "promot[ing] employees' health, reward[ing] faithful service, act[ing] as incentive to continued employment," a few more ambitiously tried to shape employees' vacations at store-subsidized facilities and through didactic advice about "how to take a vacation." Clearly, the impulse to rationalize work inside the store spilled over into organizing leisure outside it. Despite the paternalistic aspects of the vacation resorts, store workers eagerly patronized them and of course no one objected to paid vacations; exuberant vacation news was a staple of the *Echo* store-gossip columns. These notable benefits were enjoyed far less often by saleswomen's counterparts in factories. The more cynical among the clerks might well have noted, however, that paid time off was only just recompense for some of the unfavorable aspects of saleswomen's working hours.[33]

Hours: Short Weekdays, Long Saturdays, and Unpaid Overtime

From the point of view of most factory workers, women in department stores had an enviably short work day. All available data show that women in stores worked fewer hours daily than those in manufacturing plants or than the female labor force as a whole. Typical were Ohio—where, in 1922, about 95 percent of those in general mercantile stores and only 30 percent of those in all industries had daily hours of eight or less—and Texas—where, in 1932, seven in ten department-store and ready-to-wear workers had a day of under nine hours, as opposed to only four in ten of all the state's working women.[34]

Between the turn of the century and the beginning of the Great Depression, first large and then smaller stores eliminated evening shopping hours. This was partly a response to pressure from socially concerned people who condemned the cruelly long working hours caused by evening openings, but managers also perceived that shorter hours were in their self-interest. The profits of staying open did not justify the added expense: evening shoppers often came for the recreation of "looking" rather than for the express purpose of buying; and exhausted salespeople were inefficient and even ill-tempered. Retailers preferred citywide unity on store hours in order to avoid destructive competition, but some stores cut their hours even though their competitors failed to follow suit. When the Depression upset previous calculations, a number of stores broke the unwritten downtown rule of closing by 6:00 P.M. Many condemned such action as "a step backward," a return to the days when stores remained open long into the evening until the last customer had made her leisurely choice. R. H. Macy, justifying its 1934 decision to remain open on Thursdays until 9 P.M., argued that "[b]ecause [Thursday] was the maid's night out, women met their husbands downtown and had dinner out." Other Herald Square stores soon did likewise, but most large urban stores held the line on evening closings. In smaller centers of under a quarter of a million people many stores began to stay open one or two evenings a week, but it was a sign of the times that they generally used a shift system on long days so that individuals' working hours did not increase.[35]

Saleswomen were less favored in the matter of weekly working hours.

The data permit twenty-eight comparisons of weekly hours, and women in retail stores (except five-and-ten-cent stores) had a shorter-than-average work week in fifteen cases, a longer one in ten, and about an average week in three. Weekly hours were usually shorter in large cities; in 1921, for example, virtually all Baltimore saleswomen had a work week of under forty-eight hours, while only one in five of their counterparts elsewhere in Maryland had as short a week. The cause of the longer week in stores was the long Saturday. In fifteen of sixteen comparisons, stores had longer Saturday hours than the average. By the turn of the century the short Saturday of six hours or less was increasingly common in factories, while the Saturday half-holiday in retailing prevailed only in the larger urban stores. In Massachusetts in 1906 and in the District of Columbia in 1913, women in stores worked a notably longer sixth day than their sisters in factories or in stenographic positions except during the summer. The short summer Saturday in retailing never became universal; a 1926 study showed that only half of stores surveyed closed on a summer afternoon.[36]

The fact that some but not all mercantile women had longer weeks resulted from managers' efforts to please both their customers and their salespeople. They catered to the former by maintaining, in general, a Saturday as long as their other days, but they mollified their saleswomen and complied with maximum-hours laws by dividing the work into shifts with overlapping schedules. Sometimes women were assigned split shifts, with a few hours off in the afternoon or extra-long meal breaks. The sources are silent on store women's response to this arrangement, but telephone operators faced with the split shift complained bitterly that it lengthened the overall working day and led either to wasted time on a short break or to wasted money in extra carfare to go home and return during a longer break.[37]

Scheduled hours, on which the foregoing comparisons are based, do not reflect all of the demands on saleswomen's time; the bane of their existence was unpaid overtime. Their salaries required them to be at their posts during certain hours, but various contingencies expanded their working day beyond the store's opening and closing hours. Because stores failed to make the same provisions for their employees' convenience as for their customers', saleswomen lost a great deal of time getting to and from their counters. Delays at overcrowded time desks, elevators, and locker rooms lengthened their days on each end and in between chipped away at their lunch hours. Stores insisted that customers in the store at closing time not be rushed but dealt with as patiently, as one saleswoman

put it, "as if it were 9 o'clock in the morning." Store meetings, inventories, replacing stock after a last-minute sale, and rearranging departments all cut into saleswomen's leisure time. Except for meetings and inventories, these exactions were unpredictable: "engagements must be
cancelled, supper must wait, anticipations of a quiet evening fade before
an unexpected summons to remain at the store." But the greatest and
most grimly inexorable demand of all was that of the Christmas rush season. Long days during the Christmas season far exceeded the worst that
most factories demanded: in New York City in 1908, for example, only
about one in five factory employees reported that her single longest day
had been over twelve hours, but three out of four store employees did. For
their overtime after November 30 of that year, about half received only
supper or a token "supper money," a quarter received nothing at all, and
a quarter received an average of $1.77 apiece. In city after city, year after
year, at all seasons of the year, the tale of unpaid overtime was retold:
Annie Marion MacLean, a sociologist, experienced it in 1899 in Chicago
stores; the saleswomen of Baltimore told Elizabeth Beardsley Butler of
working seventy-hour weeks before Christmas; and Frances Donovan,
another sociologist, took inventory late into a blistering summer night in
1928 for the meager compensation of a free supper. The practice was even
enshrined in state maximum-hours laws and in the NRA code for retailing, which allowed extended hours or unpaid overtime at stores' peak
periods.[38]

Saleswomen's scheduled weekly and daily hours both dropped between 1880 and 1920 because of the early-closing movement, although
no figures document the precise extent of the change. Through the 1920s,
saleswomen's hours stayed more or less the same while other women
workers' hours tended to become shorter. During the Depression saleswomen's hours increased both relatively and absolutely: hours for Kentucky women in general fell from 1921 to 1937, but whereas store women
in 1921 had been two and a half times as likely as all women to work
forty-eight hours or less, by 1937 the average working woman was seven
times as likely as the department-store woman to work less than forty-
four hours. In West Virginia after the end of the NRA, hours increased
for all industries but to the greatest degree for women in department and
ready-to-wear stores. Shorter hours had a double meaning during the
1920s and 1930s, sparing the worker physically and correlating strongly
with higher earnings. Those who worked longer hours usually earned less
per hour, even more so in stores than in factories. Once again, store

Fig. 15. Saleswomen View the Christmas Rush

"This store will be like the battle of Gettysboig the last three days."

Rupert Hughes, *Miss 318* (New York, 1911), following page 70.

women's earlier advantage over other women workers narrowed or disappeared during the Great Depression.[39]

Finally, breaks during the day affected saleswomen's hours. According to a 1936 study, stores were three times as likely as the average firm to allow workers to take rest periods in addition to lunch hours. In addition, women in stores almost invariably had a longer lunch period than their sisters in factories: during the 1920s and 1930s from 80 to 100 percent of store workers had a lunch period of a full hour, while from 30 to 75 percent of all employees did. Department stores clustered in livelier, more exciting districts than most factories, and the lunch hour was the saleswoman's chance to experience that world as a customer rather than as a worker. Because stores were also more likely than factories to provide lunch rooms and recreation rooms, the longer lunch hour was an opportunity for more relaxed sociability with co-workers. On busy days, however, saleswomen were often required to take shorter lunch breaks.[40]

The actual hours worked by saleswomen both contradict and support the popular image of them. On the one hand, saleswomen even before World War I usually enjoyed shorter daily hours than women in manufacturing; the extraordinarily long day was already obsolete thanks to a combination of public pressure and managers' business calculations. It was during the 1930s that saleswomen's hours increased relative to those of the average working woman. On the other hand, unpaid overtime was unfortunately not a myth but a constant burden on store women. That and the long Saturday were the most unfavorable features of saleswomen's working hours, setting them decisively apart from women in manufacturing and—in the case of Saturday work—from clerical workers as well.

Who They Were: Age and Department-Store Women

Statistical studies of saleswomen from 1880 to 1940 provide a sketchy profile of department-store saleswomen, albeit less clearly for the earlier decades than for the 1920s and 1930s. Probably their most notable feature was their tendency to be older than the typical women worker. The picture is somewhat confused by a number of pre–World War I studies which show saleswomen to have been younger than other women workers, but these and four of six later Women's Bureau studies with similar findings used a category of "saleswomen" or "selling trades" and thus included the legions of very young women who staffed the counters of five-and-ten-cent stores. By contrast, the 1909 federal report on woman and child wage earners and fifteen of twenty-one Women's Bureau case studies, all using a category such as department or general mercantile stores, found that store women were older than those in factories and in some service industries.[41]

Ironically, for an industry so closely involved with advertising campaigns linking youth and consumption, department stores not only employed older people but definitely rewarded age. Irrespective of experience, older workers tended to earn more than their younger counterparts. The 1909 study of woman and child wage earners shows that, while factory women under twenty earned more than store women of the same age, store women earned more than factory women aged twenty-five and over. Older Texas department-store women in 1932 earned over two-thirds more than the younger women, while the oldest group in the state's factories exceeded the earnings of the youngest by only one half. One study showed, in fact, that age was a slightly more accurate predictor of earnings than experience. Older workers were not only better paid than younger ones, but in at least one case they were more satisfied with their work. An anonymous questionnaire asked workers in a number of large department stores to rate their jobs on such features as autonomy, possibilities for initiative, chances for advancement, appreciation by upper management, and fairness of remuneration. On fourteen of the fifteen measures, older workers rated their jobs higher than younger workers; on the fifteenth, job security, they rated themselves at the same level as their younger colleagues.[42]

Students of the labor market repeatedly noted that retailing was more hospitable to older workers than manufacturing. While no one denied that age discrimination existed in retailing as elsewhere in a society which idealized youthful physical appearance, it coexisted with a real respect for the "thoughtful, conscientious, and thorough" mature woman. In 1929, Johanna Lobsenz asserted that "salesmanship is one of the few fields still remaining where experience and capability are held to be more important than the question of age." Managers praised older saleswomen for their neatness, dignity, graciousness, courtesy, and "real desire to be of service," valuing them highly for the expertise and customer following they built up over years of service and often keeping them on even when they became feeble or eccentric. A study of older employees in three large Springfield, Massachusetts, department stores at the depths of the Depression found not only that the stores respected long experience—40 percent of the group had worked in merchandising for twenty years or

Fig. 16. The Saleswoman as Hostess

"She acted as though she were in her own dining room at home."

more—but also that they hired people at a relatively advanced age: 60 percent of the women had been hired in their current jobs after the age of forty. Many had entered the labor force without experience or training and had chosen their jobs because they felt comfortable in stores. As one drapery saleswoman commented, "A woman feels more at ease in a department store selling things she had long used in her own home." [43]

This rosy picture was changing even as these studies appeared. Managers began to stress older women's crankiness and lack of adaptability, to argue for the value of youthful "snap." Stores which were taken over by chains or ownership groups often became less sensitive to community opinion and fired older employees without regard to their service record or customer following. Once source testified that during the mid-1930s many New York stores replaced "middle-aged" saleswomen with "young and pretty college girls with refined accents." Influenced by the growing cultural obsession with youth, store managers in general had become increasingly uneasy about their older employees by the late 1920s. Dissatisfied with the traditional practice of pensioning off each employee individually, many managers tried to rationalize their job security and pension plans. The R. H. Macy Company guaranteed employees either continued employment or a pension after fifteen years, providing medical assistance and job retraining to help people remain productive as long as possible. Other stores developed formal pension plans, but in the mid-1930s stores were still more likely than the average firm to have the older informal arrangements. The motives behind the new plans were not always laudable: some used them to painlessly get rid of less productive older workers without alienating either customers or other employees, while others cynically noted that these plans would cost little since a sizable proportion of department-store workers were still young and short-term employees. Older workers nonetheless appear to have done well overall in department stores, not just holding onto their jobs but also reaping the rewards of their maturity. Yet, as with so many other benefits of store work, this advantage began to erode during the 1930s. [44]

Who They Were: Marital Status

Like the figures on age, the record on marital status of women in department stores is skewed by the inclusion of five-and-ten-cent store women who were almost all young and unmarried. Even when allowances are made for this factor, however, department-store saleswomen differed less from the average woman worker in marital status than they did in age. Not until the 1930s did the proportions of married and once-married saleswomen surpass the proportions of married and once-married women in the United States female labor force as a whole, as Appendix F shows. The proportions of specific groups of married and once-married women in retailing tended, curiously, to fall outside but rarely within the range of the national figures for all working women in any given decade. Given the local nature of most statistics on store women, this suggests that customs about hiring married women in stores varied regionally; little else would explain why New Jersey department-store saleswomen in 1932–33 were only half as likely to be or to have been married as those in Denver at the same time. By 1940, so many married women had become saleswomen and clerks in stores that it was numerically the second largest occupational category for married working women, including nearly a third of a million married women and surpassed only by domestic service.[45]

In a number of ways, older married women were well suited to department-store selling, and vice versa. For many middle-income families who sought a higher standard of nutrition, housing, or dress, the latest laborsaving appliances, vacations, or better education for their children, the only answer was for the wife and mother of the family to go to work. Selling required little prior training, and appealed alike to those with no job experience and to those tiring of earlier careers; as one writer commented in the late 1920s, "almost all types drift into . . . selling positions and make good, with training, if they have the personality and interest in the work. There are actresses who have tired of the uncertainties of their profession; teachers who are fed up with children; trained nurses who want something sure and regular; young and middle-aged women who never before have held a position." Selling was, in fact, the only white-collar position into which middle-aged women could easily be placed. Women's Bureau figures from the early 1930s show a correlation between the proportions of married women and of women over the age of thirty, suggesting that many of the married women in department stores were mature women working to provide their families with basic support or a higher standard of living.[46]

To the department-store manager, married women were ideal candidates for skilled selling; one department-store manager remarked that "the married woman who has roots in her community will have more ideas for marketing and advertising products designed for the home." As noted earlier, married women also were ideal part-time workers, and some stores eagerly recruited them. Trade journals gave little attention to the suitability of married women as saleswomen until the late-1930s campaigns, admirably documented by Lois Scharf, against married women's work in public employment and particularly in teaching. Department stores were subject to similar public pressure for the same reasons that they had been a target of Progressive reform: anyone could observe and judge their employees at work. Legislative campaigns never focused directly on department stores' employment of married women, but in 1939 store managers felt considerable informal pressure as a by-product of attempts to outlaw the employment of married women by over half the state governments. Most department-store managers defended the right of married women to gainful employment, in part because of their own stake in the two-earner family:

[The married woman worker] is the partner in an earning combination whose combined income enables both parties to live better than if she were not working. The partners not only buy more units of merchandise, but they buy higher priced items. They contribute materially to the flow of upper bracket goods with a higher profit rate. Break the earning power of the partnership and the sales volume of better goods declines, profits tend to decrease, the buying both of the partnership and of the new worker who replaced the married woman in her job swings into the field where price competition is keenest.

Crusaders against the employment of married women wanted to spread the available work in order to assure a subsistence income for more families, while department stores stood to gain more if a smaller proportion of families had sizable discretionary income. They were, in short, firmly on the side of those middle-income wives who wanted to raise their families' standard of living with second incomes.[47]

Most stores consequently hired and retained married women during the 1930s. The *Department Store Economist* queried seventy-four stores in 1939 about their married female employees. Well over half reported that between 40 and 50 percent of their women workers were married. Only four reported "very few," and two stated firmly that women who married were fired. A third of the stores, however, took a harder line on hiring than on retention: their policies ranged from an outright refusal to hire any married women with employed husbands to a consideration of married women's economic need as a factor in hiring. Assessments of the performance of married women on the job were overwhelmingly favorable; even those who were biased against hiring them did not question their worth as employees. Three-quarters of the stores noted that they would not, even if they changed their policies on hiring married women, announce the change. Any establishment which relied for its most profitable steady trade on married women customers would have been ill-advised to take a public stand against them as workers. But not all store managers were motivated by self-interest alone; the personnel director of "one of the finest stores in the mid-west" wrote:

There are forces at work in every country, including this one, *that seek an enemy—that seek some simple panacea for the troubled times we are in.* It is not surprising to find these unthinking and disturbed forces picking married women in business for their particular focus of action. The clean-cut example in Germany alone of the destruction of the individual dignity of women by government order is enough to make this question very serious indeed. Until we restore our economy and build that form of society in which it will be possible for women to choose their lives, *we cannot, without losing many of the dignities, accept lightly this growing challenge by the unthinking.*

Clearly the progressive feminist strain in early personnel work still survived in the late 1930s.[48]

Who They Were: Home Life, Ethnicity, and Race

Social investigators often asked working women whether or not they were "adrift," as the term of the time had it—whether or not they were living independently of family. Appendix G summarizes their answers. Before 1920 there was no consistent difference in this respect between department-store women and those in other occupations. Ten of the sixteen studies from the 1920s show that women in retailing were more likely than all employed women to be living independently; five that the percentage was about the same, and one that the proportion of store workers was lower. The figures for the earlier period were probably skewed by saleswomen's unwillingness to admit to living independently because many employers would refuse to hire them, knowing that their wages would not permit them to live "honestly"—without resorting to prostitution or theft. Some women desperate for a job at any wage lied about their living situations in order to gain a position, and prudence dictated that they maintain the fiction to outside questioners.[49]

Like working women in other industries, store women living independently often maintained ties with their families, but available evidence tells only of their financial and not their affective links. Still, the former

Fig. 17. Living Independently on a Saleswoman's Salary

THE THREE GIRLS COOKED THEIR OWN BREAKFASTS AND SUPPERS

Munsey's Magazine, 50 (Nov. 1913), 257. Original in John Hay Library,
Brown University.

were substantial; in the seven cities studied in the report on woman and child wage-earners, for example, between one sixth and one fourth of store women adrift contributed from just under a quarter to well over a third of their weekly earnings to their kin. In four of the seven cities, store women were more likely than factory women to make such contributions, and in six their contributions were larger. The independent residence of these women by no means put them outside the web of family obligation. While sales work increasingly attracted women who lived away from their families, department-store employment was still woven into family and neighborhood ties. The Filene *Echo* repeatedly mentions kin connections between store workers. Two examples from 1915, noted offhand in articles about other matters: Mrs. Melynn of misses' dresses was the mother of Mrs. Huxley of ladies' shoes, and the Toomey sisters sold in the flower shop and on the second floor. One wit suggested that Julia Frangipane had so many relatives in the store that it should bear her name instead of Filene's. Filene's encouraged such links, repeatedly exhorting employees to recommend family and neighbors for employment in the store.[50]

The early studies frequently remarked that saleswomen adrift paid higher than average rent and gravitated toward the "more desirable" or "fashionable" residential districts; frequently, of course, these were near the large downtown stores and may have been chosen for convenience rather than prestige. One observer noted dourly, "where a choice was made between bad housing and bad food, . . . the store women economized on food." Another found an occupational cause at the root of their extravagance: "[e]vidently," she argued, "their personal standards are influenced by the attractive goods which they often deal in." But what, in many cases, they purchased was a tawdry bit of privacy at a distinguished address. Because the desirable districts where saleswomen clustered, such as Boston's South End and Back Bay, were customarily the most expensive, they often got less value for their money than factory women in working-class neighborhoods. Louise Bosworth, in her 1911 study of Boston working women, noted with approval that saleswomen were the most likely of all occupational groups to have a room to themselves, with six out of ten enjoying this solitude. But what she ignored was the fact that they also were the least likely to have access to the sociability of a parlor or the convenience and savings of laundry facilities.[51]

The members of so-called new immigrant families, with the exception of Jews, were not well represented in retailing. In more industrialized areas, such as Rhode Island, New Jersey, Ohio, Illinois, and Massachusetts, women in stores were less likely to be foreign-born than women in other occupations. In certain less industrialized areas, such as Florida and Montana, women in stores were slightly more likely to be foreign-born than working women as a whole. As a rule, saleswomen's national origins were not dramatically different from those of other working women; Ohio and New Jersey, with much higher proportions of native-born saleswomen, were exceptions. Immigrants from the British Isles, Scandinavia, and Germany were always well represented among saleswomen and were increasingly joined by those born in Russia. Despite some discrimination against Jews—Elizabeth Butler found in 1909 that eight out of thirty-four Baltimore stores refused to hire Jews, and Elizabeth Stern learned firsthand of informal quotas for Jews in Chicago stores owned by Jews and non-Jews alike—they were relatively welcome in department stores. In 1916 Filene's had about 250 Jewish employees, roughly 10 percent of the whole staff. By the early 1930s, some New York stores reported that half of their employees were Jews, and the *Journal of Retailing* asserted that "Jews are admirably fitted for the retail business. In fact, in the recent layoffs probably a larger proportion of Gentiles than Jews were dispensed with." [52]

Virtually no department store, on the other hand, would knowingly hire a Black woman as a saleswoman, although they were sometimes employed as elevator operators and behind-the-scenes personnel. If St. Louis was typical, however, there may have been more Black clerks than either employers or students of the labor force were aware of. Writing of employment conditions among Blacks, William A. Crossland noted that a "majority of the colored female clerks are employed in department stores. This fact, however, is not known to the employer. There are a few negro women of very light color, who are working in the finest stores in the city." In general, department stores tried as best they could to match their selling staffs to their desired clientele; this meant always excluding Black women and weeding out as much as possible those with too-obvious immigrant or working-class demeanor. Store employment offices were always on the lookout for what was referred to as the "better type" of employee—a code for a genteel but ambitious white woman. A subjective standard in itself, its attainment depended in turn on the equally impressionistic cultural image of department-store selling. [53]

Beyond Statistics: The Subjective, the Exceptional, and the Fictional

Women entering the labor market or contemplating a change of job doubtless balanced many of the factors which we have measured quantitatively, assessing such variables as financial possibilities and the opportunities for older women, weighing a paid vacation against the long Saturday. But people of course do not make decisions on strictly quantifiable grounds; the subjective always looms large. In the case of saleswomen one of the most contradictory and intriguing of these qualitative issues is that of the social status of the occupation.

Department-store selling had a thoroughly ambiguous status. On the one hand it involved behaving as a servant to the customer, being exposed to the public in a way most distressing to those who believed that woman's place was in a home, and being tarred with the brush of immorality. On the other, it offered upward mobility, glamour, and white-collar respectability. There were as many viewpoints on the social status of selling as there were individuals passing the judgments. While the reputation of store work seems to have improved between 1890 and 1940, observers were by no means unanimous on this point. In 1910 Annie Marion MacLean maintained that selling offered many young women a more "alluring" choice than the factory, while in 1940 a manager complained that retailing was regarded as a "prosaic and colorless business," a place to work "if you can't get a job anywhere else."[54]

Alice Kessler-Harris has pointed out that women workers ranked available occupations in a class-based hierarchy: professional positions and clerical work outranked department-store selling, while factory work, waitressing, and domestic service were regarded as progressively less desirable. Considerations of morality, gentility, ethnicity, cleanliness, and earnings crisscrossed this ranking, and any individual's hierarchy was likely to differ according to her personal situation and preferences. The ambiguities involved in department-store selling, however, made it more of a wild card than most other occupations. At the top of the scale, it offered some competition to professional and clerical work. One teacher, unable to find a classroom position in Buffalo and unwilling to move away from her family, chose to sell fine linens and laces in a local department store. Lucinda Wyman Prince argued that teaching and selling in fact involved the same skill: "to get the message across. I cannot see any difference between my efforts to instruct a salesperson and that salesperson's efforts to sell the merchandise." The near-certainty of a higher salary and status in clerical work was also not an infallible lure; some argued that the demand for truly competent clerical workers and their possibilities for advancement were less than for saleswomen. Especially during the 1920s and early 1930s, mechanization and division of labor made many clerical positions much less attractive, while selling was relatively unaffected by these factors. Some disdained "pound[ing] a typewriter all day"; others praised the department store for offering more sociability and greater "opportunities for self-culture and education" than the office.[55]

The excitement and gentility of department-store selling often outweighed the possibility of higher earnings in factories. In Pittsburgh, sales work was so much more desirable than factory work that women clamored for the former while the latter went begging; the labor surplus in retailing kept salaries low and, in the words of Elizabeth Beardsley Butler, "the shop girl loses financially through her desire for social esteem." Rose Schneiderman's mother felt keenly the loss of status when her daughter doubled her salary by trading her department-store sales book for a sewing machine. On the other hand, women who expected life behind a counter to be less fatiguing than in a factory were sorely disappointed by the year-round aching feet and backs and the nearly intolerable exhaustion of busy seasons. A saleswoman commanded more respect from her superiors than most blue-collar workers; if nothing else, the presence of a customer imposed a decorum not necessary behind factory walls. As one early-twentieth-century editor put it, "Maggie" in the factory became "Miss" in the store. Moreover, selling at its best provided real job fulfillment. The work offered variety, changing rhythms, a wide range of social interaction, and the chance to exercise initiative and autonomy. The women of the infants' department at Filene's were enthusiastic about suggestive selling, maintaining that it was "a study and not a hardship. It is a better type of selling than the old dull grind of selling just one article to a customer. It also means a wonderful knowledge of merchandise in other stocks." One saleswoman became so skillful that women entrusted to her the selection of whole wardrobes; she learned not just "the pleasure of selling" but "the pleasure of creating." As Leah Cramer said of her days selling gloves in the tawdriest of department stores, "I was the person who connected them with their dreams, their special saleslady. . . . [The merchandise] was the bottom of the line, imitation *schlock*, that's all, pure and simple. They knew it, I knew it, but if you don't keep the dreams alive, people themselves don't want to be alive." Few women working in the most modern factories or the most luxurious offices could say as much.[56]

Almost all women in the labor force agreed on the rock-bottom status of domestic service, regarding the life of a maid as a "final degradation," less because of the work involved than because of its class position. Domestics, complained women wage earners, lacked freedom and independence, were "bossed around" at any hour of the day or night, and were locked into virtual "slavery." Saleswomen were particularly disdainful of paid household work. In an 1898 survey almost half of the shop workers but only about a third of the factory workers mentioned the social stigma as a negative feature of domestic service. Store managers noticed the same aversion: Edward Filene flatly asserted that he had "never known of a salesgirl becoming a servant." Saleswomen's vehemence on this point suggests an eagerness to dissociate themselves from a job that shared with their own a requirement for servility and deference.[57]

Before World War I, at least those saleswomen who were living at home probably came from families slightly better off financially than those of women in manufacturing jobs. Scattered bits of evidence suggest that saleswomen were more likely to be part of home-owning families than the average woman worker and more likely than factory women to be spared household duties and to make no contribution to the family fund. During the 1920s a number of observers commented on what they saw as a change in the class of saleswomen. One school of thought held that both the work and the workers were losing status. New and lower-prestige groups were entering store work: Catholics and Jews of foreign parentage were replacing the Protestants who had once dominated department-store counters. Moreover, stores were losing favor to the factories; one corset buyer complained that "time was when the stores got the better class and those not considered fit went into the factories. Now the factories pay such a large wage, the better class go there and the store takes what is left." Others blamed not just wages but also the bad reputation the department store still carried from the prewar era: a lingering aura of wretched working conditions and immorality clung to the store, reinforced by the conviction that selling was a catchall for those with no special aptitude or training.[58]

Those who argued the opposite stressed the efforts of store managers to improve store facilities and atmosphere through welfare and personnel work, to open opportunities for promotion, and to use training programs to establish selling as skilled work. Such measures, the argument went, had begun to attract that elusive "better sort" of employee. Observers began to note the change early in the 1920s and by the middle of the decade one writer happily announced that "during the last five or six years, the class of salespeople in the average department store has improved greatly. The girls are better educated, more intelligent, and eager to learn." An occasional society woman lent glitter and prestige to store work; the newspapers took note when August Belmont's daughter-in-law became head of Saks Fifth Avenue's personal shopping bureau. Personnel directors of the 1930s noted with relief that "the gum-chewing girls who always called everybody 'Dearie,'" who affected "cheap and tawdry" dress and "extreme and frightful" hairdos seemed to be gone forever, replaced by those with "more training—such as teachers and others with technical experience or insurance training."[59]

Managers characterized the change in the work force principally as a change in its educational level. While as a rule saleswomen were better-educated than women working in factories, they were notably less educated than women in clerical work. Studies of evening schools showed that saleswomen were eager consumers of education and had better school records than most women workers. Even after World War I, some stores complained that they could not attract high school graduates, although others persisted in selecting salespeople on the basis of intuition rather than academic credentials. Still, beginning in the 1920s and accelerating in the 1930s as high unemployment levels closed off more attractive alternatives, college women began to seek department-store jobs. Some, of course, entered the new executive training programs, but more became saleswomen in the hope of working their way up to a buyer's position. One writer reported that in some of the nation's largest stores 10 percent of the saleswomen were college women. Saleswomen without much education but with valuable experience often received these newcomers with some resentment, and many college women themselves were disagreeably surprised to find that their road to success involved long hours of hard work rather than carefree glamour. However the Depression affected their sales, it certainly bettered department stores' position in the labor market. More and more often, they were able to attract their ideal types of employee: the young college graduate and the woman of thirty-five or so with many years of department store experience.[60]

The two points of view on the composition of the sales force were by no means irreconcilable; what in fact was happening was that saleswomen as a group were becoming more heterogeneous. Other immigrant groups experienced the same occupational switch that Louise Oden-crantz observed among Italian women in New York: the daughters of in-dustrial homeworkers, janitors, and factory workers became either retail clerks or factory operatives. As early as 1912, half of Massachusetts sales-women were daughters of immigrant families. A rising standard of living and increasing acculturation made the American-born acceptable in de-partment-store selling in a way that their parents had not been; economic and social barriers kept them from entering higher-prestige occupations. At the same time, a growing number of high school and college women—particularly the latter—went into store work, some with the thought of moving up, some because of narrower opportunities in the social service field. For both groups, although in different ways, department-store sell-ing could be seen as a step up.[61]

For the exceptional woman, department-store selling offered striking opportunities for wealth and power. Popular magazines ran articles with such titles as "Women in $6,000 to $30,000 Jobs" and "From Dust-Rag to Buyer's Desk." The former told of the thirty-four-year career of a woman who rose from cash girl to buyer of women's suits; the latter re-counted Bessie Harrison's twelve-year progress from dusting-girl to art needlework buyer. Even a *True-Story* article provocatively titled "What Makes Girls 'Bad' and 'Good'" held out the promise of an executive posi-tion for those who managed to be good. Women moved in increasing numbers into advertising, personnel, and the merchandising hierarchy; buying positions were the most lucrative, most numerous, and most ac-cessible of these options. A 1920 survey found that just under half of buyers were women. For the individual saleswoman, of course, the possi-bilities for dramatic upward mobility were limited but still probably greater than those in manufacturing: a 1909 study found twice as high a proportion of managerial personnel in department stores' female labor force as in factories'. Whatever the actual chances, the dream of becom-ing a well-paid, well-traveled buyer remained as alluring as the pot of gold at the end of the rainbow. For those willing to settle for smaller successes, there were numerous opportunities which carried slightly higher salaries and greater autonomy than the ordinary saleswoman's job: personal shopper, mail order shopper, head of stock, sponsor, model, and intersell-ing clerk.[62]

Finally, women's vision of sales work was also shaped by films and popular fiction. The department store was a favorite setting: glamorous, filled with activity, and easy for readers to imagine and identify with. The fictional images were as varied as the reality of department-store selling. The pre–World War I reader could choose between O. Henry's dreary shopgirl heroines and the acid-tongued but tenderhearted Miss Mooney of Rupert Hughes's widely serialized *Miss 318;* she could imagine herself giving up the excitement of department-store life for love and marriage in the manner of Edna Ferber's Gertie or renouncing domestic bliss for business success like Ferber's veteran buyer Effie Bauer. In films and a novel of the 1920s the department store, sex, and social mobility went together as saleswomen married men of a higher class whom they had met through store contacts. Dorothy Canfield's novel *The Home-Maker*, made into a film in 1924, depicts department-store selling as challenging and fulfilling work for older married women. Several novels from the 1930s combine an insider's quite accurate view of the workings of large fashionable stores with overheated plots combining sexual freedom and sexual harassment, success and failure, bitter competition and warm community, bigoted snobbery and egalitarian opportunity. A 1936 novel and a 1940 film explore labor relations and the development of class consciousness in the department store, showing women as union stalwarts adept at protecting their turf as workers. A full discussion of these fictional treatments is beyond the scope of this book, but even a cursory survey shows that they used the palace of consumption as a setting for a wide range of female fantasies about work and love, success and fulfillment, depicting department-store selling as a richly varied cultural terrain. We cannot of course know precisely what effect Clara Bow as the lingerie-selling "It" girl had on a woman's labor-force decisions, but these films and novels helped to take the department store out of the workaday world and give it a place in a women's dreams.[63]

The hope of making more money than the average factory or service worker; the desire to increase one's earnings with experience; the lure of steady work; the possibility of a shorter working day; the attraction of a paid vacation; the feeling that an older woman returning to the labor force would be welcomed; the appeal of often-luxurious store facilities; the dream of glamour and wealth as a buyer at an exclusive store, or the more modest goal of becoming a head of stock or assistant buyer; the fantasy of marrying a rich man; the allure of a white-collar job without the education required for clerical work—these were some of the factors that would attract women to department-store selling. On the negative side were lower wages than in clerical work or in certain industries such as the needle trades; a long Saturday and a six-day week; unpaid overtime and the Christmas rush. The ambiguous social status of department-store work cut both ways. All in all, in comparison to other occupations, sales work had real attractions, particularly for white native-born women with little training but a refined manner. In many respects, saleswomen's relative advantages were greatest during the 1920s; the next decade brought ominous reverses: part-time work increased, hours lengthened, and discrimination against older workers grew.

But none of this speaks to the work itself, to the appeal of what salespeople actually did on the selling floor. Of one thing we can be sure: any applicant so inclined could observe the work before committing herself. Unlike work hidden away in factories or offices, selling took place in full view of the public, and the prospective saleswoman could readily imagine herself on the other side of the counter. Managers who stuck to the older methods of driving employees and dressing them down in public thus undermined their fortunes in three ways: by offending customers, by alienating current employees, and by repelling potential applicants. Moreover, observing customers' treatment of saleswomen could frighten off the timid or embolden the stout of heart. In all likelihood, selling appealed to those with a zest for social interaction, those who enjoyed the byplay of persuasion and manipulation involved in a sales transaction. And, as we shall see in the next chapter, these social skills were at the heart of saleswomen's work culture, the unwritten code through which saleswomen governed the selling floor.

Notes

1. "From Dust-Rag to Buyer's Desk," *Forum*, 58 (July 1917), 81–90.

2. For the best general survey of women's work-force participation, see Alice Kessler-Harris, *Out to Work: A History of Wage-Earning Women in the United States* (New York, 1982). Studies on selected aspects of women's work include: Leslie Woodcock Tentler, *Wage-Earning Women: Industrial Work and Family Life in the United States, 1900–1930* (New York, 1979); Lois Scharf, *To Work or to Wed* (Westport, Conn., 1980); Barbara Melosh, *"The Physician's Hand": Work Culture and Conflict in American Nursing* (Philadelphia, 1982).

3. Valerie Kincade Oppenheimer, *The Female Labor Force in the United States*, Population Monograph Series, University of California, Berkeley, No. 5 (Berkeley, 1970), 66–77; Kessler-Harris deals with these themes throughout her book.

4. Generalizations about saleswomen's place in the female labor force are

based on Appendix A; for women's place in the store labor force, see Appendix B. On the sex-based wage differential, see *Mercantile Wages and Salaries*, in *Thirty-Third Annual Report of the Massachusetts Bureau of Statistics of Labor* (Boston, 1903), 112–13, 123–24; *Vocational Education Survey of Richmond, Virginia, August, 1915*, U.S. Department of Labor, Bureau of Labor Statistics, Bull. No. 162 (Washington, 1916), 249; Margaret L. Lovell, *The Personnel Policies of Pennsylvania Department Stores*, Pennsylvania Department of Labor and Industry, Bureau of Women and Children, Bull. No. 13 (Harrisburg, 1926), 18, 32; Mary Elizabeth Pidgeon, *Differences in the Earnings of Women and Men*, U.S. Department of Labor, Women's Bureau, Bull. No. 152 (Washington, 1938), 22–24, 32–38; *Women Wage-Earners*, Part 4 of *Second Biennial Report of the Bureau of Labor Statistics for the State of Iowa, 1887–8* (Des Moines, 1887), 195. After the first reference to each Women's Bureau or Bureau of Labor Statistics report, subsequent citations will give only bulletin and page numbers.

5. "General Type of Employee Must Be Raised, Charters Asserts," *DGE*, 74 (28 Feb. 1920), 17. Sarah Smith Malino, constructing a similar profile of department-store workers between 1870 and 1920, stresses the nonexploitive rather than the mixed nature of their work. See her "Faces across the Counter: A Social History of Female Department Store Employees, 1870–1920" (Ph.D. diss., Columbia Univ. 1982).

6. Tentler, *Wage-Earning Women*, 13–25.

7. Mary Elizabeth Pidgeon, *Wages of Women in 13 States*, U.S. Department of Labor, Women's Bureau, Bull. No. 85 (Washington, 1931), 91; the states in which general mercantile earnings were larger than those in any other industry are marked with an asterisk in Appendix C.

8. See the following publications of the U.S. Department of Labor, Women's Bureau: *Women in Kentucky Industries*, Bull. No. 29 (Washington, 1923), 30; *Women in Missouri Industries*, Bull. No. 35 (Washington, 1924), 14–15, 30; *Women in New Jersey Industries*, Bull. No. 37 (Washington, 1924), 13; *Women in Oklahoma Industries*, Bull. No. 48 (Washington, 1926), 10, 30; *Women in Tennessee Industries*, Bull. No. 56 (Washington, 1927), 8; Harriet A. Byrne, *Women's Employment in West Virginia*, Bull. No. 150 (Washington, 1937), 9, 15; Ethel L. Best and Arthur T. Sutherland, *Women's Hours and Wages in the District of Columbia in 1937*, Bull. No. 153 (Washington, 1937), 4; *Employment in Service and Trade Industries in Maine*, Bull. No. 180 (Washington, 1940), 8, 13; *Women Workers in Their Family Environment*, Bull. No. 183 (Washington, 1941), 31. Also see Iris Prouty O'Leary, *Department Store Occupations* (Cleveland, Ohio, 1916), 48; *Hours and Earnings of Women in Five Industries*, New York Department of Labor, Spec. Bull. No. 121 (Albany, 1923), 23; Barbara Mayer Wertheimer, *We Were There* (New York, 1977), 293–335; James J. Kenneally, *Women and American Trade Unions* (St. Albans, Vt., 1978), 8–9; Ruth Milkman, "Organizing the Sexual Division of Labor: Historical Perspectives on 'Women's Work' and the American Labor Movement," *Socialist Review*, 10 (Jan.–Feb. 1980), 120–21; "Fascinating Numbers," *Survey*, 53 (15 Jan. 1925), 465.

9. *Women in Ohio Industries*, U.S. Department of Labor, Women's Bureau, Bull. No. 44 (Washington, 1925), 26–27; Amy G. Maher, *Bookkeepers, Ste-*

nographers, and Office Clerks in Ohio, U.S. Department of Labor, Women's Bureau, Bull. No. 95 (Washington, 1932), 13; *Cost of Living of Working Women in Ohio*, Industrial Commission of Ohio, Department of Investigation and Statistics, Report No. 14 (Columbus, 1915), 106; Caroline Manning and Arcadia N. Phillips, *Wage-Earning Women and the Industrial Conditions of 1930*, U.S. Department of Labor, Women's Bureau, Bull. No. 92 (Washington, 1932), 10.

10. Horace G. Wadlin, *Women in Industry*, in *Twentieth Annual Report of the Massachusetts Bureau of Statistics of Labor*, Part 4 (Boston, 1889), 582; WB #85, 93, 202; see also Louise Marion Bosworth, *The Living Wage of Women Workers* (New York, 1911), 38; Marie L. Obenauer, *Hours, Earnings, and Duration of Employment of Wage-Earning Women in Selected Industries in the District of Columbia*, U.S. Bureau of Labor Statistics, Bull. No. 116 (Washington, 1913), 19; Marie L. Obenauer and Frances W. Valentine, *Hours, Earnings, and Conditions of Labor of Women in Indiana Mercantile Establishments and Garment Factories*, U.S. Bureau of Labor Statistics, Bull. No. 160 (Washington, 1914), 52; BLS #162, 45.

11. *Unemployment among Women in Department and Other Retail Stores of Boston, Mass.*, U.S. Bureau of Labor Statistics, Bull. No. 182 (Washington, 1916), 29, 62; WB #150, 14; WB #153, 22, 27; *Women in Kentucky Industries*, U.S. Department of Labor, Women's Bureau, Bull. No. 162 (Washington, 1938), 5, 21; *Women's Wages and Hours in Nebraska*, U.S. Department of Labor, Women's Bureau, Bull. No. 178 (Washington, 1940), 15, 19, 21–22.

12. O. N. Manners, "How Retail Stores Handle Holiday Trade," *System*, 6 (Dec. 1904), 488–91; Kendall Banning, "To Regulate the Supply of Labor," *System*, 10 (July 1906), 94; T. G. Goodwin, "Rush Seasons Don't Find Us With 'Green' Help," *System*, 42 (Nov. 1922), 561–62, 640–41; BLS #182, 58; Louise C. Odencrantz and Zenas L. Potter, *Industrial Conditions in Springfield, Illinois* (Springfield, Ill., 1916), 87; WB #150, 13–14; "Contingents: Distribution, Schedules, and Pay-Off," *BNRDGA*, 17 (Feb. 1935), 72.

13. Frank H. Williams, "Selecting Best Type of Salespeople Easy with This Set of Test Questions," *DGE*, 77 (21 Apr. 1923), 15; William G. Blodgett, "The Use of Part Time Employees," in Store Managers' Division, *Sixth Annual Convention*, 72; "Christmas in the Personnel," *BNRDGA*, 20 (Oct. 1938), 31; "Personnel Plans for Christmas," *BNRDGA*, 21 (Oct. 1939), 31–32.

14. D. J. Tobin, "Dividing Sales Work and Stock Work without Extra Expense," *DGE*, 80 (8 May 1926), 21; BLS #182, 60; Gertrude H. Sykes, "Employment Policy and Practice Which Takes Advantage of Experience Rating," in NRDGA, *Management Conference Proceedings, May 1939* (New York, 1939), 115.

15. Commonwealth of Massachusetts, *Report of the Commission on Minimum Wage Boards. January, 1912*, House Doc. No. 1697 (Boston, 1912), 91–92; *Variations in Employment Trends of Women and Men*, U.S. Department of Labor, Women's Bureau, Bull. No. 73 (Washington, 1930), 52–53, 105; "Share-the-Work Movement," *BNRDGA*, 14 (Nov. 1932), 838; raw data for WB #125, National Archives, Record Group 86, Box 286; see also Lovell, *Personnel Policies*, 7–8; WB #56, 22; Bertha Blair, *Women in Arkansas Industries*, U.S. Department of Labor, Women's Bureau, Bull. No. 124 (Washington, 1935), 7; Mary Loretta

Sullivan and Bertha Blair, *Women in Texas Industries: Hours, Wages, Working Conditions, and Home Work*, U.S. Department of Labor, Women's Bureau, Bull. No. 126 (Washington, 1936), 18; Ethel Erickson, *Employment of Women in Tennessee Industries*, U.S. Department of Labor, Women's Bureau, Bull. No. 149 (Washington, 1937), 21; WB #150, 13; WB #153, 21; WB #162, 16; WB #178, 15; WB #180, 6; Bess Bloodworth, "Utilization of Part-Time Workers," *BNRDGA*, 12 (July 1930), 385–86.

16. *Hours and Earnings of Women in Five Industries*, 31; WB #95, 6. Sarah Smith Malino, examining department-store women's earnings up to 1920, finds that these lagged behind those of women in other industries and those of male workers in the period from 1890 to 1914. Intriguingly, Malino suspects but cannot document a relation between lagging salaries and the introduction of welfare work in department stores. See "Faces across the Counter," 165–74.

17. Ruth Milkman, "Women's Work and Economic Crisis: Some Lessons of the Great Depression," *Review of Radical Political Economics*, 8 (Spring 1976), 75–81; Women's Work Project, "Women in Today's Economic Crisis," in Union for Radical Political Economics, *U.S. Capitalism in Crisis* (New York, 1978), 75; Kessler-Harris, *Out to Work*, chap. 9; "Editorial," *DSE*, 1 (25 May 1938), 31; "The Real Answer to Problems of Overhead," *DGE*, 75 (2 Apr. 1921), 12.

18. U.S. Congress, Senate, *Report on Condition of Woman and Child Wage-Earners in the United States*, vol. 5, *Wage-Earning Women in Stores and Factories*, 61st Cong., 2d sess., Sen. Doc. 645 (Washington, 1910), 113, 174; WB #85, 190; WB #73, 32.

19. WB #126, 18–19; WB #149, 5; Lorine Pruette, *Women Workers through the Depression* (New York, 1934), 75; WB #124, 5; WB #92, 19; Harriet A. Byrne, *The Effects of the Depression on Wage Earners' Families*, U.S. Department of Labor, Women's Bureau, Bull. No. 108 (Washington, 1936), 19; Bertha M. Nienburg, *Re-employment of New England Women in Private Industry*, U.S. Department of Labor, Women's Bureau, Bull. No. 140 (Washington, 1936), 14, 107; see also David R. Craig, "A Labor Survey," in Store Management Group, NRDGA, *1937 Mid-Year Convention Proceedings* (New York, 1937), 126–28.

20. Raw data from WB #125, Box 286; WB #152, 24.

21. *Women in Arkansas Industries*, U.S. Department of Labor, Women's Bureau, Bull. No. 26 (Washington, 1923), 33; WB #35, 29; WB #37, 30–32; WB #44, 124–25; WB #48, 27; WB #56, 34; WB #85, 85, 106; WB #126, 31; BLS #160, 49; *Wage-Earning Women in Stores and Factories*, 42, 47.

22. *Women in Rhode Island Industries: A Study of Hours, Wages and Working Conditions*, U.S. Department of Labor, Women's Bureau, Bull. No. 21 (Washington, 1922), 69; WB #126, 50. Malino, analyzing the data in a somewhat different fashion, comes to similar conclusions about department-store women's tendency to remain on the job. See "Faces across the Counter," 225–27.

23. Michael J. Carter and Susan B. Carter, "Up the Down Escalator: Internal Labor Markets and Women's Employment Patterns in Two New York City Department Stores, 1913," forthcoming in *Industrial and Labor Relations Review*, Table I; Mary Elizabeth Pidgeon, *Variations in Wage Rates under Corresponding Conditions*, U.S. Department of Labor, Women's Bureau, Bull. No. 122 (Washing-

ton, 1935), 9; raw data for *Women in Maryland Industries*, U.S. Department of Labor, Women's Bureau, Bull. No. 24 (Washington, 1922), National Archives, Record Group 86, Box 183, Bonwit-Lenman Schedule; "The Minimum Wage," *DGE*, 67 (15 Mar. 1913), 51; *Women in Georgia Industries: A Study of Hours, Wages, and Working Conditions*, U.S. Department of Labor, Women's Bureau, Bull. No. 22 (Washington, 1922), 64; *Hours and Earnings for Women in Five Industries*, 76.

24. *Wage-Earning Women in Stores and Factories*, 348–49.

25. Carroll D. Wright, *The Working Girls of Boston*, in *Fifteenth Annual Report of the Massachusetts Bureau of Statistics of Labor, 1884* (Boston, 1889), 77; Elizabeth Beardsley Butler, *Saleswomen in Mercantile Stores: Baltimore, 1909* (New York, 1912), 111–13; *Wage-Earning Women in Stores and Factories*, 107, 146, 160; O'Leary, *Department Store Occupations*, 75, 81; BLS #116, 20–21; BLS #160, 40, 46; BLS #162, 249; BLS #182, 29; *Mercantile Wages and Salaries*, 112–13; Helen Christine Hoerle and Florence B. Saltzberg, *The Girl and the Job* (New York, 1919), 25–29; WB #126, 19; Personnel Group, NRDGA, *A Report on Junior Training* (New York, 1930).

26. Butler, *Baltimore*, 105–10; BLS #160, 40, 45; BLS #162, 249; BLS #182, 29; WB #80, 36; WB #126, 19; WB #153, 22; see also "Wages of Women in Retail Stores in Massachusetts," *Bulletin of Minimum Wage Commission*, No. 6 (Mar. 1915), 35–36.

27. *Wage-Earning Women in Stores and Factories*, 107, 146, 160; New York State Factory Investigating Commission, "Mercantile Establishments," part 2 of appendix 4, *Fourth Report* (Albany, 1915), 64–65; BLS #116, 20–21; BLS #160, 40, 47; BLS #162, 39; BLS #182, 29; WB #44, 26–27; WB #95, 6; WB #162, 19; WB #178, 44; WB #180, 8, 28.

28. BLS #162, 245; New York State Factory Investigating Commission, "Mercantile Establishments," 64–65; BLS #160, 44; "Wages of Women in Retail Stores in Massachusetts," 15; Hartley Davis, "The Department Store at Close Range," *Everybody's Magazine*, 17 (Sept. 1907), 321–22; Butler, *Baltimore*, 109–10; Local 1365, Retail Clerks' International Protective Association, contract with Gimbel Brothers, National Archives, Federal Mediation and Conciliation Service Records, Record Group 280, Box 779, File 1903380.

29. Pauline Goldmark and George A. Hall, "Preliminary Report on the Employment of Women and Children in Mercantile Establishments," appendix 9, vol. 2, New York State Factory Investigating Commission, *Second Report* (Albany, 1913), 1231–33; New York State Factory Investigating Commission, "Mercantile Establishments," 85; Sue Ainslie Clark and Edith Wyatt, *Making Both Ends Meet: The Income and Outlay of New York Working Girls* (New York, 1911); *Wage-Earning Women in Stores and Factories*, 71–73; Bosworth, *Living Wage of Women Workers*, 74; *Cost of Living of Working Women in Ohio*, 53.

30. Evelyn M. Borg, "Employee Purchases," *JR*, 3 (July 1927), 27–28.

31. *Welfare Work for Employees in Industrial Establishments in the United States*, U.S. Department of Labor Statistics, Bull. No. 250 (Washington, 1919), 15; National Industrial Conference Board, *What Employers Are Doing for Employees: A Survey of Voluntary Activities for Improvement of Working Conditions in American Business Concerns* (New York, 1936), 44–45; BLS #250, 54,

68; WB #19, 43; Carroll D. Murphy, "The Blind Side of the Show Window," *System*, 16 (Aug. 1909), 141; Elizabeth G. Stern, *I Am a Woman—and a Jew* (1926; rpt. New York, 1969), 172–73; Goldmark and Hall, "Preliminary Report," 1213.

32. Carroll D. Wright, *Working Girls*, 55–57; "Social Statistics of Workingwomen," *Massachusetts Labor Bulletin*, No. 18 (May 1901), 41; Butler, *Baltimore*, 57, 97–99; BLS #116, 19, 29; BLS #160, 54; WB #21, 24; WB #24, 58; Lovell, *Personnel Policies*, 15; WB #80, 20; Grace Pugh, "Department Store Vacations," *DGE*, 80 (14 Aug. 1926), 17; BLS #182, 9, 21; National Industrial Conference Board, *What Employers Are Doing for Employees*, 56.

33. Pugh, "Department Store Vacations," 17–18.

34. WB #44, 15–16; WB #126, 10. Working hours cannot be presented as a table because the breakdown of hours differed from study to study.

35. "Early Closing Movement," *DGE*, 56 (4 Jan. 1902), 19; "Business Hours," *DGE*, 64 (16 July 1910), 71; "No More Night Hours," *DGE*, 64 (24 Sept. 1910), 41; "Change in the Retail Direction," *DGE*, 64 (24 Dec. 1910), 43; "Better for All Concerned," *DGE*, 68 (21 Feb. 1914), 47; Julia Cameron, "Shorter Working Hours," *JR*, 3 (Oct. 1927), 21–23; Mary Chamberlain, "Saturday Night Closing on Trial in Rochester," *Survey*, 33 (7 Nov. 1914), 151–52; Butler, *Baltimore*, 200; Consumers League of Oregon, *Report . . . on the Wages, Hours, and Conditions of Work and the Cost and Standard of Living of Women Wage Earners . . .* (Portland, 1913), 27–28; "Shall Stores Keep Open Saturday Evenings?" *BNRDGA*, 14 (Nov. 1932), 886; Bess Bloodworth, "Store Hours and the Five-Day Week," *BNRDGA*, 15 (June 1933), 51–52; Leona Furstenberg, "Department-Store Hours of Doing Business," *JR*, 15 (Apr. 1939), 36–37.

36. On the length of the week, see "Social Statistics of Workingwomen," 37–38; "Hours of Labor in Certain Occupations," *Massachusetts Labor Bulletin*, No. 42 (July 1906), 273; BLS #116, 15, 25; O'Leary, *Department Store Occupations*, 41; *Iowa Women in Industry*, U.S. Department of Labor, Women's Bureau, Bull. No. 19 (Washington, 1922), 70–71; WB #21, 16, 18; WB #22, 18, 62; WB #24, 52–53; WB #26, 10; WB #29, 18; *Women in South Carolina Industries*, U.S. Department of Labor, Women's Bureau, Bull. No. 32 (Washington, 1923), 22; *Women in Alabama Industries*, U.S. Department of Labor, Women's Bureau, Bull. No. 34 (Washington, 1924), 13; WB #35, 46; WB #37, 48; WB #44, 18–19; WB #48, 35; *Women in Illinois Industries*, U.S. Department of Labor, Women's Bureau, Bull. No. 51 (Washington, 1926), 16–17; WB #56, 49; *Women in Florida Industries*, U.S. Department of Labor, Women's Bureau, Bull. No. 80 (Washington, 1930), 28; WB #124, 17; WB #126, 11; WB #150, 3–14; WB #153, 3; WB #162, 4, 17; WB #178, 43; WB #180, 7, 17, 27; WB #51, 16–17. On the long Saturday, see WB #19, 23–24; WB #21, 23; WB #22, 22–23; WB #24, 56; WB #26, 10; WB #29, 21; WB #32, 24; WB #34, 14; WB #35, 52; WB #44, 20–21; WB #48, 37; WB #51, 84–85; WB #56, 51–52; WB #124, 17; BLS #116, 17, 26; "Hours of Labor in Certain Occupations," 274. "Changes in Retail Trade," in *Thirtieth Annual Report of the Massachusetts Bureau of Statistics of Labor* (Boston, 1900), 58; "Hours of Labor in Certain Occupations," 274; "Store Hours Curtailed," *DGE*, 56 (7 June 1902), 19; BLS #116, 17, 26; Lovell, *Personnel Policies*, 10–11, and Pugh, "Department Store Vacations," 17, discuss the Saturday half-holiday.

37. Consumers League of Oregon, *Report*, 28; WB #26, 10; WB #48, 37; WB #56, 51–52; WB #124, 17; Maurine Weiner Greenwald, *Women, War and Work* (Westport, Conn., 1980), 198–99.

38. Goldmark and Hall, *Preliminary Report*, 1238, 1242; Rheta Childe Dorr, "Christmas from Behind the Counter," *Independent*, 63 (5 Dec. 1907), 1340; *Wage-Earning Women in Stores and Factories*, 89, 110, 127–28, 161, 177, 207–13; Consumers League of Oregon, *Report*, 28; BLS #160, 28–29; Annie Marion MacLean, "Two Weeks in Department Stores," *American Journal of Sociology*, 4 (May 1899), 739; Butler, *Baltimore*, 76; Frances R. Donovan, *The Saleslady* (1929; rpt. New York, 1974), 72; *State Laws Affecting Working Women*, U.S. Department of Labor, Women's Bureau, Bull. No. 63 (Washington, 1927), 13–25; Florence P. Smith, *Labor Laws for Women in the States and Territories*, U.S. Department of Labor, Women's Bureau, Bull. No. 98 (Washington, 1932), 17–31; Mary Elizabeth Pidgeon, *Employed Women under N.R.A. Codes*, U.S. Department of Labor, Women's Bureau, Bull. No. 130, 42.

39. Lovell, *Personnel Policies*, 12–13; compare WB #26, 10, 14 and WB #124, 14, 17; WB #56, 49 and WB #149, 20, 23. WB #29, 18; WB #162, 4; WB #150, 17. C. C. Coulter, "Shorter Hours in Industry but Longer Hours at Retail," *RCIA*, 37 (Sept.-Oct. 1931), 8–9; "Summer Half-Holidays Threatened," *RCIA*, 38 (July-Aug. 1932), 14–15; "Don't Kid Yourselves," *RCIA*, 39 (July-Aug. 1934), 5–6; C. C. Coulter, "Increased Hours for Clerks," 34 (Sept.-Oct. 1935), 1–3. On the relation between short hours and high wages, see WB #44, 40, 48; WB #48, 24; WB #122, 50; WB #150, 10, 15; WB #162, 18; WB #178, 16.

40. National Industrial Conference Board, *What Employers Are Doing for Employees*, 56; WB #19, 23; WB #22, 72; WB #26, 16; WB #35, 55; WB #37, 54; WB #44, 107; WB #48, 38–39; WB #51, 88; WB #80, 31; WB #126, 13; Mary Loretta Sullivan, *Employment Conditions in Department Stores in 1932–33*, U.S. Department of Labor, Women's Bureau, Bull. No. 125 (Washington, 1936), 10; "Employment of Extra Help," *RCIA*, 25 (Jan. 1918), 19.

41. Carroll D. Wright, *Working Girls*, 39; "How Long Is the Woman Wage-Earner's Working Life? A New Answer," *Survey*, 31 (20 Dec. 1913), 324–25; BLS #116, 8, 11–12; and *Family Status of Breadwinning Women in Four Selected Cities*, U.S. Department of Labor, Women's Bureau, Bull. No. 41 (Washington, 1925), 28, 57, 89, 115 are the cases in which saleswomen were younger. WB #26, 83; WB #32, 75; WB #35, 58–59; WB #37, 92; WB #44, 102; WB #48, 106; WB #56, 112; WB #80, 66; Harriet A. Byrne and Cecile Hillyer, *Unattached Women on Relief in Chicago, 1937*, U.S. Department of Labor, Women's Bureau, Bull. No. 158 (Washington, 1938), 43; Mary Elizabeth Pidgeon and Margaret Thompson Mettert, *Employed Women and Family Support*, U.S. Department of Labor, Women's Bureau, Bull. No. 168 (Washington, 1939), 6; Johanna Lobsenz, *The Older Woman in Industry* (New York, 1929) 122; *Wage-Earning Women in Stores and Factories*, 39–40, 86, 104, 125, 143, 158, 173. Age, like working hours, cannot be tabulated because studies use different age classifications.

42. *Wage-Earning Women in Stores and Factories*, 41, 46; WB #126, 29; BLS #160, 44; Charles C. Stech, "Older People Happier on the Job," *DSE*, 1 (25 Jan. 1938), 13.

43. Charlotte Molyneux Holloway, *Report of the [Connecticut] Department*

of Labor on the Conditions of Wage-Earners in the State, 1919–1920 (Hartford, 1920), 29; Lobsenz, *Older Woman in Industry*, 39; Amy Hewes, "Employment of Older Persons in Springfield, Mass., Department Stores," *Monthly Labor Review*, 35 (Oct. 1932), 773–81; the quotation appears on 776. For other instances of managers' praise for older employees—"the older the employee the better the service"—see a discussion at the 1930 Store Managers' Convention, Store Managers' Division, NRDGA, *Proceedings, Seventh Annual Convention* (New York, 1930), 76.

44. Lobsenz, *Older Woman in Industry*, 65–75; *Nation*, 147 (29 Oct. 1938), 451; Delos Walker, "Meeting the Old Employees Problem," *BNRDGA*, 10 (Mar. 1928), 128–29; Ingalls Kimball, "Pension Plans in the Retail Trade Keeping a Store Young," *BNRDGA*, 11 (July 1929), 393–96; David R. Craig, "The Problem of the Superannuated Worker," *BNRDGA*, 12 (Mar. 1930), 143–44.

45. WB #218, 42–43; the following tables present the relationship between the proportions of once-married or married retail women and the proportions of such women in the labor force as a whole:

TABLE 1
Comparison of Retail Women Married
with All Working Women Married

Decade	Range of Percent Married, All Working Women	Relation of Retail Cases, Percent Married, to All		
		Below Range	Within Range	Above Range
1900–1910	15.4 to 24.7	1	—	—
1910–20	24.7 to 23.0	4	—	—
1920–30	23.0 to 28.9	6	1	4
1930–40	28.9 to 35.5	1	1	4

TABLE 2
Comparison of Retail Women Once but No Longer
Married with All Working Women

Decade	Range of Percent Formerly Married, All Working Women *	Relation of Retail Cases, Percent Married, to All		
		Below Range	Within Range	Above Range
1900–1910	18.4 to 15.0		no cases	
1910–20	15.0 to 23.0	4	—	—
1920–30	23.0 to 17.2	7	2	8
1930–40	17.2 to 21.0	1	2	3

* Figures for 1900–1930 are widowed and divorced; for 1940, widowed, divorced, and husband absent.

Sources: For column 2 of both tables, Winifred D. Wandersee Bolin, "The Economics of Middle-Income Family Life: Working Women during the Great Depression," *Journal of American History*, 65 (June 1978), 61. For other data, see Appendix F.

46. Bolin, "Economics of Middle-Income Family Life," 60–75; Mary Ross, "Can Mother Come Back?" *Survey*, 58 (1 Apr. 1927), 39; WB #125, 21–22.

47. Pruette, *Women Workers*, 109; Scharf, *Work or Wed*, chaps. 3 and 4; "Stores Come Face to Face with the Married Employee Problem," *DSE*, 2 (25 June 1939), 31.

48. "Store Attitudes on the Married Woman," *DSE*, 2 (10 Aug. 1939), 3; "'An Issue Not to Be Overlooked,'" *DSE*, 2 (25 Aug. 1939), 2–3, 22.

49. *Wage-Earning Women in Stores and Factories*, 22.

50. *Wage-Earning Women in Stores and Factories*, 91, 104, 127, 144, 158, 173; *Echo*, 13 (1 July and 24 Sept. 1915), 23 (16 Apr. 1926), 10 (15 June 1912), 15 (5 Sept. 1919), 26 (28 Oct. 1927); see also Lawrence S. Bitner, *Personnel Work in the Department Store* (New York, 1927), 14.

51. *Wage-Earning Women in Stores and Factories*, 92, 114, 133–35, 187–88; Bosworth, *Living Wage of Women Workers*, 59–63.

52. WB #21, 68; WB #35, 56; WB #37, 63; WB #41, 60, 121; WB #44, 101; WB #51, 79; and Carroll D. Wright, *Working Girls*, 34, refer to industrialized areas. WB #22, 82; WB #41, 23–27, 88; and WB #80, 65 refer to less industrialized areas. Butler, *Baltimore*, 144; Stern, *I Am a Woman*, 172–75; *Echo*, 10 (31 Aug. 1912), 13 (28 Sept. 1916); and "Maintaining the Working Force on Jewish Holidays," *JR*, 8 (Oct. 1932), 92, refer to Jewish employees. A typical ethnic distribution can be found in Holloway, *Report . . . on Conditions of Wage-Earners*, 37.

53. Jordan Marsh *Fellow Worker*, 11 (Dec. 1928), 7; William A. Crossland, *Industrial Conditions among Negroes in St. Louis* (St. Louis, 1914), 95–96; *Negro Women in Industry*, U.S. Department of Labor, Women's Bureau, Bull. No. 20 (Washington, 1922), 38.

54. Massachusetts *Report on Commission of Minimum Wage Boards*, 89–90; Annie Marion MacLean, *Wage-Earning Women* (New York, 1910), 63; George A. Palmer, Jr., "Improving Our Employment Technique for Greater Stabilization," in NRDGA, *Joint Management Proceedings—1940* (New York, 1940), 124.

55. Kessler-Harris, *Out to Work*, 128–38; "Making Good on the Sales Job," *DGE*, 80 (30 Oct. 1926), 11; "Second Day's Meetings," *DGE*, 69 (13 Feb. 1915), 39; Sharon Strom, "'We're No Kitty Foyles': Organizing Office Workers for the CIO, 1937–1950," in Ruth Milkman, ed., *Women, Work, and Protest: A Century of Women's Labor History* (London, 1985), 206–34, and "Beyond the Typewriter: The Feminization of Bookkeeping, 1910–1940," paper presented at the Berkshire Conference on the History of Women, June 1984; "A School in Salesmanship," *Framingham News*, 27 Jan. 1915, clipping in Records of the Prince School, Simmons College, Box X, File 174; "Customers Who Have Tried to Uplift Me," *DGE*, 73 (11 Jan. 1919), 105; "Which End of the Spyglass Are You Looking Through?" *DGE*, 74 (7 Feb. 1920), 53; see also Lucy L. W. Wilson, "A

New Opportunity for College Girls," *Wellesley College News*, June 1913, in Records of the Prince School, Box X, File 160. On the growing popularity of selling, see Sarah Eisenstein, *Give Us Bread but Give Us Roses: Working Women's Consciousness in the United States, 1890 to the First World War* (London, 1983), 81–83.

56. Elizabeth Beardsley Butler, *Women and the Trades: Pittsburgh, 1907–1908* (New York, 1911), 306–7; Rose Schneiderman with Lucy Goldthwaite, *All for One* (New York, 1967), 43; Goldmark and Hall, "Preliminary Report," 1214; Stern, *I Am a Woman*, 152; editor's note to William Hard and Rheta Childe Dorr, "The Woman's Invasion," *Everybody's Magazine*, 20 (Jan. 1909), 73; *Echo*, 20 (14 July 1922); Mary Curtis, "How Does a Good Saleswoman Sell?" *BNRDGA*, 17 (Aug. 1935), 17; "Mary Used Her Head, All Right; but Jean Used Her Heart," *DGE*, 74 (21 Aug. 1920), 42; Thomas J. Cottle, *Hidden Survivors* (Englewood Cliffs, N.J., 1980), 174. I am indebted to Sonya Michel for providing me with the last reference. See also "Which End of the Spyglass Are You Looking Through?" 51.

57. Helen Campbell, *Prisoners of Poverty* (1887; rpt. Westport, Conn., 1970), 182; "Social Statistics of Workingwomen," 46–48; Mary E. Trueblood, "Housework versus Shop and Factories," *Independent*, 54 (13 Nov. 1902), 2691–93; "The Objections to Domestic Service," *Massachusetts Labor Bulletin*, 8 (Oct. 1898), 27–29; Edward A. Filene, "The Betterment of the Conditions of Working Women," *Annals of the American Academy*, 27 (1906), 621; John Livingston Wright, "Confusion from Cheapness in Boston," *Arena*, 22 (Aug. 1899), 172.

58. Carroll Wright, *Working Women in Large Cities*, in *Fourth Annual Report of the [U.S.] Commissioner of Labor, 1888* (Washington, 1889), 351–67; Carroll D. Wright, *Working Girls*, 49; *Wage-Earning Women in Stores and Factories*, 19–21; Stern, *I Am a Woman*, 166, 174–76; "Corsetiere or Corset-eer—Which?" *DGE*, 74 (17 Jan. 1920), 193; Women's Educational and Industrial Union, *Training for Store Service* (Boston, 1920), 33–34.

59. Women's Educational and Industrial Union, *Training for Store Service*, 33–34; James True, "Department Stores Want You to Educate Their Clerks," *Printer's Ink*, 134 (1 Feb. 1926), 175; "Mrs. Morgan Belmont to Take Job in Store," New York *Herald Tribune*, 14 Aug. 1925, in Bureau of Vocational Information Collection, Schlesinger Library, Radcliffe College, Box 4, File 70; Marjorie Sidney, "Adaptation of Personnel Work to Present Day Problems," *BNRDGA*, 15 (July 1933), 74; Lew Hahn, "Salesmanship—The Art of Making Compromise Easy," *BNRDGA*, 21 (July 1939), 24; Bamberger questionnaire in raw data for WB # 125, Box 286.

60. Mary Van Kleeck, *Working Girls in Evening Schools: A Statistical Study* (New York, 1914), 53; Hazel Ormsbee, *The Young Employed Girl* (New York, 1927), 45; *Wage-Earning Women in Stores and Factories*, 87, 105, 127, 144, 159, 175; WB #48, 108–9; Harriet A. Byrne, *The Age Factor as It Relates to Women in Business and the Professions*, U.S. Department of Labor, Women's Bureau, Bull. No. 117 (Washington, 1934), 23; WB #183, 33; NRDGA, *Ninth Annual Convention Bulletin* (New York, 1920), 55; Frank T. Stockton, "Employee Training in

Kansas Department Stores," *Kansas Studies in Business*, 2 (Nov. 1925), 8; Paul Brown, "Shopgirls: 1930 Model," *Commonweal*, 12 (8 Oct. 1930), 577–78; "Is There a Place for College Women in the Retail Store?" *DGE*, 80 (23 Jan. 1926), 29; Mary H. Tolman, *Positions of Responsibility in Department Stores and Other Retail-Selling Organizations* (New York, 1921), 9–30, 93; "Are Stores Such Funny Places?" *Retail Bureau Bulletin*, 2 (1929), 20; *Nation*, 147 (29 Oct. 1938), 451; Robert F. Abell, "Store Management under the Retail Code," *BNRDGA*, 16 (Feb. 1934), 91.

61. Louise Odencrantz, *Italian Women in Industry* (New York, 1919), 20; Massachusetts *Report on Commission of Minimum Wage Boards*, 97.

62. "Women in $6,000 to $30,000 Jobs," *American Magazine*, 88 (July 1919), 60–61, 131–32; "From Dust-Rag to Buyer's Desk," 81–90; "What Makes Girls 'Bad' and 'Good,'" *True-Story Magazine*, 1 (July 1919), 52–53, 92 (my thanks to Christina Simmons for this reference); Tolman, *Positions of Responsibility*, 22 (see also Tolman's raw data in Bureau of Vocational Information Collection, Box 4, File 71); *Wage-Earning Women in Stores and Factories*, 43–46; "New Kind of Employee," *DGE*, 53 (25 Mar. 1899), 15; "Departmentized His Store," *DGE*, 58 (2 Dec. 1904), 15; Helen J. Kiggen, "The Future of the Co-operative Sales Pupil," *Balance Sheet*, 12 (Sept. 1930), 24; Arthur W. Einstein, "Interselling versus Specialization of Sales Efforts," in NRDGA, *Joint Management Proceedings—1940* (New York, 1940), 91.

63. Rupert Hughes, *Miss 318* (New York, 1911); Edna Ferber, *Buttered Side Down* (New York, 1912), 1–16, 102–29. The films are *It* and *Our Blushing Brides*; see Sumiko Higashi, "Cinderella vs. Statistics: The Silent Movie Heroine as a Jazz-Age Working Girl," in Mary Kelley, ed., *Woman's Being, Woman's Place* (Boston, 1979), 112–16, and Mary P. Ryan, "The Projection of a New Womanhood: The Movie Moderns in the 1920s," in Jean E. Friedman and William G. Shade, *Our American Sisters*, 3d ed. (Lexington, Mass., 1982), 500–518. The 1920s novel is Meredith Nicholson, *Broker Barriers* (New York, 1922). The 1930s novels are Claudia Cranston, *Ready-to-Wear* (New York, 1932) and *The Murder on Fifth Avenue* (Philadelphia, 1934); —*A Brilliant Future* (New York, 1932); Anne Pinchot, *Shrine of Fair Women* (New York, 1932); and Harold Morrow, *Saleslady* (New York, 1932). Dorothy Canfield, *The Home-Maker* (New York, 1924). Leane Zugsmith, *A Time to Remember* (New York, 1936) and *The Devil and Miss Jones* discuss labor militancy.

6

"The Clerking Sisterhood": Saleswomen's Work Culture

When a woman chose—for whatever reason—to become a department-store saleswoman, she moved into the orbit of a powerful work culture which helped to shape and define daily working life. The world of women's work intersected with the world of the department-store industry on the selling floor, and the culture which emerged from that conjunction built upon both elements. The heart of saleswomen's lives from every perspective was skill in social interaction. As women, they had been socialized to become adept at interpersonal relations and—lacking formal authority—to use influence. As clerks they were trained to be masters of the complex social situation involved in persuading someone of another class background to make a purchase. As members of occupational and departmental groups, they used their social skills to forge a resilient and cohesive work culture.

Saleswomen, no less than managers and customers, had their own ideas about how they should do their work. Observers of workers' conduct on the shop floor have long recognized that custom and informal rules compete with employer's prescriptions to govern day-to-day life on the job. Building on the insights of observers such as Stanley Mathewson and Frances Donovan, labor historians are now writing the history of these shop-floor practices and of the ideology and social organization which support them. Frequently focusing on a single industry or workplace, detailed studies recapture the complex history of the social relations of production as they developed through daily contact among and between workers and managers. When a third element—the patient in a hospital, for example, or the customer in a department store—enters into the equation, the possibilities for workers to manipulate the situation become that much greater. Labor history written from this point of view focuses on daily interaction within the workplace rather than upon formal union organization and dramatic events such as strikes.[1]

The concept of work culture—the ideology and practice with which workers stake out a relatively autonomous sphere of action on the job—is a useful tool for analyzing these interactions. A realm of informal, customary values and rules mediates the formal authority structure of the workplace and distances workers from its impact. Work culture is created as workers confront the limitations and exploit the possibilities of their jobs; it is transmitted and enforced by oral tradition and social sanctions within the work group. Generated partly in response to specific working conditions, work culture includes both adaptation and resistance to these structural constraints. More than simply reactive, work culture embodies workers' own definition of a good day's work, their own sense of satisfying and useful labor. While condemning oppressive aspects of the job, it also celebrates the skill it demands and the rewards it brings. Work culture is very much an in-between ground: it is neither a rubber-stamp version of management policy nor is it a direct outcome of the personal—class, sex, ethnic, race, age—characteristics of the workers. It is the product of these forces as they interact in the workplace and result in collectively formed assumptions and behaviors.[2]

The study of work culture opens the way to a fuller understanding of the formation of workers' consciousness and of the strategies through which they resist and accommodate to employers' demands. Both processes are currently the subject of much discussion among students of the labor process; the writings of Harry Braverman, Michael Burawoy, and Leslie Tentler show the range of the debate. Braverman and Burawoy, devoting their closest attention to male workers, maintain that forces inside the workplace are the prime shapers of consciousness; Braverman ignores and Burawoy discounts the influence of life beyond the factory gates. Tentler, focusing on women factory workers, argues that consciousness is formed most powerfully by gender, particularly by women's experience in the family and the home, and that women's labor-force experience only reinforced their progress toward "conventional maturity." For Braverman and Burawoy changes in the labor process are controlling; for Tentler, they are incidental to the central fact of women's workplace subordination. All three agree that, ultimately, workers' submission to the conditions of their jobs surpasses their resistance: Braverman assumes that the process of rationalization crushes workers; Burawoy affirms the transformation of resistance into consent; Tentler argues that women abandoned their grueling and demeaning jobs for the higher status and greater satisfactions of marriage and the family. In the end, of course, it is difficult to fault their shared judgment that workers' accommodation in whatever form has outweighed workers' resistance, but for students of work culture the process is as interesting as the result, the study of the small struggles, victories, and losses of daily life equal in significance to the exploration of the larger political context.[3]

My discussion of the work culture of department-store saleswomen departs from two common assumptions, often all the more powerful because implicit, made by writers on labor and the labor process. First, I view skill not as an objective category but rather as a judgment based on social and economic imperatives which may be far removed from the nature of the work itself. In studies of the working class, the notion of skill has been biased in favor of men's work and artful manual work, with jobs performed by men labeled as more skilled than those performed by women, and the highest skill attributed to those engaged in custom production. All workers, in fact, whatever the level of skill attributed to their jobs, shape their workplace experience in ways that revise and expand managers' notions of the job, using the special "working knowledge" they develop. In the case of women workers, this working knowledge is often grounded in social interaction—as it is in retailing—and is thus doubly devalued. Second, I find that the family consciousness/work consciousness dichotomy distorts and oversimplifies the process by which forces both within and outside the workplace shape the outlook of male and female workers alike. Department-store saleswomen's work culture reflected a consciousness of themselves as workers, as women, and as consumers, reflecting the complexities and contradictions of their lives.[4]

The historian faces a serious problem in writing about work culture: traditional historical sources focus on the written and the formal, and the very essence of work culture is that it is oral and informal. The most useful sources are those based on firsthand observation of people at work. Saleswomen appear in a variety of such accounts, including social investigations, theses in retailing based on field work in selling departments, and human relations studies. Store newspapers can shed valuable light on the conduct of workers and managers; the *Echo*, the newspaper of the Filene Co-Operative Association, is particularly revealing because it provides many glimpses of saleswomen's oppositional ideas and actions. Trade periodicals provide less direct evidence: department-store managers complained with gusto and candor about the failings of their employees, and careful analysis of their complaints can reveal much about the actual behavior of saleswomen.[5]

In seeking to understand the complex dialectics of the shop floor, historians have learned a great deal both conceptually and methodologically from anthropologists. They have contributed the useful notion of social network and a sensitivity to informal structure and influence in social situations. Equally important have been the vivid studies of specific workplaces in participant observation studies. Intrigued by the ability of these studies to explicate the social relations of the workplace, historians have begun a kind of historical anthropology. Since we cannot observe our subjects on the job, but can at best only question them about past experiences, we cannot study a single workplace with anthropological intensity. Instead, our work can outline the range of attitudes and behavior that arises out of a given industrial or occupational setting rather than the specific form that work culture takes in one workplace.[6]

Managers' efforts to rationalize the selling floor created the ideal conditions for the flourishing of saleswomen's work culture. Typically, department stores had conflicting lines of authority: members of the buying, operations, advertising, personnel, accounting, and sales promotion staffs all had some degree of leverage over the salespeople. In theory, this meant more thorough supervision, but in practice it meant that authority was hopelessly fragmented and frequently inconsistent. Saleswomen's work culture both exploited this weakness and mediated the contradictions in the situation. Management's decision to increase productivity by encouraging more and larger sales through "personal" or "skilled" or "suggestive" selling rather than resorting to self-service further enhanced the power of salespeople; managers relied increasingly on their initiative, originality, and skills at social interaction. This policy had a powerful double potential, since the skilled saleswoman could manipulate not just her customers but also her relationship with her bosses and her co-workers. The most valued employee could also be the most subversive.

Class and gender also played an important role in work culture. When managers tried through training and discipline to erase signs of working-class origins and to apply a veneer of middle-class or elite culture to the saleswomen, they raised the issue of class in a persistent and emphatic way. It would have been difficult for a saleswoman to avoid learning the lesson: that she was different from bosses and customers, that she and her peers formed a group apart. On the other hand, by encouraging clerks to form a womanly rapport with women on the other side of the counter, store managers set the stage for saleswomen to ally with customers and other saleswomen in ways that hurt the store's profits. Managers tried to harness class and gender to further their own ideas of selling efficiency, but in fact they unwittingly encouraged connections that could as easily do the opposite.

The Ethics of Class and Consumption

The women who joined the selling staffs of American department stores brought with them elaborate and sometimes conflicting assumptions about the meaning of work in general and of their work in particular. Perhaps most important, saleswomen shared with millions of American workers an ethic of independence: they would work but they would not serve; hence their aversion to domestic service. David Montgomery has written of an ethic of "manliness" that informed craftsmen's bearing and behavior toward their bosses and one another; while the term is obviously inappropriate to women workers, women's thoughts and actions often proceeded from a similar sense of their own dignity. Women used many of the same terms as male labor reformers and organizers to describe and analyze their experience, but they had in mind quite different points of reference.[7]

Saleswomen prized their occupation's white-collar prestige and its opportunities for initiative and creativity while resisting those features of store life which bore an uncomfortable resemblance to lower-status occupations. They resented the built-in class system in the store—the set of rules that underscored their subordinate position, casting them in servantlike roles or subjecting them to the same sort of control as factory employees faced. Rules that confined saleswomen to segregated store facilities irritated them no end, and they let management know of their resentment. Annie Marion MacLean and her co-workers were appalled that an ailing saleswoman found no better comfort than the "rough, dirty floor" of the bathroom; MacLean complained that "[a] shop girl might die on the bare, hard floor, while easy chairs and couches in another room [reserved for customers] were unoccupied." Saleswomen objected to separate employee entrances, particularly when they were tucked into dingy back streets and contrasted too obviously with the elaborate portals designed for customers. They were even unhappier when there were time clocks inside the employees' entrance because, according to a saleswoman at Rich's of Atlanta, they "make one feel more like a member of a goat herd than a human being." A number of enlightened stores responded to employee pressure and removed their time clocks during the 1920s; the manager of a major North Carolina store understood the conflict between the time clock and the development of a responsible staff: "[the time clock] was an invention of the devil to check prisoners into their cells at night, and not to check honorable boys and girls into their jobs." Saleswomen loathed stores' spy systems and especially the measures for controlling or inspecting employees' packages; one manager testified that no single measure earned more of his employee's goodwill than the abolition of the parcel-checking system. At Filene's, saleswomen cavalierly disobeyed rules restricting them to certain elevators and underlined their rebellion with boisterous behavior in front of customers. After many hours on one's feet an elevator ride was hardly a luxury and a long wait for an overcrowded employee elevator prolonged the agony of sore feet. Shifting uncomfortably from one foot to another as she waited, a New York saleswoman told a state investigator, "I'd rather be shot than walk down the stairs."[8]

But the meaning of separate elevators went beyond the practical to the social. On the one hand, the two-class system of store facilities smacked of the upstairs-downstairs division of the servant's life; on the other, it echoed the regimentation and anonymity of the factory. Servants and factory workers doubtless resented these rules and tokens of rank as much as saleswomen did; but only saleswomen could use their bosses' own pronouncements as an ideological foundation for their rebellion. When managers reminded salespeople that they were the stores' emissaries to the public, when they told them that selling was a dignified profession, they were setting the stage for saleswomen to insist that they be treated like first-class citizens.

Saleswomen similarly scorned store rules and practices that more directly mandated their subordination to the customer. Despite managers' attempts to curb unreasonable shoppers, John Wanamaker's pronouncement that the customer was always right still affected store atmosphere by prescribing servile and unquestioning demeanor for the saleswoman. One feisty woman framed the clerk's response to Wanamaker: "The customers ain't God!" The head of Lord & Taylor showed that he understood this sentiment when he explicitly renounced the notion of the customer's infallibility in favor of "policies . . . that any person we employ can loyally support without any sacrifice of self-respect." Unfortunately, some aspects of the job seemed inevitably to force the saleswoman into a servantlike role. Many, for example, objected to helping customers to try on clothing since it involved the servile intimacy associated with being a maid.[9]

Subordination to the customer especially rankled with the saleswoman since she was both an arbiter of consumption and a consumer herself. Basking in the reflected prestige of the goods over which she presided, located at the center of action of a culture in which material goods increasingly defined personal and public fulfillment, the saleswoman became a minor priestess of consumption. Her sense of her pivotal role in the palace of consumption emboldened her and formed the wiry backbone of her work culture. But she herself was also a consumer, moving easily and regularly from one side of the counter to the other. The roles dovetailed neatly: what a saleswoman learned behind the counter helped her to consume more intelligently, while what she learned from the other side of the counter enabled her to sell with extra assurance. Managers abetted saleswomen in refining these complementary skills; Macy's began in 1919 to give clerks with over a year's service two hours per month to shop their departments in other stores. By requiring written reports, the firm effectively tapped a fund of worker expertise which would otherwise have been inaccessible to them. Saleswomen combined business and recreation on buspersons' holidays; Filene's *Echo* provides two notable examples. In 1909, four saleswomen from the Boston store walked to Providence and on the following day visited the city's two major department stores, calling on ex-Filene employees and observing merchandise and display techniques. In the late 1920s, two hundred employees spent Patriot's Day—a holiday in Boston but not in Worcester—traveling to Worcester to tour Filene's new store there.[10]

Managers were well aware of the power of the saleswoman's example within the store and in her community, and exhorted her to buy where she worked. They cringed when she bought elsewhere, behaving like a "doctor who refuses to take his own medicine." What could be more embarrassing for management than to have a customer ask for a garment just like the one a saleswoman was wearing, only to be told that it was purchased in a competing store? Moreover, employee patronage was a useful early-warning system for trouble in a department, "the barometric drop presaging the storm of mark-downs and lost volume looming on [the] business horizon." Particularly because employees did not have access to the store's "free" services, their purchases were not just a business indicator but also a source of profits; one survey showed that employees accounted on the average for 4 percent of a store's total sales, and Filene's employees spent $35,000 in their store during one pre-Christmas week.[11]

Because employee patronage was important to the store in so many ways, managers gave workers incentives to shop in the store. Discounts were a nearly universal lure, with rates frequently higher on items of clothing to be worn on the job. Many stores allowed employees to charge their purchases up to a certain limit. Salespeople were frequently released from their departments to do their own shopping in the store, particularly in the early morning or late afternoon slow hours. A number of stores allowed employees to shop for marked-down merchandise before the general public, although without an employee discount. Others staged sales for employees only, sometimes featuring special lots of merchandise almost daily. Witty and flamboyant promotional campaigns, laced with insiders' irony, specially solicited salespeople's business.[12]

Discounts and charge accounts were valuable ways to stretch a salary to buy more and better quality merchandise. Few saleswomen earned enough to qualify for charge accounts except where they worked, and being able to charge things at their stores could enable them to get better value for their money than at neighborhood stores. These privileges were of great importance to saleswomen, whose possibilities for advancement depended in part upon their looking well on the job. For example, a twenty-eight-year-old Ohio woman who quit her tobacco-factory job to become a saleswoman because of "her desire for self-betterment" used her charge account to purchase a wardrobe suitable to her new calling, and a year later was in debt to the store for an amount two and a half times her weekly salary. One woman who had worked herself up to a $10,000 buyer's position by 1930 attributed part of her success to the store's discount, which had made it easier for her "to keep herself attractive and youthful in appearance." Many managers discovered to their sorrow that what they viewed as a privilege their employees saw as a right. In 1932, Filene's tried to cut costs by trimming the employee discount from 20 percent to 10 percent. The store force's intensely negative reaction forced the firm to restore the higher rate within less than a year. A store executive told a convention of retailers that this action "created a much more favorable reaction among our employees than any pay raise we have ever given." To saleswomen, the discount had become not a bonus but an entitlement, one of their marks of privilege in the female labor force.[13]

The discount and employers' eagerness for their workers' trade, however, were not unmixed blessings; shopping where one worked underlined saleswomen's second-class status. Store employees were always required to step aside for outside customers. Macy's limited the number of each item of apparel that could be purchased with the discount and set a maximum price for each article. Although the ceilings were generous— a saleswoman could pay up to $149.75 for a coat—the very idea of such a limitation conflicted with saleswomen's notions of themselves as accomplished consumers. In some cases, the store's merchandise was out of reach even with a discount and employers' urging of in-store purchases only intensified the contradiction between high-priced merchandise and low-priced labor. Miss Wisehmeyer, a saleswoman at the Scruggs-Vandervoort-Barney store in St. Louis, complained to a Women's Bureau investigator in the early 1920s that the store sold no affordable waists for store wear and that the half-hour meal break made shopping elsewhere impossible. Clerks who deciphered their store's wholesale-price code realized that the store was still making a tidy profit on their purchases, and some resented that the discount was not more generous. The charge account could be a trap as well as a boon: a saleswoman saddled with a heavy debt would think twice about leaving her job.[14]

No issue, however, so well crystallized the complicated interaction between saleswomen's roles as workers and as consumers as that of dress. Clothing had many meanings to the saleswoman. First, it was her way of narrowing the class gap between herself and the customer. As one late-nineteenth-century observer put it, "She knows far better what constitutes the life of the rich than the rich ever know of the life of the poor. From her post behind the counter the shop-girl examines every detail of costume, every air and grace of these women whom she despises, even when longing most to be one of them. She imitates where she can, and her cheap shoe has its French heel, her neck its tin dog-collar." Second, it was her ticket both to entry and to advancement in the department store; as one saleswoman put it in 1911, "Every cent aside from my living expenses has been *invested* in clothes. A poorly clad saleswoman draws a small salary and often finds it hard to obtain a position." Third, it was tangible evidence of her skill as a consumer, a way of asserting that she was not always on the worker's side of the counter. Saleswomen particularly prided themselves on their stylishness—"Prairie Parisiennes," as a Chicago writer termed them. They studied the style and construction of the latest fashions and copied them at lower cost, seeking out sewing and hat-trimming classes to improve their skills. Finally dress, as manifested in dress codes, became a battleground on which the saleswoman struggled for autonomy with her employer. Some of the employees in any type of business would probably resent such restrictions on personal freedom, but in department stores the insult of dress regulations was magnified by their coexistence with training in fashion. The one tried to make saleswomen look drab if dignified; the other tried to make them minor prophets of style. A writer in the *Journal of Retailing* correctly perceived that salespeople would resent the contradiction: "With the present interest of stores in style and color, it is natural that employees should chafe against strict and somber dress regulations." [15]

The perennial struggle over dress regulations at Filene's illustrates the last two points with particular clarity. The issue surfaced in 1902 in the *Echo* with a roving-reporter article on opinions about store dress. While resigned to wearing black, saleswomen were emphatic that management should neither prescribe the style of their dress nor provide them with uniforms. Their answers left no doubt that they viewed uniform dress as "a badge of service," in the words of Miss Wickerson of the suit department. Others complained in the same vein that uniforms would make them look, variously, like orphans, prisoners, charity patients, paupers, and waitresses. Similarly, they felt that having the store buy their clothing would undermine their dignity as workers; another woman from the suit department stated that "it gives one more reliance, independence, to furnish your own [clothing]." [16]

In 1913, four-fifths of the saleswomen voted to demand the right to wear either black or white garments the year round, on the grounds that "management owed us the right to dress as we pleased." Saleswomen waged a continuing battle to broaden the range of acceptable dress and refused to comply with narrowed regulations; two years of resistance in the early 1920s restored their right to wear either black or dark blue. By 1930, when saleswomen voted twenty to one in favor of a proposed rule stating only that they dress in "business-like styles and neutral shades," the argument integrated their rights as consumers with their rights as workers. The women of one department warned managers that they could not sell effectively if they didn't feel that they were "dressed well and look[ed] smart." [17]

Women working in other stores presented further arguments against dress regulations. A saleswoman who did not want to wear the regulation black or black-and-white garb all the time had to go to extra expense to

Fig. 18. A Prairie Parisienne

IN A STORE YOU CAN BE A MODEL,
BUT NO ONE NEEDS A MODEL IN
A HORSENAIL FACTORY.

Everybody's Magazine, 20 (Jan. 1909), 74.
Original in John Hay Library, Brown University.

buy separate clothing for social occasions, clothing that could not later be used for work. Conversely, a saleswoman who simply could not afford a dual wardrobe found that her employer was in effect dictating what she wore off the job as well as on it. Dress rules underlined the saleswoman's subordinate status in the store and her inability to consume as she wished. Tellingly, one saleswoman who became the proprietor of her own large store abolished the dress code, arguing that "this is not a prison. Why should [the saleswomen] be compelled to sink their last ounce of individuality in our employ, even to the clothes they wear?" [18]

When they could not consume in a legitimate way because of low pay or dress regulations, or when they wanted to square a grievance with their employers, some saleswomen took a logical if not laudable step: they stole. Pilferage is a fact of life in many industries, but in department stores the temptation was particularly strong. The merchandise was in finished form, it was immediately usable, and it was for the most part easy to conceal. A saleswoman who had access to stock reserves could easily appropriate a new and stylish item for her own use—or perhaps just "borrow" it for a special occasion. With huge quantities of merchandise passing into and out of the store each day, systems of control were inevitably imperfect. Stealing was an effective and satisfying form of vengeance: a wave of pilfering swept through an Illinois department store in the early 1920s after "wholesale reductions" in wages. Some alleged that married women were the most accomplished thieves, possibly because of their greater need. Whether singly, in groups, or in league with friends posing as customers, salespeople engaged in some unknown amount of thievery. One writer noted that work culture could govern even stealing: "They do not regard taking articles for their own use as theft, whereas to take them for someone else, even a member of the family, is plain robbery." A milder form of pilferage was rampant at Filene's: misuse of store discounts. The firm permitted workers to take the discount when buying things for their personal use, for dependent family members whose needs were supplied out of a Filene salary, and for Christmas gifts. But many employees purchased items for other family members and friends; a 20 percent reduction was very useful in informal reciprocal exchanges. The firm took discount abuse very seriously, dismissing those found guilty. [19]

Store managers seem to have tacitly accepted a certain amount of stealing for the same reason that they stepped cautiously in other areas: they feared to anger their employees, knowing how badly an insulted employee could damage both their immediate profits and their long-run reputation. Despite the nearly universal use of store detectives, most firms seem to have campaigned strenuously against theft only in the case of repeated or major "shortages." All in all, they viewed the problem of theft fatalistically; a Louisiana merchant opined, "I think only God Almighty can cure that leak, and no one else has the power." [20]

Still, most saleswomen doubtless kept their consumption within legal channels, which were collective as well as individual. Consumer lore circulated in female networks, with saleswomen as an expert elite supplying advice and information. Frequently, saleswomen used their position as super-consumers to further the interests of their own store. Pages of the *Echo* abound with tales of saleswomen who buttonholed friends on the subway or at social functions and regaled them with stories of the store's wares. One anecdote shows both clerks' impressive ability to improve an opportunity and the way in which their occupational identity could give them a sense of mastery in a difficult situation. A Filene saleswoman, languishing in a hospital, asserted that she was not simply a patient when she noticed a departing fellow-patient cramming her belongings into a tiny bag. She persuaded her to go to Filene's to buy a larger one from a special selection the store had just received. [21]

All the same, saleswomen did not hesitate to criticize their stores to their friends; managers repeatedly warned that they severely damaged the firm in this way. Often, they simply voted with their pocketbooks, eloquently stating their evaluation of their employer and his merchandise. Mrs. R. L. Terry, suit saleswoman at the Palais Royal in Washington, D.C., bought her clothes at a rival store; in 1916 alone, she ran up a bill of five times her weekly salary at King's in the same city. Some saleswomen attacked their employers more directly; witness this conversation between two Indiana saleswomen in front of a group of the store's customers:

"I am going over to so-and-so's and get a hat. I can't find anything in this store. Can you get off to go with me?"

The other girl said, "Sure I can get off any time. You can't get anything in this store."

True to their sense of their selling skill, saleswomen became unofficial consumer authorities, but, equally true to their sense of independence, they used their authority both to encourage and to subvert their employer's interests. In the process they also became spokeswomen for consumer capitalism. Both sellers and buyers, workers and consumers, they found themselves in a curious position bridging two worlds. Outside as well as inside the store, saleswomen's skill as administered by their work culture had a powerful double potential.[22]

The selling floor was, then, rich with possibilities for the development of saleswomen's work culture. On the one hand, selling as work offered more autonomy than most factory or office jobs. A confused authority structure and a job definition which emphasized worker initiative combined with managers' inability to control the pace of the work, creating an atmosphere highly congenial to workers' attempts to impose their own ideas about the proper way to run a department. On the other hand, selling as a social situation was fraught with contradictions which at once inspired and were manipulated by saleswomen's work culture. The social relations of department store selling involved a complicated triangle of saleswomen, managers, and customers, overlaid with the vexed issues of class and gender. Differentiated from bosses and customers alike on the basis of class, saleswomen asserted themselves as workers. Linked to their customers by a common gender experience, and particularly by their shared role as consumers in the developing economic order, saleswomen asserted themselves as women. In the process, they created a complex work culture which gave to the selling floor a tone and a structure sharply at variance with managers' plans, although sometimes working toward managers' goals along different routes.

On the Selling Floor: Work Culture in the Department

Although some aspects of saleswomen's work culture grew out of storewide links of occupation, sex, and class, the most important developed in the crucible of the department. In subdividing stores, managers had hoped to achieve economies through better control and specialization, but their actions had unintended results. Saleswomen did become more specialized, but they also became proprietary about their merchandise; accounting control was tighter in the departmentalized store, but social control was more difficult as cohesive departmental groups countered managers' efforts to create a "homogeneous business." The selling staffs of department stores sometimes split in other ways—between Catholic and Protestant or older and younger or college and noncollege women— but the major divisions within the store were almost invariably along departmental lines. Retailing students frequently remarked that saleswomen's primary loyalty was to the department.[23]

The peculiarities of different departments compounded the organizational and physical differences that separated them and helped to condition the content of work culture within each. In general, smaller articles such as jewelry, handbags, neckties, underwear, and children's clothes were sold in departments where salespeople stood behind counters; larger items were displayed on shelves, tables, or racks in a more open arrangement. In the former case, saleswomen had greater control over access to merchandise; in the latter, they had greater freedom of movement. Departments which sold a large number of small items such as hosiery, notions, and shoes demanded a great deal of stock work from salespeople; those which sold relatively few large items had very little stock work. Some merchandise attracted lookers and was often sold on impulse, such as novelties and flowers; other types were usually sold in response to a specific request, such as yard goods or ribbons. A customer would come to a toilet goods department for help with a beauty problem and expect the saleswoman to act as an advisor; a customer in an art needlework department might want instruction in embroidery stitches and expect the saleswoman to act as a teacher. A saleswoman more often built up a steady clientele in selling large and custom items such as furs, dresses, and corsets than she did in selling small, less individualized goods. Obviously, handling large or heavy goods was tiring, but selling smaller items could be physically taxing as well. One glove saleswoman recalled her first day on the job: exhausted by fitting gloves all day, "my hands ached so I couldn't lift them, and I thought if that was what I would have to go through each day I might as well become a ditch digger." Even after five years, she "often [was] so fatigued . . . she hardly [could] stay awake to eat dinner." A shoe saleswoman similarly reported that her work "was exhausting, because of the stooping, the frequent sitting down and rising, the effort of pulling shoes on and off." In each of these cases, the nature of the merchandise and the accepted ways of selling it shaped the interaction of saleswomen with one another, with their bosses, and with their customers.[24]

Store managers had fixed ideas about the supposedly appropriate types of persons to sell different sorts of merchandise. While a good appearance was necessary in general, skillful makeup was expected in the toilet goods section and tasteful, stylish dress in the better apparel departments. Experience was at a premium in some departments, such as gloves, while others, such as notions, were the bailiwick of the raw recruit. One glove department was so punctilious about training that even the most experienced saleswomen spent three weeks observing the department in action before beginning to sell. Selling prestigious merchandise such as silverware demanded a woman who understood the rituals of correct entertaining and the appropriate social usage for her wares. Managers channeled older and native-born women into higher-priced departments, and younger and immigrant women into selling cheaper goods. For the high-priced apparel department they sought out women with genteel manners and to the lower-priced sections they assigned those who were "shrewd hunters by nature—'price' saleswomen." A mature, motherly type fit in well in the children's department, and a young attractive woman found her place on the first floor. Managers usually tried to match the age of the saleswomen with that of the department's typical customer but made occasional exceptions to this rule, such as the elderly matron whose advice on weddings and trousseaux was prized by a town's young brides. Appearance remained a very important factor in hiring, especially in departments where saleswomen modeled the merchandise. At least one observer suggested caustically that the fixation on beauty was less a function of customer demands than of employer inclination:

> The naive surprise with which one floor superintendent spoke of the large "book" of a middle-aged woman who, although she was not particularly attractive or well-dressed, had won a following because she was jolly, talked well with customers and had a memory for names, suggests that men supervisors may have credited the buying public with their own personal preferences. Middle-aged women, seeking to supply family needs, are the chief purchasers of store wares, and it seems probable that service by kindly women of their own age would be acceptable.[25]

Managers were of course unable to staff their departments in complete conformity with their stereotypes, but they generally managed to give each section a certain character. As a result, the staff within a department was more homogeneous than the selling staff as a whole. This characteristic, while it did not inevitably produce departmental solidarity, certainly encouraged it—and in the process fostered divisiveness between departments. This departmental closeness emerged in personnel studies. A survey of one store's employees showed that virtually all liked the members of their own departments, while only one out of five wanted a promotion if it meant leaving their departments. In another store, women placed departmental matters highest on their list of morale factors; men, significantly, placed this factor eleventh. Department members stuck together off the floor as well as on: in store cafeterias, for example, members of a department customarily ate together, sometimes sharing lunches. The

Fig. 19. The "Better Sort" of Saleswoman

"THE HALL MARK OF ELEGANCE IS GIVEN TO SOME ESTABLISHMENTS BY THEIR SALESPEOPLE."

Munsey's Magazine, 22 (Jan. 1900), 536.
Original in John Hay Library, Brown University.

Echo carried numerous reports of whole departments going away for weekends together, and smaller groups of co-workers spent vacations together. Even more impressive was the store's waist department, whose informal alumnae association held reunions of past and present saleswomen.[26]

Departmental solidarity included a definition of the department's distinctiveness, frequently expressed in ways that reflected hierarchies of class within the store. This ranking grew in part out of departmental salary differentials; because managers linked salaries to each department's selling cost, earnings varied more according to the merchandise sold than as a function of a saleswoman's skill or effort. At Filene's, an *Echo* editorial bemoaned the widespread "social stratification—otherwise known as class feeling. This shows itself in the form of snobbishness on the part of those who feel themselves a bit superior to somebody else." But the ranking varied according to one's position in the store: while the clerk in an upstairs department might look down on basement saleswomen, the members of the basement staff had an equally firm conviction of their superiority to upstairs departments. A member of Jordan Marsh's basement staff waxed poetic about her milieu:

> Who has counted, so who can say,
> How many there are in a single day
> Hunting the bargain in its lair
> Down at the foot of the basement stair?
> Dear little brides whose incomes are small,
> Matrons without any cash at all!
> Wealthy patrons, pleasant to see—
> —equally pleasant and smiling Chinese!
> Of course we admire the vast upstairs
> With its velvet carpets and easy chairs,
> But it's nice to be serving the human throng
> Down in the Basement all day long.

Whether one valued the higher-priced goods and refinement of the main selling floors or the lively democratic atmosphere of the basement, the world of the department store was varied enough to provide validation for one's point of view.[27]

Tensions between departments reinforced saleswomen's tendency to associate almost exclusively with members of their own sections. Management's standard metaphor in deploring this situation was that each department built "a stone wall" around itself. Exclusivity easily led to outright hostility. Salespeople might willingly allow a customer to leave the store rather than recommend another department's wares to her, and they freely criticized other departments' service and merchandise to customers. A more direct form of aggression was to insult a saleswoman from another department by refusing to sell her choice merchandise or to make adjustments in her purchases. Managers to some degree encouraged this practice by excluding sales to employees from bonuses or commissions, but at least as important were a desire to make the outsider unwelcome outside her own turf and a refusal to compromise one's dignity by serving a peer as one would a customer.[28]

Cohesiveness within departments was as impressive as enmity between them. Solidarity grew out of the intense social interaction which co-workers shared; huddling, or gathering together and talking, was the most universally remarked feature of saleswomen's work culture. The uneven pace of retail trade left saleswomen a great deal of free time in which to socialize. Observers estimated that, even after taking care of the stock, most salespeople were idle one-third of their time on the job. Saleswomen fiercely defended this idle time, subverting managers' attempts to give them extra housekeeping duties or use them for low-status chores such as marking. Most managers simply despaired of squelching saleswomen's gregariousness, agreeing with the Filene's assistant buyer who moaned, "Call-downs don't work here. They quiet down for the day, but it only seems to give the jawbone a rest which improves its speed and stamina. The next day they are at it, again." A shop-floor vocabulary intensified the sociability of the huddles. A crepe-hanger was a saleswoman who ruined a sale by talking a customer out of something she had resolved to buy; a stoker was an eager-beaver saleswoman; the main squeeze was the supervisor; spiffs or kokum were premiums; a looker or a rubber-neck was a customer who didn't intend to buy; a call of "Oh, Henrietta" signaled that a customer was a hen, a hard-to-please person. One tap of a pencil announced the approach of a supervisor; two taps warned of a difficult customer. At Filene's, saleswomen also used their jargon to describe their social activities outside the store. Despite their dislike of dress regulations, women at Filene's underlined their departmental solidarity with uniform clothing or accessories: the neckwear clerks wore identical blouses with flowers matching the department's decorations at one spring opening; the women in a basement department sported rhinestone initial pins.[29]

Although some accounts note tensions within a department, all ob-

Fig. 20. The Ubiquitous Huddle

servers remarked the way in which the work groups submerged internal antagonism in collective action when the occasion demanded it. In one department, women contributed to the support of Aggie, a particularly destitute co-worker; they paid her insurance and sick-benefit premiums, brought extra food for her lunch, and helped her to stretch her meager clothing budget. But their actions went beyond self-help within the department to confront management on Aggie's behalf. When a manager halted their yearly collection to send Aggie on vacation and made them return the money, they ostentatiously collected it again outside the employees' entrance. They knew, however, that the only real solution to Aggie's problems was a higher salary, and their most impressive victory was in backing up her successful quest for a raise. Saleswomen in a department at Filene's similarly shamed the firm with their generosity: when a saleswoman gave her customer an extra $5 in change by mistake, store rules required that she pay it back to the firm out of her own salary "but her fellow clerks thought differently, and the amount was quickly subscribed among them to cover the shortage." An outside threat almost invariably awakened a department's collective spirit; many observers related the impressive ability of departments to rally for mutual support during the brutal Christmas rush.[30]

Saleswomen, like skilled male craftsmen, had genuine pride in their skill. Departments at Filene's praised their collective selling skill in doggerel in the *Echo;* typical was a coat department's vision of itself: "as a team they're hard to beat, . . . / and they're lightning on their feet. / . . . just to watch them at their work is quite a treat." Different departments emphasized the special little skills necessary in selling their merchandise. Apparel saleswomen learned to estimate a woman's size and the cost of the outfit she was wearing at a glance; those who sold yard goods, patterns, and trimmings could calculate the amounts required to the inch and give useful technical advice as well. A waist saleswoman could tell by the look of a garment whether it was cut for a customer's build. An educated whiff of a customer's perfume could reveal her budget and her tastes.[31]

Selling skill and department solidarity were inseparable, for selling skill was in large part collectively developed and transmitted. Saleswomen keenly observed one another in dealing with customers, both learning from and criticizing their sisters' performances. Frances Donovan joined the other clerks of the Mabelle frock department in the game of "Playing Customer": two among them acted out a sale, impersonating familiar types from both sides of the counter. The game was a ritual, reemphasizing the women's group solidarity against the customer and establishing the saleswomen as the masters in a complicated social situation. It was also a conduit for oral tradition, passing along and elaborating selling skill. Finally, it was a form of initiation and apprenticing: Donovan knew she was accepted into the group the first time a skit caricatured her selling style. She fully understood that "Playing Customer" was no frivolous diversion: "I was always amazed at the seriousness with which they invariably regarded it. They applauded, not with their hands, but with the attitude of their bodies, the expression in their eyes. This bit of make-believe drama enabled them to see themselves, not as saleswomen, tired with a daily routine of monotonous drudgery, but as actresses in the play of life—their part not small to them but of the utmost significance." A retailing student observed another version of the same practice in a drapery department: saleswomen would enliven slow days by corralling lookers and giving virtuoso selling performances while their co-workers looked on. The ritual even spilled over into leisure hours, with impromptu skits at department parties.[32]

Selling skill was very much a group phenomenon. Like craft workers, saleswomen collectively protected their knowledge from the boss and restricted its application on the job. As noted earlier, female clerks' notion they they had the right to control the use of their own time died hard, and they repeatedly thwarted management's efforts to fill up their idle hours with various tasks. One Filene's saleswoman directly confronted the issue when she challenged management's right to subtract the price of a returned item from her sales total because "as she had given her time, she was entitled to the credit of the sale." Her suggestion provoked a store executive to write a two-column article in the *Echo* arguing that the firm bought full control of the saleswoman's time when it paid her wages.[33]

By far the most impressive instance of saleswomen's collective action was their enforcement of the stint. They had a clear concept of the amount of sales—a "good book"—that constituted a good day's work, the amount varying from department to department according to the price level of the merchandise and the difficulty of selling it. A saleswoman deviated from the stint at her own peril: sales totals too far below it would bring management down on her head, while sales too far above it would alienate her peers. Saleswomen carefully conformed to the stint despite the uncontrollable fluctuations of their trade. Within a day, they tapered off their selling efforts as they approached the informal quota, sometimes calling other clerks with lower "books," or sales tallies, to take customers. They balanced out the number of sales they made to compensate for the size of the purchase; if they made a few large sales early in the day they might retire to do stock work. When customers were few and far between during bad weather or in the summer doldrums, saleswomen tried more aggressively to sell than during the busy season, when they could attain their quotas and still ignore some of the customers. When a few saleswomen in a girls' clothing department ran a low book, "the rest of the salespeople center[ed] their effort in helping these unfortunate individuals" at the expense of their own sales records. The worst sin the saleswoman could commit was to be a grabber: to ignore the stint and compete too energetically for customers. As an Arkansas saleswoman delicately put it, "While it is well to have an eye open for prospective buyers, undue pushing ahead of another creates an unpopularity that makes those about you unpleasant and reacts on your disposition." [34]

Saleswomen had a range of methods for enforcing the stint and the social rules of the department. Penalties for violation included messing up the offender's assigned section of stock, bumping into her, banging her shins with drawers, ridiculing or humiliating her in front of peers, bosses, or customers, and, in the final extremity, complete ostracism. At Filene's, saleswomen used the department-gossip column of the *Echo* to publicly warn those who deviated from group norms. Typical offenses included: keeping the amount of one's book a secret, habitually coming to work late, associating too exclusively with only one member of the department, never giving a customer to another clerk, and socializing with members of a more prestigious department. When informal pressure failed to bring a deviant to heel, saleswomen could try to enlist management on their side by disrupting a department's functioning, as the president of Bloomingdale's testified: "I have seen in my time salespeople . . . who were so *efficient* in grabbing all the sales in sight that their services had to be dispensed with because otherwise no other salespeople could be kept in the department." The threat of withdrawal of services was much more compatible with the saleswoman's independent stance than a direct appeal to managerial authority. [35]

The work group devoted special attention to new clerks, for department discipline would have collapsed if they were not properly socialized. Eager-to-please newly hired saleswomen often exceeded the stint and were alarmingly receptive to training programs which disrupted the selling-floor status quo. In the earlier decades, when stores' training programs were rudimentary and casual, departments seem to have welcomed new saleswomen with sisterly support and friendliness. This early initiation process was a kind of apprenticeship, as the department helpfully taught the newcomer the ropes. Later, however, as training departments more energetically socialized new employees in the art of selling, the reception of the neophyte more frequently became a trial by fire. Suspicious that she might have been successfully indoctrinated into management's dangerous ideas about a good day's work, the departments made it clear to the newcomer that she had to prove herself before she would be accepted.[36]

The life of new, part-time, or temporary clerks could be made miserable indeed as old-timers exiled them to dull corners of the selling floor, prevented them from making sales, rudely criticized them, and saddled them with the most distasteful stock work. Veterans worried that new saleswomen would take their steady customers if they gave away the department secrets too easily. Asked a waist saleswoman, "What does it get you, I want to know, to show a green girl how to take your trade away from you? What does it get you?" Even more threatening were contingents, part-time saleswomen who were in the departments only during the peak hours or on busy days. Many appeared to feel "that they [were] a bit superior, privileged above the ordinary and [could] arrive late and leave early from their assigned departments." Full-timers, in turn, resented their attitude, their cavalier disregard for stock work, and most of all their tendency to be grabbers—"taking the bread out of our mouths," as one outraged saleswoman put it. A new full-time saleswoman could eventually be integrated into the department, but a contingent remained forever a dangerous outsider.[37]

On occasion, the initiation process could include a message to management as well as to the newcomer. In one children's-wear section, the executives made the mistake of firing a popular though unproductive saleswoman and compounded the offense by immediately replacing her with another clerk. The newcomer, experienced in the ways of saleswomen's work culture and aware of the hazards of her position, tried eagerly to learn how the department defined a good book. Her co-workers, bent on revenge and willing to sacrifice her to group solidarity, ostracized her, refused to tell her what the informal sales quota was, and effectively crippled her performance in the department.[38]

Like a skilled craft, however, selling balanced the emphasis on solidarity with controlled competition and an appreciation of individual accomplishment and aptitude. Saleswomen's work groups provided for temperamental or personal quirks by allowing a degree of specialization within departments. Unofficial pecking orders allocated special privileges in unequal measures. One department elaborately divided the turf by general consensus, despite bosses' persistent efforts to change the arrangement. The group functioned peacefully because everyone knew her place and kept to it. Individual saleswomen also specialized in certain types of customers—some delighted in fitting stout women, selling to men, or giving special service to the elderly; others enjoyed the challenge of convincing resolute lookers to buy. Finally, saleswomen tended to develop their own personal rhythms of work, balancing customers and stock work in a comfortable way.[39]

Saleswomen had a respectful admiration for individuals' special talents, and their lore emphasized the need for each to develop her personal style of selling and to tailor her conduct to the wide variety of situations she faced. Mary Ellen Riley wrote to the *Echo* describing a sale which she had thoroughly bungled by repeating, parrotlike, phrases which she had heard other clerks in her department use. She pointed the moral clearly: "the next time I was careful not to use borrowed thunder." Saleswomen guarded their own transactions jealously; one of the truly serious offenses a saleswoman could commit against a sister behind the counter was to interfere in her sale and impugn her judgment. In one survey, salespeople indicated that fellow workers' most annoying habits were interrupting and eavesdropping on their sales. Only the rawest new clerk would turn over a foundering sale to another saleswoman, but clerks frequently called in co-workers as informal consultants to help them clinch a difficult sale.[40]

The line separating the exercise of individual talents and eccentricities from out-and-out competition was a fine one, the demarcation of which was a central and continuing concern of saleswomen's work culture. Selling in itself was competitive, pitting the skills of the saleswoman against the resistance of the customer; that spirit spilled over into saleswomen's relations with one another. Saleswomen competed for sales, but they did so within limits; they responded to the incentive of commissions, but they did so with one eye on their work group and the other on their pay envelope. Work culture set boundaries of acceptable conduct but not a lockstep routine. Some departments had acknowledged pacesetters, whose sales were customarily higher than those of other saleswomen but within the acceptable range defined by the stint. Saleswomen admired individual feats of selling, but only when they stayed within the limits of permissible competition. Two examples suggest the acceptable types of selling coups. One was the marathon variety, in which a saleswoman assigned to a special lot of goods outdid herself. A case in point was Charlotte Broad of Filene's, who sold 1503 boxes of hairnets in a single day, for a total of $902—over 200 boxes per hour. Another type was the stroke of genius—a single sale stupendous in its size or ingenuity. Pauline Leyman of Strawbridge and Clothier's glove department dazzled her peers by selling a dozen pair of gloves because she had remembered the exact size and shape of the hands of a woman whom she had observed only briefly a year earlier. As long as saleswomen were part of a larger culture that defined success in material terms, as long as good jobs and decent salaries were scarce, work culture had to assume the task of regulating the breadth and intensity of competition among saleswomen.[41]

Saleswomen's work culture also included shop-floor wisdom about their merchandise. Their instincts for what would sell were legendary; as the manager of Filene's put it, they could "spot a lemon quicker than a Mediterranean fruit fly." When things went well, they took great pride in their merchandise and built a strong esprit de corps around their appreciation of and expert knowledge about it. Saleswomen voluntarily enhanced the salability and attractiveness of their merchandise by concocting elaborate displays. The clerks in one ribbon department festooned its counters with fancy ornaments made of their merchandise; the observer reporting this practice made a connection between women's culture and selling skills, praising them for their "domestic, homely ability." A toy department saleswoman spent an evening learning to play a zippy rendition of "America" on a toy saxophone. Clerks eagerly awaited and enthusiastically displayed the newest fashions. In some departments, they even wore the merchandise on the job, usually with management's blessing. Finally, they prized information about their wares. When Empress Eugenie hats became the rage, for instance, Filene's saleswomen flocked to the store library to bone up on the appropriate historical background.[42]

The department where saleswomen took such pride in their merchandise was usually one where the buyer consulted them and took their opinions seriously. Buyers disregarded saleswomen at their own risk; merchandise that clerks considered unworthy of the department was doomed to languish in the stockroom and await eventual markdowns. In one toy department, for example, saleswomen refused to sell sleazy stuffed toys bought against their recommendation, dismissing them as "drug-store Easter bunnies." Even when saleswomen approved of the merchandise, they did not necessarily sell it efficiently. They frequently showed only one pet item or one category of stock. Sometimes, they enjoyed displaying goods to customers so much that they forgot to sell them; as a retailing student said of the saleswomen in a china and glassware department, "They become interior decorators at the expense of their day's total."[43]

Finally, saleswomen could become so proprietary about their stock that the issue of access to merchandise severely disrupted the department. At Filene's such a case led to a hearing before the store's Board of Arbitration. Mrs. Emerson, in charge of the higher-priced waists, had doggedly refused to allow the other saleswomen to touch her stock; in retaliation, the others sent away customers rather than refer them to her. Department sales had plummeted while the guerrilla war continued. Finally, Mrs. Emerson was dismissed. She complained to the board, alleging that she barred the others from her section because they were "throwing [stock] around." Her firing was upheld, but only after a bitter hearing that caused so much ill feeling that the board voted to omit thereafter all personal remarks from its records. In other cases of departments torn by dissension, disputes over stock work—the care and arrangement of the merchandise—figured prominently. An inequitable division of stock work; too intense a level of competition; a breakdown of mutual respect for selling skills—these were the issues most likely to shatter departmental solidarity.[44]

Work Culture Manages the Managers

Departmental work culture helped to manage the ties of interdependence between saleswomen and their buyers. Although the formal structure of the store defined clerks as simply subordinate to buyers, in fact the two were linked by almost feudal ties of dependence, loyalty, and obligation. The buyer bought the merchandise—but depended upon saleswomen to sell it. The buyer could provide the merchandise information for which saleswomen were eager—but saleswomen controlled the shop-floor knowledge about customers' wishes and demands which was vital to buyers' success. As a rule, saleswomen disliked classroom-type training and preferred to receive information from their buyers, whom they regarded as more expert than staff executives such as training directors. A good buyer was one who helped them learn about the stock; a bad buyer was one who did not. They disliked written materials and classroom lectures because their work culture and their entire work lives depended upon oral tradition and persuasion and they preferred to sharpen their skills through similar means. Older saleswomen whose stock-in-trade was experience rather than formal education especially resisted the classroom setting. Saleswomen perceived merchandise training as useful information; they scorned salesmanship training as an insult to their shop-floor skills. When training was given in a dictatorial or condescending fashion, they simply ignored it.

Buyers, for their part, came to saleswomen to learn what was selling, what customers were saying about the merchandise, what the department needed, what trends they observed in customer demand. This information was enormously important to buyers in planning for the future, in solving problems before they crippled the department, and in petitioning upper management for more merchandise, space, or personnel. Saleswomen, predictably, gave buyers this information in a way that reflected well on themselves and worked in their best interests. Merchandise managers and general managers eager to break the power of buyers and salespeople alike tried to switch the source of shop-floor knowledge from salespeople to accounting figures so that "[s]alespeople can't hornswoggle [buyers] any more with threats and cajoleries." But simple figures lacked the subtleties and the qualitative information saleswomen could provide. This exchange of knowledge about merchandise and customers formed a powerful link between buyer and saleswomen. Buyers could reward faithful and effective saleswomen with good recommendations and performance reports, juicy store gossip, and perquisites such as out-of-town buying trips and special bargains on merchandise.[45]

Buyers and saleswomen were also involved in a tacit alliance against other managers. The buyer acted as a buffer between saleswomen and floorwalkers or upper-level management. She could shield her clerks from harassment by other executives and enforce rules in a lax manner. When salespeople clashed with upper management, buyers often pleaded their cases. Saleswomen in one department at Filene's appealed the store's decision to deny them supper money on a technicality. The general manager argued to the Board of Arbitration that the sales force was uncooperative about giving overtime: "the people should be willing to do a little of the giving and not demand the last drop of blood every time anything special comes up." The department head objected angrily to the "drop of blood" phrase, asserting that "[t]his is a question of justice." Such advocacy earned the loyalty of department members; they could, moreover, reciprocate by protecting the buyer from her superiors. Managers understood that a good way to get saleswomen's compliance with a storewide procedure or rule was to make it a test of cooperation with and loyalty to the buyers. Filene's top management learned the hard way that salespeople would resist anything that smacked of betrayal of the buyers; in 1922, the store announced a "Complete Stocks" contest offering workers a 50¢ prize for each report of an article or size that was out of stock. In the first two weeks of the contest, they received only nine reports because salespeople were well aware that incomplete selections reflected badly on a buyer. Only after A. Lincoln Filene himself met with the buyers and convinced them that the information would not be used against them did the reports come rushing in—eight hundred in a single week.[46]

The gossip columns of the *Echo* are filled with notices about department parties including buyers. Sometimes the saleswomen were the hostesses—as when the suit department saleswomen held a reception for their buyer on her return from a European buying trip—and sometimes the buyer was—as when the cotton waist buyer entertained the department at her home in honor of one who was leaving to marry. One particularly beloved buyer, after casually remarking that she needed three horseshoes for good luck on the opening of her department in the new store building, found her new office filled with three huge horseshoes made of flowers, a gift from her saleswomen. But however warm department relations, a buyer was still well advised to keep her place. A little selling on the floor was fine, a sign of her willingness to work along with the rest, but any buyer who competed with saleswomen for sales or spoke disparagingly of them to customers incurred lasting enmity.[47]

Other managers—floorwalkers, staff executives, and those above buyers in the merchandising hierarchy—were equally aware of saleswomen's work culture but tended to see it as evidence of stupidity, stubbornness, or indifference to self-interest rather than as a sign of workers' informal self-government. Not unlike the slave owners of the antebellum South, they interpreted the actions of their subordinates in a self-serving fashion, refusing to acknowledge explicitly what most dimly perceived: the existence of an oppositional set of rules which simultaneously challenged and sustained the functioning of the store. On one hand, work culture helped the store to run smoothly by arbitrating intradepartmental conflicts, socializing new members, and fostering selling skill; on the other, it sanctioned the stint and various kinds of insubordination, its influence countering management's authority. To crush saleswomen's work culture would have damaged selling service by angering and alienating the saleswomen; to ignore it would have damaged selling service by giving free rein to the stint and departmental sociability. Most managers chose a middle ground which focused limited efforts on specific offenses.

Saleswomen bent rules at every turn, showing that they sensed their employers' hesitancy. Bosses and floorwalkers constantly complained of high spirits and boisterous sociability in the departments and did their unsuccessful best to stamp out loud laughing, talking, singing, and horseplay. Saleswomen openly ridiculed petty regulations and simply refused to comply with managers' demands that they complete "want slips" for every customer request they were unable to fill. They intentionally omitted their numbers from sales checks so that returned goods could not be subtracted from their sales totals. Rule-breaking was a way of life at Filene's; the *Echo* contained many exhortations to employees to be more conscientious. Saleswomen so frequently violated the dress rules with improprieties such as sleeveless dresses and sheer blouses that management began in the mid-1920s to send them home to change clothes and to dock their pay for time lost. They exploited the seasonal rhythms of retailing; twice as many arrived late for work during the summer doldrums as during the busier spring season. When an antitardiness campaign pushed too hard on the rank and file, a wit in the *Echo* suggested that the Tardiness Committee would have to hire Mechanic's Hall, a large auditorium, to hear all the cases of executive tardiness.[48]

Saleswomen most dramatically defied managers when they felt that their dignity had been attacked or their prerogatives undermined. Such was the case in a drapery department in a Pittsburgh store. When the display department assumed the task of decorating the department, saleswomen viewed it as an insult to their abilities; they criticized the display department's work and ostentatiously refused to straighten out displays which became disarranged during the day. A saleswoman whom an executive offended spread the word among her co-workers, and "in a few minutes all the salespeople [were] aroused and doing all they [could] to ignore or annoy him." In dealing with staff personnel, floorwalkers, and upper management, saleswomen maintained a stern unity.[49]

Management's major offensive against saleswomen's work culture was an effort to break the hold of the stint through incentive systems of payment. Saleswomen, like skilled craftsmen and less skilled factory operatives, resisted these tactics. Managers found to their sorrow that these plans might raise sales levels only to cause other problems. Saleswomen became more ruthless about weeding out those whom they supposed to be lookers and concentrated on the most likely prospects, particularly those who appeared to be more prosperous. They became fixated on their books; as one rueful manager put it, they "look at the records their sales are going to show this month, and they do not look at *the customer.*" They shunned stock work as if to point out to management that they would play the game of higher sales with a vengeance, to the exclusion of other aspects of their work. They kept a wary eye out for any among them who might take the incentives too seriously and become a grabber. They ignored less popular merchandise and sold along the lines of least resistance, leaving large portions of the stock untouched until it had to be marked down. And, perhaps most alarming of all, they administered collectively what was designed to be an individualistic system. One manager reported that "[t]here was a tendency for some salespeople who had no prospects of making their quota to turn their sales over to someone who had made their quota and split the commission." Despairing of material incentives, one harried buyer simply resorted to pitting one saleswoman against another with vicious gossip in order to foster a competitive selling spirit. She succeeded in the short run, but in the long run she was left with a foul-tempered and backbiting department that was unable to deliver good selling service.[50]

As universally as managers complained about the power of saleswomen's work culture, no boss testified to the successful and total elimination of its practices. Dire threats and draconian discipline might break its grip on an individual: the manager of an Ohio store told of his yearlong battle to get one saleswoman to sell occasionally in other departments. She stood firm in her refusal, affirming "I'm a coat girl," invoking work culture's pride in and identification with her merchandise. Only his threat to fire her forced her to sell other merchandise, and even then he hedged his bets by demanding that she sign a letter promising to sell anywhere in the store. But more impressive are tales of saleswomen's small, quiet, collective victories against management. In 1915, for example, a desperate floorwalker mounted a major offensive against an obstreperous and temperamental department. He succeeded in subduing the saleswomen temporarily and in whipping them on to higher sales levels, but his success was short-lived. The store manager, faced with imminent insurrection among the saleswomen, finally had to transfer him to another floor. Even in the depth of the Depression, managers lost their battles with work culture. A retailing student reported on an extremely cohesive women's shoe department where the saleswomen enforced the stint rigorously, flaunted the dress code by wearing large hoop earrings, unilaterally extended their lunch hour from forty-five minutes to an hour, and resolutely ignored all storewide activities. Not even the specter of Depression-era unemployment deterred them.[51]

Managing Customers: "Our Friend the Enemy"

However vexed saleswomen's relations with their managers, their dealings with their customers were more so. No one better realized this fact than the saleswomen themselves; a writer for the *Echo* captured all the ambiguity and ambivalence in these relationships by calling the customer "our friend the enemy." While management ingenuously maintained the fiction that all customers could expect equal service, saleswomen picked and chose among their customers and served them with widely varying degrees of interest and efficiency. There were as many views of customers as there were saleswomen: one clerk, near the end of her rope, growled "All customers are crackpots!"; another, more relaxed but still wary, grimly declared "I like a counter between me and the customer"; a third stated firmly, "[M]y customers are my friends." The customer was neither an unambiguous enemy nor a certain ally, but she was in all cases a potential threat to saleswomen individually and collectively.[52]

Class seriously complicated the saleswoman-customer relationship. The former usually came from a working-class family, and the latter from a middle- or upper-class home; even after middle-class and college-educated women entered selling during the 1920s and especially the 1930s, the conviction that the counter was the boundary between classes persisted. In saleswomen's eyes customers behaved either as mistresses to servants or as ladies bountiful to poor working drudges. In the first case, customers simply unloaded their anger and ill temper on the saleswoman as freely and contemptuously as if dealing with a servant. One early-twentieth-century saleswoman complained, "They treat us like the dirt under their feet, and seem to think that we never had anything and never will have anything, and that they can do as they please with us." Two decades later, another saleswoman suggested that perhaps this behavior grew out of the customer's anxieties about her own class and sex position: "It seems . . . as though all the women who have servants they dare not speak to, or a husband who abuses them, take special delight in asserting their independence when they come to buy from us girls, who must say, 'Yes, ma'am' and 'Thank you' in the sweetest possible way." Managers had perversely educated customers to think that they could behave outrageously in the store, and this lesson shaped the conduct of some toward the saleswoman. Even a customer who was quite nice to a clerk could unintentionally give offense or intimidate her, just as she could misunderstand the clerk's best efforts. The class-based differences in manners of saleswoman and customer were troublesome and disruptive, even with the greatest of goodwill on both sides.[53]

Saleswomen responded to this situation either by assuming the servant's role or by trying to beat the customer at her own game of snobbery. An Oregon department store manager had to take a saleswoman out of the better suit department because "[s]he didn't have the nerve to make suggestions to the people whom she waited upon. . . . Our wealthy clientele overawed her with their obvious social position and splendor, and she felt so far beneath them that her manner of showing models developed into that of the well-trained lady's maid." One saleswoman fresh from an egalitarian country store came to work in a Chicago store and was appalled at the "fawning servility" of clerks "who would think of thanking a door mat for letting you wipe your feet on it."[54]

The servant's role, however, did not sit well with the emphasis on independence in saleswomen's work culture in the long run. More frequently, they asserted either equality with or superiority to their customers. Copying the dress and manners of members of a higher class both protected their turf as workers and displayed their acumen as consumers. Moreover, selling shaded over into acting. One writer thus described her experience as a clerk: "The salesgirls seemed always trying to imitate their wealthier customers or the buyer or the coat and suit ladies. Everyone seemed to be imitating someone else and few of the girls were content to be their unvarnished selves." This, then, was the meaning of the ostentatious dress that so often galled managers; it was an attempt to copy, on a saleswoman's budget, a wealthy woman's style of dress and a way of asserting equality with her. Such habits as calling customers "Dearie" were similarly a way of breaking out of the subordinate position defined by the counter.[55]

Saleswomen became fiercely accurate observers with "an uncanny instinct for 'class,'" guessing "a customer's social standing with almost clairvoyant promptness" and treating her accordingly. If she was clearly wealthy and self-assured, they were all respectful but restrained deference; if she was of humbler station and perhaps less poised, they could intimidate her with their superior attitude. The second pattern outraged managers; they roundly condemned saleswomen's "supercilious haughtiness" and tendency to "high-hat." A saleswoman might answer a request for something that was out of stock by intimating that it was too unfashionable for the store to bother with, subtly or not so subtly putting the customer in her place. And when she considered the customer to be beneath the caliber that she and the store merited, gentle intimidation could turn to outright scorn and ridicule. Feeling themselves mistreated or looked down upon, saleswomen sometimes passed that treatment along to those whom they thought unlikely to fight back.[56]

The lady-bountiful customer was more of a mixed bag. Saleswomen owed improvements in their working conditions in part to these women, but day-to-day contact with them in the store could be trying. Socially concerned women frequently questioned them about their salaries, hours, and other aspects of store and even personal life. For the most part, saleswomen viewed their interest as patronizing and resented the familiarity. Sociologist Annie Marion MacLean relished one woman's retort: annoyed beyond endurance when she was asked her salary for the fifth time in one day, she answered the customer and then added, "How much do you get?" Another saleswoman deplored the "cloying public sympathy" of a customer who urged her to rest while she tried on blouses: "I feel so sorry for you girls. I don't see how you keep looking so well, living the life you do. I suppose it is just the necessity of acting cheerful no matter how you feel." In reply, the clerk defended the social and financial advantages of selling. And a woman who had worked her way up to be a buyer had a simple prescription for those who would help "shop-girls"—"Shop early and let them alone outside!" Public concern, whether genuine or condescending, somewhat abated during the 1920s when muckraking was out of fashion and the worker's plight not so much in the press. During the 1930s, though, customers once again began to quiz workers about their lot, particularly asking if the NRA had helped them. Saleswomen were no more grateful then than they had been in the prewar period. The public nature of saleswomen's work lives exposed them to this sort of questioning just as it had to being treated like servants. In both cases, saleswomen's work culture, with its affirmation of the skill and the dignity of the work as well as its critical distance on the customer, supported them in coping with class conflict over the counter.[57]

Even when class-related issues were not at the forefront of the saleswoman-customer interaction, there were myriad ways in which the customer could complicate the life of the clerk. Despite the fact that saleswomen depended for their livelihood on the customer, she was a stranger intruding on their turf, a disruptive factor in their work lives. She barraged them with quirky demands and moody behavior; she interrupted their socializing; she heedlessly took up their time with no thought of buying; she caused them endless extra stock work by demanding to see merchandise; she thoughtlessly got them into trouble with their superiors; and she held them responsible for store practices which were beyond their control. Perhaps the customer's greatest offense was to be a "shop tramp," to wander idly through stores examining the stock and questioning the salespeople—all "just for fun," as a Filene's customer confided to her companion in a stage whisper. When she rounded out the charade by buying something with the intention of later returning it, the sale was subtracted from the clerk's sales record. Saleswomen soon learned to tell these women from those who genuinely meant to buy; no customer was a hero to her saleswoman. Too often, a customer would spend a long time shopping for an item, go home and mull over what she saw, and then go to a different saleswoman and make a quick choice; whether it was a question of sales records or of earnings under an incentive system, this habit did a real injury to the saleswoman who had spent time with her. Saleswomen tried unsuccessfully to educate their customers on this score.[58]

Customers and saleswomen jousted over access to merchandise. The customer wanted to see everything, the widest possible assortment of goods, while the saleswoman wanted to show only a selection, both to assert her power over the customer and to avoid extra stock work in replacing merchandise. Managers repeatedly marveled at saleswomen's reluctance to show goods; even those who were proudest of and most knowledgeable about their stocks held them back from customers. Too often, they preselected merchandise and narrowed the customer's choice for her—showing goods only in a certain price range, those easiest at hand, or those which they themselves favored. Saleswomen were convinced of their customers' ignorance about merchandise and often made no secret of it; they were the professionals, their customers the amateurs.[59]

They also had other ways of putting the customer in her place, perhaps the most important of which was simple indifference. They pretended not to notice customers, alienated them with rudeness, appeared to be engrossed in stock work, or disappeared on sudden errands. When a customer succeeded in catching their attention, they lackadaisically filled her requests, often while continuing to chat with co-workers, add up their books, or arrange stock.[60]

The silent third party in saleswoman-customer interactions further complicated the situation. Customers could get saleswomen into trouble with their superiors, just as they were prone to blame saleswomen for inconveniences that were the fault of management. When a customer had to wait too long for her change or her package or when she found that advertised goods were misrepresented or unavailable, she turned her annoyance on the clerk who represented the store to her. When a customer demanded to return nonreturnable merchandise, the manager was likely to blame the saleswoman for not having made it clear that the sale was final. One saleswoman insured herself against this possibility by telling a customer loudly and pointedly in front of her sister saleswomen that certain articles were not returnable. She could then count on the backing of the work group against management. Saleswomen, for their part, vented their pique with management-caused problems on the customer. In one department the stock was stored in badly designed bins and in piles under tables; when saleswomen had to grope awkwardly for stock, they tended to become irritated with their customers. When they had inadequate merchandise information, they would invent an answer to a customer's question; one sportswear saleswoman termed any fabric with which she was unfamiliar a "novelty weave."[61]

Some saleswomen simply decided that the customer was an out-and-out enemy and treated her as such. They gloated after closing a sale, as if delighting that they had put something over on the unsuspecting purchaser. Feeling themselves victimized by their employers, they themselves delighted in victimizing customers. They loudly commented on customers' manners, dress, and taste, often within earshot of other customers as if to warn them not to commit similar blunders. A particularly disagreeable customer would be left to stew in a fitting room until her saleswoman deigned to rescue her. Clerks repeated tales of customers' offenses over and over in their huddles, perpetuating "an antagonistic attitude towards the next customer."[62]

Some customers, of course, were in fact not what they seemed to be, but rather service shoppers who were management's undercover spies. Although occasionally a department might be eager to be "shopped" as a confirmation of its collective selling skill, more often saleswomen cast the shopper as the enemy. Once managers began to pressure a department to improve service, the saleswomen became obsessed about shoppers; in a ribbon department, "every slightly tedious or exacting customer is imagined to be a shopper with horns and they consequently allow themselves to become upset." Saleswomen prided themselves on being able to spot a shopper and either ostentatiously killed her with kindness or turned on her "the fierce antagonism of the clerking sisterhood."[63]

Other saleswomen, or the same saleswomen at different times, saw the customer as a friend whom they were eager to please and accommodate, someone whose continued trade they desired. When conditions were right, dealing with a customer could be a joy rather than a trial. In addition to treating purchasers with, as a Boston saleswoman put it, "[g]raciousness, tact, and courtesy," saleswomen had a number of tactics with which they might please a customer or smooth a rough transaction. They could flatter or commiserate with a woman fresh from a bad experience with a less gracious clerk; one saleswoman found that suggesting that a woman wore a smaller size than she actually did was a sure way to soothe a ruffled temper. Saleswomen devised little tricks to please customers and sell merchandise: one saleswoman finished the bottom of a blouse with an artful series of tucks to fit it to a short woman; another helped a customer to run a colorful yarn through a skirt to match it to a sweater. Clerks urged customers to take advantage of the store's services, often incurring considerable cost to the store but winning the customer's goodwill. They suggested the delivery of small parcels to close a sale quickly; they urged the tediously undecided to send home a selection of merchandise to reflect on at leisure; they called fitters to alter, often beyond recognition, garments when nothing suitable was in stock; they made wild promises and unauthorized guarantees to quiet customers' nagging doubts; they generously overmeasured yard goods while their approving customers looked on. When customers came behind the counter to sell for the benefit of charities, saleswomen cordially welcomed them into the clerking sisterhood; class barriers dissolved as saleswomen taught them the ropes and turned sales over to them to increase the charity contribution. Yet saleswomen who saw their customers as friends and allies still tried to keep their distance. A few were willing to listen to personal problems and worries, but most tried to center the discussion on the merchandise and related topics; when a Filene saleswoman in the prestigious French Shop went to lunch with one of her wealthy customers, a note in the *Echo* sardonically suggested that this was going too far.[64]

Saleswomen who took a positive view of their customers often built up a clientele with whom they had a continuing relationship; saleswoman's work culture sternly tabooed waiting on another clerk's steady customer. Managers, of course, had long urged the development of clienteles, but saleswomen often went beyond the letter of their instructions. A Kansas City saleswoman sent out seventy-five Christmas cards to her regular customers in 1925; most of them dropped in to thank her and bought something while they were there. A San Francisco cosmetics saleswoman kept an elaborate card catalog of her customers' past purchases and complexion needs. Enterprising saleswomen routinely called their customers to alert them to new merchandise or special sales; customers who trusted "their" saleswomen would frequently purchase such items over the phone. Sometimes, clerks served their clientele too well, from managers' point of view: they would appropriate new styles for them, leaving other customers to choose from older items; they would call customers when a certain item was about to be reduced in price and even hide it in the stockroom until it was time to mark it down.[65]

When she had a large enough following to get away with it—in one Youngstown, Ohio, store each clothing saleswoman had one thousand to twelve hundred steady customers—a clerk would snub "strange" customers and concentrate exclusively on her clientele. A saleswoman in such a position could exert a great deal of control over her work life, scheduling appointments with special customers and lavishing time and attention on them. She could also threaten to quit and take her following with her to another store; managers disagreed about saleswomen's chances of accomplishing this feat, but they worried enough about the possibility to try to protect themselves against it. While saleswomen could use their selling skill to form close and mutually beneficial relationships with customers, they could not do so independently of the store, and another store's different or inferior merchandise could undermine their relationship with their steady customers. The enduring fact was that they simply had access to but did not own, could not determine the nature of, the material means of "production" of sales—the merchandise. And, even at its best, the relationship of a saleswoman with her customer was a chancy thing. As one buyer who had begun her career as a cash girl put it,

"*A customer must be made to think that it is her own good taste, not that of the saleswoman, that sends her off well dressed.* Now here is a curious contradiction which I cannot attempt to explain: The customer will want you to appear to think that she has made the choice, and she will want to go home and receive the admiration of her family and friends upon her good taste; but deep in her heart of hearts she holds you responsible. For your own protection as a saleswoman *you must learn to induce your customers to buy becoming clothes.*"

This, then, was the irreducible minimum of selling skill.[66]

Women/Workers/Consumers

Just as male craftsmen bolstered their control of the shop floor with aspects of men's culture such as sports,* so saleswomen used women's culture to defend their turf as skilled workers and to assert their presence as women. The impact of women's culture on saleswomen's work culture had the same doubleness as it had for American women's lives in general. As Nancy Cott has pointed out, two kinds of ties have linked women: those which limit them to traditional roles, and those which join them to one another and provide the basis for some measure of challenge to those roles. The clerking sisterhood integrated into the life of the selling floor the time-honored rituals of women's culture; employee newspapers reported scores of showers and parties to commemorate engagements, marriages, and births. In Boston, some of the rituals had a special twist: co-workers showered women who were about to be married with confetti. Moreover, saleswomen made a place in the store for domestic skills as well as for job skills, sharing homemaking lore which enabled them to juggle job and home responsibilities more easily. On a more prosaic note, they often brought in home-cooked food to share with co-workers, and sometimes developed friendly rivalries over cooking skill.[67]

---

* Salesmen of course had their own work culture, one which both overlapped with and diverged from that of saleswomen. First, since men were a minority in the store force and usually concentrated in a section of men's departments or in the furniture and appliance departments on the upper floors, they tended to be less departmentally oriented. Much of their store life revolved around sports and storewide events rather than centering in the intense small-group sociability of female-staffed departments. Second, competition was probably more intense among salesmen. A variety of factors can account for this difference: greater dependence upon commissions, often for their entire salary; selling "big ticket" items for which the customers were fewer and farther between than for smaller cheaper items; and male socialization's greater emphasis on competition. For whatever reason, cartoons and anecdotes about "grabbing" in the *Echo* usually cast men in the grabber's role. (See, for example, *Echo*, 13 [21 Dec. 1917], 15 [6 Aug. 1919].) In their dealings with managers and customers, however, men appear to have used the same tactics as their female co-workers.

The store was indeed a place where women traded information about their beaux and learned the rituals of courtship, as Leslie Tentler has pointed out. Women met, dated, and married men from the store force and men whom they met across the counters; tales of romantic entanglements were one of the staples of the *Echo*'s gossip columns. The occasional woman who too aggressively pursued her love life in the store was discharged. Saleswomen's interest in romance coexisted with a consciousness of themselves as workers and even as career women, as an *Echo* article about the infants' department shows: it was praised as a good place to work because its saleswomen *both* got married *and* got promoted. A saleswoman was said to have refused to marry in the summer because she would lose her vacation money, in the fall because she would lose her bonus, and in the winter because she would lose her first winter vacation; the implication was that marriage was not always the eager first choice of Filene women. The Women's Club staged evening musicales and listened to fortune tellers spin out romantic predictions, but it also provided a forum for close questioning of top management about promotion possibilities and salary increases.[68]

Saleswomen's work culture also supported and encouraged varieties of feminism. As Barbara Melosh has noted in regard to nurses, sex segregation on the job has a subversive potential. In the all-female work group, women develop close bonds of solidarity and mutual respect as well as an understanding of their skills and competence as workers. Far from being simply a source of victimization, sex segregation can provide a space where self-respect and initiative grow. Female clerks made it clear to male employees that they were on hostile ground in a woman's world; one beleaguered floorwalker got the message when he observed, "These imperious dames seemed to resent even the very presence of a 'mere male' in their sections." Because maleness coincided with higher levels of authority in the department store, women simultaneously protected their turf as workers and their turf as women. At Filene's, saleswomen used the *Echo*'s gossip columns to warn male employees to desist from behavior that we would today call sexual harassment and to chide men who used language insulting to women. An offender received this message from the women of the Basement Balcony: "Mr. Smith, our dear floorman, seems quite interested in some of our girls. We wish he wouldn't do us any favors." A manager who made the mistake of saying that an election should not be conducted "according to a woman's idea of keeping a secret" earned a stern chastisement. The suffrage movement attracted the

Fig. 21. A Timely Warning

NELLIE WAS WARNED TO BE
DISTANT IN HER ATTITUDE
TOWARD A CERTAIN
FLOOR-WALKER

Munsey's Magazine, 50 (Nov. 1913), 254. Original in John Hay Library,
Brown University.

store's saleswomen in large numbers and was frequently discussed in the departments and in the women's club. Apparently a majority of store women were eager for the vote and used store networks to recruit for the cause. From baby showers to suffrage parades, saleswomen's work culture used women's culture in both a traditional and an oppositional way, expressing and sustaining saleswomen's multivalent status as workers and women.[69]

The nature of saleswomen's work culture shows their notable ability to exploit a flexible and ambiguous situation. Because there was no rigid formula for successful selling, clerks could liberally interpret employers' rules and instructions with relative impunity. For example, managers urged saleswomen to help one another, and they went overboard in forming close-knit work groups which subverted management goals. Managers emphasized selling skill, and saleswomen made those skills the basis of a resourceful work culture. Management encouraged saleswomen to use their domestic knowledge and women's culture in the store, and they went a step further in forming the "clerking sisterhood." Management encouraged clerks to become adept at social interaction, and they huddled on the selling floor, using their social skills with their peers as well as with their customers. Management emphasized the importance of fashion, and saleswomen used their arguments to justify insurrections against dress rules.

Saleswomen's techniques for disciplining unruly customers were similar to their ways of dealing with their bosses. They withheld their knowledge about merchandise from customers, and often sullenly withheld the merchandise itself. Clerks had enormous discretion in dealing with customers as well as in dealing with their employers: they could calculatingly fawn over or condescend to them; they could terrorize them or kill them with kindness; they could ignore them or overwhelm them with attention.

The study of saleswomen's work culture not only illuminates the lives of those legions of women who were a part of it, but also suggests ways of revising the history of women workers in particular and life on the shop floor in general. At least one group of women workers, and doubtless others, developed a shop-floor culture that combined a keen sense of themselves as workers and as women. Both elements contained contradictions. As workers, saleswomen developed an appreciation of the skill of selling but an unwillingness to use that skill as their employers wished.

As women, they integrated both a traditional home-and-family outlook and a more critical feminist stance into their work culture. The long-standing assumption that women's consciousness is overwhelmingly the product of domestic imperatives oversimplifies the complicated dynamic of women workers' daily lives.

The tactics of saleswomen's work culture were those long familiar to male skilled workers, but now mobilized to protect interpersonal and consumer skills rather than artisanal or mechanical ones. It is time to ask if these tactics are less specific to skilled workers than generalized among workers under conditions of capitalist production. All workers have a knowledge of the work they do that surpasses the prescriptions of their employers; to understand the modes by which workers protect and expand that knowledge can help to fix the boundary between the struggle and the acquiescence that are part of every worker's life.

One of male skilled workers' major weapons was conspicuously absent from saleswomen's work culture: the labor union. Until the CIO-sparked drives of the middle and later 1930s, barely a handful of the nation's saleswomen carried union cards. The Retail Clerks' International Protective Association (RCIPA), the principal pre-CIO retail union, claimed only two thousand female members in the mid-1920s—an insignificant .4 percent of the nation's women sales workers, many of them in small-town shops rather than in urban department stores. The organizing efforts of the late 1930s brought the unionized proportion nearer 5 percent. For most of the half-century between 1890 and 1940, then, labor unions had very little impact on the day-to-day life of the selling floor.[70]

Far from surprising, this fact is doubly predictable because of the tendency of both women and white-collar workers to organize less often than men and blue-collar workers. Virtually all of the factors which conspire against women's unionization converged in department-store selling: high labor turnover; possibilities for upward mobility for the longer-term worker; a union (the RCIPA) which was at best paternalistic and often outright hostile to the organizing of saleswomen; and managers who were especially ruthless in firing union sympathizers uncovered by their pervasive and effective spy networks. Given the array of circumstances undermining unionization, it is remarkable not how little but how often saleswomen tried to organize. First during the pre–World War I burst of women's militancy, then after World War I, and again during the late 1930s, some department-store saleswomen saw unionization as desirable and possible. As historians begin to ask not why women fail to organize but why they sometimes try and succeed, the motivations, victories, and failures of this minority will be recaptured for the historical record.[71]

One of the questions a study of department-store saleswomen's union efforts will have to consider is that of the relation of saleswomen's work culture to labor unions. Recent writers have argued both that work culture fed into union strength and that it thwarted it; an understanding of saleswomen's work culture suggests that the two possibilities coexisted and that work culture was indeed a flexible resource. Work culture fostered persuasive skills and ease at dealing with the public which served saleswomen well in their union struggles; news reports frequently note the energy and verve that saleswomen brought to the picket line and support meetings. Even as they displayed workers' militancy, however, saleswomen could still act out their pride in their white-collar status and their vision of themselves as the arbiters of fashion and consumption: during the 1937 San Francisco strike saleswomen from the carriage-trade stores showed up for picket duty dressed to the nines, making the strike action look "like a fashion show."[72]

Seen from another point of view, of course, work culture was a hindrance to and an inferior substitute for unionization. Reinforcing the fragmentation of the store into departments, work culture's base in the departmental work group could undercut the storewide solidarity required to build a union. The aspects of work culture which provided channels for expressing hostility toward managers and customers could legitimate that anger, but could also defuse it by allowing saleswomen to act out their workers' consciousness in the sheltered context of the department rather than taking the enormous risks of union activity. Moreover, sales work did not involve the dyadic worker-manager relationship of the factory; the complex saleswoman/customer/manager triangle obscured and transformed the content of class conflict on the selling floor. It was not always clear who the enemy was. Finally, and perhaps most important of all, work culture functioned in an informal, customary fashion while unions adopted formalized legalistic agreements; shop-floor action was not always readily transferable to the bargaining table or the grievance procedure. Labor unions might regularize management practice, but work culture protected the "perks," and the two could clash as well as reinforce each other. It would be equally inappropriate to romanticize saleswomen's work culture and to blame it for their failure to unionize. Work culture in itself cannot insure dignity and justice for workers, but it did shape the daily lives of thousands of saleswomen, providing organizing principles and a sense of right even as it lacked the authority to enforce them. Placed alongside the cultural factors inhibiting the organization of white-collar women, the impotence of the RCIPA, and the grimly anti-union policies of their employers, saleswomen's work culture pales into insignificance as a block to unionization.

The work culture of saleswomen suggests that the society of mass consumption was not, and is not, a seamless whole. Consumer capitalism had created and defined saleswomen's roles as workers along with their female roles as consumers, but their patterns of independence and resistance made them less than paragons of either role. Saleswomen played both sides of the counter: on the one hand they were the finest flower of a consumers' society, yet on the other hand they were expert at subverting it. As a group, they occupied a peculiar position spanning the realms of production and consumption: just as their image of themselves as workers undermined their absolute allegiance to a life of consumption, so too did their image of themselves as priestesses of consumption circumscribe their actions as workers. Perhaps the position of the saleswoman was not in fact unique after all, but rather an extreme case of the dilemma of all workers under consumer capitalism—driven by the social relations of the workplace to see themselves as members of the working class, cajoled by the rewards of mass consumption to see themselves as middle-class. We should not dismiss this as false consciousness, but rather try to understand its contradictions by studying the complex interactions among managers, workers, and customers; between life on the job and life off the job.

Notes

1. Frances R. Donovan, *The Woman Who Waits* (1920; rpt. New York, 1974), and *The Saleslady* (1929; rpt. New York, 1974); Stanley B. Mathewson, *Restriction of Output among Unorganized Workers* (1931; rpt. Carbondale, Ill., 1969); Katherine Stone, "The Origins of Job Structures in the Steel Industry," *Review of Radical Political Economics*, 6 (Summer 1974), 113–73; Sharon Strom, " 'We're No Kitty Foyles': Organizing Office Workers for the CIO, 1937–1950," in Ruth Milkman, ed., *Women, Work, and Protest: A Century of Women's Labor History* (London, 1985), 206–34; Patricia Cooper, *Fire and Smoke: Men, Women, and Work Culture in American Cigar Factories* (forthcoming); Barbara Melosh, *"The Physician's Hand": Work Culture and Conflict in American Nursing* (Philadelphia, 1982). Melosh's is a model treatment of the three-way employer/worker/client relationship.

2. Barbara Melosh and I jointly wrote this paragraph. It grows out of a long collaboration between us.

3. Harry Braverman, *Labor and Monopoly Capital: The Degradation of Work in the Twentieth Century* (New York, 1974); Michael Burawoy, *Manufacturing Consent: Changes in the Labor Process under Monopoly Capitalism* (Chicago, 1982); Leslie Woodcock Tentler, *Wage-Earning Women: Industrial Work and Family Life in the United States, 1900–1930* (New York, 1979). For an excellent synthesis of writings on the labor process, see Jeremy Brecher et al., "Uncovering the Hidden History of the American Workplace," *Review of Radical Political Economics*, 10 (Winter 1978), 1–23. Sarah Eisenstein (*Give Us Bread but Give Us Roses: Working Women's Consciousness in the United States, 1890 to the First World War* [London, 1983]) provides a more nuanced account than Tentler, but basically agrees about the primacy of the desire for marriage and a family among working women.

4. Ken Kusterer explores working knowledge in *Know-How on the Job* (Boulder, Colo., 1978).

5. The theses were written by graduate students in retailing at Simmons College and the University of Pittsburgh during the 1920s and 1930s. The major human relations study, a rich source indeed, is George F. F. Lombard, *Behavior in a Selling Group* (Boston, 1955). The thesis on which the book is based contains additional detail: Lombard, "Executive Policies and Employee Satisfaction" (Ph.D. diss., Harvard Univ., 1941). Both grow out of shop-floor research done in Macy's children's wear department in 1940. For a general study of Filene's and the Filene Co-Operative Association, see Mary LaDame, *The Filene Store* (New York, 1930); although Filene's industrial democracy plan was highly unusual, my reading of the *Echo* has convinced me that the management of selling and the shop-floor interaction at the store were quite typical of department stores in general. Trade periodicals are more useful for the study of work culture than individual store histories, which tend to be shameless paeans to the store's founders.

6. Elizabeth Bott, *Family and Social Network*, 2d ed. (New York, 1971); Michelle Zimbalist Rosaldo and Louise Lamphere, eds., *Woman, Culture, and Society* (Stanford, Calif., 1974); James Spradley and Brenda Mann, *Cocktail Waitress* (New York, 1975); Ann Bookman, "The Process of Political Socialization among Women and Immigrant Workers" (Ph.D. diss., Harvard Univ., 1977); Nina Shapiro-Perl, "Labor Process and Class Relations in the Costume Jewelry Industry: A Study in Women's Work" (Ph.D. diss., Univ. of Connecticut, 1983); Louise Lamphere, "Fighting the Piece-Rate System: New Dimensions of an Old Struggle in the Apparel Industry," in Andrew Zimbalist, ed., *Case Studies on the Labor Process* (New York, 1979), 257–76.

7. David Montgomery, *Workers' Control in America* (Cambridge, 1979), 13–14. Women embraced the nineteenth-century idea of the labor theory of value with its assertion of the dignity and worth of labor as the source of value, but were excluded by definition from the traditions of the skilled male crafts and from the republican vision of independent citizenship. For a discussion of the labor theory of value, see Alan Dawley and Paul Faler, "Working Class Culture and Politics in the Industrial Revolution: Sources of Loyalism and Rebellion," *Journal of Social*

History, 9 (June 1976), 466–80. See also Thomas Dublin, "Working Women and the Free Labor Ideology, 1830–1850," paper presented at the annual meeting of the Organization of American Historians, Apr. 1979.

8. Annie Marion MacLean, "Two Weeks in Department Stores," *American Journal of Sociology*, 4 (May 1899), 729; "They Put Martha in the Kitchenware, and Left Her—So Someone Else Got Her," *DGE*, 74 (3 Jan. 1920), 19; *Rich Bits*, May 1938, 6, quoted in Henry Givens Baker, *Rich's of Atlanta* (Atlanta, 1953), 310; David Ovens, "Management's Job in Better Selling," *BNRDGA*, 23 (Feb. 1941), 26; Store Management Group, NRDGA, *Mid-year Convention Proceedings* (New York, 1942), 139; *Echo*, 10 (7 Dec. 1912 and 30 Apr. 1913), 14 (11 Jan. 1918), 22 (6 Feb. 1925), 24 (18 Feb. 1927); Pauline Goldmark and George A. Hall, "Preliminary Report on the Employment of Women and Children in Mercantile Establishments," appendix 9, vol. 2, New York State Factory Investigating Commission, *Second Report* (Albany, 1913), 1252. In some popular-priced department stores catering to a humbler trade, the two-class system was less noticeable. Rheta Childe Dorr, for example, worked in a store "patronized by the rank and file" where customers and saleswomen shared the same elevators and restaurant. It is impossible to know how widespread this practice was, but virtually all discussions of store facilities assume a segregated system. "Christmas behind the Counter," *Independent*, 63 (5 Dec. 1907), 1341–42.

9. Lauren Gilfillan, "Weary Feet," *Forum*, 90 (Oct. 1933), 208; Store Managers' Division, NRDGA, *Convention Proceedings, Fourth Annual Convention* (New York, 1927), 115 (the speaker was Samuel Reyburn); *Echo*, 26 (30 Mar. 1928); Susan Katherine Manning, "An Analysis of a Merchandising Department (Foundation Garments) with Organized Material for a Departmental Training Program: A Study Made in Nine Pittsburgh Stores" (M.A. thesis, Univ. of Pittsburgh, 1930), 26.

10. "A Documentary History of the R. H. Macy Company," Manuscript Division, Baker Library, Harvard Graduate School of Business Administration, 185–86; *Echo*, 7 (May 1909), 27 (27 Apr. 1928).

11. "Employees' Sales," *DGE*, 81 (2 Apr. 1927), 14; "Discounts to Employees," *DGE*, 74 (15 Nov. 1919), 5; J. R. Ozanne, "What Do You Know about Your Own Employees?" in Store Managers' Division, NRDGA, *Convention Proceedings, Fourth Annual Convention* (New York, 1927), 122; C. E. Eerkes, "The Employee—A Preferred Customer," in NRDGA, *Joint Management Proceedings—Concurrent Conventions* (New York, 1934), 78; Charles M. Edwards, Jr. and Mary L. Brower, "'Cashing In' on Employee Business," *JR*, 13 (Dec. 1937), 113; "Forging a Link between Employees and the Public," *System*, 60 (July 1931), 62; *Echo*, 24 (10 Dec. 1926).

12. "Store Instructs High School Students," *DGE*, 69 (13 Mar. 1915), 33; "Get Employees to Read Ads," *DGE*, 69 (16 Oct. 1915), 61; "Employee Purchases," *DGE*, 70 (11 Dec. 1915), 55; "Sales to Employees," *DGE*, 70 (1 Jan. 1916), 28; Evelyn M. Borg, "Employee Purchases," *JR*, 3 (July 1927), 27–30; "Documentary History of Macy Company," 2915; "Employee Shopping during Store-Wide Sales," *BNRDGA*, 13 (Dec. 1931), 737–38, 773; "Employees' Sales," *DGE*, 63 (5 Dec. 1908), 17; "The Emporium 'Sells' Important Group of

Customers—Its Own Employees," *DGE*, 80 (9 Jan. 1926), 17; *Echo*, 22 (16 May 1924).

13. *Cost of Living of Working Women in Ohio*, Industrial Commission of Ohio, Department of Investigation and Statistics, Report No. 14 (Columbus, 1915), 199; Paul Brown, "Shopgirls: 1930 Model," *Commonweal*, 12 (8 Oct. 1930), 577; Eerkes, "Employee—A Preferred Customer," 79.

14. "Documentary History of Macy Company," 2915; interview with Miss Wisehmeyer, in raw data for Women's Bureau Bulletin No. 35, National Archives, Record Group 86, Box 190; "Get Employees to Read Ads," 61.

15. Helen Campbell, *Prisoners of Poverty*, (1887; rpt. Westport, Conn., 1970), 183; Louise Marion Bosworth, *The Living Wage of Women Workers* (New York, 1911), 66; William Hard and Rheta Childe Dorr, "The Woman's Invasion," *Everybody's Magazine* 20 (Jan. 1909), 77; "Wide-Awake Retailing," *DGE*, 48 (13 Apr. 1893), 49; Elizabeth Beardsley Butler, *Women and the Trades: Pittsburgh, 1907–1908* (New York, 1911), 328–29; *Echo*, 20 (29 Sept. 1922); Gertrude H. Sykes, "Dress Regulations in New York Metropolitan Stores," *JR*, 4 (Jan. 1929), 28.

16. *Echo*, 1 (Dec. 1902).

17. *Echo*, 10 (29 Jan., 12 Feb., 19 Feb., and 26 Feb. 1913), 20 (10 Nov. and 17 Nov. 1922), 21 (8 June and 14 Sept. 1923), 22 (26 Sept. 1924), 29 (27 June and 18 July 1930); see also 11 July, 26 Sept., and 3 Oct. 1930, and 27 Mar. 1931.

18. U.S. Congress, Senate, *Report on Condition of Woman and Child Wage-Earners in the United States*, vol. 5, *Wage-Earning Women in Stores and Factories*, 61st Cong., 2d sess., Sen. Doc. 645 (Washington, 1910), 109, 129; "Martha in Kitchenware," 20.

19. H. J. Conway, "Low Wages Paid in Retail Stores Responsible for Many Evils," *RCIA*, 29 (Jan. 1922), 17–18; Hartley Davis, "The Department Store at Close Range," *Everybody's Magazine*, 17 (Sept. 1907), 321; *Echo*, 11 (20 Nov. and 4 Dec. 1913), 28 (28 June 1929).

20. A. M. Houghton, "How Store Leaks May Be Minimized," *DGE*, 65 (10 June 1911), 29–31; A. C. Helhake, "How Store Leaks May Be Minimized," *DGE*, 65 (8 July 1911), 29–31; A. G. Chaney, "How Store Leaks May Be Minimized," *DGE*, 65 (29 July 1911), 33–34; S. A. Hamburger, "How to Minimize the Store's Leaks," *DGE*, 65 (22 Sept. 1911), 59–60. These articles were for a *DGE* essay contest on the subject; they are notable in being exceptions to the rule of silence on such matters. For other examples of managers' unwillingness to confront the issue of employee theft, see "Bonding a Good Method," *DGE*, 66 (17 Feb. 1912), 55–56; "Worked Thievery Claim," *DGE*, 66 (11 Nov. 1911), 39, "Inspection Wrap vs. Clerk Wrap," *DGE*, 81 (9 Apr. 1927), 11; NRDGA, *Twenty-Five Years of Retailing* (New York, 1936), 50; S. A. Hamburger, "How to Minimize Store's Leaks," 59; Store Managers' Division, NRDGA, *Convention Proceedings, Fourth Annual Convention*, 90–91. For another, more dramatic instance of the tacit acceptance of pilfering, see Alvin Gouldner, *Patterns of Industrial Bureaucracy* (New York, 1954), 51.

21. *Echo*, 22 (3 July and 8 Aug. 1924), 23 (26 June 1925), 24 (20 Aug. 1926

and 11 Feb. 1927), 31 (15 Sept. 1933), 32 (27 Apr. 1934); the hospital anecdote is in 27 (22 Mar. 1929).

22. *Echo*, 13 (21 Sept. 1916), 15 (18 Sept. 1919), and 16 (23 Jan. 1920); Schedule No. 455, raw data for Bureau of Labor Statistics Bulletin No. 128, National Archives, Record Group 257, Box 92; Ozanne, "What Do You Know about Your Own Employees?" 122.

23. Elizabeth G. Stern, *I Am a Woman—and a Jew* (1926; rpt. New York, 1969), 174–77; Mary H. Tolman, *Positions of Responsibility in Department Stores and Other Retail-Selling Organizations* (New York, 1921), 30, 93; Helen Baker, *Personnel Programs in Department Stores* (Princeton, N.J., 1935),19–20; Emma Wilson Smith, "An Analysis of a Sportswear Department in a Department Store" (M.A. thesis, Univ. of Pittsburgh, 1935), 48; Anna May Johnston, "An Analysis of a Linen Department in a Department Store" (M.A. thesis, Univ. of Pittsburgh, 1932), 83.

24. "Operating Experiences under the NRA," *BNRDGA*, 15 (Oct. 1933), 44; "The Way with People," *BNRDGA*, 9 (Oct. 1927), 522; "Sales Chats," *DGE*, 81 (21 May 1927), 88; "Saleswoman's View of Department Heads," *DGE*, 72 (6 Apr. 1918), 153; "Making Good on the Sales Job," *DGE*, 81 (27 Nov. 1926), 12; Sue Ainslie Clark and Edith Wyatt, *Making Both Ends Meet: The Income and Outlay of New York Working Girls* (New York, 1911), 14.

25. Interview with Ethel Calhoun, in raw data for Women's Bureau Bulletin No. 22, National Archives, Record Group 86, Box 182; interview with Lora Smith, in raw data for Women's Bureau Bulletin No. 35, Record Group 86, Box 190; "Educate Help and Customer," *DGE*, 63 (23 Jan. 1909), 31; "The Question of Personnel in the Silverware Department," *DGE*, 81 (27 Aug. 1927), 71; Philip J. Reilly, "The Bases Used by Department Stores in Establishing Wage-Rates," *Annals of the American Academy*, 100 (Mar. 1922), 31; "Mr. Newmaier Speaks His Piece about Making First Floor Departments Pay," *DGE*, 78 (10 May 1924), 15; Stern, *I Am a Woman*, 177; Johnston, "Analysis of Linen Department," 83; Alice Hughes, "A Customer's Idea of Good Store Service," *BNRDGA*, 17 (Feb. 1935), 75, 179; Margaret Durand, "A Study of a Millinery Department (with Special Emphasis on Personnel and Sales Promotion Factors)" (M.Sc. thesis, Simmons Coll., 1937), 16; Stanley Roth, "The Selection and Placement of Salespeople," in NRDGA, *Confidential Bulletin*, 7 (Mar. 1925), 40; Sarah Johnson, "An Analysis of a Drapery Department in a Department Store" (M.A. thesis, Univ. of Pittsburgh, 1934), 97; B. J. May, "Round Pegs Can Fit Too Well," *DSE*, 1 (10 May 1938), 28; "How to Sell Veilings," *DGE*, 55 (29 May 1901), 15; *Training for Store Service* (Boston, 1920), 46–47; see also "Good Looks Help Sell Cosmetics," *DGE*, 75 (3 Sept. 1921), 55; Isabel B. Wingate, "Getting a Job in a Retail Store," *JR*, 4 (July 1928), 26; "An Assistant That Was 'O.K.,'" *DGE*, 65 (20 May 1911), 69.

26. NRDGA, *Joint Management Proceedings—1940* (New York, 1940), 17; F. R. Lamb, "How to Develop an Interchangeable Sales Force," *BNRDGA*, 8 (May 1926), 25; "'Clinic' Prescribes Treatment for Ailments of Employee Morale," *BNRDGA*, 21 (Feb. 1939), 41, 122; Mary Barnett Gilson, *What's Past Is*

Prologue (New York, 1940), 43; "From Dust-Rag to Buyer's Desk," *Forum*, 58 (July 1917), 83; *Echo*, 13 (22 June and 20 July 1917), 17 (11 Mar. 1921), 23 (6 Nov. 1925). Sue Ainslie Clark and Edith Wyatt entered a lone dissent about the sociability of saleswomen, noting that some women held themselves apart for fear that their co-workers were of low moral character (*Making Both Ends Meet*, 28–29).

27. *Echo*, 14 (19 July 1918); Gilson, *What's Past*, 43; *Echo*, 13 (30 Nov. 1917); Jordan Marsh *Fellow Worker*, 11 (Feb.-Mar. 1928), 6.

28. *Echo*, 1 (May 1903), 13 (3 June 1915), 15 (18 Sept. 1919), 9 (Mar. 1912), 22 (16 May 1924); "An Influential Class of Customers," *DGE*, 79 (25 Apr. 1925), 9–10; "Employees' Sales," *DGE*, 81 (2 Apr. 1927), 13.

29. References to huddling abound in all varieties of retailing literature. See, for example, "On Both Sides of the Counter," *DGC & FGR*, 7 (15 June 1889), 7; "Wide-Awake Retailing," *DGE*, 48 (11 Mar. 1893), 57 and (13 Apr. 1893), 49; "Hints for December," *DGE*, 64 (4 Dec. 1909), 43; "Harmony Essential," *DGE*, 66 (3 Aug. 1912), 39; "What It Means to Be a Department-Store Girl—As Told by the Girl Herself," *Ladies' Home Journal*, 30 (June 1913), 8; *Echo*, 11 (26 June 1913); Rowena Elizabeth Hoisington, "Analysis of a Hosiery Department" (M.Sc. thesis, Simmons Coll., 1931), 107; Florence L. Luman, "An Analysis of the China and Glassware Department in a Department Store" (M.A. thesis, Univ. of Pittsburgh, 1932), 84. George E. Bittner, *Analyzing Retail Selling Time: Cost of Selling Commodities over the Retail Counter*, U.S. Department of Commerce, Bureau of Foreign and Domestic Commerce, Domestic Commerce Division, Distribution Cost Studies No. 2 (Washington, 1928), 3–4; David R. Craig, "A Labor Survey," in Store Management Group, NRDGA, *1937 Mid-Year Convention Proceedings* (New York, 1937), 124; "In Their Spare Time," *DGE*, 76 (17 Dec. 1921), 14; D. J. Tobin, "Dividing Sales Work and Stock Work without Extra Expense," *DGE*, 80 (8 May 1926), 21; *Echo*, 11 (26 June 1913); "Do PMs Really Pay?" *DGE*, 53 (10 June 1899), 18; Mabel Potter Daggett, "Cash Girl No. 63," *Delineator*, 83 (July 1913), 5–6; MacLean, "Two Weeks," 726; "Teach Salespeople How to Serve 'Looker,'" *DGE*, 70 (5 Aug. 1916), 15; "What Would *YOU* Do with the Crepe Hanger?" *DGE*, 76 (4 Mar. 1922), 37; "Here Is the Clam—What Would *YOU* DO?" *DGE*, 76 (1 Apr. 1922), 119; W. H. Leffingwell, "Sizing Up Customers from behind the Counter," *American Magazine*, 94 (July 1922), 150; *Echo*, 13 (13 July 1917), 12 (11 Mar. 1915), 21 (19 Oct. 1923), 24 (23 Apr. 1926).

30. Mary Alden Hopkins, "The Girls behind the Counter," *Collier's*, 48 (16 Mar. 1912), 17; "A Salesgirl's Story," *Independent*, 54 (31 July 1902), 1819; Goldmark and Hall, "Preliminary Report," 1252; *Echo*, 1 (Dec. 1902); Clark and Wyatt, *Making Both Ends Meet*, 29–34; Dorr, "Christmas," 1346–47.

31. *Echo*, 15 (18 Sept. 1919); "Lace and Embroidery Selling Hints," *DGE*, 67 (8 Nov. 1913), 47, 51; "Her Sun Is a Frosted Electric Globe and Her Queen Is Fashion," *DGE*, 77 (13 Jan. 1923), 69; Felix Koch, "Making the Customer Happy with Her Purchase, Is Mabley's Selling Keystone," *DGE*, 78 (5 Jan. 1924), 33; "Making Good on the Sales Job," *DGE*, 80 (26 June 1926), 17; "Sales That I Wished I Hadn't Made," *DGE*, 73 (5 Apr. 1919), 277; untitled note, *RCIA*, 35 (Nov. 1928), 9.

32. Frances R. Donovan, *The Saleslady* (1929; rpt. New York, 1974), 76–77; Ruth Farquhar, "The Analysis of a Drapery Department in a Department Store" (M.A. thesis, Univ. of Pittsburgh, 1932), 109; *Echo*, 16 (18 Oct. 1935).

33. *Echo*, 1 (July 1903).

34. Nina Lambert, "An Analysis of a Girls' Wear Department in a Department Store" (M.A. thesis, Univ. of Pittsburgh, 1935), 41–42; Edward Mott Woolley, "A Short Cut to Salvation," *McClure's Magazine*, 40 (Dec. 1912), 231; "Study of a Ribbon Department," *BNRDGA*, 9 (Oct. 1927), 524; Donovan, *Saleslady*, 48; Anne Bezanson and Miriam Hussey, *Wage Methods and Selling Costs* (Philadelphia, 1930); Mathewson, *Restriction of Output*, 20–21; Ruth Farquhar, "Analysis of Drapery Department," 87; Charlotte Anne Feazel, "An Analysis of a Women's Shoe Department in a Department Store" (M.A. thesis, Univ. of Pittsburgh, 1933), 51; Katherine Barbara Fetterman, "An Analysis of a House Dress Department in a Department Store" (M.A. thesis, Univ. of Pittsburgh, 1933), 55, 60; Georgia Wittich, "Constructive Use of the Shopping Report," in NRDGA, *Joint Management Proceedings—Concurrent Conventions* (New York, 1934), 14–20; Charlotte Collins, "A Study of the Oxford Shop" (M.Sc. thesis, Simmons Coll., 1938), 73; Lombard, *Behavior*, 147–67; "Making Good on the Sales Job," *DGE*, 81 (7 May 1927), 16.

35. Lombard, *Behavior*, 147–67; *Echo*, 16 (16 Jan. and 16 Apr. 1920), 20 (26 May 1922), 24 (21 Jan. and 25 Feb. 1927); Michael Schaap, "Building an Efficient Selling Organization," *BNRDGA*, 23 (Feb. 1941), 27; Diana Hirschler, "The Aisles of Trade," *Collier's*, 51 (23 Aug. 1913), 33.

36. Margaret Holbrook Titcomb, "Selling to the Selling Force," *DGE*, 80 (5 Dec. 1925), 15; MacLean, "Two Weeks," 727; "Training Program Packs Dynamite," *DSE*, 4 (10 Mar. 1941), 3; Lombard, "Executive Policies," 318–28. Compare MacLean, "Two Weeks," 721–41; Goldmark and Hall, *Preliminary Report*, 1227; and Stern, "*I Am a Woman*," 152–57 with those describing later initiations.

37. "Putting a Punch into the Departments," *DGE*, 69 (8 May 1915), 33; Imogene McIlvain, "Merchandise Training for Contingents" (M.Sc. thesis, Simmons Coll., 1927), 7–10; Irene Winifred Gallagher, "An Analysis of a China and Glassware Department" (M.Sc. thesis, Simmons Coll., 1929), 75; Alice Paul Fehr, "An Analysis of a Merchandise Department (Electrical Appliances) with Organized Material for a Training Program" (M.A. thesis, Univ. of Pittsburgh, 1931), 17–18; Emma Wilson Smith, "Analysis of Sportswear Department," 48; Helen Johnson, "The Employment and Subsequent Handling of Extra Salespeople" (M.Sc. thesis, Simmons Coll., 1939), 37–38; "Sales That I Wished I Hadn't Made," 273; Harold Caile, "Those Damned Contingents," *DGE*, 82 (24 Dec. 1927), 9; "How I Want to Be Taught, and Why," *DGE*, 77 (14 Apr. 1923), 26; Anne Gletne, "The Contingent's Job," *BNRDGA*, 17 (Jan. 1935), 100; Fehr, "Analysis of Merchandise Department," 17–18.

38. Lombard, "Executive Policies," 327.

39. "Retailers Condemn Clerk Control Coupons," *DGE*, 66 (20 April 1912), 49, 51. The allocation of turf is a central concern of Lombard's thesis and book. See also Arthur W. Einstein, "Interselling versus Specialization of Sales Efforts," in NRDGA, *Joint Management Proceedings—1940* (New York, 1940),

91–92, for a description of a similar situation. "Distribution of Help," *DGE*, 61 (15 Dec. 1906), 3; "'How to Sell It' Problem from Various Angles," *DGE*, 72 (5 Oct. 1918), 7; "Making Good on the Sales Job," *DGE*, 81 (8 Jan. 1927), 14, (12 Feb. 1927), 15, (19 May 1926), 14; *Echo*, 24 (9 July 1926), 25 (6ay 1927); Julia Campbell, "An Analysis of a Girls' Wear Department in a Department Store" (M.A. thesis, Univ. of Pittsburgh, 1933), 53; *Echo*, 35 (23 Aug. 1935); Wittich, "Constructive Use of Shopping Report," 19.

40. *Echo*, 4 (Mar. 1907); M. Bridgman, "How We Rebuilt an Unprofitable Department," *System*, 33 (Feb. 1918), 213; Vita S. Putter, "The Salesperson Looks at Selling," *JR*, 14 (Feb. 1938), 32; *Echo*, 2 (Apr. and Oct. 1904), 5 (May 1907); Ruth M. Cunningham, "An Analysis of an Interior Decorating Department of a Department Store" (M.A. thesis, Univ. of Pittsburgh, 1932), 211.

41. B. Kirk Payne, "An Analysis of a Foundation Garment Department in a Department Store" (M.A. thesis, Univ. of Pittsburgh, 1935), 39; *Echo*, 24 (30 Apr. 1926); "A Valuable Asset," *DGE*, 71 (6 Oct. 1917), 14.

42. NRDGA, *Joint Management Proceedings—Concurrent Conventions* (New York, 1934), 78; Johnston, "Analysis of Linen Department," 83; Leffingwell, "Sizing Up Customers," 152; Elizabeth Nickolls, "Inquiry into Departmental Methods of a Department Store for the Purpose of Making Constructive Criticism" (M.Sc. thesis, Simmons Coll., 1929), 73–74; Daggett, "Cash Girl," 5; *Echo*, 23 (26 June 1925); C. K. MacDermut, "That's Aggressive Selling," *RCIA*, 37 (Mar.-Apr. 1932), 4; "How to Consult Salespeople," *DGE*, 62 (12 Sept. 1908), 55; "Moving Slow Selling Merchandise," *DGE*, 62 (10 Oct. 1908), 95; "Told to the Salespeople," *DGE*, 67 (8 Mar. 1913), 93; *Echo*, 23 (12 Mar. 1926); "Making Good on the Sales Job," *DGE*, 81 (12 Feb. 1927), 15; Margaret J. Accipter, "An Analysis of an Intimate Apparel Department in a Department Store" (M.A. thesis, Univ. of Pittsburgh, 1933), 21–22; Emma Wilson Smith, "Analysis of Sportswear Department," 43; John H. Leh, "The Store Wide PM," *DSE*, 1 (10 Oct. 1938), 1; *Echo*, 30 (7 Aug. 1931).

43. "The Way with People," 522; Accipter, "Analysis of Intimate Apparel Department," 21–22; Mildred Farquhar, "An Analysis of a Toy Department in a Department Store" (M.A. thesis, Univ. of Pittsburgh, 1933), 14; Wittich, "Constructive Use of Shopping Report," 19; Ruth Farquhar, "Analysis of Drapery Department," 89; Luman, "Analysis of China and Glassware Department," 82.

44. Filene Co-Operative Association Arbitration Records, manuscript in possession of the store, 8 and 13 Oct. 1903; Sarah Johnson, "Analysis of Drapery Department," 99; Emma Wilson Smith, "Analysis of Sportswear Department," 50.

45. *Vocational Education Survey of Richmond, Virginia, August, 1915*, U.S. Department of Labor, Bureau of Labor Statistics, Bull. No. 162 (Washington, 1916), 254; "Saleswoman's View of Department Heads," *DGE*, 72 (6 Apr. 1918), 153; Laura Van Dorn Harter, "Value of Educational Work in Store," *DGE*, 73 (5 Apr. 1919), 9–10; Wittich, "Constructive Use of Shopping Report," 14; Julia Campbell, "Analysis of Girls' Wear Department," 69, 73; Fetterman, "Analysis of House Dress Department," 57; A. H. Wehmeier, "Disinterested Selling," *BNRDGA*, 19 (Jan. 1937), 19; Virginia Gerding, "A Study of a Women's and Misses' Coat and Suit Department (with Special Emphasis on Personnel and

Sales Promotion Factors)" (M.Sc. thesis, Simmons Coll., 1937), 47; Annette M. Law, "True-to-Life-Teaching," *DSE*, 3 (25 Feb. 1940), 2, 10; "Making Good on the Sales Job," *DGE*, 81 (7 May 1927), 16; Ruth Farquhar, "Analysis of Drapery Department," 83–86; "'Up with the Controller, Down with the Guesser,' Safety Motto," *DGE*, 79 (1 Aug. 1925), 17; "Careful Buying and an Eye on Reserve Stocks Keep Lines Always Interesting," *DGE*, 77 (17 Feb. 1923), 32; "Salespeople Know Public Better than Buyer, So They Go to Market, Too," *DGE*, 77 (17 Feb. 1923), 26; *Echo*, 26 (17 Feb. 1928).

46. Elizabeth Ann McCune, "An Analysis of the Women's Shoe Department in a Department Store" (M.A. thesis, Univ. of Pittsburgh, 1932), 72; Filene Arbitration Records, 8 Oct. 1903; "Want Slip Policies and Systems in Department Stores," *BNRDGA*, 18 (Apr. 1936), 13–22; *Echo*, 20 (1 and 15 Sept. 1922); "Goods Not in Stock," *DGE*, 56 (1 Mar. 1902), 17.

47. *Echo*, 5 (Oct. 1907), 12 (Apr. 1909), 1 (Apr. 1903); "Saleswoman's View of Department Heads," 153.

48. "Promote the Deserving," *DGE*, 62 (12 Sept. 1908), 40; "Harmony Essential," 39; Luman, "Analysis of China and Glassware Department," 84; Eva Bassingwaite, "An Analysis of the Women's Coat Department in a Specialty Store" (M.A. thesis, Univ. of Pittsburgh, 1932), 57; "'Want' Slip Problem," *DGE*, 64 (25 Mar. 1910), 33; "Store Rules," *DGE*, 67 (22 Feb. 1913), 2; *Echo*, 13 (23 Mar. 1917), 15 (21 Feb. and 23 May 1919), 16 (19 Mar. 1920), 21 (7 Mar. 1924), 22 (18 Apr. 1924), 20 (16 June 1922), 27 (21 Jan. 1921).

49. Ruth Farquhar, "Analysis of Drapery Department," 83.

50. "Sidelights on the Bonus System," *DGE*, 73 (27 Sept. 1919), 315; Store Management Group, NRDGA, *Trends in Compensating Salespeople* (New York, 1938), 12–15; B. S. White, "Effect of Compensation Methods on Management Operation and Employee Production," in Store Management Division, NRDGA, *Compensation Methods and Selling Costs*, Report No. 3 of *Store Management Convention Proceedings* (New York, 1936), 14; Ruth Leigh, *Elements of Retailing* (New York, 1923), 327–28. Managers noted a similar problem with the use of PMs or premium payments for selling certain pieces of merchandise. "PMs and Salesforce," *DGE*, 63 (13 Feb. 1909), 14–17; "They Cooed like Turtle Doves," *DGE*, 81 (13 Aug. 1927), 87, 94.

51. Einstein, "Interselling versus Specialization," 91–92; "Putting a Punch," 33–34; "What Happened to Aggressive Floorman," *DGE*, 69 (22 May 1915), 31, 34; Feazel, "Analysis of Women's Shoe Department," 47–57.

52. *Echo*, 3 (Feb. 1906); "The Still Tongue," *DGE*, 65 (8 July 1911), 28; Lombard, "Executive Policies," 348, 355; "The 'Little Old Lady Who Lived in the China Department,'" *DGE*, 77 (25 Nov. 1922), 15.

53. "A Salesgirl's Story," 1819; Leffingwell, "Sizing Up Customers," 152.

54. "Service vs. Sales, Which Pays Best?" *DGE*, 81 (1 Jan. 1927), 13; "Martha in Kitchenware," 19.

55. Gilson, *What's Past*, 45.

56. Stern, *I Am a Woman*, 167; "Putting a Punch," 33; Store Managers' Division, NRDGA, *Proceedings, Seventh Annual Convention* (New York, 1930), 171; Anne Shannon Monroe, "What I Don't Like When I Go Shopping," *System*,

37 (May 1920), 962; "The Covert Sneer," *DGE*, 66 (1 June 1912), 41; "On Teaching Saleswomen," *New York Commercial*, 21 Sept. 1916, in Records of the Prince School, Simmons College, Box XI, File 218; "Her Sun Is a Frosted Globe," 13; "Sales Chats," 88.

57. MacLean, "Two Weeks," 733; Annie Marion MacLean, *Wage-Earning Women* (New York, 1910), 66–67; "Customers Who Have Tried to Uplift Me," *DGE*, 73 (11 Jan. 1919), 105, 113; "From Dust-Rag to Buyer's Desk," 81, 90; "Can Your Salespeople Justify Increased Prices?" *BNRDGA*, 15 (Dec. 1933), 46.

58. MacLean, *Wage-Earning Women*, 66; *Echo*, 15 (7 Nov. 1919); Mary Rankin Cranston, "The Girl behind the Counter," *World To-Day*, 10 (Mar. 1906), 271; MacLean, "Two Weeks," 724–26; "Sidelights on the Bonus System," 315.

59. "Moving Slow Selling Merchandise," 95; "As to Salesmanship," *DGE*, 63 (9 Jan. 1909), 87; Carroll D. Murphy, "The Blind Side of the Show Window," *System*, 16 (Aug. 1909), 139–41; Westlaw Keene, "Fabrics," *BNRDGA*, 22 (May 1940), 48; NRDGA, *Joint Management Proceedings—1940* (New York, 1940), 99; Johnston, "Analysis of Linen Department," 85; *Echo*, 21 (31 Aug. 1923); Stern, *I Am a Woman*, 158.

60. "Right Handling of Help," *DGE*, 64 (14 May 1910), 46; "Teach Salespeople How to Serve 'Looker,'" 35; "Decrease Expense Ratio by Average Sale Increase," *DGE*, 75 (19 Mar. 1921), 13–14; "Her Sun Is a Frosted Globe," 13; "The Way with People," 522–24; Accipter, "Analysis of Intimate Apparel Department," 21–22, 80.

61. "Decrease Expense Ratio," 13; MacLean, "Two Weeks," 726–27; "Sales That I Wished I Hadn't Made," 273; Ruth Farquhar, "Analysis of Drapery Department," 85; "Wide-Awake Retailing," *DGE*, 48 (30 Mar. 1893), 51; Winifred E. Drach, "A Study of the Sportswear, Sweater, and Blouse Departments of Store A" (M.Sc. thesis, Simmons Coll., 1934), 49.

62. MacLean, "Two Weeks," 725; "Making Good on the Sales Job," *DGE*, 81 (8 Jan. 1927), 14; Drach, "Study of Sportswear, Sweater, and Blouse Departments," 48; untitled note, *RCIA*, 39 (Nov.-Dec. 1935), 7; "The Way with People," 524.

63. "The Way with People," 524; see also Sears, Roebuck, and Company, *Division Management* (n.p., 1940), 90; *Echo*, 14 (13 Dec. 1918); Zelie Leigh, "Shopping Round," *Atlantic Monthly*, 138 (Aug. 1926), 205.

64. "Making Good on the Sales Job," *DGE*, 81 (15 Jan. 1927), 17; *Echo*, 21 (11 May and 22 June 1923); "Must Have Exact Sizes," *DGE*, 64 (17 Sept. 1910), 45; Helhake, "How Store Leaks May Be Minimized," 29–31; Hamburger, "How to Minimize Store's Leaks," 59; C. Angus Wright, "Minimizing the Store's Leaks," *DGE*, 66 (1 June 1912), 29; "Right, and Wrong, Suggestions," *DGE*, 65 (14 Oct. 1911), 36; "That Word 'Guarantee,'" *DGE*, 67 (1 Mar. 1913), 35; "Economy in the Alterations Room," *DGE*, 68 (24 Jan. 1914), 63; "Test Discloses Waste in Piece Goods Department," *DGE*, 72 (11 May 1918), 47; "Caution Employees as to Making Promises," *DGE*, 73 (1 Nov. 1919), 2; McCune, "Analysis of Women's Shoe Department," 64, 71; Cora Bohlen, "Floorwalker's Job 'Softest' Thinks Society Saleswoman," *RCIA*, 23 (May 1916), 13–14; "Making Good on

the Sales Job," *DGE*, 80 (30 Oct. 1926), 11; "Making Good on the Sales Job," *DGE*, 81 (27 Nov. 1926), 12; *Echo*, 50 (1 Apr. 1927).

65. Natalie Kneeland, "Keeping Up Department Morale," *BNRDGA*, 14 (Nov. 1932), 884, 920; "Making Good on the Sales Job," *DGE*, 80 (31 July 1926), 9; "Making Good on the Sales Job," *DGE*, 80 (4 Sept. 1926), 13; "Making Good on the Sales Job," *DGE*, 80 (18 Sept. 1926), 17; Titcomb, "Selling to Selling Force," 13, 53; Henry A. Breithaupt, "Putting Personality into a Store," *System*, 48 (Aug. 1925), 222–24; "A Simple Way to Help Your Employees Address Customers by Name," *BNRDGA*, 9 (Mar. 1927), 168; Caroline Spalding, "Case Studies in Training," *BNRDGA*, 18 (Feb. 1936), 86–87.

66. Einstein, "Interselling versus Specialization," 91–93; Gerding, "Study of Coat and Suit Department," 20; "Employee Rating System Maintains White House Personnel's Reputation," *DGE*, 79 (23 May 1925), 13; D. J. Tobin, "Dividing Sales Work and Stock Work," 102; "Wide-Awake Retailing," *DGE*, 56 (8 Mar. 1902), 205; "Tabulator Prevents Loss of Customers," *Management Methods*, 61 (May 1932), 286–87; "Women in $6,000 to $30,000 Jobs," *American Magazine*, 88 (July 1919), 131.

67. Nancy F. Cott, *The Bonds of Womanhood* (New Haven, 1977), 1. Notices of these social occasions appear in virtually every issue of the *Echo* as well as in the Jordan Marsh newspaper variously titled *The Fellow Worker, Store Topics,* and *The Tally*. Confetti-throwing is mentioned, for example, in *Echo*, 6 (Apr. 1909) and 26 (12 Aug. 1927). Stern, *I Am a Woman*, 156–57; *Echo*, 15 (14 Feb. 1919), 26 (30 Mar. 1928).

68. Filene Arbitration Records, 8 Oct. 1903; *Echo*, 13 (8 Sept. 1916), 23 (3 July 1925), 13 (10 Feb. 1916), 17 (21 Jan. 1921).

69. Barbara Melosh, "Doctors, Patients, and 'Big Nurse': Work and Gender in Post-War Hospitals," in Ellen Condliffe Lagemann, ed., *Nursing History: New Perspectives, New Possibilities* (New York, 1983); "Putting a Punch," 33; *Echo*, 15 (24 Oct. 1919), 20 (2 Mar. 1923); Anne O'Hagan, "The Shop-Girl and Her Wages," *Munsey's Magazine*, 50 (Nov. 1913), 253; *Echo*, 1 (Apr. 1903). Some examples from *Echo* of the interest in suffrage: a third-floor department took a suffrage play on tour (11 [4 June 1913]); a notice urged attendance at a suffrage meeting (12 [24 Dec. 1914]); a suffrage poem appeared (12 [28 Jan. 1915]); straw votes in several departments showed a majority favoring suffrage (13 [28 Oct. 1915]). Perhaps most interesting of all was a suffragist's link of the vote with women's rights within the store: she asserted that women should be allowed to vote just as men did outside the store, and to wear the clothes they chose just as men could inside the store (14 [6 Dec. 1918]).

70. Theresa Wolfson, *The Woman Worker and the Trade Unions* (New York, 1926), 118–19; "Store Signs Union Check-Off Pact," *Business Week*, 10 Dec. 1938, 32–33.

71. The best discussion of factors inhibiting women's union organizing is Alice Kessler-Harris, "Where Are the Organized Women Workers?" in Nancy F. Cott and Elizabeth H. Pleck, eds., *A Heritage of Her Own: Toward a New Social History of American Women* (New York, 1979), 343–66.

72. "News from the St. Louis Press Relating to Strike of Department Store Clerks," *RCIA*, 25 (Apr. 1918), 7–9; "The Department Store Strike in San Francisco," typescript in "Department Store Organizing—Statistics and History of the San Francisco Strike" file, Department Store Organizing in the 1930s box, Tamiment Library.

Conclusion

Many worlds intersected in American department stores between 1890 and 1940, sometimes smoothly and sometimes jarringly. Saleswomen, customers, and managers had different agendas and different points of departure, but all were part of the same drama of consumer capitalism played out in the great theater of the store. Class and gender provided the central tensions; the pursuit of loyalty, control, monetary advantage, and personal gratification electrified the plot; a kaleidoscope of shifting alliances kept the players on their toes; the script rang variations on the themes of service and consumption. Like the audience-involvement theater of the 1970s, the drama of the department store brought together people of disparate backgrounds and provided an arena for them to play out their hopes and anxieties. Unlike theater, however, the department store was not neatly set off from daily life but bound up in its intricate fabric. The stakes were real and the roles people played were not dissimulations but compounds of their own personalities and the social system of the store.

Managers pursued profits by seeking closer control over the operations of their firms and the people who worked and shopped in them. Using an eclectic mixture of accounting systems, technology, services, advertising, display, training, welfare work, and material incentives, they strove for predictable and systematic organization and loyal saleswomen and customers. Customers traded their dollars for merchandise which they assessed—at different times and under different circumstances—on the basis of quality, fashion, its reflection on their personal appearance and status, and the milieu in which they purchased it. Whether crankily demanding special considerations, coolly requesting information on which to make intelligent decisions, or cannily gauging the real worth of a bargain, customers were constantly asking more and more of saleswomen and managers. Saleswomen exchanged their labor power for an ambiguous status and a complex mix of advantages and disadvantages in pay, hours, and working conditions. Determined to insulate their departmental turf from the full force of customers' and managers' demands, they used their work culture to define and administer selling skill and to control interaction on the sales floor.

Each of these three major groups pursued its own ends in opposition to pressures from the other two, but under the right conditions would ally with another against the third. Saleswomen and customers could unite in the name of service against managers' cost-conscious policies, manipulating both merchandise and services to produce cordial interaction—and sometimes a lasting and mutually beneficial relationship—across the counter. Saleswomen and managers could join in opposing the more trying and expensive of customers' exactions, invoking "store policy" and an insiders' community of interest against the interlopers. Customers and managers could condemn with one voice the apathy and impertinence of the sales force, asserting the primacy of the store's raison d'être of selling merchandise.

Encounters among the three were not simply economic—related to profit, value, and income—but cultural. Department-store managers were torn between a pervasive business culture which valued system and efficiency and a retail culture which stressed service and amenity. Moreover, their gender socialization as men told them that they could and should dominate women while their experience in the store often required them to submit to the machinations of women and the sway of women's culture. Managers shared with customers an urban bourgeois culture which led the store into onerous costs for buildings and services and customers into imperious and demanding conduct. At the same time, this class-based culture set them off from saleswomen, whose working-class demeanor they condemned. Women's culture provided common ground for saleswomen and customers, a slice of shared consciousness and experience which could build bridges across the class gap of the counter. In their element in the women's world of the department store, they could make the male manager feel an alien in his own domain. Even here, though, class could intervene, for saleswomen also partook of a workers' culture which scorned the condescension of well-to-do reformers and provided patterns of shop-floor resistance from which they forged their own occupational culture. All three groups, finally, were linked by the growing influence of the culture of consumption even as it set them against one another in the tense triangle of department-store life.

The shifting coalitions among saleswomen, managers, and customers produced an uncertainty about who was an ally and who an adversary; Filene workers termed the customer "our friend the enemy" but the phrase could well have been used by any of the three about the others. The contest for primacy in the department store was not a directly engaged tooth-and-claw battle which would meet the more rigid standards of class struggle; frequently the process was masked by competing uses of the ideology of service and manipulation of the rewards of a consumption-oriented society. Each member of the triad could marshal a variety of tactics to ease or complicate the lives of the others; even the saleswoman had far greater latitude than might be expected of one at the bottom of the hierarchy.

Such ambiguities and contradictions in fact pervaded the department store. When managers switched from the stick to the carrot as a means of gaining saleswomen's cooperation, they became somewhat more manipulative but also less unpleasant and tyrannical. Welfare work was at once paternalist and the source of genuine benefits. Better design of stores led to tighter stock control and demands for greater efficiency while providing a more attractive and convenient workplace. Lavish services pleased and attracted the public to the department store, but they also spoiled customers and fomented discord. Department stores took the lead as fashion authorities but in the process risked losing steady customers' trade in staples. Managers devised the notion of skilled selling in order to maximize their profits and impose their definition of the work process, but in doing so they inadvertently expanded saleswomen's range of action. Life behind the counter offered wage-earning women employment involving autonomy as well as regimentation, possibility as well as constraint. The rhetoric about the professional nature of skilled selling contrasted sharply with saleswomen's actual position in the labor market. Moreover, the social status of department store selling was quite unclear: it enjoyed the respectability of white-collar work but commanded a lower wage than similar jobs in the clerical field and overlapped uncomfortably with aspects of domestic service. Saleswomen's work culture was both oppositional and accommodating, ordering life on the selling floor in ways that protected saleswomen's turf yet served the selling goals of the store. It was extraordinarily difficult to assess what went on in department stores: quantitative standards were either narrow or inappropriate and qualitative standards were slippery and ambiguous. Too exclusive a concentration on high sales volume obscured vital questions of profitability and service; an insistence on short-term profitability imperiled the long-term reputation of the store; no reliable standard measured the effectiveness of the store's selling efforts and service appeals. The department store as a social and economic institution was enduringly contradictory, at once a vibrant center of the delights of consumption and an arena of persisting class and gender conflict, a business that was highly profitable yet torn between its roles as vendor of merchandise and purveyor of culture.

A detailed look at daily life in department stores suggests that this, at least, was one industry where the conception and implementation of new systems of control had more mixed and contradictory effects than in the manufacturing industries discussed by Braverman, Edwards, and Clawson. The most important features distinguishing retailing from manufacturing were variability and service. The pace as well as the content of the work load varied in a relatively uncontrollable way in department stores. Customers came and went according to seasonal, weekly, daily, and personal rhythms; they brought an almost infinite variety of whims and needs to sales transactions. By the 1930s, department-store managers had begun to control the pace of the work by the more deliberate use of part-time workers, but even so saleswomen continued to have a great deal of "free" time that was not absorbed either by waiting on customers or by stock work. Managers had little if any success, however, in controlling the substance of customer-salesperson interactions; the attempt to maximize and satisfy each customer's needs enduringly resisted routinization.[1]

Equally important was the fact that department stores based their appeal both on the goods they stocked and on the service they provided. They wanted not just to sell one dress, but also an idea of fashion that required the purchase of matching accessories; they wanted the customer to be attracted not just by their merchandise but by the store as a whole; they wanted not simply to make individual sales but to attract steady and loyal customers. The lavish store buildings and complimentary services with which they seduced customers imposed astronomical fixed costs for both plant and labor, expenditures which increased managerial pressure for more and larger sales. Manufacturers of consumer goods were also, of course, concerned with fostering a culture of consumption, but they had the luxury of relegating this effort to advertising and sales departments; it did not suffuse the central work process of factories as it did in department stores.

Committed to a unified view of their economic and cultural role, department-store managers resolutely rejected the idea of self-service selling or any of its variants. Instead of freeing themselves from reliance on sales-women's behavior and skills, they sought to expand those skills. They were trying to purvey an idea of skill which was their own creation, but in fact this skill was grounded in shop-floor practice and was relatively diffi-cult to supervise and evaluate. Its basis was not mechanical or manual facility, but social and interactive ability; they wanted their saleswomen to be resourceful, to take the initiative, to adapt to ever-changing circum-stances, to produce not just a standard amount but to maximize output in each and every sale. There was, however, no clear measure of output: a particularly large sale might have been made with high-pressure tactics which alienated the customer from the store; a small transaction in which a saleswoman helpfully and sympathetically satisfied a customer might earn her future patronage and enduring loyalty.

The attempt to serve simultaneously a cultural function—the long-run encouragement of a culture of consumption—and an economic func-tion—the short-term efficiency and profitability of the firm—led depart-ment-store managers into a difficult position. Measures to stimulate the culture of consumption were often costly and had uncertain results. Mea-sures to cut costs threatened the service aspects of their businesses. Store managers therefore pursued an erratic course on the road to rationaliza-tion of their practices. With a few exceptions, such as store and fixture re-design, most of their policies had unforeseen countereffects, and execu-tives vacillated between pursuing first one of their goals and then the other. Repeatedly they found that policies useful in moderation, such as better accounting procedures, merchandise control, and elaborate customer ser-vices, were dangerous indeed if implemented too single-mindedly.

But managers' most enduring problem was that they were trying to manage and influence the behavior of large numbers of people over whom they exerted limited control. All managers function through a combina-tion of influence and authority, but in the factory the day-to-day emphasis was decidedly on authority: a manager could specify what a given worker should be doing, when, and at what pace. In department stores—and in other service industries where there were a number of discretionary tasks to be performed and a variety of situations to respond to—the balance between influence and authority was more nearly equal. Department-store managers could require a clerk to be at a counter between stated hours, to obey store rules, to maintain certain levels of sales, and to keep merchandise in order. They could not extend that level of control into the uncharted territory of the individual sales transaction because of the sheer magnitude of supervision that would require and the dangers of angering saleswomen and customers by standing over them. The only practical solution was to train clerks in acceptable selling techniques and then hope that loyalty to the store would inspire them to perform effectively. In that context, persuasion and not command became crucial. Department-store managers exerted even less control over customers, setting only the store's hours, prices, and policies on such matters as deliveries and exchanges. Beyond that they had only influence—and, moreover, influence primarily exerted secondhand through the medium of the sales force. Managers' control of both customers and saleswomen was further undermined by their attempts to co-opt their gender characteristics. By encouraging the use of nonbusiness values of empathy and cooperation in a business setting that stressed competition and profit, managers provided common ground on which saleswomen and customers could meet in a way that excluded male executives and their concerns.

The study of department stores suggests that taxonomies of management practice derived primarily from manufacturing may not be readily applicable to service industries with their more complicated social reality and greater variability. One task of those who study workplace dynamics is to develop a more accurate historical understanding of service industries and the ways in which managers and workers try to shape them. At minimum, that new framework should give a central place to the ambiguities and subtle dynamics of class and gender.

The vibrant and enduring work culture of department-store saleswomen suggests that women's historians should frame a broader understanding of women's wage-earning experience. Many scholars have argued that women's jobs are the most uncompromising and eloquent teachers of their secondary status, the workplace an arena where their subordination is more sharply defined than in the home or family. Advocates of this view maintain that women's paid work conveys only the most conservative lessons: that wage-earning cannot be a source of fulfillment or autonomy and that women gain power only through their roles at home. While saleswomen's lives included many features which gave credence to this argument—the sex-based wage differential, the male-administered disciplinary systems, the relentless assault on their class-based culture— there was also much counterevidence. Women in department stores had numerous role models of women in positions of authority: buyers, who competed directly with men on their own ground, and personnel and welfare workers, who carved out a women's specialty within the men's world of staff management. Buyers furnished particularly powerful examples of female success since most had started behind the counter and risen through the ranks.[2]

But perhaps more influential in saleswomen's daily lives was the fact that department-store selling provided opportunities for them to exercise initiative, creativity, and autonomy—within the limited arena of the department, to be sure, but nonetheless to a greater extent than the vast majority of women in the labor force. Selling skill valued women's culture, rewarding both typically female personality traits and expertise in matters of dress and domestic management. The social system of the department demonstrated to women each day that their work culture could administer complex interaction and govern the selling floor more effectively than managers' prescriptions. While in the formal hierarchy of the store saleswomen were near the bottom in pay and authority, they in fact wielded enormous influence over the daily operations of the store. Their actions and attitudes played a critical role in determining which merchandise sold rapidly and which remained on the shelves; whether a customer returned eagerly to the store or refused to cross its threshold again; whether a department was a lively money-maker or a lackluster drain on the store's profits. They successfully delineated protected space in which their work culture mediated the demands of customers and managers. The lessons of department-store selling, then, surpassed simple precepts about women's subordination to men and included validation for female values and competence, bolstering women's confidence and self-esteem.

As Barbara Melosh has persuasively argued, nursing conveyed a similarly contradictory message to its practitioners; the combined evidence from the study of department store selling and nursing reopens the question of the role of women's paid work in their lives. A more nuanced view of the implications of women's jobs will not only strengthen our historical understanding of women's lives but also provide part of the groundwork for a more accurate and respectful view of women's contemporary labor-force experience.[3]

The department store was the product of a particular historical era in which large cities grew and flourished and in which the realm of consumption expanded but still encompassed a limited sphere of life and—in its department store form—a limited segment of the population. Since World War II, this context has changed dramatically, and the department store with it. Central cities have decayed, losing population and institutions to growing suburbs. Mass consumption has moved inexorably into new areas of life, supplanting even further the role of home and family in providing goods and services. Consumption is no longer so exclusively the province of adult women—as children and men join them—or of the financially comfortable—as consumer credit and expanding production draw in members of the working classes. As more and more women have entered the labor force, the leisurely genteel style of shopping has declined. Department stores have adjusted to these shifts by making major alterations in their notions of service and selling; through it all women have continued to fill the evolving role of salesperson.

Beginning with World War II, when personnel shortages mandated new selling arrangements, self-service schemes—in which the customer has direct access to merchandise—proliferated. Virtually every department store in the country has implemented some form of self-service, sometimes eliminating human salesmanship by leaving customers to wander unassisted among open displays, sometimes using saleswomen as adjuncts to the displays. When managers finally turned to self-service, they found many advantages in it. First, it led to lower costs, as customers began to do work that had formerly been done by saleswomen. Self-service also lessened—but did not end—managers' social dependence on saleswomen. As one New England store manager recently confessed, "I spend half my waking hours trying to figure out ways to become less dependent on labor." Third, because the industry as a whole underwent a major postwar transformation, it was relatively easy to implement new operating practices in new settings. As suburbs mushroomed, downtown stores declined while branches proliferated and even eclipsed their parent stores. In Baltimore in the mid-1970s, Hochschild Kohn and Company closed its center-city store and became a purely suburban operation; Jordan Marsh, which halved the size of its downtown Boston store in 1977, acknowledges that its Warwick (Rhode Island) Mall branch is now the company's "flagship"; the J. L. Hudson store, once one of the nation's three largest, stands empty in downtown Detroit. The new suburban stores were generally smaller, more austere, and less service-oriented than the older palace of consumption. They dramatically intensified the trend toward part-time work, using housewives during the day and students in the evenings and on weekends. Finally, self-service helped department stores to respond to competition from discount merchandisers during the 1950s, 1960s, and 1970s.[4]

Despite their conversion in practice to self-service, managers continued to write fervent tributes to skilled selling and service in the industry journals; typical was the trade association report which maintained bluntly in 1962 that "[t]here is no substitute for good salespeople." Yet few followed in the footsteps of carriage-trade stores such as Saks Fifth Avenue and Bonwit Teller which maintained their air of luxury and their tradition of service, albeit on a more modest scale. By the mid-1960s, most managers would probably have admitted in their franker moments that the self-service discount store was the model for the future, with its salespeople reduced to mere stock handlers and cash register operators.[5]

Within the last decade or so, however, the picture has again become more complicated. The revival and gentrification of central cities has sparked something of a renaissance of downtown retailing with an emphasis on elegance, high style, and service. Even Macy's, long known for serviceable merchandise at competitive prices, has redecorated its Herald Square store in an elegant Art Deco motif, vying in style and luxury with the likes of Bloomingdale's. At first, it appeared that these central-city stores would rely primarily on dramatic display and decoration techniques—known in the trade as theatrical selling—to sell merchandise, but in recent years managers have begun to talk more like their predecessors in the years before 1940. They complain today about high employee turnover, lackluster selling efforts, salespeople's ignorance about their merchandise, and the enormous costs of doing business in today's economy. Moreover, they face a problem peculiar to the post–World War II period: the standardization of merchandise.[6]

Increasingly, they are reviving an early-twentieth-century strategy to cope with these problems—training employees in skilled selling. As one manager described the situation: "Since all stores carry the same goods today, the only difference is how well you help the customer." Today's manager is learning anew the important lesson that millions of dollars spent on elegant stores, displays, and advertising avail little unless they are backed up by an effective sales force. The message from customers also echoes that from decades past; a recent survey of the attitudes of women shoppers concluded that "efforts to attempt to change the 'salesclerk' to a 'professional salesperson' will be rewarded." The message is not entirely a welcome one for it puts managers back in the uncomfortable position of depending upon the goodwill of the sales force. The switch to self-service was in some ways a retreat from defeat, as managers despaired of supplanting saleswomen's version of skilled selling with their own. There is little reason to think that contemporary managers will be any more successful in combating the work culture of the selling floor than were those of the past, especially given their intensified commitment to trimming selling costs.[7]

For many saleswomen, however, the vision of selling skill and serving the customer well never waned. In interviews, saleswomen of the post–World War II era frequently comment that they feel that management is standing between them and their customers, making it impossible to deliver good service because of store rules or merchandising policies. These comments echo those of teachers who say that school administrators are undermining the quality of education, or of nurses who maintain that hospital administrators and physicians limit their ability to give first-rate patient care. A woman retiring from a carriage-trade store after thirty years of selling comments acidly that management is transforming the store into a pale copy of the city's largest popular-price emporium. Still, until the day she left the store she maintained a large file of special customers to whom she gave personalized service, even though she was one of but four saleswomen on a floor where there had once been twenty-three. Another woman, after selling for nineteen years, transferred to a clerical position because a combination of management policies and personal circumstances prevented her from giving her customers the kind of high-quality service she demanded of herself and her store. Significantly, she refused to leave the store although she could have much improved her earnings elsewhere.[8]

The persistence of the ideal of service and skilled selling among some (particularly older) saleswomen and the revival of that ideal among managers suggests that the pre-1940 history of the department store is of more than historical interest. Still, a relatively recent development—the advent of the computer in retailing—may bode ill for the future of skilled selling. Point-of-sale terminals, the beeping replacements for cash registers, have enabled managers to maintain closer control of staffing on a day-to-day and even an hour-to-hour basis, providing information that allows them to shift personnel as customer volume fluctuates and hence to minimize clerks' idle time. In addition, they provide detailed and immediate information about what is selling, freeing managers from their dependence upon salespeople's shop-floor knowledge of customers' wishes and preference. Still, the computer gives only a partial picture of what happens on the selling floor; it cannot tell managers what a customer asked for but could not find, nor how saleswomen cajoled customers into buying more than they had intended. The most advanced computer system has some of the same shortcomings of earlier systems of evaluation, and cannot compete with salespeople in being the eyes and ears of managers.[9]

Even without the arrival of the computer on the selling floor, the revived emphasis on skilled selling would not bring back the pre–World War II world of the department-store saleswoman. The department store no longer holds an unchallenged place at the pinnacle of American retailing; pressures from discount stores on one side and from exclusive boutiques on the other have put it into a defensive posture. Moreover, the expansion of the service sector in recent years has meant a degradation of working conditions for many of its workers. Like other service-industry workers, saleswomen can expect a continuation of the trend toward part-time work, pressures for increased productivity, closer surveillance through computers and industrial espionage, and low pay. But the picture is not totally gloomy. A renewed interest in union organizing, bolstered by feminism, among women white-collar workers may help to reverse the decline in wages and working conditions. The new attitude toward selling suggests that the possibilities for satisfaction in giving good service and in using initiative and creativity may expand. And, finally, saleswomen have never lost their grip on the bulwark of their daily lives on the job— their work culture.

Notes

1. Harry Braverman, *Labor and Monopoly Capital: The Degradation of Work in the Twentieth Century* (New York, 1974); Richard C. Edwards, *Contested Terrain: The Transformation of the Workplace in the Twentieth Century* (New York, 1979); Dan Clawson, *Bureaucracy and the Labor Process: The Transformation of U.S. Industry, 1860–1920* (New York, 1980).

2. For major statements of this position, see Louise A. Tilly and Joan W. Scott, *Women, Work, and Family* (New York, 1978) and Leslie Woodcock Tentler, *Wage-Earning Women: Industrial Work and Family Life in the United States, 1900–1930* (New York, 1979).

3. Barbara Melosh, *"The Physician's Hand": Work Culture and Conflict in American Nursing* (Philadelphia, 1982). Other studies, less relevant to the immediate discussion, which also emphasize the positive aspects of women's wage-earning experience are Thomas Dublin, *Women at Work: The Transformation of Work and Community in Lowell, Massachusetts, 1826–1860* (New York, 1979) and Evelyn Nakano Glenn, "The Dialectics of Wage Work: Japanese-American Women and Domestic Service, 1905–1940," *Feminist Studies*, 6 (Fall 1980), 432–71.

4. Barry Bluestone, Patricia Hanna, Sarah Kuhn, and Laura Moore, *The De-*

partment Store Industry in New England: An Analysis of Market Transformation, Investment, and Labor (Cambridge, Mass., 1979), 164; Isadore Barmash, "Associated Dry Goods Shifting Its Retail Appeal," *New York Times*, 22 Dec. 1978, D1; Gwynne Morgan, "Jordan Marsh 'Steps Up' Quality, Prices," *Providence Sunday Journal*, 12 Sept. 1982, F1.

5. Store Management Group, National Retail Merchants Association, *Speeding Selling Service* (New York, 1962), 89.

6. Jesse Kornbluth, "The Department Store as Theater," *New York Times Magazine*, 29 Apr. 1979, 65–66; Paul Goldberger, "Macy's Elegant New Main Floor," *New York Times*, nat'l ed., 1 Dec. 1983, 19–20; Barbara Ettore, "Stores Try Theatrical Selling Techniques," *New York Times*, 23 Jan. 1979, D1, D4.

7. "Retailers Discover an Old Tool: Sales Training," *Business Week*, 22 Dec. 1980, 52; Isadore Barmash, "Selling—Retailing's Lost Art," *New York Times*, 15 Mar. 1983, D1, D4; John J. Burnett, Robert D. Amason, and Shelby D. Hunt, "Feminism: Implications for Department Store Strategy and Salesclerk Behavior," *Journal of Retailing*, 57 (Winter 1981), 82.

8. Interview with S. M., 12 Jan. 1980; interview with C. E., 17 Nov. 1981.

9. Morgan, "Jordan Marsh," F4; Clyde H. Harrington, "Outlet Co. Installing $3 Million Computer System in Its Stores," *Providence Sunday Journal*, 6 Nov. 1977, F1; Leonard S. Edgerly, "Retailers Check Out Computers as Tools to Build Business," *Providence Sunday Journal*, 8 July 1979, F1, F12–13.

APPENDIXES

APPENDIX A

Saleswomen and the Female Labor Force

Year	Category of Women Sales Workers[a]	Women Sales Workers				Women in the Labor Force	
		Number Women in Category	Women as Percent of All Sales Workers	Saleswomen as Percent of Female Labor Force	Percent Increase in Saleswomen by Decade	Women as Percent of Total Labor Force	Percent Increase in Female Labor Force by Decade
1880	Saleswomen	7,744	24.0	0.3	—	15.2	—
1890	Saleswomen	58,451	22.1	1.5	654.8	17.2	51.3
1900	Saleswomen	149,230	24.4	2.8	155.3	18.3	32.8
1910	Saleswomen (stores) and clerks in stores	362,081	28.6	4.5	142.6	19.9	52.3
1920	Saleswomen (stores) and clerks in stores	526,718	34.2	6.2	45.5	20.4	8.2
1930	Saleswomen and clerks in stores	705,793	29.5	6.6	34.0	22.0	26.7
1940	Saleswomen (stores) and clerks in stores	799,360	41.1	6.1	13.3	24.4	25.2

[a]"Clerks in stores" were first set off from "clerks" in the 1910 census. Despite instructions to the contrary, enumerators persisted in returning salespeople as clerks in stores. For this reason, statisticians customarily assume that a majority of the latter were salespeople and lump the two groups together.

Sources: Janet M. Hooks, *Women's Occupations through Seven Decades*, WB #218 (Washington, 1947), 34, 86, 243; U.S. Department of the Interior, Census Office, *Compendium of the Eleventh Census: 1890*, Part 3 (Washington, 1897), 396–97; U.S. Bureau of the Census, *Thirteenth Census of the U.S. Taken in the Year 1910*, vol. 4, *Population 1910—Occupation Statistics* (Washington, 1914), 48–49, 54–55; U.S. Bureau of the Census, *Fourteenth Census of the United States Taken in the Year 1920*, vol. 4, *Population 1920—Occupations* (Washington, 1923), 697–98.

Appendix B

Women and Sales Workers in the Store Labor Force

Year	Place	Type of Store[a]	Women as Percent of All Employees	Women as Percent of Sales Workers	Sales Workers as Percent of All Employees	Saleswomen as Percent of All Women Employees
1871–74	R. H. Macy Co.	DS	88.0	—	40–45	—
1901	Fall River, Holyoke, Pittsfield, Worcester, Mass.	DG	55.5 to 67.6	—	—	—
1902	Boston	DS	58.3	—	—	—
1902	Boston	DS	—	64.6	—	—
1902	Boston	DG	—	76.2	—	—
1908	Chicago/New York City/Philadelphia	DS	—	—	—	46.2
1909	Baltimore	GM	68.6	86.2	43.6	54.8
1911	R. H. Macy Co.	DS	61.0	—	—	—
1911	New York City	DS	56.9	—	—	45.2
1912	New York State	DS	61.6	—	—	66.1
1913–14	New York State	DS	60.4	77.4	38.8	49.8
1913	District of Columbia	DS+	—	—	—	65.9
1914	Indiana	DS+	—	76.0	—	60–70
1915	Richmond, Va.	DS, DG, Spec.	77.5	—	—	—
1916	Cleveland	DS	70.0	—	51.0	—
1920	Kansas	GM	72.4	—	—	—

Year	Location	Store type				
1920	Iowa	DS, DG	75.9	83.3	60.2	66.1
1920	Rhode Island	GM	60.8	—	—	—
1921	Maryland	GM	66.6	—	—	—
1924	Oklahoma	GM	72.4	—	—	—
1924	Chicago	GM	50.7	—	—	—
1924	Illinois	GM	54.5	—	—	—
1925	Tennessee	GM	60.9	—	—	—
1926	Pennsylvania	DS	66.4	76.5	39.4	45.4
1928	Florida	GM	70.8	—	—	—
1932	Arkansas	GM	65.7	—	—	—
1932	Texas	DS, RTW	69.5	—	—	—
1933	U.S.	DS	66.9	—	—	—
1933	U.S.	GM, DG	61.3	—	—	—
1933	U.S.	RTW, Spec.	83.4	—	—	—
1937	District of Columbia	DS	70.4	—	—	60–97
1937	District of Columbia	RTW	77.9	—	—	60.0
1937	District of Columbia	DS	65.7	—	—	76.8
1937	Kentucky	DS	73.2	—	—	66.0
1937	Kentucky	RTW	87.0	—	—	58.0
1938	Nebraska	DS	—	—	—	79.0
1938	Nebraska	RTW	—	—	—	74.0
1940	Maine	DS	69.1	—	—	—
1940	Maine	App.	89.4	—	—	—

[a]DS—department store
GM—general mercantile store
Spec.—specialty store
RTW—women's ready-to-wear store

DG—dry goods store
DS+—department store and other retail
App.—apparel store

(Appendix B, *continued*)

Sources: Ralph M. Hower, *History of Macy's of New York, 1858–1919* (Cambridge, Mass., 1943), 190–93, 383; *Massachusetts Labor Bulletin*, No. 20 (1901), 119–20; Massachusetts Bureau of Statistics of Labor, *Thirty-Third Annual Report* (Boston, 1903), 86–87, 112–13; U.S. Congress, Senate, *Wage-Earning Women in Stores and Factories*, vol. 5 of *Report on Condition of Women and Child Wage-Earners in the United States*, 61st Cong., 2d sess., Sen. Doc. 645 (Washington, 1910), 41; Elizabeth Beardsley Butler, *Saleswomen in Mercantile Stores* (New York, 1912), 57; *National Civic Federation Review*, 4 (15 July 1913), 1, 22; New York State Factory Investigating Commission, *Second Report*, vol. 2 (Albany, 1913), 1199; *Fourth Report*, vol. 2 (Albany 1915), 53, 54, 62; Marie L. Obenauer, *Hours, Earnings, and Duration of Employment of Wage-Earning Women in Selected Industries in the District of Columbia*, BLS #116 (Washington, 1913), 9; Marie L. Obenauer and Frances W. Valentine, *Hours, Earnings, and Conditions of Labor of Women in Indiana Mercantile Establishments and Garment Factories*, BLS #160 (Washington, 1914), 8, 37; *Vocational Education Survey of Richmond, Virginia, August, 1915*, BLS #162 (Washington, 1916), 44; *Women's Wages in Kansas*, WB #17 (Washington, 1920), 9; *Iowa Women in Industry*, WB #19 (Washington, 1922), 55; *Women in Rhode Island Industries*, WB #21 (Washington, 1922), 4; *Women in Maryland Industries*, WB #24 (Washington, 1922), 9; *Women in Oklahoma Industries*, WB #48 (Washington, 1926), 3; *Women in Illinois Industries*, WB #51 (Washington, 1926), 4–5; *Women in Tennessee Industries*, WB #56 (Washington, 1927), 3; Margaret L. Lovell, *The Personnel Policies of Pennsylvania Department Stores*, Pennsylvania Department of Labor and Industry, Bureau of Women and Children, Bull. No. 13 (Harrisburg, 1926), 7; *Women in Florida Industries*, WB #80 (Washington, 1930), 4; Bertha Blair, *Women in Arkansas Industries*, WB #124 (Washington, 1935), 2; Mary Loretta Sullivan and Bertha Blair, *Women in Texas Industries*, WB #126 (Washington, 1936), 2; U.S. Bureau of the Census, *Census of American Business: 1933, Retail Distribution, United States*, vol. 2 (Washington, 1937), 72; Ethel L. Best and Arthur T. Sutherland, *Women's Hours and Wages in the District of Columbia in 1937*, WB #153 (Washington, 1937), 2; raw data for WB #153, Record Group 86, National Archives; *Women in Kentucky Industries*, WB #162 (Washington, 1938), 2; *Women's Wages and Hours in Nebraska*, WB #178 (Washington, 1940), 15.

Appendix C

Women's Earnings in Retail Stores and Elsewhere

Year	Place	Retail Category[a]	Weekly Earnings[b]	Yearly Earnings[b]	Nonretail or Summary Category[c]	Weekly Earnings	Yearly Earnings
1880	Boston	Saleswomen	6.20	—	AOS	6.35	—
					Mfg.	6.47	—
					Personal Service	6.13	—
1908	Boston	Stores	7.15	—	Factories	6.53	—
1908	Chicago	Stores	8.10	—	Factories	7.25	—
1908	Minneapolis/St. Paul	Stores	6.95	—	Factories	6.69	—
1908	New York City	Stores	6.07	—	Factories	6.12	—
1908	Philadelphia	Stores	7.64	—	Factories	6.71	—
1908	St. Louis	Stores	6.78	—	Factories	6.92	—
1911	Kentucky	Mercantile	6.76	—	Mills	5.84	—
1913	District of Columbia	Saleswomen	6.55	—	Mfg./Mechanical	7.13	—
1913	New York	Mercantile	7.25	—	Factories	6.25	—
1913	Oregon	DS	—	465.86	Factories	—	412.97
					Offices	—	595.25
					Laundries	—	453.75
					Miscellaneous	—	447.89
1913	Ohio	Mercantile	7.00	—	—	—	—
1914	Ohio	Saleswomen	—	369.84	Factories	—	408.06
					Offices	—	468.07
					AOS	—	417.37
1914	Indiana	Saleswomen	7.44	—	—	—	—
1915	Richmond, Va.	DS Saleswomen	6.62	—	—	—	—
		Spec. Saleswomen	7.67	—	—	—	—

(Appendix C, *continued*)

Year	Place	Retail Earnings			Other Earnings		
		Retail Category[a]	Weekly Earnings[b]	Yearly Earnings[b]	Nonretail or Summary Category[c]	Weekly Earnings	Yearly Earnings
1918	New York	Mercantile	11.75	—		11.75	—
1920	Georgia	Stores	10.50	*758.00	Factories	13.40	752.00
					Factories	10.90	463.00
					Laundries	12.95	748.00
					AOS		
1920	Atlanta	Stores	*15.35	*812.00	Factories	11.40	689.00
					Laundries	14.70	713.00
					AOS	13.05	721.00
1920	Kansas	GM	11.95	730.00	AOS	11.80	770.00
					Office	13.55	830.00
1920	Rhode Island	GM	13.20	727.00	AOS	16.85	829.00
1921	Kentucky	GM	11.65	688.00	AOS	10.65	618.00
1921	South Carolina	GM	*15.50	*856.00	AOS	9.50	605.00
1922	Alabama	GM	12.45	*731.00	AOS	10.40	532.00
1922	Arkansas	GM	*15.15	808.00	AOS	11.60	698.00
1922	Missouri	GM	14.45	810.00	AOS	12.65	743.00
1922	St. Louis	GM	14.60	—	AOS	13.50	—
1922	New Jersey	GM	16.75	*1085.00	AOS	14.95	—
1922	Ohio	GM	14.05	801.00	AOS	13.80	726.00
1923	Ohio	—	—	—	Offices	21.02	—
1923	New York	Mercantile	16.25	—	Factories	15.25	—
1923	New York City	Mercantile	18.25	949.00	Confectionery	15.25	793.00
					Paper box	16.75	871.00
					Shirts & collars	19.25	1001.00
					Tobacco	20.50	1066.00
					Factory average	18.25	948.00

1923	New York excluding New York City	Mercantile	12.75	663.00	Confectionery	14.25	741.00
					Paper box	14.75	767.00
					Shirts & collars	15.25	793.00
					Tobacco	15.25	793.00
1924	Oklahoma	GM	17.35	*914.00	AOS	13.00	666.00
1925	Tennessee	GM	14.15	780.00	AOS	11.10	629.00
1928	Florida	GM Sales	*18.10	1020.00	AOS	15.00	—
1929	U.S.	FT DS	—	1243.00	—	—	—
		FT DG & GM	—	1083.00	—	—	—
		FT RTW	—	1293.00	—	—	—
		FT FC	—	1450.00	—	—	—
1931	U.S. (sample)	Saleswomen	—	915.00	Business & professional women	—	1625.00
1931	Arkansas	GM	*15.45	—	AOS	9.25	—
1932	Arkansas	GM	*12.90	—	AOS	8.45	—
1931	Texas	DS Sales	*15.40	—	Factories	9.40	—
1932	Texas	DS Sales	*13.40	—	Factories	7.45	—
1933	U.S.	FT DS	—	990.00	—	—	—
		FT DG & GM	—	891.00	—	—	—
		FT RTW	—	991.00	—	—	—
		FT FC	—	1141.00	—	—	—
1934	Tennessee	DS	12.70	—	AOS	12.00	—
1935	Tennessee	DS	12.75	—	AOS	12.25	—
1936	West Virginia	DS	12.70	—	All mfg.	12.70	—
		Spec.	15.25	—			
1937	District of Columbia	DS sales	16.95	—	Beauty shops	17.80	—
		RTW sales	18.90	—	Beauty shops (stores)	19.65	—
					Offices	16.65	—
1937	Kentucky	DS sales	*13.75	—	Mfg.	13.00	—
		RTW sales	*15.25	—			

Year	Place	Retail Category[a]	Retail Earnings Weekly Earnings[b]	Yearly Earnings[b]	Nonretail or Summary Category[c]	Other Earnings Weekly Earnings	Yearly Earnings
1938	Nebraska	DS	14.80	91.50	Mfg.	14.90	244.00
		RTW	14.90	115.50	Offices	22.19	792.00
					Laundries	10.65	212.50
					Beauty shops	15.45	469.00
					Hotels	8.80	39.50
					Store restaurants	9.55	104.00
					Other restaurants	8.90	138.50
1939	Cleveland	Stores	—	56.00/mo.	Factories	—	72.00/mo.
					Beauty shop	—	67.00/mo.
					Laundries	—	58.00/mo.
					Hotels & restaurants	—	55.00/mo.
					Misc. service	—	34.00/mo.
1940	Maine	DS & DG	14.80	676.00	Hotels & restaurants	12.20	—
		App.	15.50	687.00	Offices	15.25	—
1940	Portland, Maine	DS & DG	15.80	—	Beauty shops	17.15	—
		App.	16.00	—	Laundries	13.25	—
1940	Maine excluding Portland	DS & DG	14.20	—	Beauty shops	15.00	—
		App.	14.25	—	Laundries	10.30	—

[a] DS—department store; Spec.—specialty store; GM—general mercantile store; FT—full-time; DG—dry goods store; RTW—women's ready-to-wear store; FC—family clothing store

[b] An asterisk indicates that retail earnings were higher than those in any other category used in the given study.

[c] AOS—all occupations surveyed; Mfg.—manufacturing

Sources: Carroll D. Wright, *The Working Girls of Boston* (Boston, 1889), 83; U.S. Congress, Senate, *Wage-Earning Women in Stores and Factories*, vol. 5 of *Report on Condition of Woman and Child Wage-Earners in the United States*, 61st Cong., 2d sess., Sen. Doc. 645 (Washington, 1910), 25, 86, 104, 125, 143, 158, 173; Commission to Investigate the Conditions of Working Women in Kentucky, *Report* ([Louisville], 1911), 5–6; Marie L. Obenauer, *Hours, Earnings, and Duration of Employment of Wage-Earning Women in Selected Industries in the District of Columbia*, BLS #116 (Washington, 1913), 20–21, 30; New York Department of Labor, *Hours and Earnings of Women in Five Industries*, Spec. Bull. No. 121 (Albany, 1923), 23, 29, 111, 112; Consumers League of Oregon, *Report . . . on the Wages, Hours and Conditions of Women Wage Earners in Oregon . . .* (Portland, 1913), 21; Industrial Commission of Ohio, Department of Investigation and Statistics, *Wages and Hours of Labor of Women and Girls Employed in Mercantile Establishments in Ohio in 1913*, Report No. 1 (Columbus, Ohio, 1914), 9, and *Cost of Living of Working Women in Ohio*, Report No. 14 (Columbus, Ohio, 1915), 104; Marie L. Obenauer and Frances W. Valentine, *Hours, Earnings, and Conditions of Labor of Women in Indiana Mercantile Establishments and Garment Factories*, BLS #160 (Washington, 1914), 40; *Vocational Education Survey of Richmond, Virginia, August, 1915*, BLS #162 (Washington, 1916), 249; *Women's Wages in Kansas*, WB #17 (Washington, 1920), 26, 102; *Women in Rhode Island Industries*, WB #21 (Washington, 1922), 27, 36; *Women in Georgia Industries*, WB #22 (Washington, 1922), 64–65; *Women in Kentucky Industries*, WB #29 (Washington, 1923), 30, 49; *Women in South Carolina Industries*, WB #32 (Washington, 1923), 33, 44; *Women in Arkansas Industries*, WB #26 (Washington, 1923), 29, 39–40; *Women in Alabama Industries*, WB #34 (Washington, 1924), 35, 51; *Women in Missouri Industries*, WB #35 (Washington, 1924), 14, 30; *Women in New Jersey Industries*, WB #37 (Washington, 1924), 13, 37; *Women in Ohio Industries*, WB #44 (Washington, 1925), 26–27, 124–25; Amy G. Maher, *Bookkeepers, Stenographers, and Office Clerks in Ohio*, WB #95 (Washington, 1932), 13; *Women in Oklahoma Industries*, WB #48 (Washington, 1926), 10, 30; *Women in Tennessee Industries*, WB #56 (Washington, 1927), 8, 37; *Women in Florida Industries*, WB #80 (Washington, 1930), 34, 36, 48; U.S. Bureau of the Census, *Census of American Business: 1933, Retail Distribution, United States*, vol. 5 (Washington, 1937), 206; Harriet A. Byrne, *The Age Factor as It Relates to Women in Business and the Professions*, WB #117 (Washington, 1934), 29, 51; Bertha Blair, *Women in Arkansas Industries*, WB #124 (Washington, 1935), 5; Mary Loretta Sullivan and Bertha Blair, *Women in Texas Industries*, WB #126 (Washington, 1936), 19; Ethel Erickson, *Employment of Women in Tennessee Industries*, WB #149 (Washington, 1937), 8, 21, 23; Harriet A. Byrne, *Women's Employment in West Virginia*, WB #150 (Washington, 1937), 9, 14, 15; Ethel L. Best and Arthur T. Sutherland, *Women's Hours and Wages in the District of Columbia in 1937*, WB #153 (Washington, 1937), 4, 22; *Women in Kentucky Industries*, WB #162 (Washington, 1938), 5, 19, 20; *Women's Wages and Hours in Nebraska*, WB #178 (Washington, 1940), 5, 15, 25, 31, 38, 44, 47; *Employment in Service and Trade Industries in Maine*, WB #180 (Washington, 1940), 8, 9, 12, 13, 18; *Women Workers in Their Family Environment*, WB #183 (Washington, 1941), 31.

APPENDIX D

Percentages Women's Highest Earnings Were above Starting Earnings

Year	Place	Retailing		Nonretailing	
		Percent	Years of Experience at Maximum	Percent	Years of Experience at Maximum
1908	7 major cities	184.2	16–21	84.8	16–21
1914	Indiana	179.0	—	—	—
1920	Rhode Island	22.9	15+	16.6	1–2
1921	South Carolina	52.9	5–10	14.4	2–3
1921	Georgia except Atlanta	54.9	5–10	9.4	2–3
1921	Kentucky	78.7	10–15	4.5	1–2
1922	Missouri	51.8	15+	29.0	5–10
1922	New Jersey	86.2	15+	14.9	2–3
1922	Ohio	44.8	10–15	19.7	5–10
1922	Alabama	100.9	15+	11.1	2–3
1922	Arkansas	74.9	15+	13.6	1–2
1924	Delaware	59.8	15+	6.7	1–2
1924	Oklahoma	101.8	15+	11.1	1–2
1925	Tennessee	87.2	15+	4.9	2–3
1932	Texas	57.3	15+	44.0	—

Sources: U.S. Congress, Senate, *Wage-Earning Women in Stores and Factories*, vol. 5 of *Report on Condition of Woman and Child Wage-Earners in the United States*, 61st Cong., 2d sess., Sen. Doc. 645 (Washington, 1910), 42, 47; Marie L. Obenauer and Frances W. Valentine, *Hours, Earnings, and Conditions of Labor of Women in Indiana Mercantile Establishments and Garment Factories*, BLS #160 (Washington, 1914), 49; Mary Elizabeth Pidgeon, *Wages of Women in 13 States*, WB #85 (Washington, 1931), 106; Mary Loretta Sullivan and Bertha Blair, *Women in Texas Industries*, WB #126 (Washington, 1936), 31.

Percentage of Women Workers with Ten Years or More Experience

Year	Place	Basis of Calculation	Retail		Other	
			Category[a]	%	Category	%
1908	7 major cities	Time in industry	Stores	14.9	Factories	11.2
1911	Massachusetts	Time in the trade	Stores	9.5	Candy factories	7.0
					Laundries	19.2
1915	Richmond, Va.	Time in industry	DS	8.7[c]	—	—
			DS & Spec.	14.0	—	—
1920	Rhode Island	Time in the trade	GM	24.2	AOS[b]	12.7
1921	Maryland	Time in the trade	GM	20.8	AOS	18.0
1922	New Jersey	Time in industry	GM	14.3	AOS	15.4
1922	Ohio	Time in industry	GM	20.8	AOS	16.0
1924	Oklahoma	Time in industry	GM	26.9	AOS	9.2
1925	Tennessee	Time in the trade	GM	27.1	AOS	16.0
1928	Florida	Time in the trade	GM sales	35.4	AOS	15.5
1932	Texas	Time with firm	DS	17.3	AOS	10.9
1932–33	New Jersey— 10 cities	Time with firm	DS	11.9	—	—
1932–33	Little Rock	Time with firm	DS	15.5	—	—
1932–33	Denver	Time with firm	DS	10.6	—	—
1932–33	Los Angeles	Time with firm	DS	20.5	—	—
1932–33	San Francisco	Time with firm	DS	20.6	—	—

[a] DS—department stores
Spec.—specialty stores
GM—general mercantile stores
Note that category "stores" includes five-and-ten-cent stores, with their very high rate of turnover, significantly lowering the proportion of those with long experience.
[b] AOS—all occupations surveyed
[c] Percent of women with over 9.5 years of experience

Sources: U.S. Congress, Senate, *Wage-Earning Women in Stores and Factories*, vol. 5 of *Report on Condition of Woman and Child Wage-Earners in the United States*, 61st Cong., 2d sess., Sen. Doc. 645 (Washington, 1910), 42, 47; Commonwealth of Massachusetts, *Report of the Commission on Minimum Wage Boards. January, 1912*, House Doc. No. 1697 (Boston, 1912), 269, 287, 322; *Vocational Education Survey of Richmond, Virginia, August, 1915*, BLS #162 (Washington, 1916), 242; *Women in Rhode Island Industries*, WB #21 (Washington, 1922), 69; *Women in Maryland Industries*, WB #24 (Washington, 1922), 95; *Women in New Jersey Industries*, WB #37 (Washington, 1924), 30–32; *Women in Ohio Industries*, WB #44 (Washington, 1925), 51; *Women in Oklahoma Industries*, WB #48 (Washington, 1926), 27; *Women in Tennessee Industries*, WB #56 (Washington, 1927), 34; *Women in Florida Industries*, WB #80 (Washington, 1930), 69; Mary Loretta Sullivan and Bertha Blair, *Women in Texas Industries*, WB #126 (Washington, 1936), 50; Mary Loretta Sullivan, *Employment Conditions in Department Stores in 1932–33*, WB #125 (Washington, 1936), 23.

Appendix F
Marital Status of Women in the Labor Force

Year	Place	Retail Category[a]	Percent Married	Percent Widowed, Divorced, Separated[b]	Nonretail Category[c]	Percent Married	Percent Widowed, Divorced, Separated[b]
1900	Massachusetts	Saleswomen	5.93	—	Mfg.	14.64	—
					Clerical	2.59	—
					Telephone	5.06	—
					AOS	11.72	—
1905	Massachusetts	Saleswomen	13.2[d]	—	—	—	—
1913	District of Columbia	DS+	7.8	6.7	Mfg. & mechanical	14.8	10.7
					Hotel & restaurant	28.0	28.0
1913–14	New York	Mercantile	5.9	6.9	—	—	—
1914	Indiana	Mercantile	5.8	4.9 w / 3.2 d & s	—	—	—
1915	Richmond, Va.	DS	10.0	14.4 w	—	—	—
1920	Kansas	GM	21.4	15.0	AOS	22.5	16.3
1920	Rhode Island	GM	21.1	10.4	AOS	14.8	7.9
1920–21	Georgia	All stores	20.2	18.5	AOS	29.1	21.1
1921	Maryland	GM	11.0	14.5	AOS	18.0	14.4
1921	Kentucky	GM	14.5	19.9	AOS	19.9	19.3
1921	South Carolina	GM	20.6	14.9	AOS	35.5	14.8
1922	Arkansas	GM	28.5	20.9	AOS	25.3	24.9
1922	Alabama	All stores	15.0	14.1	AOS	26.7	20.7
1922	Missouri	GM	16.3	20.5	AOS	20.2	16.2
1922	New Jersey	GM	14.5	13.5	AOS	21.9	10.9
1922	Ohio	GM	25.0	18.5	AOS	28.4	17.2
1924	Illinois	GM	20.7	21.2	AOS	22.4	12.3
1924	Oklahoma	GM	38.9	24.0	AOS	33.2	20.7

1925	Tennessee	GM	29.0	19.2	AOS	30.2	20.4
1928	Florida	GM sales	38.8	20.1	AOS	36.8	22.1
1930	South Bend, Ind.	Saleswomen	39.7	7.3	Mfg.	48.9	10.6
					Clerical	22.4	6.1
					AOS	43.7	10.2
1932	Texas	DS	35.6	16.0 w 8.6 d & s	Factories	45.8	17.1 w 7.8 d &'s
1932–33	New Jersey	DS Saleswomen	22.0	8.6	—	—	—
1932–33	Little Rock	DS Saleswomen	39.7	24.9	—	—	—
1932–33	Denver	DS Saleswomen	46.3	17.8	—	—	—
1932–33	Los Angeles	DS Saleswomen	33.3	32.4	—	—	—
1932–33	San Francisco	DS Saleswomen	40.8	18.9	—	—	—

[a] DS+—department stores and other retail stores
DS—department stores
GM—general mercantile stores
[b] w—widowed
d & s—divorced and separated
[c] Mfg.—manufacturing
AOS—all occupations surveyed
[d] Includes all women ever married

Sources: Massachusetts Bureau of Statistics of Labor, *Thirty-Third Annual Report* (Boston, 1903), 251–54; Commonwealth of Massachusetts, *Report of the Commission on Minimum Wage Boards. January, 1912*, House Doc. 1697 (Boston, 1912), 99; Marie L. Obenauer, *Hours, Earnings, and Duration of Employment of Wage-Earning Women in Selected Industries in the District of Columbia*, BLS #116 (Washington, 1913), 10–13; New York State Factory Investigating Commission, *Fourth Report*, vol. 2, *Report of Wage Investigation* (Albany, 1915), 60; Marie L. Obenauer and Frances W. Valentine, *Hours, Earnings, and Conditions of Labor of Women in Indiana Mercantile Establishments and Garment Factories*, BLS #160 (Washington, 1914), 11; *Vocational Education Survey of Richmond, Virginia, August, 1915*, BLS #162 (Washington, 1916), 242; *Women's Wages in Kansas*, WB #17 (Washington, 1920), 58; *Women in Rhode Island Industries*, WB #21 (Washington, 1922), 70; *Women in Georgia Industries*, WB #22 (Washington, 1922), 84; *Women in Maryland Industries*, WB #24 (Washington, 1922), 96; *Women in Kentucky Industries*, WB #29 (Washington, 1923), 109; *Women in South Carolina Industries*, WB #32 (Washington, 1923), 127; *Women in Arkansas Industries*, WB #26 (Washington, 1923), 84; *Women in Alabama Industries*, WB #34 (Washington, 1924), 63; *Women in Missouri Industries*, WB #35 (Washington, 1924), 60; *Women in New Jersey Industries*, WB #37 (Washington, 1924), 93; *Women in Ohio Industries*, WB #44 (Washington, 1925), 103; *Women in Illinois Industries*, WB #51 (Washington, 1926), 76; *Women in Oklahoma Industries*, WB #48 (Washington, 1926), 107; *Women in Tennessee Industries*, WB #56 (Washington, 1927), 113; *Women in Florida Industries*, WB #80 (Washington, 1930), 67; Caroline Manning and Arcadia N. Phillips, *Wage-Earning Women and the Industrial Conditions of 1930: A Survey of South Bend*, WB #92 (Washington, 1932), 8; Mary Loretta Sullivan and Bertha Blair, *Women in Texas Industries*, WB #126 (Washington, 1936), 30; Mary Loretta Sullivan, *Employment Conditions in Department Stores in 1932–33*, WB #125 (Washington, 1936), 22.

Living Conditions of Women Workers

Year	Place	Retail Category[a]	Percent Living Independently	Nonretail Category[b]	Percent Living Independently
1889	Boston	Trade	25.2	Mfg.	31.7
1895	Boston	Saleswomen	20.1	Personal service	36.1
				Clerical	21.3
				Mfg.	21.7
1895	Worcester, Mass.	Saleswomen	16.3	Clerical	14.7
				Mfg.	13.3
1895	Brockton, Mass.	Saleswomen	25.0	Clerical	14.8
				Mfg.	16.9
1895	Waltham, Mass.	Saleswomen	17.6	Clerical	30.3
				Mfg.	33.9
1907	Pittsburgh	Mercantile	20.0	AOS	10.5
1908	Boston	DS+	35.8	Factories	25.3
1908	Chicago	DS+	20.3	Factories	16.4
1908	Minneapolis/St. Paul	DS+	27.7	Factories	18.5
1908	New York	DS+	7.9	Factories	13.0
1908	Philadelphia	DS+	22.2	Factories	18.0
1908	St. Louis	DS+	21.0	Factories	21.6
1908	7 cities above	DS+	26.1	Factories	21.3
1909	Baltimore	Merc.	17.0	—	—
1911	Chicago	DS	13.5	—	—
1913	District of Columbia	DS+	22.3	AOS	25.6
1914	Indiana	Merc.	8.3	—	—
1920	Kansas	GM	16.9	AOS	15.7
1920	Rhode Island	GM	8.9	AOS	7.8
1920–21	Georgia	All stores	18.1	Mfg. & laundries	13.1

Year	Place	Type	Category		
1921	Maryland	GM	AOS	16.4	12.1
1921	Kentucky	GM	AOS	9.2	10.1
1921	South Carolina	GM	AOS	16.8	6.0
1922	Arkansas	GM	AOS	14.9	17.0
1922	Alabama	Stores	AOS	14.2	9.3
1922	Missouri	GM	AOS	17.9	12.6
1922	New Jersey	GM	AOS	8.3	6.1
1922	Ohio	GM	AOS	13.9	11.3
1922	Manhattan	Merc.	Factories	38.0	30.0
			Office		18.0
1924	Oklahoma	GM	AOS	17.8	14.7
1924	Illinois	GM	AOS	17.9	10.6
1925	Tennessee	GM	AOS	14.8	13.1
1928	Florida	GM Sales	AOS	14.2	14.2

aMerc.—mercantile
DS—department stores
DS+—department stores and other retail stores
GM—general mercantile stores
bMfg.—manufacturing
AOS—all occupations surveyed

Sources: Carroll D. Wright, *The Working Girls of Boston* (Boston, 1889), 20; "Residential Conditions of Women and Girls Employed in Trade and Manufactures," *Massachusetts Labor Bulletin*, No. 18 (May 1901), 63–66; Elizabeth Beardsley Butler, *Women and the Trades: Pittsburgh, 1907–1908* (New York, 1911), 320–21; U.S. Congress, Senate, *Wage-Earning Women in Stores and Factories*, vol. 5 of *Report on Condition of Woman and Child Wage-Earners in the United States*, 61st Cong., 2d sess., Sen. Doc. 645 (Washington, 1910), 25; Elizabeth Beardsley Butler, *Saleswomen in Mercantile Stores* (New York, 1912), 146; Louise DeKoven Bowen, *The Department Store Girl* (Chicago, 1911), 2; Marie L. Obenauer, *Hours, Earnings, and Duration of Employment of Wage-Earning Women in Selected Industries in the District of Columbia*, BLS #116 (Washington, 1913), 8, 11; Marie L. Obenauer and Frances W. Valentine, *Hours, Earnings, and Conditions of Labor of Women in Indiana Mercantile Establishments and Garment Factories*, BLS #160 (Washington, 1914), 10; *Women's Wages in Kansas*, WB #17 (Washington, 1920), 103; *Women in Rhode Island Industries*, WB #21 (Washington, 1922), 70; *Women in Georgia Industries*, WB #22 (Washington, 1922), 84; *Women in Maryland Industries*, WB #24 (Washington, 1922), 96; *Women in Kentucky Industries*, WB #29 (Washington, 1923), 110; *Women in South Carolina Industries*, WB #32 (Washington, 1923), 127; *Women in Arkansas Industries*, WB #26 (Washington, 1923), 84; *Women in Alabama Industries*, WB #34 (Washington, 1924), 65; *Women in Missouri Industries*, WB #35 (Washington, 1924), 61; *Women in New Jersey Industries*, WB #37 (Washington, 1924), 94; *Women in Ohio Industries*, WB # 44 (Washington, 1925), 104; Katharine Bement Davis, *Housing Conditions of Employed Women in the Borough of Manhattan* (New York, 1922), 44; *Women in Oklahoma Industries*, WB #48 (Washington, 1926), 107; *Women in Illinois Industries*, WB #51 (Washington, 1926), 77; *Women in Tennessee Industries*, WB #56 (Washington, 1927), 114; *Women in Florida Industries*, WB #80 (Washington, 1930), 68.

BIBLIOGRAPHIC ESSAY

I have been particularly fortunate in being able to draw on an extensive body of sources. The backbone of my analysis is retail trade literature. It describes the methods and the goals of managers and owners who looked beyond their store doors to the larger issues of retailing and became involved in the ongoing discussions about transforming the industry along the lines of modern management.

The most important agency in helping large-scale retailers to form a national identity was the *Dry Goods Economist,* a weekly publication which changed its name in 1938 to the *Department Store Economist.* Founded in 1852, it began in 1889 to focus its appeal on department stores with a threefold campaign: "how to buy," "how to sell it," and the problems of managing and operating a large store. The magazine advocated systematic practices, published testimonials from retailers about their own methods, and provided a variety of consulting services on fashion, advertising, display, store layout and fixtures, and training. It also gathered and published the first systematic and standardized data on the operation of typical stores, thus giving retailers a yardstick against which to measure their own operations. Businessmen were invited to visit or write the *DGE* offices for consultations, and *DGE* staff members traveled throughout the country to observe retail practices and offer advice.

Active and successful as the *DGE* was, its editors and constituency recognized that the industry needed the organized power of a formal trade association, In 1911, with the active encouragement of the *DGE,* thirty-seven stores formed the National Retail Dry Goods Association. Relations between the NRDGA and the *DGE* continued to be cordial and cooperative. By the end of 1911, the NRDGA included 10 percent of all U.S. department stores, particularly larger and medium-sized establishments. With aims and concerns similar to the *DGE,* the NRDGA added an echo rather than a choice to the industrial options of the retailer; self-conscious managers interested in new methods gravitated toward both.

In its early years, the major new contributions of the NRDGA were the forum of a yearly convention and support for the work of Lucinda Wyman Prince in retail training. Nineteen nineteen was a turning point for the association in two respects. First, its membership more than doubled to 1362 stores between early 1919 and early 1920; one observer noted that after that point most major stores belonged to the NRDGA. Second, Lew Hahn became the association's executive secretary, a post he retained under a variety of titles until his retirement in 1948. Under his energetic direction, the NRDGA developed a functional organization corresponding to each of the major store tasks. Between 1920 and 1925, the Controllers' Congress, the Traffic Group, the Sales Promotion Division, the Retail Delivery Association, the Store Management Group, the Personnel Group, and the Merchandising Division were established; in 1934 the Credit Management Division completed the roster of the NRDGA's special-interest caucuses.

The association had published a brief bulletin sporadically since its founding, but in 1925 it began to appear regularly and to offer expanded coverage of industry matters in somewhat the same vein as the *DGE*. The NRDGA also published the proceedings of all its conventions and many useful topical reports. Both the *DGE* and the *Bulletin* of the NRDGA offer an excellent view of the most foward-thinking of large-scale retailers. Used with care, these journals reveal managers' views of themselves, their customers, and their saleswomen as well as shed light on the behavior and outlook of customers and saleswomen themselves.

In 1925 the New York University School of Retailing began to publish the more academically oriented *Journal of Retailing*. Presenting mostly the work of the school's faculty and students, the *Journal* is a welcome supplement to the *DGE* and *Bulletin* of the NRDGA because many of its articles detail department-store practices through systematic surveys rather than case studies. The graduate schools of retailing at Simmons College and the University of Pittsburgh did not produce a regular journal, but during the 1920s and 1930s their students wrote masters' theses based on field work in department stores. Virtually all of these provide useful pictures of life in selling departments, and the best of them are perceptive ethnographies. While the writers clearly envisioned management careers for themselves, the theses reflect their present status as students more often than their hopes for the future. They are frequently frank and sympathetic portraits of saleswomen's attempts to make the best of a difficult situation. Similarly vivid material about life on and off the job can be found in the *Echo*, the newspaper of the Filene Cooperative Association. Because it was not a unilateral voice of management, the *Echo* often published views critical of the firm along with the standard house-organ fare of gossip, cautionary tales, and policy announcements.

Department stores were the object of public attention as well as of management concern, and popular or general-interest magazines had a great deal to say about them. This literature fell into two categories. The first, investigations that grew out of the struggles to improve working women's conditions through legislation or unionization, provides information about saleswomen's lives and jobs. The second focused less on saleswomen than on the department store as an urban or commercial phenomenon and a colorful backdrop for romance and intrigue. A wide range of writers produced this body of work: reformers, academic researchers, reporters, participant observers, fiction writers, and industry insiders.

The scarcity of secondary literature on department stores counterbalances the richness of the primary sources. Until historians of the early 1980s began to turn their attention to the study of consumption, most writing about department stores was in the form of store histories. Often thinly disguised advertisements for a given firm, these histories nonetheless provide a wealth of useful if unsystematic information. The only scholarly store histories are Ralph M. Hower's *History of Macy's of New York, 1858–1919: Chapters in the Evolution of the Department*

Store (Cambridge, Mass., 1943) and Robert W. Twyman's *History of Marshall Field & Co., 1852–1906* (Philadelphia, 1954), and both focus on the formative years of the late nineteenth century rather than the mature years of the twentieth century.

Department stores have recently begun to attract their historians. Elaine S. Abelson's dissertation, "'When Ladies Go A-Thieving': Shoplifting, Social Change, and the City, 1870–1914" (New York Univ., 1985), studies shoplifting and relates it to the class and gender dynamics of urban life. William R. Leach looks at the department store as a cultural institution, analyzing the forms in which it presented itself and the possibilities it offered ("Transformations in a Culture of Consumption: Women and Department Stores, 1890–1925," *Journal of American History*, 71 [Sept. 1984], 319–42). Sarah Smith Malino's dissertation, "Faces across the Counter: A Social History of Female Department Store Employees, 1870–1920" (Columbia Univ., 1982), focuses on saleswomen, emphasizing the positive aspects of their jobs and stressing the way in which department-store selling shaped and was shaped by changing cultural notions of women's place. While I have benefited from the work of all three scholars, and especially from Malino's, my perspective differs from each of theirs as I have placed my work at the intersection of women's, labor, and business history.

Finally, two books which unconsciously situate themselves at this intersection provide a rich store of information and insight for historians, sociologists, and anthropologists who want to explore further the daily life of department stores: Frances R. Donovan's *The Saleslady* (1929; rpt. New York, 1974) and George F. F. Lombard's *Behavior in a Selling Group: A Case Study of Interpersonal Relations in a Department Store* (Boston, 1955).

INDEX

317

A Note on the Author

SUSAN PORTER BENSON received her doctorate in history from Boston University, chaired the Department of History at Bristol Community College, and is now a member of the history department of the University of Missouri–Columbia. She has also taught social history for the Amalgamated Clothing and Textile Workers Union and in 1984 was Visiting Senior Lecturer at the University of Warwick. She recently edited, with Stephen Brier and Roy Rosenzweig, *Presenting the Past: Essays on History and the Public.*